YEAR C ▪ 2004

workbook

FOR LECTORS AND GOSPEL READERS

Aelred R. Rosser

LTP
LITURGY
TRAINING
PUBLICATIONS

Liturgy Training Publications
1800 North Hermitage Avenue
Chicago, IL 60622-1101
1-800-933-1800
fax 1-800-933-7094
orders@ltp.org
www.ltp.org

Editor: David A. Lysik
Production editor: Audrey Novak Riley
Typesetter: Jim Mellody-Pizzato
Original book design: Jill Smith
Revised design: Anna Manhart and Jim Mellody-Pizzato
Cover art: Barbara Simcoe
Interior art: Steve Erspamer, SM

Printed in the United States of America.

ISBN 1-56854-424-3
WL04

CONTENTS

The Author

Aelred Robert Rosser was born and reared in an evangelical tradition of Christianity that has always centered its religious experience on the Bible, the word of God. Since becoming a Catholic at the age of 20, he has spent 40 years promoting the best of those two religious traditions—a profound love for scripture expressed in a nourishing liturgical celebration of the sacraments. Aelred holds degrees in philosophy, religion, and theology, and a doctorate in rhetoric, linguistics, and literature from the University of Southern California. He has conducted lector workshops and preaching seminars nationwide. He is also certified as a teacher of English as a foreign language (TEFL) and has taught in Central America and the Middle East. His other writings on the ministry of proclamation are among the resource works listed at the end of the introduction.

Dedication

This book is affectionately dedicated to my two brothers Bill and Chuck. Bill, the eldest, is an ordained minister in the evangelical tradition and an ardent proclaimer of God's word. Chuck, the youngest, is an astute and thoughtful skeptic, always prepared to pose articulate and challenging questions to organized religion. Appropriately, I fall between them, as I always have—both chronologically and theologically. As a convert to Catholicism, I cherish the primacy of place the Bible has had in my life since my youth, as well as the sacramental life I learned to love later on. And I zealously guard the right and duty we have to question, critique, and examine our Christianity in practice. Unloved faith is lifeless and unexamined faith is blind. Thank you, my brothers, for your inspiration, your encouragement, and your love.

INTRODUCTION

Those who proclaim God's word in the liturgy are ministers. When you answer the call to be a minister of the word, you enter a deeper relationship with God revealed in sacred scripture. You take upon yourself the awesome duty and privilege of bringing the printed word to life, making it flesh. Your proclamation enables God's word to achieve the purpose for which it was sent. In short, you become a prophet, one who speaks for God. John the Baptist is your model, preparing the way of the Lord, making crooked paths straight and rough places smooth. You cry out with every breath, "See, there is the Lamb of God!" Finally, you join yourself to the Jewish tradition, which sees prayerful study of God's word as the worthiest of all endeavors. And as a Christian you believe that God's words find their fullest expression in that one perfect Word—Jesus, the Word made flesh.

The Word

"The Word of God" means more to us than a simple "word." It means "all the words of God." Or perhaps it means "the Bible." And certainly for Christians it means Jesus Christ, "the Word made flesh," the "incarnate Word." The familiar liturgical proclamation that follows every reading, "The word of the Lord," and the response to it, "Thanks be to God," have a formative influence on us over time. They create in our hearts and minds an association between the words of the reading and the benevolent actions of the God who revealed them.

That association is even more vivid in the languages in which the words of God were originally written. The Hebrew word for "word" is *dabar,* and it means "deed" (an action) as well as "word." In this definition, words are not merely sounds or symbols that describe deeds; they are themselves deeds. Contemporary language scholars have formulated a similar view. They argue that words are not always just sounds or written symbols that *refer* to something, as in "There is the house where I live." In some usage, words actually *do* something. In these cases they are called "performative speech acts." For example, the words "I baptize you" or "I forgive you" or (at the eucharist) "this is my body" do not simply refer to an action; they actually accomplish the action.

We understand the words of liturgical proclamation more accurately when we view them as "performative," as accomplishing the work of salvation they describe even as the reader proclaims them. The word of God is not a history lesson, though there is history in it. It is not a story, though it is full of stories. It is not a set of rules to live by, though there is much in it to guide our choices. No, the word of God is a living and dynamic presence, achieving the salvation it describes, even as the reader proclaims it. The church's own teaching expresses this view: "[Christ] is present in his word since it is he himself who speaks when the holy scriptures are read in church"; and, again, "[I]n the liturgy God speaks to his people, Christ is still proclaiming his gospel" (Second Vatican Council, *Constitution on the Liturgy,* 7, 33).

The Words of the Word

All of sacred scripture is written in exalted language because its writers were always engaged in communicating something more than their actual words. Even what appears to be the most straightforward narrative has a deeper purpose. The deeper purpose explains, in part, why the gospel narratives of Matthew, Mark, and Luke differ so much from each other. Each writer had a governing purpose, not only in recording events in the life of Jesus but in recording them *in a certain way.* And the gospel of John is radically different from the other three. In John's account of the passion, for example, Jesus is very much in control of the situation. He is not victim; he is king and ruler. A loyal band of followers stands at the foot of his cross. In the other accounts, a mocking crowd witnesses Jesus' death. John's purpose is different, so he portrays the passion of Jesus differently. Such controlling themes elevate prose far beyond the merely literal and project it into the realm of the figurative, even the poetic.

The point is that casual attempts to "translate" scripture into colloquial, informal, or even "everyday" expressions reveal a lack of understanding of scripture and the subtleties of its original forms. More serious still is the effect of such attempts, no matter how well-intentioned or motivated: They invariably and inevitably trivialize sacred scripture. They also underestimate the sensitivities of the hearers and emphasize the proclaimer at the expense of the word of God.

The Shapes of the Word

The Bible is a collection of many different kinds of literature: narratives (stories), poetry, sermons, hymns, and so on. Your instincts will tell you that different kinds of literature require different treatments. Trust your instincts, but avoid stereotypes. There is no reason to imitate bad Shakespearean actors when reading poetry, or Mother Goose when reading a story.

There is an important reason for recognizing and respecting the different literary styles in the Bible, and it has been alluded to above. The writer's message is told in a particular way (literary form) because the writer is making a particular point or appealing to the audience in a particular way. The choice of style is not arbitrary. A poetic account of the creation story, for example, may not be in accord with what science has shown to be factual. The writers of the Bible were seldom concerned with scientific data. The author of Genesis has but one point: to demonstrate that the Creator God is responsible for all that is. The facts of the case are beside that point—presenting a problem for those who like their logic tight. But poetry is usually not the style of choice for logicians.

Readers who have studied literature in high school and college should not hesitate to approach the Bible as a collection of literature written in a variety of genres. Concepts such as metaphor, simile, narrative, plot, and denouement (resolution) all apply to scripture. Understanding poetic structure, word order, alliteration, and onomatopoeia can be helpful when studying biblical poetry. Yes, many poetic elements such as these are lost in translation, but the better translations today have tried to preserve them.

The point here is that readers often bring to the ministry of proclamation a wealth of experience that should be capitalized upon, not tossed aside in the mistaken notion that the literature of the Bible—and effective proclamation of it—is so rarefied that it requires a whole new frame of reference.

The Proclaimer

The reader proclaims God's word to the assembled faith community. It's that simple and that sublime. Although the ministry is a simple one, that does not mean it's easy to do well or requires little energy or effort. Simplicity refers to the mode of the ministry, the reader's ability to proclaim the word transparently, which allows the word itself, and not the proclaimer, to take center stage. Simplicity does not, however, refer to the reader's task, for the task itself is quite challenging. Not everyone is equal to it.

But there is an element of the sublime in the work of the reader as well. To be chosen to proclaim God's word to one's fellow believers is to participate in the mystery and struggle of their individual journeys of faith. There can be no more sublime ministry than that. And there can be no more humbling responsibility, for the quality of the reader's proclamation determines whether his or her service will help or hinder the hearers.

Women and men who take on the ministry of reader are presumed to be of good faith, eager to serve their fellow Christians, and willing to engage in ongoing formation for effective service. But it is not presumed that they are particularly holy, exceptionally gifted, or highly skilled in communication techniques. Basic abilities are required, and these are the subject of part of this book. Highly developed communication skills related to certain professions (public speaking, broadcasting, and acting, for example) must be developed by the reader, but they do not in themselves render a person capable of effective liturgical proclamation. The purpose of liturgical worship is different from the objectives we find in the work of professional communicators: conveying information, entertaining, persuading to action, and so forth. The liturgy may do all of these things, of course, but they are not its purpose, which is to celebrate the faith shared by the worshipers.

Finally, the mere wish or willingness to serve as reader does not qualify one for the ministry. This statement sounds harsh. No one wants to discourage a volunteer. But the fact remains that the ministry of reader is a charism for the building up of the community. It requires certain native abilities that some do not have, such as an adequate vocal instrument, for example. It also requires self-possession and confidence, maturity, poise, and sensitivity to diversity in one's audience. Such qualities can be enhanced in a formation program, but should already be present to a significant degree in the potential reader.

Like all ministries in the church, liturgical proclamation of the word is an awesome responsibility to which one is called and into which one is formed. Fifteen hundred years ago, Saint Benedict wrote in his *Rule:* "They should not presume to read who by mere chance take up the book. . . . Only those are to discharge these duties who can do so to the edification of the hearers."

The Proclaimer's Book

As a proclaimer of God's word, you know that your best friend is a book called the lectionary (from the Latin word *lectio,* which means "reading" or "lesson"). It is a collection of Bible texts arranged for proclamation according to the church's liturgical calendar. Seasoned lectors and gospel readers should have a thorough knowledge of the lectionary and be able to use it with ease. More than that, the committed proclaimer respects this holy book as the medium through which God's word is lavished upon the people of God for their comfort and inspiration, and as an invitation to respond to God's love more fully.

When the Second Vatican Council insisted that the riches of sacred scripture be opened more lavishly for the faithful, we had lived for centuries with one set of Bible readings that were the same each year and for every day of the year. The lectionary compiled after Vatican II nearly tripled our exposure to the Bible during liturgical worship with a collection of readings covering a three-year cycle for the Sunday liturgy and a two-year cycle for weekdays.

In order to abide by the Council's directive, two major changes were made. The Sunday liturgy of the word was expanded from two readings (epistle and gospel) to include an additional selection, what we know now as the first reading, almost always from the Old Testament except during the Easter season, and chosen with the gospel of the day in mind. The second reading is taken from New Testament books other than the gospels. No particular relationship to the other readings guides its choice; it is often a *lectio continua,* which means that part of a New Testament book is proclaimed in sections in semi-continuous fashion over a number of weeks.

When the cycle of readings was expanded from one year to three (Years A, B, and C), gospel readings from the three synoptic gospels—Matthew, Mark, and Luke—were assigned for each year, respectively. These three evangelists write a kind of "synopsis" of Jesus' life and ministry, a more or less sequential narrative. The gospel of John, very different in character and purpose from the synoptics, fills in occasionally, but it is primarily reserved for the Easter season in all three years.

Part of the lectionary we have been using for the past 30 or so years has recently been revised (the part containing the readings for Sundays, solemnities, and certain feasts). Even this, we hope, is not a final revision. We will continue to see improvements in the selection of scripture texts (and the way they are edited for public proclamation) for several more years to come. We will also see improved translations in the

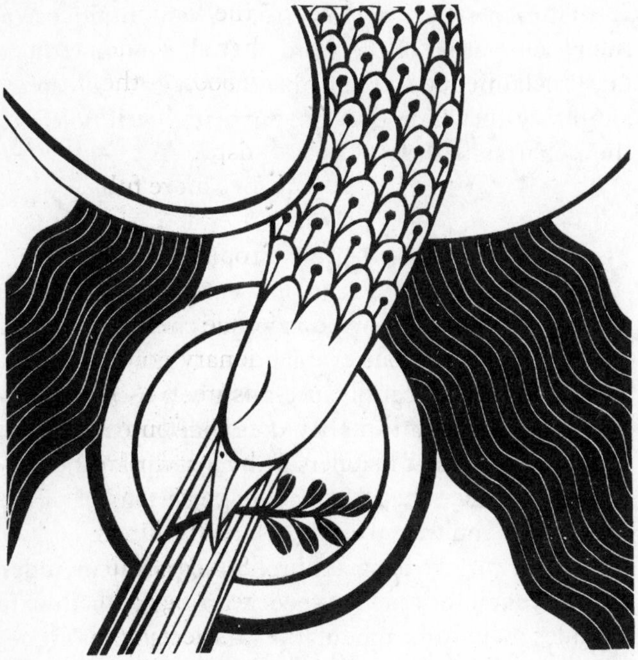

future, translations that take into even greater consideration such issues as inclusive language, oral presentation, and other existing lectionaries.

The most obvious feature of the lectionary is its organization in accord with the liturgical calendar. There is a three-year cycle of readings for Sundays that begins with the seasons of Advent and Christmas, and continues with Lent, Easter, and Pentecost. Between Christmas and Lent, and again between Pentecost and Advent, are the Sundays in Ordinary Time, divided into two parts. Incidentally, the word "ordinary" here does not mean "plain" or "common" or the opposite of "extraordinary." The root word involved is "ordinal" (as in the ordinal numbers) and indicates that Ordinary Time is composed of those Sundays we number consecutively from the Second Sunday in Ordinary Time (the "first" Sunday is the feast of the Lord's baptism, the last day of the Christmas season) to the Thirty-fourth Sunday in Ordinary Time, the solemnity of Christ the King.

Notice that each group of readings is numbered in the lectionary (and in *Workbook*) for easy reference. Thus, the First Sunday of Advent (Year A) is #1, the First Sunday of Advent (Year B) is #2, and so on. Readers who are unaware of how the lectionary is laid out run the risk of proclaiming the wrong reading (Year C instead of Year A, for example).

Clearly, the lector who knows the "why" and "how" of the lectionary is better equipped to perform the ministry of reader effectively. No reading is completely isolated from the others at a given celebration. Each is carefully chosen for its relevance to a particular season, its relationship to the other readings at the same celebration, or its appropriateness for a particular feast day. Lectors and gospel readers who are truly committed to their important ministry will take some time to learn more about how the church's book of readings is put together. Knowledge of the lectionary is nothing less than knowledge of the means by which God speaks to the Sunday assembly through your voice.

The Proclaimer's Instrument

Our personal experience is sufficient evidence for the power of the human speech. We know that it can heal, destroy, provoke to anger. We have used it to express love, hate, disgust, ecstasy, anger, joy—the full range of human emotions. We have heard others speak and have known that it can affect us quite profoundly, for good or ill. We have heard strong arguments spoken by trustworthy speakers who have changed our way of thinking and our choices. We have seen others swayed to poor choices by charlatans who have misused the power of speech.

In our ministry as readers we need to become more aware of the power of our speech. Our proclamation of the word is *never* without effect. The poorest proclamation, the mediocre proclamation, the most compelling proclamation—each affects the hearers. What is true of liturgical worship is true of proclamation during that worship: Poor liturgy diminishes faith; good liturgy augments it. A time-proven Latin axiom sums it up best: *lex orandi, lex credendi*—as we pray, so we believe.

But it is the potential of our speech's power for good that we want to emphasize here. And to do that we need to consider another aspect of human speech as it applies to our ministry: *sacramentality*. The familiar definition of sacrament as "an outward sign of an inward reality" can help us appreciate why the church invests the proclamation of the word with such significance: "It is Christ himself who speaks." Christ's word is creative and causative. The water poured at baptism and the words that are spoken ("I baptize you in the name of . . .") are the outward sign of the sacrament of baptism. The inward reality is the incorporation of the newly baptized into the church, the Body of Christ. Similarly, when the reader proclaims the Good News in a liturgy, the word goes forth from the reader and is fulfilled in the hearing of the assembly. An action takes place. The "sign," the proclamation, is outward. The fulfillment of the word even as it is proclaimed is the "inward reality."

This is not to say that proclamation of the word is itself a sacrament. But it does have a sacramental character and effect, like the liturgy of which it is a part. In the words of the apostle Paul, "As often as you eat this bread and drink the cup, you proclaim the Lord's death until he comes" (1 Corinthians 11:26). The eucharist is more than a simple recollection of what Christ accomplished in his death and resurrection. It is a continuation of that accomplishment throughout history and into the future. Proclamation of the word is more than a retelling or rereading. It is a continuation of God's saving presence in human history.

Human speech is powerful. When employed in the proclamation of the word of God, it is sacramental. Proclaimers who recognize the power and responsibility with which they are entrusted will not take their charism lightly.

The Proclaimer's Tools

Many factors are involved in producing speech that meets the expectations of the hearers. They all add up to what communication specialists tell us is the single most important quality demanded by listeners: vocal variety. What listeners find most difficult to listen to is a voice that lacks color, variations of pitch, animation, and warmth.

Vocal variety is an umbrella term that includes all the characteristics of speech discussed below. It includes melody (or modulation), rate, pause, volume, and articulation—and this list is not exhaustive. Each term is elusive and imprecise. What is "too fast"? How loud is "too loud"? When does a pause become "dead air"? In our discussion of vocal variety, keep in mind that the complexities of human speech sounds do not fit into precise categories. Matters of taste, individual preference, and many other considerations make the esthetics of speech an imprecise science! Nevertheless, we can certainly speak of what is effective and pleasant and generally considered "listenable." By the same token we can certainly identify undesirable characteristics: monotony, dullness, inaudibility, lack of clarity, and "phoniness," to name a few.

As you experiment with the individual components of vocal variety, keep in mind that they are interdependent. After all, they cannot be considered or experienced in isolation. The melody of the passage will influence the rate at which it is proclaimed; effective pausing depends on how fast or slow the text is read, as does good articulation. Although the volume at which you read must always be adequate and appropriate, it should not always be the same. Melody, rate, and articulation all affect considerations of loudness and softness.

The Listener

Both speaker and listener are constantly sending signals; the circular flow of information and feedback is constant. The difference between the two is that the communicator is ordinarily sending verbal signals, whereas the listener is sending nonverbal signals. The effective communicator must remain constantly alert to this feedback. We have all experienced readers in the liturgy who cannot be heard and yet seem unaware of it. They seem, in fact, to be oblivious to the fact that they have an assembly of listeners. Such readers conceive of their task as one-sided. They send out signals but do not receive them. The communication act is incomplete.

As reader, you must remain aware of how your listeners are responding. Are they attentive? Are they distracted by something else? Are they nodding off? Are they finding seats because they came late? Are they searching in pamphlets to find the printed text of what they can't hear?

The reason contemporary listeners will not tolerate insufficient volume is that they ordinarily do not have to. In informal conversation they can ask their communication partner to speak up. Radios, televisions, and other devices have volume controls. If your reading is simply not loud enough, then something else is being perceived as louder. That could be crying infants, the air-conditioning system, a restless assembly, or the "inner noise" that we all have playing in our heads at every moment. The point is, if something is louder (let alone more interesting and commanding of attention), the reading will not be heard.

But sheer volume is not the answer. Indeed, excessive volume is more disagreeable than insufficient volume. The kind of volume required in public communication situations is more complex than turning a knob—either on the microphone system or in the human body! Just as important as volume is sound "height" and "weight," or pitch and projection. Depending on the environment in which your ministry is exercised (Gothic cathedral or tiny chapel), the "height" or pitch of the voice must be elevated accordingly. And the voice must take on a proportionate degree of "weight" or strength of projection as well. Experimentation and feedback can help you find and discover the vocal tools that are best for you and your hearers.

Beyond the esthetics of a well-employed vocal instrument, there is another matter the proclaimer must take very much to heart: credibility with the listeners. Before they can believe in your proclamation, they must believe in you. And credibility with the members of the assembly is your responsibility alone. The assembly may owe you courtesy and attention, but you must earn the one and capture the other.

What is involved in building credibility with the assembly? Everything from your conduct as a member of the parish community to the way you arrange your hair. If either borders on the bizarre, your credibility will suffer. However, leaving most of the obvious things aside, consider some of the common problems that compromise the proclaimer's credibility—and therefore detract from the assembly's participation in the liturgy.

Mispronounced words, especially proper biblical names, are intolerable. You simply cannot stumble over these, even though some of them are quite foreign to the modern ear and difficult to pronounce. The instant you announce a reading from "Deuteromony" instead of "Deuteronomy," you will be branded inept. Even to stumble once during a list of place names (Cappadocia, Emmaus, Galatia, Thessalonica, Horeb, Caesarea, and Philippi) is not acceptable. The point is made so strongly because the solution is so easy. Consult a dictionary or any of a dozen pronunciation guides available. *Pronunciation Guide for the Sunday Lectionary* by Susan E. Myers is a good reference tool, readily available from Liturgy Training Publications for a couple of dollars. If you underestimate the importance of this point, you are underestimating the members of your assembly and your power for good.

Overly dramatic (theatrical, gooey, self-centered, or bombastic) proclamation is a severe disservice to the assembly and to God's word. Though you may be convinced of your power to instill joy or dread or comfort or obedience by means of a "powerful" presentation, you will have to lay aside such insensitive arrogance. In every assembly there are those who are sad, distraught, happy, excited, bored, weary, full of pep, and grieving. How can you enable the word of God to reach all of them? A degree of restraint and sincere involvement with the text will let it work on its own merits and allow all these various moods to hear God's message.

Excessive solemnity, dullness, monotonous delivery, and inaudibility are perhaps even worse than showiness. They communicate a lack of care and involvement that will not be tolerated by a more or less captive listener. In some cases, dullness is the effect of stage fright. Our voice is as petrified as we are. Experience is the solution; stage fright itself is repressed energy that can be released through the proclamation, empowering both text and reader.

More obvious threats to the proclaimer's credibility need only be mentioned: gaudy or sloppy dress, poor posture, nonverbal noise (uhs, ahs, jingling pocket change, losing one's place, rushing to and from the ambo). Consider all these dangers, even the ones you think are not a problem for you.

If your response to these warnings is, "It's the assembly's problem if they are so picky and can't overlook a mistake or two," you are partially right. The assembly's members should not be so picky, and you will find that most are extraordinarily tolerant and forgiving. But consider this: Did the members of the assembly come to church to exercise tolerance of the proclaimer or to hear the word of God proclaimed in a way that will alter their lives for the good? Certainly, liturgical celebration is not an antiseptic experience. After all, it's done by human beings. But the better we do it, the better it can work its miracle of transforming individual lives to transform in turn the world we live in.

The Proclaimer's Dialogue with the Assembly

Liturgical dialogue is effective when the principle of "expected form" is observed: "The word of the Lord"; "Thanks be to God"; "A reading from the holy gospel according to Luke"; "The gospel of the Lord"; "Praise to you, Lord Jesus Christ." The dialogue loses its ritual power when the proclaimer departs from it for the misguided purpose of making it literal, relevant, "warm," or informative. Thus it is important that readers be faithful to the dialogue assigned to them, not embellishing or augmenting it in any way. Doing so destroys the appeal of liturgy and ritual as an expected form of worship. Ritual works its long-term and subtle effect on us precisely because of its repetition and predictability. The constant search for new and potentially disarming ways to alter liturgical dialogue violates liturgy's purpose and function.

In recent years, we have heard readers at pains to "refresh" liturgical dialogue by creating their own versions of it. "The word of the Lord" has seen such permutations as "And this, my brothers and sisters, is the word of the Lord." The content of the two statements is arguably the same, but the form, function, and purpose are all radically different. Aside from the fact that the assembly will be caught off guard and so will be unable to respond with spontaneity, the casting of the dialogue in this literal and "informative" way misses the mark in at least two ways. First, it destroys the expectations with regard to "form" that are essential to ritual, and, second, it "tells" us something instead of "doing something."

It is only recently that the ritual form has been officially changed by the church. You may recall that at the end of the reading the reader used to say, "This is the word of the Lord." The formula was reduced to "The word of the Lord" not only in the interests of a better translation of the Latin *(Verbum Domini)*, as some have asserted, but to render it more appropriate to ritual (performative) and less referential (literal, informative). "This is . . ." clearly carries a feeling of the demonstrative, which explains in part the tendency of some readers to hold the lectionary aloft as they spoke the words. This practice confused things further by drawing attention to the book when the proper focus of the assembly's attention should have been the living proclamation of the word.

The fact that the shorter formula *is* closer to the Latin simply shows that the Latin carries the non-referential, non-demonstrative sense of a text that is more acclamation than explanation. The simple change has a subtle and important effect over time. It lessens our tendency to see the liturgy as a gathering in which we "learn" about our faith and intensifies our experience of the liturgy as a gathering in which we "celebrate" our faith.

A Word of Caution

You will notice that we have continued the practice of marking certain words in the scriptural text to help the proclaimer emphasize them in an effort to communicate the overall context more effectively. We do so because experience has told us that users of the *Workbook* appreciate this aid. However, the markings are not to be taken slavishly or considered obligatory. Effective proclamation can never be quite so rigidly orchestrated. If the markings help you in the development of sensitive vocal variety, use them; if not, ignore them.

Pronunciation Key

Most consonants in the pronunciation key are straightforward: The letter B always represents the sound B and D is always D, and so on. Vowels are more complicated. Note that the long I sound (as in kite or ice) is represented by *ī*, while long A (skate, pray) is represented by *ay*. Long E (beam, marine) is represented by *ee;* long O (boat, coat) is represented by *oh;* long U (sure, secure) is represented by *oo* or *yoo*. Short A (cat), E (bed), I (slim), and O (dot) are represented by *a, e, i,* and *o* except in an unstressed syllable, when E and I are signified by *eh* and *ih*. Short U (cup) is represented by *uh*. An asterisk (*) indicates the schwa sound, as in the last syllable of the word "stable." The letters *oo* and *th* can each be pronounced in two ways (as in cool or book, thin or they); underlining differentiates between them. Stress is indicated by the capitalization of the stressed syllable in words of more than one syllable.

bait = bayt	thin = thin
cat = kat	vision = VIZH-*n
sang = sang	ship = ship
father = FAH-ther	sir = ser
care = kair	gloat = gloht
paw = paw	cot = kot
jar = jahr	noise = noyz
easy = EE-zee	poison = POY-z*n
her = her	plow = plow
let = let	although = awl-THOH
queen = kween	church = church
delude = deh-LOOD	fun = fuhn
when = hwen	fur = fer
ice = īs	flute = floot
if = if	foot = foot
finesse = fih-NES	

Recommended Works

Guides for Proclaiming God's Word

Connell, Martin. *Guide to the Revised Lectionary.* Chicago: Liturgy Training Publications, 1998.

Lector Training Program: This Is the Word of the Lord. Audio tapes and booklet. Chicago: Liturgy Training Publications, 1988.

The Lector's Ministry: Your Guide to Proclaiming the Word. Mineola, New York: Resurrection Press, 1990.

Lee, Charlotte I., and Galati, Frank. *Oral Interpretation,* 9th ed. Boston: Houghton Mifflin, 1997.

Myers, Susan E. *Pronunciation Guide for the Sunday Lectionary.* Chicago: Liturgy Training Publications, 1998.

Proclaiming the Word: Formation for Readers in the Liturgy. Video. Chicago: Liturgy Training Publications, 1994.

Rosser, Aelred R. *A Well-Trained Tongue: Formation in the Ministry of Reader.* Chicago: Liturgy Training Publications, 1996.

——. *A Word That Will Rouse Them: Reflections on the Ministry of Reader.* Chicago: Liturgy Training Publications, 1995.

——. *Guide for Lectors.* Chicago: Liturgy Training Publications, 1998.

General Reference Works on the Bible

Boadt, Lawrence. *Reading the Old Testament: An Introduction.* New York, New York/Mahwah, New Jersey: Paulist Press, 1984.

Brown, Raymond E. *An Introduction to the New Testament* (The Anchor Bible Reference Library). New York: Doubleday, 1997.

Collegeville Bible Commentary, Old Testament Series. Diane Bergant, general editor. Collegeville, Minnesota: The Liturgical Press, 1985.

Collegeville Bible Commentary, New Testament Series. Robert J. Karris, general editor. Collegeville: The Liturgical Press, 1991.

The Collegeville Pastoral Dictionary of Biblical Theology. Carroll Stuhlmueller, general editor. Collegeville: The Liturgical Press, 1996.

The New Jerome Biblical Commentary. Raymond E. Brown, Joseph Fitzmyer, and Roland E. Murphy, editors. Englewood Cliffs, New Jersey: Prentice Hall, 1990.

New Testament Message: A Biblical-Theological Commentary. Wilfrid Harrington and Donald Senior, editors. Collegeville: The Liturgical Press, 1980.

The Women's Bible Commentary, expanded edition. Carol A. Newsom and Sharon H. Ringe, editors. Louisville: Westminster/John Knox Press, 1998.

Commentaries on the Gospel of Luke

Craddock, Fred B. *Luke.* Louisville: John Knox Press, 1990.

Danker, Frederick W. *Luke.* Philadelphia: Fortress Press, 1987.

Dornisch, Loretta. *A Woman Reads the Gospel of Luke.* Collegeville: Liturgical Press, 1996.

Johnson, Luke Timothy. *The Gospel of Luke* (Sacra Pagina). Collegeville: Liturgical Press, 1991.

LaVerdiere, Eugene. *Dining in the Kingdom of God: The Origins of the Eucharist according to Luke.* Chicago: Liturgy Training Publications, 1994.

Tiede, David L. *Luke* (Augsburg Commentary on the New Testament). Minneapolis: Augsburg, 1998.

1ST SUNDAY OF ADVENT

Lectionary #3

READING I Jeremiah 33:14–16

A solemn announcement; indeed, a warning for those who do not practice and foster justice!

Israel = IZ-ray-el (not IZ-rye-el, which is the Latin pronunciation).

Let the repeated formula work its effect: "In those days . . . ." A tone of warning can become an exhilarating promise.

Again, the formula. And notice the parallelism: Judah/safe; Jerusalem/secure.

A reading from the Book of the Prophet Jeremiah

The days are *coming*, says the LORD,
when I will *fulfill* the *promise*
I made to the house of *Israel* and *Judah*.

In *those* days, in that *time*,
I will *raise up* for David a *just* shoot;
he shall do what is *right* and *just* in the land.

In *those* days *Judah* shall be *safe*
and *Jerusalem* shall dwell *secure*;
this is what they shall *call* her:
"The LORD our *justice*."

READING I Each Advent we begin a new liturgical year, so today is our own special "new year's day." The season of Advent looks back to the promise of our redemption and forward to the fulfillment of that promise. "The days are coming . . . when I will fulfill the promise!" With these words we welcome another year of grace.

This text appears twice in Jeremiah (chapter 23 and chapter 33). We heard the earlier version not long ago—last July, on the 16th Sunday in Ordinary Time—when it appears in the context of a condemnation of corrupt leaders, "bad shepherds." Scholars tell us that the comforting text was reiterated by a later disciple of Jeremiah in order to remind God's flock that the promise would, indeed, be fulfilled, despite the long delay.

We can appreciate the need to be reminded. Even in our awareness that God has intervened in history we are looking for that day when all *is* history—the end of the world as we know it and the time when God's face is revealed to all the world. "The Lord our justice" attempts to describe that day when God fulfills the promise and is the only measure of mercy.

Like our ancestors, we are "people of the promise." We live in hope—the kind of hope that not only longs for fulfillment, but expects it, watches for it, even hastens it. The beauty of the promise is that it enables us to keep things in perspective. It is precisely in the midst of our suffering and doubt that Jeremiah says to us: "Look back to the promise and to the undeniable evidence that our God has brought us this far. Look forward to the day when God will bring us home!"

READING II 1 Thessalonians 3:12—4:2

A reading from the first Letter of Saint Paul to the Thessalonians

Be sure not to toss off the opening greeting.

"Increase and abound" together refer to growth in love. Don't separate them by pausing after "increase."

The sentence is long, but the subordinate clauses make it manageable.

Brothers and sisters:
May the Lord make you *increase* and *abound* in *love*
for one *another* and for *all*,
just as *we* have for *you*,
so as to strengthen your *hearts*,
to be blameless in *holiness* before our God and *Father*
at the coming of our *Lord Jesus* with all his *holy* ones. Amen.

Again, a long sentence. Vocal variety will keep the various levels of thought clear.

Finally, brothers and sisters,
we *earnestly* ask and *exhort* you in the Lord *Jesus* that,
as you *received* from us
how you should *conduct* yourselves to please *God*
—and as you *are* conducting yourselves—
you do so even *more*.
For you *know* what *instructions* we gave you
through the Lord *Jesus*.

READING II Notice that Paul uses the word "Lord" four times in this reading, and the phrase "Lord Jesus" three times. There is more here than meets the eye. For Paul, and for us, there is a difference between the historical person "Jesus," who lived and died, and the "Lord Jesus," who rose from the dead, who transcends all history and is present in every time and place. The difference is not that there are two persons involved, but that the same person is now present and active among us in a different way. It is precisely this conviction about the timeless "Lord Jesus" that infuses all the encouragement Paul offers here. It is the Lord who is at work among the new Christians, the Lord who is responsible for their increase in number and in love for one another.

Paul is eager to remind his new converts that the message he gave them came not *from* him, but *through* him from the living Lord. And therein lies the justification for their faith and trust. With the Lord as authority it is indeed possible to be blameless before "our God and Father" when that same Lord returns to earth at the end of time.

The message of Advent is twofold: (1) The Lord Jesus who rose from the dead and ascended into heaven will come again in glory to establish his reign upon the earth for all eternity; and (2) This *Lord* Jesus is the same Jesus who came nearly two thousand years ago to inaugurate that kingdom. Advent begins with the cosmic fulfillment of the great plan of salvation. And it ends with Christmas. We must not lose sight of what the Advent/Christmas celebration is about. It recalls the historical birth of Jesus in time, but always looks ahead to eternity to grasp the full meaning of that birth.

GOSPEL Luke 21:25–28, 34–36

A reading from the holy Gospel according to Luke

Avoid the tendency to toss off this initial formula. It should be an attention-getter.

The entire reading is a quotation, and a very solemn announcement.

Jesus said to his *disciples*:
"There will be *signs* in the *sun*, the *moon* and the *stars*,
and on *earth* nations will be in *dismay*,
perplexed by the roaring of the *sea* and the *waves*.
People will *die* of *fright*
in *anticipation* of what is *coming* upon the world,
for the powers of the *heavens* will be *shaken*.
And then they will *see* the Son of *Man*
coming in a *cloud* with *power* and great *glory*.
But when these signs begin to *happen*,
stand *erect* and raise your *heads*
because your *redemption* is at *hand*.

Don't let "die of fright" sound too colloquial.

"But" can be misleading, implying a switch in thought rather than a development of it.

"*Beware* that your hearts do not become *drowsy*
from *carousing* and *drunkenness*
and the *anxieties* of daily *life*,
and that day *catch* you by *surprise* like a *trap*.
For that day will assault *everyone*
who lives on the face of the *earth*.
Be *vigilant* at all *times*
and *pray* that you have the *strength*
to escape the *tribulations* that are *imminent*
and to *stand* before the Son of *Man*."

The meaning here is that preoccupation with the worries of the present makes us sluggish, so that we are not alert to the signs of the Lord's presence.

"To stand before the Son of Man" implies "to stand firm and strong" in the face of trial, as well as to appear before the Lord in good grace.

GOSPEL There's no one like Luke when it comes to telling the Christmas story. But we do not begin with that part of Luke's gospel, for the season dictates that we first recall Jesus' words concerning the end of time. Advent and Christmas are about both comings (advents) of Jesus: as the king of glory at the end of history as well as the babe of Bethlehem.

Though we sense the darkness and foreboding in this passage, we must look beyond these frightening words to the real message. Actually, the picture painted here is not much different from what is currently going on in various parts of the world. As this commentary is written, famine and poverty are decimating the peoples of more than one nation, and AIDS has reached epidemic proportions in Africa. Luke had in mind the signs of the end of time, but the devastation around us can serve as signs as well. The underlying Christian message is the same: "Be alert; do not lose hope; hold tight to your faith and hope!" The worst course of action in the face of tragedy is to try to escape it through drunkenness (of any kind) or despair.

Authentic Christianity is realistic. It faces up to the fact that the world is imperfect but is never discouraged. Indeed, the Christ-like view sees imperfection as an opportunity for redemption—for proving over and over again that the love God has for the world will triumph. Joseph Campbell perhaps said it best when he asserted that the greatest human quest is "to participate joyfully in the sorrows of the world." What better way to define the kind of Christian hope that colors our celebration of Advent.

2ND SUNDAY OF ADVENT

Lectionary #6

READING I Baruch 5:1–9

Baruch = BAIR-ook (not bar-ROOK)

Begin with all the poetic joy and dignity this passage exudes.

A reading from the Book of the Prophet Baruch

Jerusalem, take off your robe of *mourning* and *misery*;
put on the splendor of *glory* from *God forever*:
Wrapped in the *cloak* of *justice* from *God*,
bear on your *head* the *mitre*
that displays the *glory* of the eternal *name*.
For God will show all the *earth* your *splendor*:
you will be *named* by God *forever*
the peace of *justice*, the *glory* of God's *worship*.

It is difficult to begin a sentence with an exclamatory "Up!" Practice it until you are comfortable.

Up, Jerusalem! *stand* upon the *heights*;
look to the *east* and see your *children*
gathered from the *east* and the *west*
at the word of the *Holy* One,
rejoicing that they are *remembered* by *God*.

Notice and emphasize the lovely contrast: exiled on foot, but carried home aloft as on a throne!

Led away on *foot* by their *enemies* they *left* you:
but *God* will bring them *back* to you
borne *aloft* in *glory* as on royal *thrones*.

A very strong passage. The reason why all this is happening is that "God has commanded."

For God has *commanded*
that every lofty *mountain* be made *low*,
and that the age-old *depths* and *gorges*
be filled to *level* ground,
that *Israel* may advance *secure* in the *glory* of God.

READING I As a call to hope, there aren't many more effective scripture passages than this one. Baruch is writing during a time of enormous suffering (during the exile) and reminding the People of God of the glory to come when Israel is restored to the promised land. The imagery in this reading has captivated the hearts of poets and musicians over and over again.

A striking concept here is the giving of a new name to Jerusalem, a name that reflects its new status and privilege. The imposition of a new name to indicate a new kind of life is commonplace in scripture. In the Bible (and in the contemporary Middle East) there is a much greater identity between the name and the person than in modern Western parlance. Thus, to "praise the name of the Lord" is, in effect, to "praise the Lord." And in Jewish devotion still today, the name of God is considered far too sacred to be uttered. Descriptive names are used, such as "the Most High." You have probably seen the word "God" written as "G-d." It is an admirable way to remind us of God's holiness. There is some irony that some use blanks to indicate words too *bad* to be written, and others use them for words too *good* to be uttered!

The point Baruch is making is that the People of God (personified as Jerusalem) will become the embodiment of peace and justice, and Godly glory, not merely be described so. In other words, Baruch's words are much more than pretty poetry. The writer is making a vivid and comforting statement about the future of the chosen people. Biblical images of victory are employed here: robes, miter, throne. And these are complemented

A lovely ending—and quiet after the exaltation that has preceded it.

The *forests* and every fragrant kind of *tree*
have *overshadowed* Israel at God's *command*;
for God is *leading* Israel in *joy*
by the *light* of his *glory*,
with his *mercy* and *justice* for *company*.

READING II Philippians 1:4–6, 8–11

A reading from the Letter of Saint Paul to the Philippians

Paul has many moods. Here is supreme joy, and a message of comfort to your hearers.

Brothers and sisters:
I pray *always* with *joy* in my every *prayer* for *all* of you,
because of your *partnership* for the *gospel*
from the *first* day until *now*.

This should be very confident, with the intention of instilling confidence in the listeners. It is a promise of God's fidelity.

I am confident of *this*,
that the one who *began* a good *work* in you
will *continue* to *complete* it
until the day of Christ *Jesus*.

The prayer is long. Take it slowly, not fearing to pause at the end of each line, but nevertheless keeping up the momentum. Every phrase is a gem.

God is my *witness*,
how I *long* for all of you with the *affection* of Christ *Jesus*.
And this is my *prayer*:
that your *love* may *increase* ever *more* and *more*
in *knowledge* and every kind of *perception*,
to *discern* what is of *value*,
so that you may be *pure* and *blameless* for the day of *Christ*,
filled with the fruit of *righteousness*
that *comes* through Jesus Christ
for the *glory* and *praise* of *God*.

by images of peace: level paths, fragrant shade trees, and light. It is precisely in our darkest moments that we need to be reminded of the bright promises God has made—and will keep.

READING II When Paul speaks of the knowledge that makes love overflow, he has in mind something more subtle than intellectual activity. Indeed, he goes on to imply the wisdom found in keenness of perception. Rules are not enough, as every honest person knows. It takes insight, discernment, a kind of sixth sense to put faith into practice in the myriad circumstances that life puts in our path.

There are times in all our lives when we are tempted to make choices based on unrealistically clear distinctions between right and wrong, good and evil. We are tempted to strictly categorize words, deeds and people for many reasons: Perhaps we are tired of the struggle, perhaps we are blinded by emotion, perhaps we have been poorly taught. Whatever the reason, we have to return to understanding that it is a continuing struggle to sort things out. With that approach, guided always by the God-like principles of love and mercy, we will never be far from the truth.

GOSPEL John the Baptist always appears on the 2nd and 3rd Sundays of Advent. Luke's treatment of John is unique. Here we see not the first figure in the inauguration of the Christian era, but the last of the great prophets who preceded and foretold of the Messiah's coming. In Luke, John has an elaborate history; his birth to

This is exalted formula, not history; don't rush through it. It builds to the end.

GOSPEL · Luke 3:1–6

A reading from the holy Gospel according to Luke

Tiberius Caesar = tī-BEER-ee-uhs SEE-zer

In the fifteenth *year* of the reign of Tiberius *Caesar*,
when Pontius *Pilate* was governor of *Judea*,
and *Herod* was tetrarch of *Galilee*,
and his brother *Philip* tetrarch of the region
of *Ituraea* and *Trachonitis*,
and *Lysanias* was tetrarch of *Abilene*,
during the high *priesthood* of *Annas* and *Caiaphas*,
the word of *God* came to *John* the son of *Zechariah*
in the *desert*.

Ituraea = ih-too-REE-ah
Trachonitis = trak-uh-NĪ-tis
Lysanias = lī-SAY-nee-uhs
Abilene = ab-uh-LEE-nee (it's not the city in Kansas; note the extra syllable!)
Annas = AN-uhs
Caiaphas = KAY-uh-fuhs
Zechariah = zek-uh-RĪ-uh

Pause before beginning the narrative sentence about John's mission.

John went throughout the whole *region* of the *Jordan*,
proclaiming a *baptism* of *repentance* for the *forgiveness*
of *sins*,
as it is written in the *book* of the words of the *prophet Isaiah*:
"A *voice* of one crying *out* in the *desert*:
'Prepare the *way* of the *Lord*,
make *straight* his *paths*.
Every *valley* shall be *filled*
and every *mountain* and *hill* shall be made *low*.
The *winding* roads shall be made *straight*,
and the *rough* ways made *smooth*,
and all *flesh* shall *see* the *salvation* of *God*.'"

The rest of the reading is poetry, not narrative. Proclaim it with vigor and dignity. The familiarity of the text challenges you to make it sound fresh and new.

Elizabeth and Zachary is accompanied by signs and wonders. These things he has in common with the great prophets of the Old Testament. Even as John announces the beginning of a new period in salvation history, he is cast as the central figure in the conclusion of what has gone before.

Though Luke's complex historical references present a challenge to the reader, they must not be rushed through or taken lightly. The details of rulers and places all serve to anchor the coming of the Messiah firmly in human history—and that is Luke's purpose. He achieves it in exalted language that names the important persons who will witness in one way or another the advent of Jesus. Once the pronunciation of the proper names is mastered, the reader should try to communicate something of the majesty of this passage. Notice that it all leads up to the very definition of prophet and yet another intervention of God in human life and history: The word of God *came to* John the son of Zechariah.

The quotation from Isaiah is an Advent song *par excellence*. The final words "all flesh shall see the salvation of God" are not quoted in Mark's gospel account (which Luke used in writing his own) or in Matthew's. It is significant that Luke chooses to include them, for they tell us something Luke will remind us of over and over again: the universality of salvation. That is, the entire world is included in God's plan. It may be difficult for us to understand, but the chosen people were amazed to discover that even the Gentiles are to be saved!

IMMACULATE CONCEPTION

Lectionary #689

READING I Genesis 3:9–15, 20

A reading from the Book of Genesis

The reading begins with a story. But the second half (except for the last sentence) is God's judgment on the situation. Prepare yourself for the change in tone.

After the man, *Adam*, had eaten of the *tree*,
the LORD God *called* to the man and *asked* him,
"Where *are* you?"
He answered, "I *heard* you in the garden;
but I was *afraid*, because I was *naked*,
so I *hid* myself."

Then he asked, "Who *told* you that you were *naked*?
You have *eaten*, then,
from the *tree* of which I had *forbidden* you to eat!"
The man replied, "The *woman* whom you put here with me—
she gave me *fruit* from the tree, and so I *ate* it."
The LORD God then asked the *woman*,
"Why did you *do* such a thing?"
The woman answered, "The *serpent* tricked me *into* it,
so I ate it."

Allow for a significant pause before pronouncing the terrible sentence of exile and punishment.

Then the LORD God said to the *serpent*:
"Because you have *done* this, you shall be *banned*
from all the *animals*
and from all the wild *creatures*;
on your *belly* shall you crawl,
and *dirt* shall you eat
all the *days* of your *life*.

READING I The ancient story of Adam and Eve and the serpent is an unforgettable way of explaining how evil came to be in the world—and why it continues to this day. How should we approach such a story? How should we tell it? Well, first we should remember that it is hallowed by the ages, like all good stories that have stood the test of time. It should be told lovingly, with all the vigor necessary to enable the hearers to relish the familiarity—even as they are encouraged to penetrate the meaning more deeply.

And what is the meaning of the story in the context of today's feast? It was chosen to be proclaimed today because of the symbolism of the relationship between Eve and Mary. As Eve was mother of all life, Mary becomes mother of Life itself in giving birth to Christ. Eve's offspring continue to battle the serpent, and the serpent's attack upon the world continues today. Evil still strikes at the heels of Eve's offspring; we still keep our foot on its ugly head. Though evil has been cursed by God, we are still living under the collective curse of sin—banned like Adam and Eve from the garden of God's intimate presence. Mary opened the way back to the garden when she uttered her obedient *fiat,* which we hear in today's gospel: "May it be done to me according to your word."

I will put *enmity* between *you* and the *woman*,
and between *your* offspring and *hers*;
he will *strike* at your *head*,
while *you* strike at his *heel*."

Add another pause here before adding the final part of the narrative, which reminds us that we all share in the effect of the sin of disobedience.

The man called his wife Eve,
because she became the mother of all the living.

READING II Ephesians 1:3–6, 11–12

A reading from the Letter of Saint Paul to the Ephesians

Sustain the energy level throughout this brief hymn/poem—and take it slowly! Every line is loaded with good news.

Notice that the reading is composed of three long sentences. But, since it's poetry, let the sense of each line (not the punctuation) guide you.

Brothers and sisters:
Blessed be the *God* and *Father* of our Lord Jesus *Christ*,
who has *blessed* us in Christ
with every *spiritual* blessing in the *heavens*,
as he *chose* us in him, before the foundation of the *world*,
to be *holy* and without *blemish* before him.

In *love* he *destined* us for *adoption* to himself
through Jesus *Christ*,
in accord with the *favor* of his *will*,
for the *praise* of the *glory* of his *grace*
that he *granted* us in the *beloved*.

In *him* we were also *chosen*,
destined in accord with the *purpose* of the One
who accomplishes *all* things according to the intention
of his *will*,
so that we might *exist* for the praise of his *glory*,
we who *first hoped* in Christ.

"The word of the Lord" must always be preceded by a pause—especially after this reading—and then delivered with firmness and conviction while looking at the assembly.

Her obedience cancels the disobedience of Eve and deals the death blow to our old enemy, sin.

It is a wonderful story you are proclaiming, full of familiar figures and phrases. But remember that it is as relevant today as ever. It packs a wallop, reminding us that obedience to the loving commands of God is the only effective antidote to the ills of our world.

READING II The good news has never sounded better than in this exultant outburst of joy. What a revelation to discover that we have been chosen—from all eternity—to be holy and without blemish! And what a challenge! Who can be holy and without blemish? The answer is found in a deeper understanding of the text, and of the good news itself. In Christ we have been given every spiritual blessing, and we have been *made* holy and without blemish. Christianity is never so much about what we are supposed to do and be; it is always much more about who God is and what God has done for us. Just as Adam and Eve were created sinless, so we have been re-created sinless. And why has God done this? Pure love and gratuitous goodness are God's motives, and we exist in Christ to reflect that goodness.

This reading deserves a careful preparation and proclamation. Every word is precious and carefully chosen. Your best skills will be required to communicate the full meaning of this scriptural gem.

GOSPEL Luke 1:26–38

A reading from the holy Gospel according to Luke

Avoid letting the familiarity of this story rob your voice of fresh energy. Proclaim it so that your hearers will be able to hear it with fresh ears—and hearts.

The angel *Gabriel* was sent from *God*
to a town of *Galilee* called *Nazareth*,
to a *virgin* betrothed to a man named *Joseph*,
of the house of *David*,
and the virgin's *name* was *Mary*.
And coming to her, he said,
"*Hail*, full of *grace*! The *Lord* is with you."

The angel's greeting perplexes Mary. Here begins a pattern of conflict and resolution.

But she was greatly *troubled* at what was said
and *pondered* what sort of greeting this might *be*.
Then the angel said to her,
"Do not be *afraid*, *Mary*,
for you have found *favor* with God.
Behold, you will conceive in your womb and bear a *son*,
and you shall *name* him *Jesus*.
He will be *great* and will be called *Son* of the Most *High*,
and the Lord God will give him the *throne* of *David* his *father*,
and he will *rule* over the house of *Jacob forever*,
and of *his* kingdom there will be *no end*."

Mary asks a second perplexing question: "How can this be?" The angel resolves the question.

But *Mary* said to the *angel*,
"How can this *be*,
since I have no *relations* with a *man*?"

GOSPEL **The stigma of evil in the Adam and Eve story is swept away in the gospel story. The good news summarized in the second reading is inaugurated and acted out in the gospel narrative. Imagine yourself to be a witness to this dialogue. Listen to the feeling and tone of the words as they are spoken by Mary and the angel. You cannot help but sense the solemnity and gravity of the moment. Even Mary's question is an obligatory formula, not to be spoken lightly, as if Mary is just satisfying her curiosity.**

Luke has structured the narrative with great genius. Notice that each pronouncement of the angel is followed by a sense of conflict that must be resolved. The angel greets Mary; she is troubled by the nature of the greeting. The angel calms her and reveals her role in the redemption of the world; she is troubled by the obvious contradiction in conceiving a child without sex. The angel not only explains how this will be accomplished but offers Elizabeth's unlikely pregnancy as testimony to the inevitability of God's plan. Nothing as paltry as human

And the angel said to her in *reply*,
"The Holy *Spirit* will come upon you,
and the *power* of the Most *High* will *overshadow* you.
Therefore the *child* to be *born*
will be called *holy*, the Son of *God*.
And *behold*, *Elizabeth*, your *relative*,
has *also* conceived a son in her *old age*,
and this is the sixth *month* for her who was called *barren*;
for *nothing* will be *impossible* for *God*."

You must emphasize "old age" more than "also." Otherwise it sounds like Mary is old as well.

Mary said, "*Behold*, I am the *handmaid* of the *Lord*.
May it be *done* to me according to your *word*."
Then the angel *departed* from her.

Mary utters the words that resolve all conflict—and ushers in the messianic age. Let your voice communicate the import of her response. And be careful not to let the last sentence (the angel's departure) be too anti-climactic. If spoken as an afterthought, it can compromise what has gone before.

limitations or frailty can hinder God's loving will to redeem us.

The narrative structure of revelation, conflict and resolution should be clearly discernible in your proclamation. Then the final resolution—Mary's "may it be done"—will have its intended effect. It's all over in a moment. The angel comes, the angel leaves, and the world will never be the same. Let your listeners experience the full weight of the moment.

3RD SUNDAY OF ADVENT

Lectionary #9

READING I Zephaniah 3:14–18a

Zephaniah = zef-uh-NĪ-uh

The poetic text is almost a series of acclamations. A bright and exalted tone is necessary. Anything less would render the text comical.

Here begins the repetition of "the Lord" and its counterpart "he will." If dealt with sensitively, these can create a steady build right through to the end. Try to create that sense of crescendo—not with volume, but with intensity. The effect needs to be subtle, however; nothing overly dramatic is recommended.

Don't miss the uniqueness and power of this imagery: *God* is rejoicing, *God* is singing joyfully!

A reading from the Book of the Prophet Zephaniah

Shout for *joy*, O daughter *Zion*!
Sing *joyfully*, O *Israel*!
Be *glad* and *exult* with all your *heart*,
O daughter *Jerusalem*!
The LORD has removed the *judgment* against you,
he has turned *away* your *enemies*;
the King of *Israel*, the *LORD*, is in your *midst*,
you have no further *misfortune* to fear.

On *that* day, it shall be said to *Jerusalem*:
Fear *not*, O Zion, be not *discouraged*!
The LORD, your *God*, is in your *midst*,
a mighty *savior*;
he will *rejoice* over you with *gladness*,
and *renew* you in his *love*,
he will sing *joyfully* because of you,
as one sings at *festivals*.

READING I **Joy, joy, joy! The first two readings today are filled with exultant rejoicing. We are halfway through the Advent season and the church finds it difficult to exercise restraint in anticipating the feast of Christmas.**

The first reading is not typical of Zephaniah's writings. Ordinarily he gives us the wrathful side of the "end times." But today's selection is just the opposite, and is perfect for the latter part of Advent, when our expectation begins its crescendo toward the celebration of Christmas—Epiphany.

The text is pure poetry, a hymn of acclamation, a celebration in the present tense of the Lord's triumph on behalf of Israel in the future. Notice the repetition of the phrase "the Lord." The well-practiced reader can use such repetition with great effect—letting the phrase become a little bigger each time it is heard, and thereby sustaining a sense of mounting joy through to the end. If "the Lord" sounds the same each time, the opposite effect is produced and a sense of dull repetition results.

The style of the passage serves to heighten its message: Great and wonderful things are coming, and they all come from the heart of a God whose mercy and love are unfathomable. Notice that Israel's joy is based on God's joy. Here is an unusual image of our God rejoicing and singing. The growing excitement of Advent is perfectly expressed in this exultant text.

READING II **Before we had a lectionary with a three-year cycle of readings, when the readings for each Sunday**

READING II Philippians 4:4–7

A reading from the Letter of Saint Paul to the Philippians

Read slowly. This reading is classic. It begins with a directive to be happy! The greeting "Brothers and sisters" can weaken the strong opening. Pause after it, and begin afresh with "Rejoice . . ."

Brothers and sisters:
Rejoice in the Lord *always*.
I shall say it *again*: *rejoice*!

First instruction: Get a reputation for kindness.

Your *kindness* should be known to *all*.
The Lord is *near*.

Second instruction: Worry is worthless.

Third instruction: Let thanksgiving be the hallmark of your prayer.

Have no anxiety at *all*, but in *everything*,
by *prayer* and *petition*, with *thanksgiving*,
make your requests *known* to God.

Final result: You will know a kind of peace you never thought possible.

Then the *peace* of God that surpasses all *understanding*
will *guard* your *hearts* and *minds* in Christ *Jesus*.

GOSPEL Luke 3:10–18

A reading from the holy Gospel according to Luke

The *crowds* asked John the *Baptist*,
"What should we *do*?"
He said to them in *reply*,
"Whoever has *two* cloaks
should *share* with the person who has *none*.
And whoever has *food* should do *likewise*."

It must be clear that this is a surprise. "Even *tax collectors*!"

Even *tax* collectors came to be baptized and *they* said to him,
"*Teacher*, what should *we* do?"

were the same every year, this passage gave the 3rd Sunday of Advent a special name: *Gaudete,* Latin for "rejoice." The first words of the second reading were used as the entrance song. There were other indications that this Sunday was special: The vestments worn by the clergy could be rose-colored, rather than violet or purple; flowers could adorn the sanctuary; and the organ, which was silent during this season, pealed forth again for this day only—and was then silent again until the Gloria of the Midnight Mass on Christmas. These practices are still observed in some communities, and they serve to heighten the sense of joyful expectation that is at the heart of Advent.

Beyond considerations for the season, notice how effective this text is as a touchstone or slogan for the Christian. If joy is the basic expression of our faith and our kindness is known to all; if we refuse to surrender to anxiety, and if thanksgiving is the substance of our prayer—then the peace of God, which is beyond anything we can imagine, will guard our hearts and minds. What a witness we can be to an anxious world if we live by these words!

In your proclamation of this beautiful reading, let each element stand out clearly. There is not one unnecessary word or thought here. Each one is a message of comfort, inspiration, and authentic Christian joy. Though Paul is quite capable of expressing himself as an old curmudgeon, this text shows us that his fundamental response to the Lord's good news is optimism and joy. It should be ours as well.

GOSPEL **John the Baptist's dialogue with the people who come**

He answered them,
"Stop collecting *more* than what is *prescribed*."

Another surprise: "*Soldiers* also asked him!"

Soldiers also asked him,
"And what is it that *we* should do?"
He told them,
"Do not practice *extortion*,
do not falsely *accuse* anyone,
and be *satisfied* with your *wages*."

Pause slightly; a new section—and a new controversy—begins here.

Now the *people* were filled with *expectation*,
and all were asking in their hearts
whether *John* might be the *Christ*.
John answered them *all*, saying,
"*I* am baptizing you with *water*,
but one *mightier* than I is coming.
I am not *worthy* to loosen the *thongs* of his *sandals*.
He will baptize you with the Holy *Spirit* and *fire*.

The reference to a winnowing fan is meaningless to most; but its function is explained.

A strong statement; don't shy away from it. Sometimes the good news sounds like bad news.

The last sentence gives us a hint of the scope of John's ministry. It was far greater than we might think and explains the high praise Jesus reserves for him later on.

His *winnowing* fan is in his *hand* to clear his *threshing* floor
and to gather the *wheat* into his *barn*,
but the *chaff* he will *burn* with unquenchable *fire*."
Exhorting them in many *other* ways,
he preached good *news* to the *people*.

to him reveals several points that the evangelist Luke wants to make strongly. First, notice that the people who approach John with the question, "What should we do?" are a motley crew. We hear clearly the low esteem in which tax collectors were held in the words, "*Even* tax collectors came to be baptized!" And soldiers too? Yes, the soldiers whose job it was to keep the chosen people subject to Rome! Who would have thought that such riff-raff would be interested in repentance?

Well, that's one of Luke's favorite themes: All human expectations of the coming of the Messiah will be shaken—even reversed. It's as though Luke says to his readers, "If you think the Lord is interested only in preaching to the already converted, think again!"

Second, a related point: the Messiah toward whom John points is coming for the salvation of the whole world, yes, even beyond the chosen people. A shocking revelation to Luke's contemporaries! Even the Gentiles will hear the good news and receive the unbounded favor of the Lord. Luke's universalism is a favorite theme.

Third, a notion that must be corrected: John the Baptist had quite a following. In fact, as we shall see later, there was a strong contingent that initially rejected Jesus in favor of John. But John himself was the strongest opponent of such a notion. Again and again he had to make it clear that "one mightier" than he was coming. John baptized with water (for cleansing); the "one mightier" would baptize with fire (for purifying).

4TH SUNDAY OF ADVENT

Lectionary #12

READING I Micah 5:1–4a

The reading is an oracle, an exalted prophecy in poetic form. It must be proclaimed with warm solemnity.

Ephrathah = EF-ruh-thuh

This sentence is parenthetical. A change of tone, slightly more explanatory, will help. Then the description of the ruler's role continues.

The emphasis is that the *Lord's* strength, not his own, is what makes him a good shepherd.

"He shall be peace" requires a dramatic sense of closure and resolution. Although the verb "be" is not marked for emphasis, you might experiment with it.

A reading from the Book of the Prophet Micah

Thus says the *LORD*:
You, Bethlehem-Ephrathah
too *small* to be among the clans of *Judah*,
from *you* shall come *forth* for me
one who is to be *ruler* in Israel;
whose *origin* is from of *old*,
from *ancient* times.

Therefore the Lord will give them *up*, until the time
when she who is to give *birth* has *borne*,
and the *rest* of his kindred shall *return*
to the children of *Israel*.
He shall stand *firm* and *shepherd* his flock
by the strength of the *LORD*,
in the majestic *name* of the LORD, his *God*;
and they shall *remain*, for now his *greatness*
shall reach to the *ends* of the *earth*;
he shall be *peace*.

READING I This oracle begins gently and rises to majesty. It foretells the appearance of an ideal messianic king in Ephrathah (Bethlehem, the city of David) who will inaugurate a new and wonderful era after Israel's period of exile. One of the central points of the text is that, contrary to expectations, this ruler will come from a relatively insignificant tribe. Clearly, the passage is chosen for this Sunday because it mentions Bethlehem and because of its use of childbirth as a sign of a new age. More generally, it is redolent of the tradition that the messiah would rise up from the lineage of David. Thus the text complements the gospel reading, which finds Mary visiting Elizabeth immediately after the revelation that Mary is to bear a son.

The description of the promised king is interrupted by a parenthetical comment that tells of a waiting period (until the mother of the promised one has borne him), and then a reunification of all the scattered tribes of Israel. The image of this ideal ruler is that of a good shepherd who protects his flock. Finally, peace will prevail. And that concept is strongly personified. This new king will himself *be* peace.

READING II This passage from the epistle to the Hebrews is not particularly easy to proclaim, but it contains important theology. Placed on the 4th Sunday of Advent between the promise of a "king of peace" (first reading) and the joy of the visitation (gospel), it is a powerful reminder that Jesus was born in the flesh in order to offer that flesh in sacrificial atonement for the world.

READING II Hebrews 10:5–10

A reading from the Letter to the Hebrews

This reading is a series of quotations and explanations. Be sure to distinguish between the two. If not dealt with correctly, the greeting "brothers and sisters" can weaken the strong opening of the reading. Pause after it, and begin afresh with "When Christ . . ."

Brothers and sisters:
When *Christ* came into the *world,* he said:
"*Sacrifice* and *offering* you did not *desire,*
but a *body* you prepared for me;
in *holocausts* and *sin* offerings you took no *delight.*
Then I said, 'As is *written* of me in the *scroll,*
behold, I come to do your *will,* O God.'"

The first part of the quote is repeated and then explained. Make "These are offered . . ." sound like an explanation, and not like a continuation of the quote.

First he says, "*Sacrifices* and *offerings,*
holocausts and *sin* offerings,
you neither *desired* nor *delighted* in."
These are offered according to the *law.*

The second part of the quote is repeated and then explained. Notice that the explanation begins with "He takes away . . ." Don't make it sound like part of the quote.

Then he says, "*Behold,* I come to do your *will.*"
He takes *away* the *first* to *establish* the *second.*

The concluding sentence explains how we are affected by all this.

By this "*will,*" we have been *consecrated*
through the offering of the *body* of Jesus *Christ* once for *all.*

Suddenly, we seem a very great distance from images of Christmas. The reason Jesus came into the world was to be obedient to the Father's will that he die for the world. The manger is never far from the cross. Thus, in Advent and Christmas we already foresee a hint of Good Friday—and then Easter Sunday.

Recall that Hebrews was written for the instruction of those whose roots lay in the ancient traditions of sacrificial offerings. The controlling purpose in the writer's mind is to show that Christ's perfect sacrifice (perfect because it was complete) has rendered the old rituals superfluous.

The concluding sentence indicates the effect of Jesus' sacrifice: We have been consecrated. The effect is like that of the old sacrificial offerings that Jesus' death replaced. Those, too, were to cleanse and consecrate the people. The great difference is that the old sacrifices had to be repeated over and over. The sacrifice of Christ is offered "once for all."

GOSPEL The account of the visitation is of one of the richest stories in the Bible. It has won a favored place in the hearts of many artists and writers. Young Mary, having just conceived a son, hastens to the hill country to visit her older relative, Elizabeth, who is six months pregnant with John, the one who will "prepare the way of the Lord." It is a scene rich with human poignancy and divine revelation. And yet, on closer examination, it is clear that the divine truths implied by the visit far outweigh any merely human considerations.

GOSPEL Luke 1:39–45

A reading from the holy Gospel according to Luke

The first sentence sets the scene. The rest of the passage is Elizabeth's response.

Mary set out
and traveled to the *hill* country in *haste*
to a town of *Judah*,
where she entered the house of *Zechariah*
and greeted *Elizabeth*.

Communicate the wonder of this moment. It is the moment of recognition that is at the heart of Luke's purpose.

When Elizabeth *heard* Mary's greeting,
the *infant leaped* in her *womb*,
and *Elizabeth*, filled with the Holy *Spirit*,
cried out in a loud *voice* and said,
"*Blessed* are you among *women*,
and *blessed* is the *fruit* of your *womb*.

The question is rhetorical, not literal. The sense is, "How wonderful that the mother of my Lord should come to me!"

And how does this *happen* to *me*,
that the mother of my *Lord* should *come* to me?
For at the moment the sound of your *greeting* reached my *ears*,
the *infant* in my *womb* leaped for *joy*.

Do not let your voice fall at the end of this short, dramatic scene. Mary's blessedness is that she believed! It is ours too.

Blessed are you who *believed*
that what was *spoken* to you by the Lord
would be *fulfilled*."

We must look to Luke's purpose in telling the story the way he does. Most of its meaning lies beneath the surface. First, it is necessary to bring Jesus and John together for that moment of recognition. John leaps in Elizabeth's womb to signal that recognition of the savior in Mary's womb. It is not an original image with Luke. The Hebrew scriptures record similar instances, predicting a future relationship between the figures involved.

Second, Elizabeth, "filled with the Holy Spirit," is able to interpret the sign. That is, the insight she has comes from God. Though we might become preoccupied with the human beings involved in this scene (all four of them), Luke clearly wants us to understand that these events are all manifestations of God's activity.

Third, Elizabeth's praise of Mary is based solely on Mary's obedience and faith. The greatness of Mary and her role in salvation history are thus defined by her cooperation with God's will. Mary's visit is not about attending to Elizabeth's needs as she approaches childbirth. Though it is surely not excluded, far more than hospitality is at stake here. Mary stays with Elizabeth about three months (until John's birth?) and then returns home. But to interpret Luke's story as a simple lesson in hospitality, as is often done, misses the much larger purposes mentioned above.

Here we have yet another example of how we must read the scriptures with an eye to the deeper meaning. The sacred writings are always more than history. The writers are not chroniclers, not historians. They are theologians, who use storytelling techniques, poetry and other literary forms to reveal the truth about our relationship to God and God's fidelity toward us.

CHRISTMAS VIGIL

Lectionary #13

READING I Isaiah 62:1–5

A reading from the Book of the Prophet Isaiah

Notice the poetic device called parallelism. The thought of every line is echoed in the line that follows it. Let this poetic structure be heard, but avoid a repetitious pattern of intonation.

The text is clearly divided into four brief sections. Begin each section with new energy.

For *Zion's* sake I will not be *silent*,
for *Jerusalem's* sake I will not be *quiet*,
until her vindication shines *forth* like the *dawn*
and her *victory* like a burning *torch*.

Nations shall *behold* your vindication,
and all the *kings* your *glory*;
you shall be called by a *new* name
pronounced by the mouth of the LORD.
You shall be a glorious *crown* in the hand of the LORD,
a royal *diadem* held by your *God*.

No *more* shall people call you *"Forsaken,"*
or your land *"Desolate,"*
but you shall be called "My *Delight*,"
and your land *"Espoused."*
For the LORD *delights* in you
and makes your land his *spouse*.

The word "you" must be emphasized above the rest, for that is the point.

As a young *man* marries a *virgin*,
your *Builder* shall marry *you*;
and as a *bridegroom* rejoices in his *bride*
so shall your *God* rejoice in *you*.

READING I **We have been hearing the songs of Isaiah all through Advent, and we continue to hear them at all four of the Masses of Christmas—vigil, midnight, dawn, and day. Portions of these exultant canticles have been unforgettably set to music in Handel's *Messiah*. They all celebrate Israel's return from exile, the restoration of the holy city of Jerusalem, and a new intimate relationship with God.**

To describe this new relationship adequately, Isaiah has to resort to metaphors that paint a picture of total intimacy: young lovers, bride and bridegroom, married couple. Such relationships are the only ones tender enough to describe God's loving care for Israel. And we still use this kind of language to describe our relationship with God. We speak of the marriage of heaven and earth at the incarnation, the church as bride and Christ as bridegroom at the resurrection, and the wedding banquet of heaven that awaits us.

The challenge of this reading is to find just the right combination of ecstatic joy and tenderness in your proclamation. A further challenge is to give each image its due; don't rush through the text, but give each line and its parallel restatement time to be absorbed before going on to the next. This does not mean the reading will be punctuated with lengthy pauses, but it will need breadth in proclamation, expansiveness in delivery, and largeness in tone. In other words, share these words with the broadness and exultation the text clearly demands. Such readings are not for lightweights!

READING II Acts 13:16–17, 22–25

A reading from the Acts of the Apostles

Antioch = AN-tee-ahk
Pisidia = pih-SID-ee-uh

When *Paul* reached *Antioch* in *Pisidia* and entered
the *synagogue,*
he stood up, *motioned* with his hand, and said,

Pause after the first sentence, which sets the scene, then launch into Paul's exposition.

"Fellow *Israelites* and you *others* who are God-fearing, *listen.*
The God of this people *Israel* chose our *ancestors*
and *exalted* the people during their *sojourn*
in the land of *Egypt.*
With uplifted *arm* he led them *out* of it.

"Then he removed *Saul* and raised up *David* as *king;*
of him he *testified,*
'I have found *David,* son of *Jesse,* a man after my own *heart;*
he will carry out my every *wish.*'

Come to a rest here before going on, then renew the energy and let your voice carry the conviction of the text.

"From this man's *descendants* God, according to his *promise,*
has brought to Israel a *savior, Jesus.*
John heralded his *coming* by proclaiming a *baptism* of *repentance*
to all the people of *Israel;*
and as John was *completing* his course, he would say,
'What do you suppose that I *am*? I am not *he.*
Behold, one is coming *after* me;
I am not worthy to unfasten the *sandals* of his *feet.*'"

READING II **Paul is preaching to his fellow Jews, laying out a case for seeing in Jesus the Messiah foretold by the prophets, prefigured in historical events, and testified to by that latter-day prophet, John the Baptist. From a logical and scientific point of view, Paul's argument proves nothing, just as from that point of view we can prove nothing about our faith. That's the difference between faith and knowledge. Believing is not the same as knowing. We might say, "In my heart of hearts I *know* Jesus rose from the dead," but of course we don't *know* it; we believe it strongly and allow it to guide our lives accordingly.**

Paul's audience probably didn't distinguish between believing and knowing as we do today. The ancient Near Eastern way of thinking was different from our own Western approach—more intuitive, less rationalistic—and we must remember this when we read the scriptures. Many came to believe in Jesus because of the strength of Paul's argument, but they weren't forced into belief by hard logic. The evidence presented to them in no way compelled them to draw Paul's conclusions.

Such is always the case with you as a proclaimer of the word. You invite your listeners over and over again to hear the evidence of God's love for us and respond to it. The invitation will be most effective when it comes from the heart of your own faith. It was probably Paul's fervent faith, as much as his so-called "argument," that won the people over.

GOSPEL Matthew 1:1–25

If you decide to proclaim the genealogy, practice the names so that you can proclaim each one with ease, so the members of the assembly can relax and listen instead of rooting for you!

Perez = PAIR-ez

Zerah = ZEE-rah

Tamar = TAY-mahr

Hezron = HEZ-ruhn

Ram = ram

Amminadab = uh-MIN-uh-dab

Nahshon = NAH-shuhn

Salmon = SAL-muhn

Boaz = BOH-az

Rahab = RAY-hab

Obed = OH-bed

Uriah = yoo-RĪ-uh

Rehoboam = ree-huh-BOH-uhm

Abijah = uh-BĪ-juh

Asaph = AY-saf

Jehoshaphat = jeh-HOH-shuh-fat

Joram = JOHR-uhm

Uzziah = uh-ZĪ-uh

A reading from the holy Gospel according to Matthew

The book of the *genealogy* of Jesus *Christ*,
the son of *David*, the son of *Abraham*.

Abraham became the father of Isaac,
Isaac the father of Jacob,
Jacob the father of Judah and his brothers.
Judah became the father of Perez and Zerah,
whose mother was Tamar.
Perez became the father of Hezron,
Hezron the father of Ram,
Ram the father of Amminadab.
Amminadab became the father of Nahshon,
Nahshon the father of Salmon,
Salmon the father of Boaz,
whose mother was Rahab.
Boaz became the father of Obed,
whose mother was Ruth.
Obed became the father of Jesse,
Jesse the father of David the king.

David became the father of Solomon,
whose mother had been the wife of Uriah.
Solomon became the father of Rehoboam,
Rehoboam the father of Abijah,
Abijah the father of Asaph.
Asaph became the father of Jehoshaphat,
Jehoshaphat the father of Joram,
Joram the father of Uzziah.

GOSPEL Most will decide to take the shorter version of this gospel passage, choosing to leave the long list of Jesus' ancestors for silent meditation. And that's a good decision if the genealogy is read poorly. Only those who have mastered the reading's many names and have acquired a deep understanding of why Matthew included this genealogy in the first place should attempt to proclaim it! A sloppy stumbling through the names, or a bored and boring rattling off of them, will do more harm than omitting it altogether. In such a case, it is better to be content with proclaiming the last eight verses (the shorter version).

Having said that, let's consider what the genealogy can teach us when masterfully proclaimed and opened up a little by the homilist. First of all, the genealogy says, "If you want to know this Jesus, you have to know the Hebrew scriptures, the Old Testament, which is a record of the lives of his ancestors." Second, it makes specific mention of several women who played important roles in salvation history—something we can hear with great profit, given the patriarchal society of Jesus' forebears and our male-dominated notions about God and church. Third, it demonstrates, with that special kind of intuitive logic found in the second reading, that God's goodwill on our behalf is documented all the way back to Abraham. God's plan to save us has not been and will not be thwarted.

Jotham = JOH-thuhm
Ahaz = AY-haz
Hezekiah = hez-eh-KĪ-uh
Manasseh = muh-NAS-uh
Amos = AY-m*s
Josiah = joh-SĪ-uh
Jechoniah = jek-oh-NĪ-uh

Uzziah became the father of Jotham,
Jotham the father of Ahaz,
Ahaz the father of Hezekiah.
Hezekiah became the father of Manasseh,
Manasseh the father of Amos,
Amos the father of Josiah.
Josiah became the father of Jechoniah and his brothers
at the time of the Babylonian exile.

Shealtiel = shee-AL-tee-uhl
Zerubbabel = zuh-ROOB-uh-b*l
Abiud = uh-BĪ-uhd
Eliakim = ee-LĪ-uh-kim
Azor = AY-zohr
Zadok = ZAY-dok
Achim = AH-kim
Eliud = ee-LĪ-uhd
Eleazar = el-ee-AY-zer
Matthan = MATH-uhn

After the Babylonian exile,
Jechoniah became the father of Shealtiel,
Shealtiel the father of Zerubbabel,
Zerubbabel the father of Abiud.
Abiud became the father of Eliakim,
Eliakim the father of Azor,
Azor the father of Zadok.
Zadok became the father of Achim,
Achim the father of Eliud,
Eliud the father of Eleazar.
Eleazar became the father of Matthan,
Matthan the father of Jacob,
Jacob the father of Joseph, the husband of Mary.
Of her was born Jesus who is called the Christ.

Thus the total number of generations
from Abraham to David
is fourteen generations;
from David to the Babylonian exile,
fourteen generations;
from the Babylonian exile to the Christ,
fourteen generations.

But many people on that list tried to thwart it! Here's something else we learn from the genealogy: There are some heavy-duty sinners among Jesus' ancestors. God works through human agents—even through their sinfulness. Here's the antidote to that recurring malady that makes us think that only saints can be channels of grace, that seals up God's activity behind church walls and corrals divine wisdom into official pronouncements. God is at work, God's wisdom is to be found, in the people of God, that motley crew of both saints and sinners that God dotes on as newlyweds dote on each other.

The story of how the birth of Jesus came about is presented here in an eight-verse mini-drama. The potentially idyllic scene of the young married couple is marred by the scandal of a pregnancy before marriage. But divine intervention brings a happy resolution, and Joseph's dilemma is solved. Proclaim this material as the story it is while remembering its solemn consequences for the future of all creation!

The break here is obvious, but connect it to what comes before by emphasizing the word "birth." Jesus has already been mentioned above, as have Mary and Joseph. The following story does not introduce them. If you begin here (taking the shorter version), then emphasize both "birth" and "Christ."

Now *this* is how the *birth* of Jesus *Christ* came *about*.
When his mother *Mary* was betrothed to *Joseph*,
but before they *lived* together,
she was found with *child* through the Holy *Spirit*.

Joseph her *husband*, since he was a *righteous* man,
yet unwilling to *expose* her to *shame*,
decided to *divorce* her *quietly*.
Such was his *intention* when, *behold*,
the angel of the *Lord* appeared to him in a *dream* and said,
"*Joseph*, son of *David*,
do not be *afraid* to take Mary your *wife* into your *home*.

The genealogy tells of Jesus' human origins. Now we hear of his divine origin as well.

For it is through the Holy *Spirit*
that this child has been *conceived* in her.
She will bear a *son* and you are to *name* him *Jesus*,
because he will *save* his people from their *sins*."

All this took *place* to fulfill
what the Lord had said through the *prophet*:
"*Behold*, the *virgin* shall conceive and bear a *son*,
and they shall *name* him *Emmanuel*,"
which means "God is *with* us."

The final lines are filled with peaceful resolution. Matthew's remark about Mary and Joseph having no "relations" emphasizes his point that Jesus is of divine origin.

When Joseph *awoke*,
he did as the angel of the Lord had *commanded* him
and took his *wife* into his *home*.
He had no *relations* with her until she bore a *son*,
and he *named* him *Jesus*.

[Shorter: Matthew 1:18–25]

CHRISTMAS MIDNIGHT

Lectionary #14

READING I Isaiah 9:1–6

Pause before and after the announcement. You must have the assembly's attention.

A reading from the Book of the Prophet Isaiah

Maintain an exalted tone throughout. This is poetry.

The people who walked in *darkness*
have seen a great *light*;
upon those who dwelt in the land of *gloom*
a *light* has shone.
You have brought them abundant *joy*
and great *rejoicing*,
as they *rejoice* before you as at the *harvest*,
as people make *merry* when dividing *spoils*.

For the yoke that *burdened* them,
the *pole* on their *shoulder*,
and the *rod* of their *taskmaster*
you have *smashed*, as on the day of *Midian*.

For every *boot* that tramped in *battle*,
every *cloak* rolled in *blood*,
will be *burned* as fuel for *flames*.

Here are the words the assembly is waiting for. Make their delivery special.

For a *child* is born to us, a *son* is given us;
upon *his* shoulder *dominion* rests.
They name him Wonder-*Counselor*, God-*Hero*,
Father-*Forever*, Prince of *Peace*.
His *dominion* is *vast*
and forever *peaceful*,

READING I Christmas Midnight Mass is special in Christian tradition. You will probably be proclaiming God's word to a church full of people whose attention is drawn by many things: the decorations, the children, the crèche, the music. It is important that you begin in such a way that you capture the attention of those present. A strong announcement of the reading preceded and followed by a brief silence may do the trick. The text before you has been immortalized by writers, readers, composers, and musicians. It deserves special treatment.

Isaiah writes about Israel's liberation from oppression through the ascendancy of King Hezekiah. The yoke, pole, and rod of the oppressor all symbolize Assyria, and because God sides with Israel, the oppressor will be conquered. Hezekiah is supposed to bring to his reign a kind of justice that will make him truly great, a man after God's own heart. But the expectations of him are too high, and he doesn't live up to the prophecy.

There is one who does, however, and that is the Messiah-king whose birth we celebrate this night. The yoke, pole, and rod of oppression that he will smash are the yoke of sin, the pole of punishment, and the rod of death—the ultimate enemies of all humankind. The birth of Christ ushers in the messianic age, the age in which we live. The second coming of Christ will bring the fullness of that age—forever peaceful, ruled in justice, brought about by the zeal of the Lord of hosts. Here is the full meaning of Christmas. Import as much of it as possible into your proclamation.

from *David's* throne, and over his *kingdom*,
which he *confirms* and *sustains*
by *judgment* and *justice*,
both *now* and for*ever*.
The *zeal* of the LORD of *hosts* will *do* this!

READING II Titus 2:11–14

A reading from the Letter of Saint Paul to Titus

This reading is brief but packed with meaning. Do not rush. Be sure you understand the meaning of every phrase, and give each its proper weight. Punctuation is not your best guide here. The meaning of the text is.

Beloved:
The grace of *God* has *appeared*, saving *all*
and *training* us to *reject* godless *ways* and worldly *desires*
and to live *temperately*, *justly*, and *devoutly* in this age,
as we await the blessed *hope*,
the *appearance* of the glory of our great *God*
and *savior* Jesus *Christ*,
who *gave* himself for us to *deliver* us from all *lawlessness*
and to *cleanse* for himself a people as his *own*,
eager to do what is *good*.

GOSPEL Luke 2:1–14

A reading from the holy Gospel according to Luke

The gospel proclamation is particularly significant tonight. Bring that significance to your proclamation.

Quirinius = kwih-RIN-ee-uhs

In those days a *decree* went out from Caesar *Augustus*
that the whole *world* should be *enrolled*.
This was the *first* enrollment,
when *Quirinius* was governor of *Syria*.

READING II **The first reading and the gospel both celebrate the birth of a child. This brief passage from Titus identifies the child and looks far ahead—beyond the historical event itself—to the moment toward which all history is aimed: the appearance of the glory of God in the coming of Jesus Christ. Clearly we live between two singular events. The first has saved us and "trained" us how to live in expectation of the second. It's a wonderful way of looking at the grace of God, which trains us to live godly lives, to await the age to come with eager longing, and meanwhile to be enthusiastic about doing good deeds.**

The author of this passage has packed it with meaning. Because it is so brief, take great care lest it end before it has had a chance to work its intended effect. This is a thinking person's formulation of the good news: Give the members of the assembly time to think, especially on this night when the spirit of the season makes us more receptive than ever.

GOSPEL **Perhaps the most familiar text of the entire Bible, this passage will be gratefully received simply because it is so beloved. But the danger for the reader is that familiarity will bring over-confidence. Strive for an energetic, fresh approach that makes the old story new. A deeper understanding of the text can help a reader achieve this.**

Every single fact recounted here has a second level of meaning. Luke is not so much interested in history as in its interpretation. The significance of each event is more important than its historical accuracy.

So *all* went to be *enrolled*, *each* to his own *town*.
And Joseph *too* went up from *Galilee* from the town of *Nazareth*
to *Judea*, to the city of *David* that is called *Bethlehem*,
because he was of the *house* and *family* of David,
to be enrolled with *Mary*, his *betrothed*, who was with *child*.

While they were there,
the *time* came for her to have her *child*,
and she gave birth to her firstborn *son*.
She wrapped him in *swaddling* clothes and laid him in a *manger*,
because there was no *room* for them in the *inn*.

Pause. A new section begins here.

Now there were *shepherds* in that region living in the *fields*
and keeping the *night watch* over their *flock*.
The angel of the *Lord* appeared to them
and the *glory* of the Lord *shone* around them,
and they were struck with great *fear*.
The angel said to them,
"Do not be *afraid*;
for *behold*, I proclaim to you good *news* of great *joy*
that will be for *all* the people.
For *today* in the city of *David*
a *savior* has been born for you who is *Christ* and *Lord*.
And this will be a *sign* for you:
you will find an infant wrapped in *swaddling* clothes
and lying in a *manger*."

Again, this is clearly a new section. Give it renewed energy.

And *suddenly* there was a *multitude* of the heavenly host
with the angel,
praising *God* and saying:
"*Glory* to God in the *highest*
and on *earth peace* to those on whom his *favor* rests."

Indeed, some of the facts are disputed. But this does not alter the meaning or significance one bit. For example, Caesar Augustus may or may not have ordered that a census be taken. There is no evidence from any other source that he did. But the meaning is that Caesar Augustus was known as a bringer of peace, and Luke wants to point out that the real bringer of peace is Jesus. There was no room for the Holy Family in the inn—a fitting and consistent circumstance for one who would be spurned, despised, and rejected. Whether or not Jesus was laid in a manger, Luke means to say that this child is food for the world. Were the shepherds truly the first to hear of the birth of this lowly Messiah? The question misses the point. The point is that shepherds were part of the lowest social class of the time—the kind of people for whom this humble Messiah will show preference and special love. The wonderful events happened in Bethlehem because it is the "city of David," and all the prophets knew the Messiah would be born from that royal line.

You will be amazed by the change in your proclamation of this text when you are attentive to the significance of every detail, rather than to the detail itself. Simply holding in your mind the meaning of the events will affect your reading in a wonderful way. Above all else, read the passage lovingly, for this story reveals just how much God loves us.

CHRISTMAS DAWN

Lectionary #15

READING I Isaiah 62:11–12

A reading from the Book of the Prophet Isaiah

Notice that there are three levels here: (1) The Lord proclaims; (2) "Say to daughter Zion; (3) 'Your savior comes!'" Make sure this is clear.

See, the LORD proclaims
to the *ends* of the *earth*:
say to daughter *Zion*,
your *savior* comes!

Place stress on "reward" and "recompense," not on the prepositions "with" and "before."

Here is his *reward* with him,
his *recompense* before him.

They shall be called the *holy* people,
the *redeemed* of the LORD,

"Frequented" is odd and weak. Give it special attention.

and you shall be called *"Frequented,"*
a city that is not *forsaken*.

READING II Titus 3:4–7

A reading from the Letter of Saint Paul to Titus

Beloved:

In two sentences, Paul gives us a thumbnail sketch of the good news. Be sure every phrase is carefully nuanced. There are no spare words here.

When the *kindness* and generous *love*
of God our *savior* appeared,
not because of any righteous *deeds we* had done
but because of his *mercy*,
he *saved* us through the bath of *rebirth*
and *renewal* by the Holy *Spirit*,

READING I Isaiah's context is the great Feast of Lights (Tabernacles), so it is appropriate that at dawn on the day we celebrate the birth of Christ, the light of the world, we should hear this lovely poetry. It must be read slowly, joyfully, and with great dignity. The message is that the people of God ("daughter Zion") are made holy by God's presence in their midst. They are no longer to be considered "forsaken" or "abandoned," just the opposite. Emmanuel ("God-with-us") has pitched his tent among them. God has made of Zion a tabernacle, a dwelling place, and all the nations of the world will seek this holy place, filling it with eager pilgrims.

READING II If there is a "bottom line" in Christian faith, here it is. We believe that a God of infinite love lavished the Spirit upon us through Jesus Christ to open eternity and make us happy. God did not do this to reward us for a life of obedience, or to redeem us from the wicked things we have done, or even obligate us to a life of good deeds. No, God offers this gift only out of kindness and love.

Let the good news ring out in all its blissful simplicity. God's loving kindness has appeared in Jesus Christ, lavished upon the creation that God looked upon when he made it and saw it was good.

GOSPEL In this brief gospel, pay particular attention to these words: "made known to us"; "they made known the message that had been told them"; "all they had heard and seen." Notice

whom he richly *poured out* on us
through Jesus *Christ* our *savior*,
so that we might be *justified* by his *grace*
and become *heirs* in hope of eternal *life*.

GOSPEL Luke 2:15–20

A reading from the holy Gospel according to Luke

When the angels went *away* from them to *heaven*,
the shepherds *said* to one another,
"Let us *go*, then, to *Bethlehem*
to *see* this thing that has taken place,
which the Lord has made *known* to us."

There is a trap here. Pause after the comma to avoid making it sound like Mary, Joseph, and Jesus are all lying in the manger.

So they went in *haste* and found *Mary* and *Joseph*,
and the infant lying in the *manger*.
When they *saw* this,
they made *known* the message
that had been *told* them about this child.
All who *heard* it were *amazed*
by what had been *told* them by the *shepherds*.

Pause here. Give special emphasis to Mary's response; it is different from that of the shepherds.

And *Mary kept* all these things,
reflecting on them in her *heart*.
Then the shepherds *returned*,
glorifying and praising *God*
for all they had *heard* and *seen*,
just as it had been *told* to them.

how much "hearing and telling" there is in this passage. The shepherds hear the good news and immediately pass it on. There is clearly no suggestion that this news should be kept a secret. It's so wonderful that one's instant reaction is to tell others.

Notice, though, that Mary's response is different. She "kept" the news, "reflecting" on it. Hers is the contemplative response, and it shows us that not everyone reacts in the same way to the gospel. There are people whose nature practically compels them to shout out the good news of God's love for us. There are others whose natural response is to fall silent in the face of such news.

The mature Christian probably does both, realizing that to share one's faith effectively, one must have done some serious reflection on it first. By emulating both the shepherds' enthusiasm and Mary's contemplation, we will find that brand of joy that has been called the surest sign of God's presence within us.

CHRISTMAS DAY

Lectionary #16

READING I Isaiah 52:7–10

A reading from the Book of the Prophet Isaiah

Begin with strong conviction and a big voice. This text is not for the timid.

How *beautiful* upon the *mountains*
are the *feet* of him who brings glad *tidings*,
announcing *peace*, bearing good *news*,
announcing *salvation*, and saying to *Zion*,
"Your *God* is *King*!"

Do not shout "Hark" or make it sound stern, but pause slightly before it.

Hark! Your sentinels raise a *cry*,
together they *shout* for *joy*,
for they see *directly*, before their *eyes*,
the LORD *restoring* Zion.

Break out together in *song*,
O *ruins* of Jerusalem!
For the LORD *comforts* his people,
he *redeems* Jerusalem.
The LORD has *bared* his holy *arm*
in the sight of all the *nations*;
all the ends of the *earth* will behold
the *salvation* of our *God*.

The last two lines are crucial; they express one of the major themes of Christmas.

READING I Does it seem odd to you that this reading begins by talking about "beautiful feet"? A special poetic device is being employed here. The feet of the messenger symbolize the whole experience of receiving glad tidings: expecting the message, seeing the messenger from afar, hearing the footsteps as the messenger draws closer. And that experience is surely beautiful.

The sentinels see the effect of the good news: The Lord is restoring Zion, comforting the people, and demonstrating his power to save. And finally the whole people are encouraged to break out in song. Notice that this reading builds upon itself. The message gets bigger and bigger as more and more voices join in, until "all the ends of the earth" behold God's salvation.

If you are one of those lectors who feels inhibited by emotion-laden and poetic texts like this one, take comfort. You are not expected to dramatize or reenact the feelings expressed here. In fact, it would be a great mistake if you tried to. Liturgical proclamation is different from oral interpretation of literature or dramatic reading. The purpose of liturgical proclamation is to allow the power of God's word to do its work. You are involved, but you should be transparent. In dramatic reading, the text is interpreted in a certain way so that the actor and the text both become part of the audience's experience. The lector in the liturgy does not interpret but should remain objective and permit the text to have its intended effect. The text is always in the foreground; the proclaimer serves it in the background. This does not mean that the proclaimer is cold or that the proclamation is without feeling. It means that

READING II Hebrews 1:1–6

A reading from the Letter to the Hebrews

Brothers and sisters:
In times *past*, God spoke in *partial* and *various* ways
to our *ancestors* through the *prophets*;
in these *last* days, he has spoken to us through the *Son*,
whom he made *heir* of all *things*
and *through* whom he created the *universe*,
who is the *refulgence* of his *glory*,
the very *imprint* of his *being*,
and who *sustains* all things by his mighty *word*.

Be as precise and emphatic as the author is here: This Son is the "refulgence" of God's glory, the "very imprint" of God's being. See how different translations try to capture the writer's point.

When he had accomplished purification from *sins*,
he took his *seat* at the right hand of the *Majesty* on *high*,
as far *superior* to the *angels*
as the *name* he has inherited is more *excellent* than theirs.

Beware of a scoffing here; the mood is one of wonder!

For to which of the *angels* did God ever say:
"You are my *son*; this day I have *begotten* you"?
Or again:
"I will be a *father* to *him*, and he shall be a *son* to *me*"?
And again, when he leads the *firstborn* into the world, he says:
"Let all the *angels* of God *worship* him."

the reader serves the text's purpose rather than the text serving the reader's purpose. Take full charge of your ministry by letting the word of God take full charge of you.

READING II For the first time in this liturgical year we hear a reading from the letter to the Hebrews. The entire work is an *apologia*—that is, a demonstration that all the prophesies and hopes of the Hebrew scriptures have their fulfillment in Jesus the Christ. The reading also shows us that the relationship of the Father and the Son has existed for all eternity—well before the Son took flesh and came to live among us. Clearly, this reading leads us to a fuller and richer meaning of the Christmas celebration.

This is not an easy reading, however. The sentences are long and layered with subordinate clauses. The text requires a great deal of study and preparation before justice can be done to it in proclamation, and it contains some semi-apocalyptic imagery that we may never fully understand. But once we have mastered its structure and glimpsed the depth of its meaning, we can read it with the conviction and nobility the text demands.

One thing is quite clear. The author of the letter to the Hebrews was very much concerned with teaching us about the divinity of Jesus and his exalted origin as the Son of God. This is a dimension of Christmas that is often neglected but should not be. The "babe in the manger" is a compelling image, but remembering that this babe is the firstborn Son of the Father makes it all the more compelling.

GOSPEL John 1:1–18

This is a huge reading, laden with important truths of Christianity. Take great pains to help the assembly listen attentively. Communicate the uniqueness of this special text by making its message your own.

A reading from the holy Gospel according to John

In the *beginning* was the *Word*,
and the Word was with *God*,
and the Word *was* God.
He was in the *beginning* with God.
All things came to *be* through him,
and *without* him *nothing* came to be.
What came to *be* through him was *life*,
and this *life* was the *light* of the human *race*;
the light *shines* in the *darkness*,
and the darkness has not *overcome* it.

A man named *John* was sent from *God*.
He came for *testimony*, to testify to the *light*,
so that all might *believe* through him.
He was *not* the light,
but came to *testify* to the light.

The *true* light, which enlightens *everyone*,
was coming into the *world*.
He was *in* the world,
and the world came to *be* through him,
but the world did not *know* him.
He came to what was his *own*,
but his own *people* did not *accept* him.

GOSPEL John opens his gospel with the same words that open the book of Genesis, the book of creation, thus putting Jesus Christ (the Word) in the context of eternity and revealing him as the one through whom all things came to be. Here again, as in today's second reading from Hebrews, we are jolted into an awareness of the full meaning of Christmas: The eternal Word that was *with* God and *is* God become flesh. Here is the awesome mystery of the incarnation: the divine becoming human.

As you might suspect after a close reading of this gospel passage, John has more to accomplish here than simple instruction. He strongly emphasizes Christ's divinity and his involvement in the creation of the world because there were schools of thought at the time of his writing that denied both. There were Christians who tried to reconcile an understanding of God as pure, perfect spirit and a material world that is flawed by evil by saying that the two had nothing to do with each other; God could not be associated with anything imperfect. There were other Christians who could not believe that Christ, who is God, could really be mortal. They decided that the Jesus who walked the earth only appeared to be human—his body wasn't a real human body.

John seeks to show Christ (the Word of God who is God) both deeply involved with the creation of the world and, through the wonder of the incarnation, truly flesh and blood. Jesus Christ existed from all eternity as God and chose to become a human being at a particular moment in time.

But to those who *did* accept him
he gave *power* to become children of *God*,
to those who believe in his *name*,
who were born not by *natural* generation
nor by *human* choice nor by a *man's* decision
but of *God*.

And the Word became *flesh*
and made his *dwelling* among us,
and we saw his *glory*,
the glory as of the Father's only *Son*,
full of *grace* and *truth*.

John *testified* to him and cried out, saying,
"This was he of whom I said,
'The one who is coming *after* me ranks *ahead* of me
because he *existed* before me.'"

From his *fullness* we have *all* received,
grace in place of *grace*,
because while the *law* was given through *Moses*,
grace and *truth* came through Jesus *Christ*.
No one has ever *seen* God.
The only *Son*, God, who is at the Father's *side*,
has *revealed* him.

[Shorter: John 1:1–5, 9–14]

The closing lines, beginning with "No one has ever seen God," are important. They mean, "No one has ever seen God until *now!* The Son, who is God, has shown us God!"

But what's the motive for this divine being to become human? John gives us the answer: grace. The grace of God has appeared in Jesus Christ. We toss the word "grace" around a lot. But what does it mean? Synonyms for grace include kindness, decency, favor, mercy, mercifulness, charity, benevolence, clemency, and leniency. I particularly like the last two: clemency and leniency. The grace of God is the face of God, seen in Jesus. No longer do we have to guess what God is like. Jesus shows us that the face of God is clement, lenient, merciful, benevolent, loving.

What about God as sometimes described in the Old Testament—vengeful, merciless, angry, even petulant? Of course, we no longer believe that these traits describe God. But our understanding of God's nature has developed over time and was incomplete until Jesus appeared. It's not that the God of the Old Testament is supplanted by the God of the New Testament. It's the same God, and God does not change. But our notion of God has definitely changed across the centuries! The writers of the Old Testament wrote about God as they understood God to be. But as we heard in the second reading, in times past we knew God only partially and in various ways. Now the grace and the face of God have appeared in fullness and clarity in Jesus Christ. That's what we celebrate on Christmas Day.

HOLY FAMILY

Lectionary #17

READING I 1 Samuel 1:20–22, 24–28

A reading from the first Book of Samuel

The reading is pure narrative. Use your best story-telling techniques.

In those days *Hannah conceived*, and at the end of her *term*
bore a *son*
whom she called *Samuel*, since she had asked the *LORD*
for him.
The next time her husband *Elkanah* was going up
with the *rest* of his household
to offer the customary *sacrifice* to the Lord and to fulfill
his *vows*,
Hannah did *not* go, *explaining* to her husband,
"Once the child is *weaned*,
I will *take* him to *appear* before the *LORD*
and to *remain* there *forever*;
I will *offer* him as a perpetual *nazirite*."

Consider the depth of Hannah's gratitude. She is so grateful to be a mother that she willingly gives her son to the Lord.

The word "nazirite" refers to one who has taken a vow of special consecration to God's service.

Customary sacrificial offerings accompanied the consecration of the nazirite.

Once Samuel was *weaned*, Hannah brought him *up* with her,
along with a three-year-old *bull*,
an ephah of *flour*, and a skin of *wine*,
and *presented* him at the temple of the *LORD* in *Shiloh*.
After the boy's *father* had sacrificed the young bull,
Hannah, his mother, approached *Eli* and said:
"*Pardon*, my lord!
As you *live*, my lord,
I am the woman who stood *near* you here, *praying* to the *LORD*.

There is a choice of first readings today. Speak with the liturgy coordinator or homilist to find out which reading will be used.

READING I The feast of the Holy Family is of very recent origin, introduced into the Catholic liturgy early in the twentieth century. As an encouragement to Christian families, it has merit. But the real power of this feast is that it encourages us to look beyond the family unit and glimpse the wider implications of family. Indeed, if we think beyond time into eternity, the nature and experience of family will be very different indeed.

The word "family" is one of the richest in our language. We use it to mean many different things, many kinds of relationships, many degrees of kinship, both distant and intimate. In combination with other words, the word "family" becomes even more flexible and rich. We speak of "family circle," "family tree," "family name." We speak of "extended family," "church family" and even the "human family."

It is in this widest sense of family that we see the true meaning of today's feast of the Holy Family. For the emphasis is not so much on Mary, Joseph, and Jesus in Nazareth as it is on the family of God, we who have become one family in the miracle of Christmas. The Word became flesh. The creator of all human beings became a human being—uniting us to each other in the most intimate and inclusive family ever known in human history.

1 SAMUEL. The first reading in today's liturgy presents us with Samuel, one who (like Jesus) was consecrated even before his birth for a special mission. The story of his conception, birth, and consecration to

Eli had prophesied that Hannah would bear a son—God's response to her earnest prayer.

"I prayed for this *child*, and the Lord *granted* my request.
Now *I*, in turn, *give* him to the LORD;
as long as he *lives*, he shall be *dedicated* to the LORD."
Hannah *left* Samuel *there*.

Or:

READING I Sirach 3:2–6, 12–14

Sirach = SEER-ak

Remember that you are reading a series of proverbs—related, of course, but not like a prose development of a theme. Take care that each kernel of insight and wisdom gets its due, and that the assembly gets enough time to let them sink in.

A reading from the Book of Sirach

God sets a *father* in *honor* over his *children*;
a *mother's authority* he *confirms* over her *sons*.
Whoever honors his *father* atones for *sins*,
and *preserves* himself from them.
When he *prays*, he is *heard*;
he stores up *riches* who reveres his *mother*.
Whoever honors his *father* is gladdened by *children*,
and, when he *prays*, is *heard*.
Whoever reveres his *father* will live a long *life*;
he who *obeys* his father brings *comfort* to his *mother*.

My son, take *care* of your father when he is *old*;
grieve him *not* as long as he *lives*.
Even if his *mind* fail, be *considerate* of him;
revile him *not* all the days of his *life*;
kindness to a *father* will not be *forgotten*,
firmly *planted* against the debt of your *sins*
—a house raised in *justice* to you.

God's service has many parallels with other great leaders, prophets, judges—important figures in Israel's growth and development as the Family of God. It is worth noting that Hannah's song of thanksgiving (in response to the blessing of motherhood) is the pattern and inspiration of Mary's great hymn of praise, the Magnificat. In many ways, the first reading today predicts and echoes the fulfillment, in Jesus, of God's plan of salvation for the family of humankind. The more we appreciate the vast sweep of that plan through individual families and peoples, the more we will glimpse the true meaning and power of today's feast.

SIRACH. The book of Sirach is the work of a sage who had traveled widely and pondered the scriptures before setting down this collection of proverbs. The book is no longer included in the Hebrew scriptures, nor is it included in the canon of sacred writings recognized by Christian denominations other than Catholic. But we have always drawn extensively from Sirach in our liturgical texts and catechesis, so much so, in fact, that the book goes by another name: Ecclesiasticus (literally, the church book).

Sirach is a charming work, filled with timeless wisdom set down in the form of aphorisms—sayings, maxims, kernels of truth. Today's passage is clearly chosen for its observations about familial relationships, the mutual duties of children and parents—appropriate enough for the feast of the Holy Family. There is great poignancy in some of these lines, and harsh reality as well: "Take care of your parents when they are old; even if their minds fail, be considerate of them." The author clearly knew some of the difficulties of family life.

READING II 1 John 3:1–2, 21–24

A reading from the first Letter of Saint John

Beloved:
See what *love* the Father has *bestowed* on us
that we may be called the *children* of *God*.
And so we *are*.
The reason the *world* does not *know* us
is that it did not know *him*.
Beloved, we are God's *children now*;
what we *shall* be has not yet been *revealed*.
We *do* know that when it *is* revealed we shall be *like* him,
for we shall *see* him as he *is*.

Beloved, if our hearts do not *condemn* us,
we have *confidence* in God and *receive* from him
whatever we *ask*,
because we keep his *commandments* and do what *pleases* him.
And his commandment is *this*:
we should *believe* in the *name* of his *Son*, Jesus *Christ*,
and *love* one another just as he *commanded* us.
Those who *keep* his commandments *remain* in him, and he
in *them*,
and the way we *know* that he remains in us
is from the *Spirit* he *gave* us.

Or:

God's love makes us God's children. Our love is the natural response.

The repetition of the word "Beloved" can be very effective.

We receive (as Hannah did) because we obey God's commandments.

Our only duty: believe in Jesus and love one another.

God's Spirit dwelling in us makes both belief and love possible.

Texts like this one call for a strong and exalted proclamation. Nothing offhand or casual will do. Equally inappropriate would be a haughty or distant rendition. Between those extremes is a noble and solid proclamation that gives the text its full weight and elicits thoughtful listening on the part of the members of the assembly.

There is a choice of second readings today. Speak with the liturgy coordinator or homilist to find out which reading will be used.

READING II **1 JOHN. John is ecstatic when he proclaims that it is because the Father loves us so much that we are called "children of God." Further, if the world does not recognize why we are so close to one another as God's children, it is because they do not (yet!) know the love of God that makes such closeness possible. The kind of love John urges us to show one another is the kind that springs spontaneously from the belief that God loves us infinitely. People who are loved in this way become loving.**

Notice, too, that John foresees that our relationships with each other and with the Father will change once we are all united with God in heaven. Yes, we have a relationship of parent/child now, but what will it be when we see God face to face? And what will our relationship to one another be? Blood may be thicker than water, but the Spirit of God is thicker still and will bind us together in relationships even stronger than the ones we now know in family.

We will truly become the family of humanity, the family of church, the family of God, when all the stereotypes are gone,

READING II Colossians 3:12–21

A reading from the Letter of Saint Paul to the Colossians

Brothers and sisters:
Put *on*, as God's *chosen* ones, *holy* and *beloved*,
heartfelt *compassion*, *kindness*, *humility*, *gentleness*,
and *patience*,
bearing with one another and *forgiving* one another,
if one has a *grievance* against another;
as the Lord has forgiven *you*, so must you *also* do.
And over *all* these put on *love*,
that is, the *bond* of *perfection*.
And let the *peace* of Christ *control* your hearts,
the *peace* into which you were *also* called in one *body*.
And be *thankful*.

Pause here. This is a crucial point: Above all and over all and most important of all, put on love!

Let the *word* of Christ dwell in you *richly*,
as in all *wisdom* you *teach* and *admonish* one another,
singing *psalms*, *hymns*, and spiritual *songs*
with *gratitude* in your hearts to *God*.
And *whatever* you do, in *word* or in *deed*,
do *everything* in the name of the Lord *Jesus*,
giving *thanks* to God the *Father* through *him*.

A new section begins here as Paul describes the virtues he has listed above with the example of married couples.

Wives, be *subordinate* to your husbands,
as is *proper* in the Lord.
Husbands, *love* your wives,
and avoid any *bitterness* toward them.

when all the ancient grudges and prejudices and fears are gone, when we look at ourselves and every human being as the family member each one of us is. Different, certainly. But differences seem bad only when I think my way is the norm. I need to be loved into leaving behind this ridiculous notion and experience the delight of being drawn back into the challenge of faith: keeping God's commandments!

There is no better example for us to follow than Jesus, of course, the one whose birth at Christmas altered the universe forever—and made us all one family. Jesus cherished differences and saw great potential in the weak and the sinful, the odd and the outcast. He also saw potential in the proud and obstinate, the coldhearted and the cynical, the angry and the resentful. He could do this—and we can too—because he saw that pride is really insecurity, obstinacy is really fear, hardheartedness and cynicism and resentment are simply pain in disguise. By faith we see through such disguises and recognize ourselves behind all of them. There's a pretty good guarantee that the more of us whose vision is lighted by faith, the more the human race will become a human *family.*

COLOSSIANS. Paul gives us in fewer than a dozen verses a fine recipe for living together in peace and harmony. One would think we could do much better than our record indicates. Surely nothing here is beyond human capacity—and certainly not beyond the ability of anyone who embraces Christian values: mercy, kindness, humility, patience, love, thankfulness. Paul even admits how difficult we can be for each other when he counsels us to bear with and forgive one another. He knows human

Children, obey your *parents* in *everything*,
for this is *pleasing* to the Lord.
Fathers, do not *provoke* your children,
so they may not become *discouraged*.

[Shorter: Colossians 3:12–17]

GOSPEL Luke 2:41–52

A reading from the holy Gospel according to Luke

Appropriate vocal variety will enable you to distinguish the *events* from their *significance*.

In effect, it is time for Jesus' bar mitzvah.

Each *year* Jesus' *parents* went to *Jerusalem* for the feast of *Passover*,
and when he was twelve years *old*,
they went *up* according to festival *custom*.

Conflict and tension are introduced into the narrative. We can sense their increasing concern.

After they had *completed* its days, as they were *returning*,
the boy *Jesus* remained *behind* in *Jerusalem*,
but his *parents* did not *know* it.
Thinking that he was in the *caravan*,
they journeyed for a *day*
and *looked* for him among their *relatives* and *acquaintances*,
but not *finding* him,
they returned to *Jerusalem* to *look* for him.

Luke makes the point that Jesus' wisdom is beyond his years.

After three *days* they *found* him in the *temple*,
sitting in the midst of the *teachers*,
listening to them and asking them *questions*,
and all who *heard* him were *astounded*
at his *understanding* and his *answers*.

nature well enough to presume the occasional necessity of putting up with each other—not the highest of virtues, of course, but as much as we can muster sometimes.

Imagine the family who adopted Paul's words as their charter for living! That would truly be a holy family—not a pietistic one but a real family who knows that the heat created by friction is better than the cold resulting from resentment.

Of course, it is genuine love that binds all our good efforts together and makes them one, and it is love that is the fruit of all those good works. But perhaps most striking here is the final admonition in Paul's list: "And be thankful." The grateful heart is the one that most spontaneously gives itself away. Thankfulness is clearly the most appropriate mode of living for the Christian. We have a God who loves us exactly as we are, warts and all. Isn't that reason enough to live in thankfulness?

The last paragraph will rankle some hearers. It is hopelessly archaic and even inflammatory to speak of "subordinate" wives today, but it wasn't in Paul's time, and we need to keep that in mind. Paul's views, here and elsewhere, about the submission of wives to husbands spring from his culture, not from the mind of God. Things have changed a bit for the better—another reason to be thankful.

GOSPEL The gospel for the celebration of the Holy Family is chosen so that in Years A, B, and C three major events of Jesus' childhood may be recounted. In Year A we read from Matthew's gospel the account of the flight into Egypt, wherein Matthew demonstrates the fulfillment of prophecy ("Out of Egypt I have

When his parents *saw* him,
they were *astonished*,
and his *mother* said to him,

Mary's disappointment and pain soon become contemplative love.

"*Son*, why have you *done* this to us?
Your *father* and I have been *looking* for you with great *anxiety*."
And *he* said to *them*,
"Why were you *looking* for me?
Did you not *know* that I must be in my *Father's* house?"
But they did not *understand* what he *said* to them.

The ending is lovely. A picture of serenity.

He went *down* with them and came to *Nazareth*,
and was *obedient* to them;
and his *mother* kept all these things in her *heart*.
And Jesus *advanced* in *wisdom* and *age* and *favor*
before *God* and *man*.

called my son") and Jesus' identity with the people of Israel called out of exile. Last year (Year B) we heard Luke's story of Jesus' presentation in the Temple, in fulfillment of ancient Mosaic law dictating that every firstborn male was to be dedicated to the Lord. Today (in Year C) Luke presents us with the story we have come to know as the finding of the child Jesus in the Temple.

There is very little in these three gospel stories to support the view that today's feast is meant to serve Christian families with a model of family life. We do see Mary, Joseph, and Jesus return to their home in Nazareth where Jesus is obedient and grows to maturity in a simple and God-centered family setting. That is certainly a glimpse of domesticity, but the wider intent of the writer in all three stories is obvious and should not be sacrificed for a homily that dwells on a family setting about which we can only speculate.

In light of our meditations on the first two readings, we must read this gospel story with a view that sees beauty and inspiration in the humble home of Nazareth, but sees far beyond it as well.

Perhaps the most striking words in this passage are those of the child Jesus himself, when he responds to his mother's question with two questions of his own. Luke clearly has Jesus address these questions to his readers. "If you understood who I am and what my mission is, you would know where to find me—in the house of my true Father and the Father of all that is." These words alone take us beyond the family of Nazareth and into considerations of Jesus' cosmic role in re-claiming the children of God for their true Father.

MARY, MOTHER OF GOD

Lectionary #18

READING I Numbers 6:22–27

A reading from the Book of Numbers

With such a brief reading you need to be sure the assembly is listening before you begin. Pause after announcing the reading until silence prevails.

The LORD said to *Moses*:
"Speak to *Aaron* and his *sons* and *tell* them:
This is how you shall *bless* the Israelites.
"Say to them:

Give each invocation sufficient emphasis and time to sink in.

The LORD *bless* you and *keep* you!
The LORD let his *face* shine upon you,
and be *gracious* to you!
The LORD *look* upon you *kindly*
and give you *peace*!

Pause slightly before and after the word "peace."

"So shall they invoke my *name* upon the Israelites,
and I will *bless* them."

READING II Galatians 4:4–7

A reading from the Letter of Saint Paul to the Galatians

Brothers and sisters:
When the *fullness* of time had *come*, God sent his *Son*,
born of a *woman*, born under the *law*,
to *ransom* those under the law,
so that we might receive *adoption* as *sons*.

Bring out the point that Jesus is born under the law to redeem us from it.

READING I This reading is a rich summary of God's attitude toward the people of the covenant. Keep in mind the following implications of this profound message as you proclaim it.

First, formal blessings are generally reserved to persons chosen for spiritual leadership. The descendants of Aaron were entrusted with this blessing to show how essential it is for the people's well-being.

Second, there are dark days in everyone's life, when it seems that the Lord's face is hidden. The blessing has this in mind when it asks that the Lord's face shine upon us.

Third, our word "peace" is a weak translation of *shalom*, a word that implies "every good thing in full measure." You can communicate something of the special character of this word by pausing slightly before and after saying the word "peace."

Finally, God's promise is irrevocable. When this blessing is invoked with sincerity and received gratefully, God says with utter certainty, "I will bless them." Pronounce the final words with great conviction, optimism, and strength. This is wonderful to hear as we begin a new year.

READING II Paul was a master at creating summaries of what Christians believe. This is such a text. The "fullness of time" implies the arrival of a predesignated moment in history and reminds us that we are involved in a divine plan that stretches back into eternity. There is a mission implied in the words "God sent his Son." The Son did not appear arbitrarily, but came for a purpose. And this Son was born of a woman, that is, fully human, sharing completely in our weakness—as well as our subjection to the law.

Abba = AH-bah

As *proof* that you are sons,
God sent the *Spirit* of his Son into our *hearts*,
crying out, "*Abba, Father*!"
So you are no longer a *slave* but a *son*,
and if a *son* then also an *heir*, through *God*.

GOSPEL Luke 2:16–21

A reading from the holy Gospel according to Luke

Beware of a trap here that makes it sound like the entire Holy Family is in the manger! Pause after "Joseph," and do not pause after "infant."

The *shepherds* went in haste to *Bethlehem*
and found *Mary* and *Joseph*,
and the infant lying in the *manger*.
When they *saw* this,
they made *known* the message
that had been *told* them about this child.
All who *heard it* were *amazed*
by what had been *told* them by the *shepherds*.

Pause before this new section. Single out the words about Mary.

And Mary *kept* all these things,
reflecting on them in her *heart*.
Then the shepherds *returned*,
glorifying and praising *God*
for all they had *heard* and *seen*,
just as it had been *told* to them.

Emphasize that the name Jesus is of divine origin.

When *eight days* were completed for his *circumcision*,
he was named *Jesus*, the name given him by the *angel*
before he was *conceived* in the *womb*.

Paul is playing with words here. It is ironic that Jesus had to be subject to the law so that he could liberate us from it. He participated in all that the law required so that he could show us he is master of all law and came to give us something beyond a law-based relationship with God. He transforms our legal relationship to God into a parent-child relationship.

Elevation from the rank of slave to the rank of child is a dramatic move indeed. And becoming an heir to the Father's riches is even more dramatic. There can be a note of amazement in your proclamation of this text. It is as if you are saying, "I know this is hard to believe, but in Christ we see that God loves us as children and wants us to call out, 'Abba.'"

GOSPEL This is the same gospel passage proclaimed at the Mass at dawn on Christmas Day. However, a final sentence has been added to show us that Jesus was circumcised in accordance with Mosaic law. It was important for Jesus to follow the law of Moses so that he would be credible when he revealed himself to be the fulfillment of the law.

In Jesus' time, the Mosaic law was terribly complex, and the extent to which it was fulfilled indicated the goodness of a person. There is no clearer presentation of the folly of such thinking than the exchanges throughout the gospels between Jesus and the scribes and Pharisees.

Jesus came to show us that God has called us to far more noble tasks than obeying the law. Jesus enables us to become the kind of people for whom law is unnecessary.

EPIPHANY OF THE LORD

Lectionary #20

READING I Isaiah 60:1–6

Be aware of the parallelism in this poetry. Almost every line is echoed, restated, or developed in the line that follows it. You will avoid a sing-song effect if you relish each line of text and allow its unique meaning to shine through.

A reading from the Book of the Prophet Isaiah

Rise up in *splendor*, Jerusalem! Your *light* has come,
the glory of the *LORD* shines upon you.
See, *darkness* covers the earth,
and thick *clouds* cover the *peoples*;
but upon *you* the LORD *shines*,
and over *you* appears his *glory*.

A new but related section begins here. Pause slightly.

Nations shall walk by your *light*,
and *kings* by your shining *radiance*.
Raise your *eyes* and look *about*;
they all *gather* and *come* to you:
your *sons* come from *afar*,
and your *daughters* in the arms of their *nurses*.

Another new section begins here.

Then you shall be *radiant* at what you see,
your *heart* shall *throb* and *overflow*,
for the riches of the *sea* shall be *emptied out* before you,
the wealth of *nations* shall be *brought* to you.
Caravans of *camels* shall fill you,
dromedaries from *Midian* and *Ephah*;
all from *Sheba* shall come
bearing *gold* and *frankincense*,
and proclaiming the *praises* of the *LORD*.

Midian = MID-ee-uhn
Ephah = EE-fah
Sheba = SHEE-buh

READING I Some years ago we started celebrating the feast of the Epiphany on the Sunday nearest January 6 rather than on that date itself. So today we actually celebrate the twelfth day of Christmas on the tenth day of Christmas! But partridges and pear trees are not our concern here.

This beautiful text from the church's Evening Prayer summarizes today's feast: "Three mysteries mark this holy day: today the star leads the Magi to the infant Christ; today water is changed into wine for the wedding feast; today Christ wills to be baptized by John in the river Jordan to bring us salvation." Obviously, these three events did not occur on the same day. The point is that in all three events the divinity of Jesus was manifested to the world—and that's even what the word "epiphany" means.

Isaiah, too, is concerned with the epiphany (the showing forth) of God's glory, and wants to emphasize especially that God's glory shines upon Jerusalem (the chosen people) even when darkness and clouds cover it. The prophet encourages the people of Israel to see beyond appearances and glimpse the glory of God's action in their midst, guiding them through whatever difficulties threaten to blind them to God's favor. It is an exultant hymn that looks into the future and confidently announces that God will be faithful.

This, of course, is the message of Advent, Christmas, and Epiphany. During Advent we remember the promises that foretell the coming of the Messiah. At Christmas we celebrate that coming in history. On Epiphany we stand in awe of the revealed mystery of the Word made flesh.

It is important that you build up to the dramatic statement that is the point of this reading. The buildup rises through "to his holy prophets and apostles by the Spirit," and then the climax reveals that the Gentiles are part of the plan!

READING II Ephesians 3:2–3a, 5–6

A reading from the Letter of Saint Paul to the Ephesians

Brothers and sisters:
You have *heard* of the *stewardship* of God's *grace*
that was *given* to me for your *benefit*,
namely, that the mystery was made *known* to me
by *revelation*.

It was *not* made known to people in *other* generations
as it has *now* been revealed
to his holy *apostles* and *prophets* by the *Spirit*:
that the *Gentiles* are *coheirs*, members of the same *body*,
and *copartners* in the promise in Christ *Jesus*
through the *gospel*.

Every detail in this story is important. Tell it with great care.

GOSPEL Matthew 2:1–12

A reading from the holy Gospel according to Matthew

When *Jesus* was born in *Bethlehem* of *Judea*,
in the days of King *Herod*,
behold, magi from the *east* arrived in Jerusalem, saying,
"Where is the newborn *king* of the *Jews*?
We saw his *star* at its *rising*
and have come to do him *homage*."

READING II It may be difficult for us to think of the message of Christ being limited to a certain people, and yet realizing that even Gentiles are included in God's plan of salvation was one of the earliest struggles faced by the church. In fact, it took some years before the universality of Christ's mission was fully understood. Remembering that the earliest Christians were mostly Jews, we can appreciate just how startling Paul's assertion in this reading really is: The Gentiles are coheirs, members of the body, sharers of the promise.

One of the great theme songs of the season of Christmas is "All the ends of the earth have seen the salvation of God." There can be no more appropriate day than Epiphany to sing this song, for this feast celebrates God's unlimited glory, shining from east to west, illuminating all of creation. With the manifestation of divinity through the humanity of Christ, every living thing appears in a different light.

Though the epistle writer speaks of God's secret plan, it was not God's intention to keep things secret. The point is that until Christ came we did not know God's plan. We had no idea how universal it was, nor did we fully know the nature of God until Christ revealed it in himself. In Christ, all the world has seen God, and all peoples have become coheirs of the ancient promises.

As you proclaim this message, imagine yourself sharing an ambassador's delight over a successful mission, an effort at reconciliation that has exceeded even the highest hopes. Groups with apparently irreconcilable differences have come together to embrace a common belief, reach for a common goal and share a wondrous destiny.

When King Herod *heard* this,
he was greatly *troubled*,
and all Jerusalem *with* him.
Assembling all the chief *priests* and the *scribes* of the people,
he *inquired* of them where the *Christ* was to be born.
They said to him, "In *Bethlehem* of *Judea*,
for thus it has been written through the prophet:
'And *you*, Bethlehem, land of *Judah*,
are by no means *least* among the rulers of Judah;
since from *you* shall come a *ruler*,
who is to *shepherd* my people Israel.'"

The conflict begins with Herod's hypocrisy.

Then Herod *called* the magi *secretly*
and *ascertained* from them the *time* of the star's *appearance*.
He sent them to *Bethlehem* and said,
"*Go* and search *diligently* for the child.
When you have *found* him, bring me *word*,
that I *too* may go and do him *homage*."

After their audience with the king they set *out*.
And *behold*, the star that they had seen at its *rising*
preceded them,
until it came and *stopped* over the place where the *child* was.

The conflict recedes for a moment in the joy of finding the child.

They were *overjoyed* at seeing the star,
and on entering the *house*
they saw the *child* with *Mary* his *mother*.

They *prostrated* themselves and did him *homage*.
Then they opened their *treasures*
and offered him *gifts* of *gold*, *frankincense*, and *myrrh*.

The conflict resumes and includes more than a hint of the troubles ahead.

And having been warned in a *dream* not to *return* to Herod,
they *departed* for their country by another *way*.

GOSPEL **Matthew's purpose in telling this story is the same one that governs his entire gospel: to demonstrate that every prophecy and promise of old has come to fulfillment in Christ. Your objective is the same as Matthew's, namely, to show the members of the assembly that their faith in Christ is well placed.**

As promised by the prophets, the humble town of Bethlehem (the city of King David's ancestor Ruth) has become the Messiah's birthplace. As promised, Gentile sages from foreign lands, guided by a miraculous star, have acknowledged Jesus' birth with gifts of gold, frankincense, and myrrh. Although Matthew quotes the prophets for only one of these fulfilled promises, it is clear that he has many ancient texts in mind.

The rich splendor of "Herod's city" (Jerusalem) stands in sharp contrast to the lowliness of Bethlehem, just as Herod's jealousy is the opposite of the humility of the Gentile magi. And the joy of birth is more than a little diminished by the hint of danger and impending doom. The foreign visitors have to avoid the envious and hypocritical Herod.

Clearly, this child brings into the world a new dimension of the inevitable struggle between good and evil. When light shines out in the darkness, the darkness does not always flee willingly. When faced with news that seems too good to be true, some resist it. That resistance, too, is part of God's plan, since only the death of this Messiah will bring that plan to its mysterious fulfillment.

BAPTISM OF THE LORD

Lectionary #21

READING I Isaiah 40:1–5, 9–11

A reading from the Book of the Prophet Isaiah

One of the most tender passages in the Bible. Relish it.

Comfort, give *comfort* to my *people*,
says your *God*.
Speak *tenderly* to *Jerusalem*, and *proclaim* to her
that her *service* is at an *end*,
her *guilt* is *expiated*;
indeed, she has received from the hand of the *LORD*
double for all her *sins*.

Pause. Change of mood here to expectation.

A *voice* cries out:
In the *desert* prepare the way of the LORD!
Make straight in the *wasteland* a *highway* for our *God*!
Every *valley* shall be *filled* in,
every *mountain* and *hill* shall be made *low*;
the *rugged* land shall be made a *plain*,
the *rough* country, a broad *valley*.
Then the *glory* of the LORD shall be *revealed*,
and *all* people shall *see* it *together*;
for the mouth of the *LORD* has *spoken*.

There is a choice of first readings today. Speak with the liturgy coordinator or homilist to find out which reading will be used.

READING I **ISAIAH 40. The poetic text from Isaiah today is a favorite of the church's liturgy during the Advent and Christmas seasons. We always hear it proclaimed on the 2nd Sunday of Advent in Year B. It has captured the hearts of poets and musicians for generations. Anyone who has heard the Christmas section of Handel's *Messiah* will read (and listen to) these words with special affection—and with unforgettable melodies echoing in their minds.**

Isaiah's poem celebrate the return of the Israelites from Babylonian exile 700 years before Christ. Isaiah himself is the voice crying in the wilderness and the heart of his message is that the word of God accomplishes what it speaks.

When we hear the middle section of this reading on today's feast, we immediately think of John the Baptist and realize that Isaiah's poetry is being applied to the coming of Jesus as Messiah. Now John the Baptist is the voice in the wilderness, and his good news is that we can look at Jesus and say, "Here is your God!"

A Christian interpretation of this passage takes nothing away from its historical significance. In fact, when the return of Israel is seen as a foreshadowing of the event we celebrate at Christmas, our appreciation for our spiritual heritage in Israel's history is heightened. The point may be well made that we Christians need to remind ourselves that our record of God's movement in

Another pause. Now the mood is exultation and joy.

Go *up* on to a high *mountain*,
Zion, *herald* of glad *tidings*;
cry *out* at the top of your *voice*,
Jerusalem, *herald* of good *news*!
Fear *not* to cry out
and say to the cities of *Judah*:
Here is your *God*!

Here comes with *power*
the Lord GOD,
who *rules* by his strong *arm*;

Emphasize "reward" and "recompense," not the prepositions after them.

here is his *reward* with him,
his *recompense* before him.
Like a *shepherd* he feeds his *flock*;
in his *arms* he gathers the *lambs*,

The final sentence is quieter. There is no more tender image of God's provident love.

carrying them in his *bosom*,
and leading the *ewes* with *care*.

Or:

love toward humankind begins with the Jews. And it is through the Jews that, as Isaiah so beautifully writes, "the glory of the Lord shall be revealed."

ISAIAH 42. There are four sections in the book of Isaiah that are called the "suffering servant songs." They depict in poignant poetry a chosen servant who must suffer much because of fidelity to God. This reading is taken from the first of those songs. Isaiah describes the election, anointing and mission of the servant, as well as the way the servant will go about accomplishing the objectives set out by God.

Who was this servant? An individual person, or the personification of the whole people of Israel? Whatever the answer to these questions, the suffering servant songs have been applied to Jesus Christ from the beginning of his ministry, which we celebrate in today's feast. Authors and preachers from the first days of the Christian era have seen in Jesus the perfect image of the suffering servant. Indeed, Jesus himself quotes from the songs and sees himself as their fulfillment.

As you proclaim this reading, it should be easy for the assembly to recognize the kind of ministry Jesus undertook following his baptism, the inauguration of his mission on earth. But remember that you are reading a poetic text, not a literal or prosaic description. The tone is exalted throughout and each image deserves to be relished. Isaiah clearly did not formulate these lines without effort. They deserve your most careful preparation and energetic proclamation.

READING I Isaiah 42:1–4, 6–7

A reading from the Book of the Prophet Isaiah

Some of Isaiah's most important poetry appears here. Let your voice signal its significance.

Thus says the *LORD*:
Here is my *servant* whom I *uphold*,
my *chosen* one with whom I am *pleased*,
upon whom I have put my *spirit*;
he shall bring forth *justice* to the nations,
not crying out, *not* shouting,
not making his voice heard in the *street*.
A *bruised* reed he shall not *break*,
and a smoldering *wick* he shall not *quench*,
until he establishes *justice* on the earth;
the *coastlands* will *wait* for his *teaching*.

A new section begins here. Prepare for it with a pause.

I, the *LORD*, have *called* you for the victory of *justice*,
I have grasped you by the *hand*;
I *formed* you, and set you
as a *covenant* of the people,
a *light* for the *nations*,

A quiet (not weak!) resolution seems appropriate here.

to open the eyes of the *blind*,
to bring out *prisoners* from *confinement*,
and from the *dungeon*, those who live in *darkness*.

There is a choice of second readings today. Speak with the liturgy coordinator or homilist to find out which reading will be used.

READING II **TITUS. These two passages from Titus identify the moment in time when God's grace appears in Jesus, look beyond the historical event itself, and peer into that future event toward which all history is aimed: the appearance of the glory of God in the second coming of Jesus Christ. Clearly, we live between two singular events. The first has saved us and shown us how to live in expectation of the second. It is training us to live godly lives, to await the age to come with eager longing, and meanwhile to be enthusiastic about doing good.**

The second part of the text makes the point that the gift of salvation is given out of love. We have great difficulty remembering that salvation is not something we earn, not something we can ever deserve, not something given in answer to need or petition. True, we were in need of redemption. But the grace we receive at baptism (in that "bath of rebirth") is pure gift—motivated by divine love alone. It justifies us, yes, and takes away our sins. But far more than that, it makes us rightful heirs of eternal life with God. Do we need more than that to make us eager and zealous for doing good?

The author of this passage has packed it with meaning. Because it is brief, take great care lest it be over before it has had a chance to work its intended effect. This is a thinking person's formulation of the Good News: Give us time to think—especially on this feast that brings the Christmas season to a close and, in a way, recapitulates its meaning.

READING II Titus 2:11–14; 3:4–7

A reading from the Letter of Saint Paul to Titus

A very strong opening. Yes! God's grace is now plain to see!

The sentences are long. Let the sense units, not the punctuation, be your guide.

Beloved:
The grace of *God* has *appeared*, saving *all*
and *training* us to reject *godless* ways
and worldly *desires*
and to live *temperately*, *justly* and *devoutly* in this age,
as we *await* the blessed *hope*,
the *appearance* of the *glory* of our great *God*
and *savior* Jesus *Christ*,
who *gave* himself for us to *deliver* us from all *lawlessness*
and to *cleanse* for himself a people as his *own*,
eager to do what is *good*.

Important pause here. God's motive is proclaimed.

Every phrase is packed. Proclaim with great deliberateness.

Prepare for a clear sense of closure. The ending is upbeat.

When the *kindness* and generous *love*
of God our savior *appeared*,
not because of any righteous deeds *we* had done
but because of his *mercy*,
he *saved* us through the bath of *rebirth*
and *renewal* by the Holy *Spirit*,
whom he richly *poured out* on us
through Jesus *Christ* our *savior*,
so that we might be *justified* by his *grace*
and become heirs in *hope* of eternal *life*.

Or:

ACTS. This reading echoes the struggle referred to in last Sunday's second reading from Ephesians, the struggle involved in recognizing that God is not partial to any one people. Anyone who approaches God with a sincere heart is acceptable. More than that, God wills that all the world hear the good news of his plan to save the world: Jew, Gentile, all nations. And how did Peter come to this realization? It came through Jesus Christ, of course, who is Lord of all.

Again we are told that in Jesus we see clearly for the first time the nature of God's heart and the divine plan for the universe. Peter is making the point that the revelation of God's universal love began at the Jordan River, when a divine anointing made clear that, in Jesus, the establishment of God's reign on earth has begun.

Jesus' works testify that he fits Isaiah's portrait of the suffering servant: Jesus brings sight to the blind and freedom to prisoners; and Jesus suffers for the sins of the people, taking on himself the burden that only divine love can bear.

Your voice should express an eagerness to explain all this when you proclaim Peter's words in this reading. You want to make it clear that when Jesus went down into the waters of the Jordan he began a journey that would end only when he returned to the Father in glory, having accomplished the salvation of the world.

GOSPEL The feast of the baptism of Jesus—the culmination of the Christmas feast—has never been celebrated in the western church with the same solemnity and significance as it has been in the east. We might say that in the west, our Christmas emphasizes more the humanity of

READING II Acts 10:34–38

A reading from the Acts of the Apostles

Make Peter's words and convictions your own. Explain to the assembly this new insight.

A new section begins here, more conversational than before.

Peter proceeded to speak to those gathered
in the house of *Cornelius*, saying:

In *truth*, I see that *God* shows no *partiality*.
Rather, in *every* nation whoever *fears* him and acts *uprightly*
is *acceptable* to him.
You *know* the word that he sent to the *Israelites*
as he proclaimed *peace* through Jesus *Christ*, who is Lord of *all*,
what has happened all over *Judea*,
beginning in *Galilee* after the baptism
that *John* preached,
how God anointed *Jesus* of *Nazareth*
with the Holy *Spirit* and *power*.
He went about doing *good*
and *healing* all those oppressed by the *devil*,
for *God* was with him."

Jesus—the babe in the crib; and in the east, the divinity of Christ is the emphasis. Thus, the Christmas feast in the eastern church is the Epiphany, when we see the three kings (representing the rulers of the world) paying homage to the divine savior. Today is also a feast of the divinity of Jesus—the manifestation to all the world, in a public way, that "Here is the Messiah God has promised through the ages. Here is my servant in whom I am well pleased."

If we study the history of the Middle East, we learn that Jesus' appearance was perfectly timed. For instance, until John the Baptist's appearance, no Jew had ever been baptized with a baptism of repentance. Such was for proselytes—those who came over into the Jewish faith from Gentile background. A Jew was a child of Abraham, already saved, chosen, assured of election. There was no need for a penitential rite to signify the chosen state that already existed for a Jew.

But the moment Jesus chooses to enter public life is a unique moment in Jewish history: A great wave of penitence is sweeping the Hebrew nation, a great willingness to admit sin and to reform one's life interiorly to match the external law—which in itself means only an opportunity to be saved, not a guarantee.

Never before had there been such a national movement of penitence and of earnest search for God. And now here he is in the form of Jesus of Nazareth. The Word of God made flesh.

The meaning of the divine voice that accompanies Jesus' baptism is clear. "You are my beloved Son" (Psalm 2: he shall rule the nations); "with you I am well pleased" (Isaiah 42: he is my suffering servant). That thunderous voice proclaims to the world

GOSPEL Luke 3:15–16, 21–22

A reading from the holy Gospel according to Luke

There are two parts to this gospel. Verses 17–20 have been omitted. Let the division be clear. The first part defines who John is and who he isn't.

The *people* were filled with *expectation*,
and all were asking in their *hearts*
whether *John* might be the *Christ*.
John answered them *all*, saying,
"*I* am baptizing you with *water*,
but one *mightier* than I is coming.
I am not *worthy* to loosen the *thongs* of his *sandals*.
He will baptize you with the Holy *Spirit* and *fire*."

Luke does not record the actual baptism; he is more interested in its significance, as revealed in the voice from heaven.

After all the *people* had been baptized
and Jesus *also* had been baptized and was *praying*,
heaven was *opened* and the Holy *Spirit*
descended upon him
in bodily *form* like a *dove*.
And a *voice* came from heaven,
"*You* are my beloved *Son*;
with *you* I am well *pleased*."

These words are full of power, but a booming voice is inappropriate. Simple and quiet strength is more effective.

that God has become king in human form and that the throne of this king will be suffering, sacrificial love, not oppression or temporal power. This sacrificial love is the kind of love we promise in our own baptism; and we do so with joyful conviction.

The baptism of Jesus is the event that ushers eternity into the world of time. It is the promise fulfilled, the end of the beginning and the beginning of the end time that is the dawn of eternity.

In Matthew's gospel the voice that comes from heaven is meant for all to hear. He used the earlier gospel of Mark to compose his narrative and chose to change Mark's words from "You are my beloved Son," to "*This* is my beloved Son." His intention is to proclaim this divine epiphany as something for all to witness and not a private revelation to Jesus alone. Luke maintains Mark's formula.

Now that the significance of this event is clear, we need to note the brevity of the text that describes it—a brevity that is seen in Matthew and Mark as well. Brevity demands a slower reading pace, a more deliberate pace. Remember that the story is very familiar. How can you get your hearers to listen carefully to something they have heard over and over? The answer is that you, the reader, must hear the story with fresh ears, glean from it all the significance it contains, and proclaim it with such vividness and strength that you draw the assembly into it.

One final caveat: the voice from heaven should not sound like your imagination of what God's voice is like. This kind of thing is never done in liturgical proclamation. Sometimes a gentle delivery of strong words makes them stronger.

2ND SUNDAY IN ORDINARY TIME

Lectionary #66

READING I Isaiah 62:1–5

A reading from the Book of the Prophet Isaiah

These are the Lord's words, not Isaiah's. The literary style here is poetic. The appropriate tone is an exalted one, clear and firm and strong.

For *Zion's* sake I will *not* be *silent*,
for *Jerusalem's* sake I will not be *quiet*,
until her *vindication* shines *forth* like the *dawn*
and her *victory* like a burning *torch*.

A familiar theme from the Christmas–Epiphany season.

Nations shall *behold* your vindication,
and all the *kings* your *glory*;
you shall be called by a *new* name
pronounced by the mouth of the *LORD*.

"Crown" and "diadem" are the same; the poetic device is parallelism.

You shall be a glorious *crown* in the hand of the LORD,
a royal *diadem* held by your *God*.

A new idea begins a new section. Pause, then renew the vigor.

No *more* shall people call you *"Forsaken,"*
or your land *"Desolate,"*
but you shall be called "My *Delight*,"
and your *land "Espoused."*
For the LORD *delights* in you
and makes your land his *spouse*.

A dramatic image for the intimate love God has for us. Make it bright.

As a *young* man marries a *virgin*,
your *Builder* shall marry *you*;
and as a *bridegroom* rejoices in his *bride*
so shall your *God* rejoice in *you*.

READING I **The prophet Isaiah is speaking for God. That is, the personal pronouns refer to God, not the prophet. And such words God speaks! What promises are made! Zion and Jerusalem are the same—the people of God, represented by the city—the intended bride of the Eternal One. The reading is one long exalted promise of the restoration of Israel after the exile. The intimate marital imagery between God and the people is not new here. It exists in earlier literature, but is taken to new heights in this passage.**

It is an impatient God who speaks, a God eager to restore the beloved to her rightful place in the world and in right relationship to her divine spouse. Several images are used to indicate the bride's beauty and privilege.

First of all, she is a "glorious crown, a royal diadem." Second, she receives new names, which change her degradation into glory. "Forsaken" and "Desolate" become "My Delight" and "Espoused."

A young man, a builder, a bridegroom—all roles played by the Lord in this strikingly intimate expression of relationship with the chosen people. Jerusalem has no choice but to revel in the boundless love that envelops her. Few passages in the Bible equal this one as a statement of the degree and kind of love that motivates God toward earth. Little wonder that such love is never withdrawn.

READING II **This reading is Paul's classic statement of unity in diversity. It is a message much needed in**

READING II 1 Corinthians 12:4–11

A reading from the first Letter of Saint Paul to the Corinthians

Repetition is what makes this reading work; relish it. The first three lines say exactly the same thing in different words. Make each line fresh.

Brothers and sisters:
There are different *kinds* of spiritual *gifts* but the same *Spirit*;
there are different *forms* of *service* but the same *Lord*;
there are different *workings* but the same *God*
who produces *all* of them in *everyone*.

This statement must stand out. Pause before and after it.

To each *individual* the manifestation of the Spirit
is given for some *benefit*.

Here the list begins. Great vocal variety will keep it from sounding dull. Each item gets equal (but not identical) treatment. Take lots of time in rehearsing it and proclaiming it.

To *one* is given through the Spirit the expression of *wisdom*;
to *another*, the expression of *knowledge* according
to the same Spirit;
to *another*, *faith* by the same Spirit;
to *another*, gifts of *healing* by the one Spirit;
to *another*, mighty *deeds*;
to *another*, *prophecy*;
to *another*, *discernment* of spirits;
to *another*, varieties of *tongues*;
to *another*, *interpretation* of tongues.

Here is Paul's point again about equality. It is a strong conclusion.

But one and the *same* Spirit produces *all* of these,
distributing them *individually* to each *person* as he *wishes*.

GOSPEL John 2:1–11

A reading from the holy Gospel according to John

The gospel is a narrative, a story. Every image is important.

There was a *wedding* at *Cana* in *Galilee*,
and the *mother* of Jesus was there.
Jesus and his *disciples* were *also* invited to the wedding.

every period of the church's history. It seems to be a difficult message to learn and live by. Clearly then, this text deserves your best efforts. And it is not easy to proclaim effectively. In effect, you have a *list* to read, and the challenge in such cases is always to keep it from *sounding* like a list! The solution is vocal variety, which will enable you to let each item on the list carry its own weight and remain distinct from the other items.

Paul did not write these words as a general instruction; they arose out of a genuine need. The Christians at Corinth were engaged in an energetic competition with one another, some convinced that their gift was worthier than the gifts of others. The gift of tongues particularly was held to be a gift of greater value. Paul sets out to teach what every Christian community throughout the ages needs to learn: that the gift itself is less important than the giver and the recipient—and the purpose for which the Holy Spirit imbues us with grace. That is, all gifts are given for the good of the community. To rank and rate them according to importance misses the point. All are important; none is unimportant. All are needed for a thriving community. None can be dismissed as insignificant. Remembering that gifts are given in order to be shared will make for more peaceful and loving communities.

GOSPEL Although Luke is the source of most of our gospel readings during Year C, we have a selection from John's gospel today to carry on the theme of Epiphany and make a seamless transition into Ordinary Time.

John's purpose in recording the events at Cana is far larger than a casual interest in

When the *wine* ran short,
the *mother* of Jesus said to him,
"They have no *wine*."
And Jesus said to *her*,
"*Woman*, how does your concern affect *me*?
My *hour* has not yet *come*."
His mother said to the *servers*,
"Do whatever he *tells* you."

There is no harshness here; John has Jesus make the point that only God's will, not a human being's request, guides his actions. Mary's response explains why we call her "Mother of Good Counsel."

The narrative continues after the dialogue.

Now there were six stone *water* jars there for Jewish *ceremonial* washings,
each holding twenty to thirty *gallons*.
Jesus told them,
"*Fill* the jars with *water*."
So they *filled* them to the *brim*.
Then he told them,
"Draw some *out* now and take it to the *headwaiter*."
So they took it.

This is the climax of the story. Renew the vigor.

And when the headwaiter *tasted* the water that had become *wine*,
without *knowing* where it *came* from
—although the servers who had *drawn* the water knew—
the headwaiter called the *bridegroom* and said to him,
"Everyone serves *good* wine *first*,
and then when people have drunk *freely*, an *inferior* one;
but *you* have kept the *good* wine until *now*."

The fact is, drunk people aren't very discriminating. Yes, that's the point.

Jesus did this as the *beginning* of his *signs* at *Cana* in *Galilee*
and so revealed his *glory*,
and his *disciples* began to *believe* in him.

Here John explains the point of the story. Help him make the point by proclaiming it boldly.

a wedding feast or in the miraculous changing of water into wine. Perhaps the best way to understand this reading is to recall the text of an antiphon from the Liturgy of the Hours and the feast of the Epiphany: "Three mysteries mark this holy day: Today the star leads the Magi to the infant Christ; today water is changed into wine for the wedding feast; today Christ wills to be baptized by John in the river Jordan to bring us salvation."

These three events mark the appearance, that is the manifestation, the epiphany, of Jesus inaugurating his divine mission on earth. Each is accompanied by a theophany—startling evidence of divine intervention: the star, the water into wine, the voice from heaven and the dove. The point of the story of the wedding at Cana, then, belongs to John's body of evidence that this Jesus truly is the son of God and the bringer of God's redeeming love.

But there is more. Specifically, the Cana event foretells the way in which Jesus will accomplish his mission, namely, by shedding his blood on the cross. The most obvious foreshadowing is Jesus' response to Mary's request: "My hour has not yet come." In other words, it was not time yet to reveal his identity and mission completely.

Jesus' words to Mary are not the only clue to what this story is really about, however. The miracle itself, the changing of water into wine, means (for John and for us) that the old covenant between heaven and earth will be changed into something entirely new. And, finally, the gospel writer gives us his reason for telling this story in the very words which conclude it: In this way Jesus revealed his glory and his disciples believed in him.

3RD SUNDAY IN ORDINARY TIME

Lectionary #69

READING I Nehemiah 8:2–4a, 5–6, 8–10

Nehemiah = nee-uh-MĪ-uh

Ezra = EZ-ruh

A solemn liturgical gathering is described here. The setting is detailed and awe-inspiring.

A reading from the Book of Nehemiah

Ezra the *priest* brought the *law* before the *assembly*,
which consisted of *men*, *women*,
and those children *old* enough to *understand*.
Standing at one end of the *open* place that was before
the *Water* Gate,
he *read* out of the book from *daybreak* till *midday*,
in the *presence* of the *men*, the *women*,
and those children *old* enough to *understand*;
and all the people listened *attentively* to the book of the *law*.
Ezra the *scribe* stood on a wooden *platform*
that had been *made* for the occasion.

He *opened* the scroll
so that all the people might *see* it
—for he was standing *higher up* than any of the people—
and, as he *opened* it, all the people *rose*.
Ezra blessed the *LORD*, the great *God*,
and all the *people*, their hands raised *high*, answered,
"Amen, amen!"
Then they bowed *down* and *prostrated* themselves
before the LORD,
their *faces* to the *ground*.

The word of God is worthy of veneration. We continue this custom today.

Ezra read *plainly* from the book of the law of God,
interpreting it so that all could *understand* what was read.

READING I All three readings today have a similar setting: an assembly of people hearing a speaker encourage them to fuller, richer lives. Ezra reads the law to the assembled Israelites. Paul's letter to the Corinthians addresses the new Christian community at Corinth, who no doubt were assembled at some point to hear his words read aloud. And in the gospel we see Jesus in the synagogue at Nazareth proclaiming the fulfillment of a prophecy of Isaiah. All three readings will be heard in your parish's Sunday assembly. Faith depends on hearing, and hearing depends on someone to speak. We might call today "Lector's Sunday," for your ministry is in evidence everywhere.

Notice the basic liturgical structure in this first reading. The people assemble, make a prayer of blessing along with Ezra, hear the word of God read, receive an explanatory instruction and encouragement, and then respond in worship, prayer, and feasting. The framework of our own liturgy today is not very different.

Ezra reads the law to a people who are very much in need of hearing it. Their heart-rending response indicates that they need both the encouraging words of the law's promise as well as, perhaps, the discipline that the law required of them. The combination of sorrow for sin and the joy of being forgiven always produces healing tears.

The occasion represented here is certainly a high holy day, perhaps Yom Kippur—the New Year. Notice that the long and arduous ceremony (from dawn until noon) is followed by a feast that is celebrated in the

Then *Nehemiah*, that is, His *Excellency*, and Ezra
the *priest-scribe*
and the *Levites* who were *instructing* the people
said to all the people:
"Today is *holy* to the LORD your *God*.
Do not be *sad*, and do not *weep*"—
for all the people were *weeping* as they heard the words
of the law.

The sadness and weeping arise from a combination of repentance and joy.

He said further: "*Go*, eat rich *foods* and drink sweet *drinks*,
and allot *portions* to those who had nothing *prepared*;
for today is *holy* to our LORD.
Do not be *saddened* this day,
for *rejoicing* in the LORD must be your *strength*!"

The conclusion is strong. Proclaim it vigorously.

READING II 1 Corinthians 12:12–30

A reading from the first Letter of Saint Paul to the Corinthians

Brothers and sisters:
As a *body* is *one* though it has many *parts*,
and all the *parts* of the body, though *many*, are *one* body,
so also *Christ*.

The opening assertion is crucial. Make sure you have the assembly's attention before beginning.

For in one *Spirit* we were all *baptized* into one *body*,
whether *Jews* or *Greeks*, *slaves* or *free* persons,
and we were all given to *drink* of one *Spirit*.

The second sentence is the foundation for all that follows.

classic way: rich food, good drink, and special provisions for the poor. It is a tradition to follow.

READING II **Paul is writing to a contentious group embroiled in a fruitless debate about rank, privilege, and special status. In his instruction he formulates a theology of Christian community that has enriched the church's self-awareness immeasurably. It is the doctrine of the church as the body of Christ, a definitive study of unity in diversity, and contains all the insights we need to belong to our faith communities in the most productive and supportive way imaginable. There is no greater statement in Christian literature about mutual responsibility and individual dignity than this text. Likewise, there is no greater indictment of Christians who look with disdain on those they feel to be inferior to themselves. Such superiority is a direct and horrible affront to Christ himself.**

Our membership in the body of Christ is the result of baptism, when the Spirit of God filled us with divine love, without regard to racial or social distinction. Baptism is the great leveler. But it levels by exalting. Anyone who belongs to the body through baptism shares equal dignity with all the other members.

And there are no insignificant members. Indeed, the doctrine is more radical

The analogy that explains Paul's doctrine begins here.

Now the *body* is not a *single* part, but *many*.
If a *foot* should say,
"Because I am not a *hand* I do not *belong* to the body,"
it does *not* for this reason belong any *less* to the body.
Or if an *ear* should say,
"Because I am not an *eye* I do not *belong* to the body,"
it does *not* for this reason belong any *less* to the body.

Rhetorical questions are a strong literary device that invite energetic involvement from the hearers.

If the whole body were an *eye*, where would the *hearing* be?
If the whole body were *hearing*, where would the sense of *smell* be?

But as it *is*, God placed the parts,
each *one* of them, in the body as he *intended*.
If they were all *one part*, where would the *body* be?
But as it *is*, there are many *parts*, yet one *body*.
The *eye* cannot say to the *hand*, "I do not *need* you,"
nor again the *head* to the *feet*, "I do not need *you*."

This sub-section shows the dramatic difference between secular values and faith values. The weaker members deserve more attention.

Indeed, the parts of the body that seem to be *weaker*
are all the more *necessary*,
and those parts of the body that we consider *less* honorable
we surround with *greater* honor,
and our less *presentable* parts are treated with greater *propriety*,
whereas our *more* presentable parts do not *need* this.

But God has so *constructed* the body
as to give *greater* honor to a part that is *without* it,
so that there may be no *division* in the body,
but that the parts may have the same *concern* for one another.
If *one* part *suffers*, *all* the parts suffer *with* it;
if one part is *honored*, all the parts *share* its joy.

than that. It reminds us that those members who, by secular standards, might seem less important are, by Christ's standards, all the more important. The weaker members are all the more necessary for being weak. Paul refers to our natural sense of modesty for this analogy. The more vulnerable and less presentable parts of the body are all the more protected by clothing. Those people whom society may see as less presentable must be treated with all the more honor.

The unity among the members of Christ's body is an organic unity. There can be no choosing among members with regard to their relationship with other members. Can the eye say to the hand, "I don't need you"? Of course not. Can we fool ourselves into thinking we are not in need of one another? Of course not.

The final section of this text reminds us that there are different roles to be filled in this great drama of Christian life. Paul ranks the gifts according to their function for the church, not according to any personal privilege these roles bestow on the recipient. His concern here is not with rank. His concern is with pastoral function. Members of the church's hierarchy do well to remind themselves often that their vocation is to serve, not to reign.

Now *you* are *Christ's* body, and individually *parts* of it.
Some people God has designated in the church
to be, *first, apostles; second, prophets; third, teachers;*
then, mighty *deeds;*
then gifts of *healing, assistance, administration,*
and varieties of *tongues.*

The ranking here is of gifts and service, not persons.

Are all *apostles*? Are all *prophets*? Are all *teachers*?
Do all work mighty *deeds*? Do all have gifts of *healing*?
Do *all* speak in tongues? Do all *interpret*?

Seven rhetorical questions! Avoid the temptation to rush through these. Let each one sink in.

[Shorter: 1 Corinthians 12:12–14, 27]

GOSPEL Luke 1:1–4; 4:14–21

A reading from the holy Gospel according to Luke

A classic periodic sentence. The main point is deferred until several assertions have prepared for it. The length of the sentence is no problem if you employ lots of vocal variety and let each sense line come through clearly.

Since *many* have undertaken to compile a *narrative* of the events
that have been *fulfilled* among us,
just as those who were *eyewitnesses* from the *beginning*
and *ministers* of the word have handed them *down* to us,
I *too* have decided,
after *investigating* everything accurately *anew,*
to write it down in an orderly *sequence* for you,
most excellent *Theophilus,*
so that you may realize the *certainty* of the teachings
you have *received.*

Jesus returned to *Galilee* in the power of the *Spirit,*
and *news* of him *spread* throughout the whole *region.*
He taught in their *synagogues* and was *praised by all.*

GOSPEL **Now that we have made the transition into Ordinary Time, we go back to the beginning of Luke's gospel and hear his purpose for writing it. Then we skip over the story of Jesus' birth, baptism (which we heard during Advent–Christmas), and temptation in the desert (which we will return to in Lent) and witness the beginning of his ministry in Galilee.**

The opening paragraph of Luke's gospel tells us a great deal about the writer's purpose. His primary objective is to provide evidence that will encourage his audience toward faith in Jesus as the fulfillment of all God's promises. And he proposes to do so in an orderly fashion, after having studied the earlier accounts (including Mark's) of Jesus' life and work. This should not lead us into the mistaken notion that Luke's gospel is a simple chronological biography. Like the other gospels, it is a theological treatment—which is to say that the meaning of the events he relates takes precedence over historical fact or sequence. He sets out to show that we can believe in Jesus with full confidence.

Theophilus may be a specific historical person or it may represent any and all who are "lovers of God," for that is how the name

A significant pause is necessary here.

Then launch into the story. "In the power of the Spirit," is one of Luke's central beliefs about Jesus. All that he did was prompted by the Spirit of God.

A regular liturgical gathering; unremarkable until Jesus makes his dramatic announcement.

He came to *Nazareth*, where he had grown *up*,
and *went* according to his *custom*
into the *synagogue* on the *sabbath* day.

He stood up to *read* and was handed a *scroll* of the prophet *Isaiah*.
He *unrolled* the scroll and found the passage where it was *written*:

Lift your voice. The quotation from Isaiah is in poetic form.

"The Spirit of the LORD is upon me,
because he has *anointed* me
to bring glad *tidings* to the *poor*.
He has sent me to proclaim *liberty* to *captives*
and recovery of *sight* to the *blind*,
to let the *oppressed* go *free*,
and to proclaim a year *acceptable* to the *Lord*."

Rolling up the scroll, he handed it back to the *attendant* and sat *down*,
and the eyes of *all* in the synagogue looked *intently* at him.

He said to them,

Pause. Then proclaim Jesus' words with forceful conviction.

"*Today* this *Scripture* passage is *fulfilled* in your *hearing*."

translates. Another of Luke's aims is to show that the word of God that Jesus speaks is for all people the world over, not only the chosen people (Israel). We will see over and over that Luke emphasizes the universal aspect of God's plan of salvation. Such a radical position does not receive immediate acclaim!

The theme of fulfillment is clearly seen in Jesus' interpretation of the scripture passage from Isaiah. He applies the personal pronouns to himself and announces that he himself is the fulfillment of Isaiah's prophecy. It is a dramatically controversial claim, not easy for the hearers to accept, even those who up to this point have been favorably impressed by Jesus' teaching. But the remainder of Luke's gospel will concern itself with proving the claim true—despite any and all opposition.

With this passage from Luke, we again embark on the wonderful and awful journey toward the paschal mystery. "Today this Scripture passage is fulfilled!" That "today" is every day and all days from the beginning of the Christian era. The passage is fulfilled again on January 25, 2004.

4TH SUNDAY IN ORDINARY TIME

Lectionary #72

READING I Jeremiah 1:4–5, 17–19

Jeremiah = jair-uh-MĪ-uh

The text is poetry, not prose. The exalted language demands an exalted proclamation.

To gird the loins is to secure one's clothing about one's body. Figuratively, it means to prepare for work, or battle. "But do you" does not signal the introduction of a question. Its meaning here is "therefore."

Is this a message of comfort to the prophet; or is it a warning? Either reading is possible.

It is the prophet's own people who will resist him.

Stress the verbs here, not the prepositions: "*fight* against you . . . *prevail* over you." The final line is the ultimate promise.

A reading from the Book of the Prophet Jeremiah

The word of the *LORD* came to me, saying:
Before I formed you in the *womb* I *knew* you,
before you were *born* I *dedicated* you,
a prophet to the *nations* I *appointed* you.

But do you *gird* your *loins*;
stand *up* and *tell* them
all that I *command* you.
Be not *crushed* on their account,
as though I would *leave* you crushed before them;
for it is *I* this day
who have made you a fortified *city*,
a pillar of *iron*, a wall of *brass*,
against the whole *land*:
against Judah's *kings* and *princes*,
against its *priests* and *people*.
They will *fight* against you but not *prevail* over you,
for I am *with* you to *deliver* you, says the LORD.

READING I **The call creates the prophet. Jeremiah's call to prophecy is a classic. Only part of the dialogue between Jeremiah and God forms this reading, but enough to show us God's resolve on behalf of the prophet even in the face of resistance. And it shows us that the prophet's mission is universal ("to the nations"), that is, beyond his own people. Thus it provides a parallel to the same thought expressed by Jesus in today's gospel reading.**

The fact that the Lord has chosen Jeremiah for his task even before Jeremiah was born says something of God's eternal plan of salvation. In other words, it has always been (and will always be) God's intention to redeem the world—and that message will continue for all time to come through spokespersons especially chosen to reveal it. There are many examples in the scriptures of being chosen in the womb (John the Baptist and Jesus, of course, and several figures in the Hebrew scriptures as well). Indeed, the idea is not unique to the Judeo-Christian tradition.

Another inevitability: The prophet will encounter resistance. Given the difference between our ways and God's ways, we can expect men and women of all time to resist a message of radical peace and justice. Given that prophets of all ages speak to an imperfect world, we cannot expect such a message to gain immediate acceptance—for that implies a degree of unselfishness that does not seem to come easy to human nature. Only faith is capable of converting hearts to the degree a prophet demands.

A final inevitability: The prophet will ultimately triumph over resistance. And the

READING II 1 Corinthians 12:31—13:13

A reading from the first Letter of Saint Paul to the Corinthians

Brothers and sisters:
Strive *eagerly* for the *greatest* spiritual gifts.
But I shall show you a still *more* excellent way.

The introduction prepares for something special. It is an invitation to listen.

If I speak in *human* and *angelic* tongues,
but do not have *love*,
I am a resounding *gong* or a clashing *cymbal*.
And if I have the gift of *prophecy*,
and comprehend all *mysteries* and all *knowledge*;
if I have all *faith* so as to move *mountains*,
but do not have *love*, I am *nothing*.
If I give away everything I *own*,
and if I hand my *body* over so that I may *boast*,
but do not have *love*, I gain *nothing*.

Still preparing for the main point. Three "if" situations show how primary love is.

Love is *patient*, love is *kind*.
It is not *jealous*, it is not *pompous*,
it is not *inflated*, it is not *rude*,
it does not seek its *own* interests,
it is not *quick*-tempered, it does not *brood* over *injury*,
it does not *rejoice* over *wrongdoing*
but rejoices with the *truth*.
It *bears* all things, *believes* all things,
hopes all things, *endures* all things.

Here is the list of phrases describing love. Each one deserves its own space. Avoid the temptation to hurry through this section. It must not sound like a list.

Love never *fails*.
If there are *prophecies*, they will be brought to *nothing*;
if *tongues*, they will *cease*;
if *knowledge*, it will be brought to *nothing*.

A new section, devoted to the enduring power of love. Pause before it.

guarantee of that triumph is the great "I am with you"—the promise God has made to all messengers from the beginning. It is the Emmanuel promise. The same promise was made to Abraham and to Moses and to Jacob. The same promise is made to us.

READING II It is not difficult to understand why this text has been a favorite for centuries. Love is a difficult reality to understand, though we have no difficulty knowing it when we are truly loved. Love is a difficult thing to do well, though we know full well when we are doing it. And unconditional love is even difficult to accept, though we realize fully that it is the one thing in life we all desire.

In his historical context, Paul is trying to show the Christians at Corinth that their squabbles over rank and privilege, their competition regarding spiritual gifts, are all meaningless when measured by the *unum necessarium* (the one thing necessary). It is easy to lose sight of priorities in our daily dealings with one another. Modern Christian communities are just as much in need of Paul's reminder. Love must be the gauge by which all our activities and energies are measured.

Notice the structure of the reading: The first section asserts the supremacy of love. The second section defines love by distinguishing it from less honorable human impulses (jealousy, selfishness, and so on). The third section further defines love by comparing it to good things, the other gifts of the Spirit (prophecies, knowledge, and the like). And finally, Paul admits (for our encouragement) that the pursuit of love is

The concluding section contains comparisons.

For we know *partially* and we *prophesy* partially,
but when the *perfect* comes, the *partial* will pass *away*.
When I was a *child*, I used to *talk* as a child,
think as a child, *reason* as a child;
when I became a *man*, I put *aside* childish things.
At *present* we see *indistinctly*, as in a *mirror*,
but *then* face to *face*.
At *present* I know *partially*;
then I shall know *fully*, as I am fully *known*.

Let this familiar final line ring out with special energy.

So *faith, hope, love* remain, these *three*;
but the *greatest* of these is *love*.

[Shorter: 1 Corinthians 13:4–13]

GOSPEL Luke 4:21–30

A reading from the holy Gospel according to Luke

The opening sentence picks up where the gospel ended last Sunday and establishes the context.

Jesus began speaking in the *synagogue*, saying:
"*Today* this Scripture passage is *fulfilled* in your *hearing*."

The initial approval of the people makes the conflict to come all the more dramatic.

And all spoke *highly* of him
and were *amazed* at the gracious *words* that came
from his *mouth*.
They also asked, "Isn't this the son of *Joseph*?"

The amazement of the people prompts Jesus to challenge them.

Capernaum = kuh-PER-nay-'m

He said to them, "*Surely* you will quote me this *proverb*,
'Physician, *cure* yourself,' and say,
'Do *here* in your *native* place
the things that we heard were done in *Capernaum*.'"

not easy. It involves growing up and struggling with vagueness—in the sure hope of one day seeing love's true greatness clearly.

We might ask ourselves why the name of God does not appear in this text. Why does Paul speak of love without reference to Christ? The answer is that Paul is a superb rhetorician. That is, he is addressing a Greek audience familiar with an elaborate existing literature of just this kind. Love here is an abstract concept, concretely applicable to any and every relationship.

GOSPEL **Even the Gentiles will be saved! This gospel narrative is replete with themes dear to Luke's heart. And it develops themes we saw in today's first reading. Notice that the context is the synagogue (the perfect place for Jesus to assert his controversial position)—a gathering of people perhaps too comfortable with their position as "chosen." Just as Jeremiah was promised that he would encounter resistance but escape from it, so Jesus encounters life-threatening resistance and yet escapes unharmed.**

What is the controversy? As Jeremiah was to be a voice to the nations so Jesus makes it clear that God's will to save extends beyond Israel and includes the lands of Sidon and Syria. The prophet Elijah was sent to a foreigner (and a woman at that!) because his own people had rejected him. Elisha is sent to cure the leprosy of a foreigner, though many of his own people stood in need of the same healing. Luke is intent on showing us

"Amen, I say to you" is a formula that precedes words of special importance. Let the formula do its work.

And he said, "*Amen*, I *say* to you,
no *prophet* is *accepted* in his own native *place*.
Indeed, I tell you,
there were many *widows* in Israel in the days of *Elijah*
when the sky was *closed* for three and a half years
and a severe *famine* spread over the entire *land*.
It was to *none* of these that Elijah was *sent*,
but only to a widow in *Zarephath* in the land of *Sidon*.
Again, there were many *lepers* in Israel
during the time of Elisha the prophet;
yet not one of them was cleansed, but only Naaman
the Syrian."

The rest of Jesus' words must build throughout and come to an energetic climax.
Elijah = ee-LĪ-juh
Zarephath = ZAIR-uh-fath
Sidon = SĪ-duhn
Elisha = ee-LĪ-shuh
Naaman = NAY-uh-muhn
Syrian = SEER-ee-uhn

When the people in the synagogue heard this,
they were all filled with fury.
They rose up, drove him out of the town,
and led him to the *brow* of the *hill*
on which their town had been *built*,
to hurl him *down headlong*.
But Jesus *passed* through the *midst* of them and went *away*.

After the fury, the ending is peaceful, assured, confident.

that the salvation offered by Jesus is universal and, when rejected by those to whom it is first offered, will be offered to the world.

The rage that fills those who hear Jesus' words is not difficult to understand. It stems from their complacency. Nothing is as frightening as the complacent who are jolted from their smugness. The sin of these people is the sin of presumption—not unknown in our own day. Without malice, but with grave consequences, we have a tendency to think of our way to God as the best or only way. Certainly we have to believe in what we believe. Otherwise we wouldn't make one choice over another. But we must believe generously, with minds and hearts open to the conscientious choices other make. Otherwise we cannot hope to understand the greatness of God, nor can we love as God loves.

Our presumptions inevitably blind us to moments of grace and make us impervious to promptings of the Spirit. When we are convinced that God will reveal the divine presence only in expected ways, we guarantee ourselves the shock of learning otherwise.

The best antidote for presumption is vulnerability—remaining open to all possibilities in the arena of faith. It is not a comfortable position, for it robs us of predictability. It makes the adventure of Christianity truly an adventure—full of surprises and risks. But people of good will realize that it also alerts us to the sovereignty of God. We cannot put limits on divine love, nor can we predict how that love will express itself.

5TH SUNDAY IN ORDINARY TIME

Lectionary #75

READING I Isaiah 6:1–2a, 3–8

A reading from the Book of the Prophet Isaiah

Uzziah = yuh-ZĪ-uh

The scene is majestic and awe-inspiring. An exalted poetic tone is best.

In the year King *Uzziah* died,
I saw the *LORD* seated on a *high* and *lofty throne*,
with the train of his *garment filling* the *temple*.
Seraphim were stationed *above*.

They *cried* one to the *other*,
"*Holy, holy, holy* is the *LORD* of *hosts*!
All the *earth* is *filled* with his *glory*!"
At the *sound* of that cry, the *frame* of the *door shook*
and the *house* was *filled* with *smoke*.

The scene shifts to personal awed fear, but the tone remains majestic. We are dealing with poetry here, not literal prose.

Then I said, "*Woe* is *me*, I am *doomed*!
For I am a man of unclean *lips*,
living among a *people* of unclean lips;
yet my *eyes* have seen the *King*, the LORD of *hosts*!"

The tone becomes more explanatory.

Then one of the seraphim *flew* to me,
holding an *ember* that he had taken with *tongs* from the *altar*.

He touched my *mouth* with it, and said,
"*See*, now that this has touched your *lips*,
your *wickedness* is *removed*, your *sin purged*."

Pause slightly before Isaiah's response, then end strongly but quietly.

Then I heard the voice of the *LORD* saying,
"Whom shall I *send*? Who will *go* for us?"
"Here *I* am," I said; "send *me*!"

READING I **Isaiah's call to prophecy comes during a period of protracted war and the bitterness of defeat. There is great need for a spokesperson for God. King Uzziah's death provides a convenient event for placing the call at a clear point in history. Much of the imagery of the heavenly court is a reflection of the temple liturgy in Jerusalem where Isaiah's vision occurred. The threefold "Holy" has made its way down through the ages into our own liturgy. The seraphim are winged human-like figures who serve and worship in God's royal court.**

The exalted passage is a study in contrast between the glory of God and the humility of human experience—expressed vividly in Isaiah's cry, "I am doomed," and reminding us of the ancient belief that no one could look upon the face of God and live. And yet, when the call from God comes, it creates the prophet—despite any human insufficiencies or fears of being inadequate to the task. Again and again in Hebrew literature we see that the call is not an invitation but an act of creation. The call actually renders the one called capable of performing the assigned task. Whatever is necessary to empower the prophet (in Isaiah's case, a purge of his sinfulness) comes with the call.

Notice that Isaiah's reluctance and fear become a cry of utter willingness and courage. In response to God's question, Isaiah volunteers himself enthusiastically. And why not? The call has created him a prophet, has made irrelevant all that could stand in the way of his vocation. In the gospel reading today we see a similar call. Simon Peter's initial reluctance and sense of unworthiness are swept away, and his call is confirmed.

READING II 1 Corinthians 15:1–11

A reading from the first Letter of Saint Paul to the Corinthians

The first two sentences are a preface; Paul tells us what he is going to tell us.

I am *reminding* you, brothers and sisters,
of the *gospel* I preached to you,
which you indeed *received* and in which you also *stand*.
Through it you are *also* being *saved*,
if you hold *fast* to the word I preached to you,
unless you believed in *vain*.

Take this section slowly. It is a summation of Christian belief. Make the series of "thats" work for you—they build to a higher and higher level. They are not all the same.

For I handed *on* to you as of first *importance* what I also *received*:
that Christ *died* for our *sins* in *accordance* with the *Scriptures*;
that he was *buried*;
that he was *raised* on the third *day*
in accordance with the *Scriptures*;
that he appeared to *Cephas*, then to the *Twelve*.

Paul presents his evidence; it builds throughout.

After *that*, Christ appeared to more
than five *hundred* brothers at *once*,
most of whom are still *living*,
though *some* have fallen *asleep*.
After *that* he appeared to *James*,
then to *all* the apostles.

Last of *all*, as to one born *abnormally*,
he appeared to *me*.
For I am the *least* of the apostles,
not fit to be *called* an apostle,
because I *persecuted* the *church* of *God*.
But by the *grace* of God I *am* what I *am*,
and his *grace* to me has not been *ineffective*.

READING II In this reading, Paul mentions his calling as part of the evidence he offers the Corinthians that the good news they have received is trustworthy. Some of the Christian community at Corinth had contested the idea of resurrection after death—not so much scoffing at the idea as holding the opinion that it was unnecessary in view of the spiritual rebirth that occurs at baptism. Thus, it was necessary for Paul to present them with testimony asserting the literal resurrection of Jesus and the promise of a like resurrection for all of us.

In addressing the doubts of the Corinthians, Paul has provided the church with a thumbnail sketch of fundamental Christian doctrine (in Greek, the *kerygma*—the earliest and constant tradition handed down from the apostles). Paul claims no original material here and that is part of the selling point of his words. He insists that what he has preached in Corinth is not his own, but the tradition he received. The essential points are these: Christ died to save us, just as the scriptures foretold; he died and was buried; and, again just as the scriptures foretold, he was raised up from the dead. To believe less than this is be something other than Christian.

But Paul does not stop there. He repeats stories of post-resurrection appearances by Christ to Kephas (Peter) and many others. The last bit of proof offered is personal: "Last of all, he appeared to me." The story of this amazing encounter is recorded in the Acts of the Apostles. The entire reading reminds us of a courtroom scene: In answer to charges that parts of his testimony may be held in doubt, Paul presents a tightly sketched summation of Christian tradition,

Indeed, I have toiled *harder* than *all* of them;
not *I,* however, but the grace of *God* that is *with* me.

The conclusion is that the greatest evidence is God's grace at work.

Therefore, whether it be *I* or *they,*
so we *preach* and so you *believed.*

[Shorter: 1 Corinthians 15:3–8, 11]

GOSPEL Luke 5:1–11

A reading from the holy Gospel according to Luke

Begin by setting the scene. You are establishing the context in which the story takes place.

Gennesaret = geh-NES-uh-ret

While the *crowd* was pressing *in* on Jesus and *listening*
to the word of *God,*
he was *standing* by the Lake of *Gennesaret.*
He saw two *boats* there alongside the *lake;*
the *fishermen* had *disembarked* and were washing their *nets.*

Getting *into* one of the boats, the one belonging to *Simon,*
he asked him to *put out* a short distance from the *shore.*
Then he sat *down* and *taught* the crowds from the *boat.*
After he had finished *speaking,* he said to *Simon,*
"Put out into *deep* water and lower your *nets* for a *catch.*"
Simon said in *reply,*
"*Master,* we have worked hard all *night* and have
caught *nothing,*
but at your *command* I will lower the *nets.*"
When they had *done* this, they caught a great *number* of fish
and their *nets* were *tearing.*

The tone shifts here to a more personal (one-on-one) encounter.

Peter's response is both dubious and obedient.

supported by the testimony of witnesses, including himself.

GOSPEL "Woe is me, I am doomed!" said Isaiah. "I am the least of the apostles!" said Paul. "Depart from me. Lord, for I am a sinful man," said Peter. Three responses to the same challenge, "Put out into deep water and lower your nets for a catch." Those of us who are old enough might remember the tight economy of the Latin form of this command: *Duc in altum.* Launch out into the deep; put out into deep waters.

It would seem that God never calls us to the safety of the harbor until our lives are over. During life the call is always a challenge: *Duc in altum.* Launch! Venture forth! Break new ground! Rouse yourself from that posture of torpor! Move on!

"Here I am, send me!" said Isaiah. But only after considerable anxiety: "Woe is me! I am a man of unclean lips." I'm not worthy to launch out. "I am the least of the apostles," said Paul. I don't deserve the name of apostle. "Leave me, Lord. I am a sinful man!" said Peter.

Human nature recoils at the thought of being asked to do something great, or even something different. We seem by nature to be in constant search of safety, of a degree of comfort, of rest, of peace, of security. Perhaps oddest of all is the tendency of Christians to see their faith as a safe refuge—a security blanket—an insurance policy against any major disturbance. And our faith is all those things in a way. It is all those things for those who have crossed the deep and reside in the peace of eternity. But probably not for us until we join them.

They *signaled* to their *partners* in the *other* boat
to come to *help* them.
They *came* and filled *both* boats
so that the boats were in danger of *sinking*.

The description of the great catch needs to build, communicating more and more amazement.

When Simon Peter *saw* this, he fell at the *knees* of Jesus and said,
"*Depart* from me, Lord, for I am a *sinful* man."

For *astonishment* at the catch of *fish* they had made *seized* him
and all those *with* him,
and likewise *James* and *John*, the sons of *Zebedee*,
who were *partners* of Simon.

Zebedee = ZEB-uh-dee

A sudden shift is heard in Jesus' words of assurance. Prepare for it with a slight pause.

Jesus said to Simon, "Do *not* be afraid;
from now *on* you will be catching *men*."

The final words are striking; this event has altered lives forever. Sustain the energy.

When they brought their boats to the *shore*,
they left *everything* and *followed* him.

Life walked in the footsteps of Christ—if the gospel is our guide—is never very safe or secure or stable. That command just keeps on coming: "Launch out into deeper waters." And we recoil. "Ah, Lord, we've been hard at it all night long. There's nothing out there."

Here we come to the point of Luke's story. Why take the risk? Why take the plunge into deeper waters? Why resist the tendency to hang back and be comfortable? Why fight that whiney voice inside that says, "There's nothing out there"?

Well, simply because bearing the name Christian makes us all apostles. Luke is showing us how the world is changed at Jesus' coming. With his love as the bait, all his followers are to catch human beings and bring them to new life. All Christians are to launch out into the deep and lure the world to Christ by deed, by example, by whatever means available.

The presumption is that you and I have taken the bait—hook, line, and sinker—and will spend our lives charting new waters to bring the world to the love of Christ. It's easy to get stuck. It's tragic to let ourselves be imprisoned. It's lethal to seek the safety of a shore than can only be an illusion. Our own faith or religion can seem a false security. Our own fellow Christians can put limits on us. And our own sense of guilt and unworthiness can mire us on a muddy shore where there is no catch to be made whatever. If this is the case, we need to let the Lord's words ring in our hearts. "Launch out into deeper waters." Do what we need to do. Break the habit. Shatter the glass ceiling. Cut the cords that fear or the past or guilt or convention or laziness or pride has wrapped us in.

6TH SUNDAY IN ORDINARY TIME

Lectionary #78

READING I Jeremiah 17:5–8

A reading from the Book of the Prophet Jeremiah

"Cursed" (one syllable) is a strong word; do not shy away from it. Remember that you are reading a pair of opposites. The "cursed" paragraph prepares for the contrast of the "blessed" paragraph. The barren bush comparison begins; let each image sink in.

Thus says the *LORD*:
Cursed is the one who *trusts* in human *beings*,
who seeks his *strength* in *flesh*,
whose *heart* turns *away* from the LORD.
He is like a barren *bush* in the *desert*
that enjoys no change of *season*,
but stands in a *lava* waste,
a *salt* and *empty* earth.

"Blessed" (one or two syllables) begins the contrast. Pause before it.

Blessed is the one who *trusts* in the LORD,
whose *hope* is the LORD.
He is like a *tree* planted beside the *waters*
that stretches out its *roots* to the *stream*:
It fears *not* the heat when it comes;
its *leaves* stay *green*;
in the year of *drought* it shows no *distress*,
but *still* bears *fruit*.

READING I In a pair of neatly matched metaphors, we see the contrast between those who trust in God and those who trust in merely human powers.

The metaphor of the barren bush is vivid. It merits contemplation. Consider the image of a desert shrub, struggling to stay alive in a wasteland where sustenance is scarce and no rains come to nourish it. The soil from which it tries to draw life is itself lifeless, made sterile by salt. Yet the shrub hangs on to a meager existence, unable to alter its arid environment. The analogy prompts us to recognize the difference between the shrub and ourselves. We have a choice; the shrub has none.

The tree planted beside the waters is a vivid contrast. The source of its nourishment is abundant and unfailing. It undergoes the same vicissitudes of harsh weather and periods of drought, but flourishes in spite of these things—for its roots have stored up strength for the trials. Again we recognize that the tree, unlike ourselves, has no choice. It is a happy accident that the seed from which it sprouted landed by a stream in good soil.

No happy accidents are involved in our free choice to place our trust in God. The vivid images in this reading prompt us to make that choice.

READING II Paul's goal here is not to prove anything. Rather, it is to clarify how resurrection of the dead is an inevitable consequence of everything else we already believe about Jesus. Approached in this way, Paul's words have a compelling force. He bases his position on the present

READING II 1 Corinthians 15:12, 16–20

A reading from the first Letter of Saint Paul to the Corinthians

The reading is made up of a series of conditional statements, "If . . . (then)." The greeting "brothers and sisters" can dilute the cadence of the argument. Pause after it and begin anew with "If Christ . . ."

The second statement has multiple "If . . . (then)" constructions. Read slowly and clearly.

Brothers and sisters:
If *Christ* is *preached* as *raised* from the *dead*,
how can *some* among you say there *is* no resurrection
of the dead?

If the *dead* are not raised, neither has *Christ* been raised,
and if *Christ* has not been raised, your *faith* is *vain*;
you are still in your *sins*.
Then those who have fallen *asleep* in Christ have *perished*.

The third "If . . . (then)" is the strongest of all!

A strong contrast, resolving all the previous "If . . . then" conditions.

If for *this* life *only* we have hoped in Christ,
we are the most *pitiable* people of *all*.
But now Christ *has* been raised from the dead,
the *firstfruits* of those who have fallen *asleep*.

GOSPEL Luke 6:17, 20–26

A reading from the holy Gospel according to Luke

Setting the scene: notice that not only is the crowd large, it is also diverse, made up of people from different regions.

Judea = joo-DEE-uh
Tyre = tīr
Sidon = SĪ-dun

Jesus came down with the *twelve*
and stood on a stretch of *level* ground
with a great *crowd* of his *disciples*
and a *large* number of the *people*
from all *Judea* and *Jerusalem*
and the *coastal* region of *Tyre* and *Sidon*.

state of Christians. We have already experienced a kind of resurrection—we have been reborn in baptism. We have been given a share in divine life and have been transformed by it. But for what purpose if our existence is limited to an earthly one? Why be forgiven and redeemed if natural death is the end of everything? Why believe in the resurrection of Jesus if we are not to share in that resurrection?

With this kind of logic, Paul asserts that Jesus' resurrection is the guarantee of our own. His resurrection is the first and best of the harvest (the first fruits); ours is the rest of the harvest. To follow Christ must include hope in the resurrection; otherwise, we're following a notion of Jesus' mission that is incomplete. Our faith is meaningless if it does not include faith in the resurrection of the dead. The lives we now lead in Christ (forgiven and redeemed) make no sense if they do not include an existence beyond this present one.

GOSPEL Luke is not so much interested in making a social statement about the economically poor and hungry. Rather, he points out that those who realize their need for God are blessed; those who feel themselves to be self-sufficient are to be pitied. Further, only the severely neurotic person literally takes joy in being excluded and insulted. Luke's point is that such treatment will inevitably come. It is part of the cost of discipleship. Indeed, it is proof of discipleship, a guarantee that our lives

There are four "blesseds" with four matching "woes." And the structure is in poetic form. The repetition of the formula or structure has the effect of making the assertions memorable. Let each assertion and its contrast (hungry/full, full/hungry, weep/laugh, laugh/weep, and so on) sink in.

And raising his *eyes* toward his *disciples* he said:
"*Blessed* are you who are *poor*,
for the kingdom of *God* is *yours*.
Blessed are you who are now *hungry*,
for you will be *satisfied*.
Blessed are you who are now *weeping*,
for you will *laugh*.
Blessed are you when people *hate* you,
and when they *exclude* and *insult* you,
and denounce your *name* as *evil*
on account of the Son of *Man*.

Notice how you must prepare now for the contrast between "prophets" and "*false* prophets" (in the final line).

"*Rejoice* and *leap* for joy on that day!
Behold, your *reward* will be *great* in *heaven*.
For their *ancestors* treated the *prophets* in the same *way*.

We know the "woes" are going to match the "blesseds." The pleasure in hearing comes partly from knowing what is coming—and then hearing it arrive! Rhetoricians call this the fulfillment of "expected form."

"But *woe to* you who are *rich*,
for *you* have *received* your consolation.
Woe to you who are filled *now*,
for *you* will be *hungry*.
Woe to you who *laugh* now,
for *you* will *grieve* and *weep*.
Woe to you when all speak *well* of you,
for their *ancestors* treated the *false* prophets in this *way*."

are radically Christian enough to prompt such ridicule. The joy comes from knowing through our sufferings that we have truly become united to the sufferings of Christ—and so will share in his ultimate joy.

A word of caution about proclaiming formulaic texts like this one. First, the ideas are familiar, so you are immediately challenged with the need to make them sound fresh. However, your aim is not to make them sound new. Perhaps the distinction seems subtle, but the point is to avoid anything odd or overdone in your attempts to make a familiar text come alive again for the hearers. Remember that part of the pleasure of hearing some texts is their familiarity. That's why formulas like "Once upon a time" take their place in our language.

On the other hand, avoid the tendency to rattle off a text simply because it is familiar ("Everybody knows this and has heard it a thousand times"). To surrender to this temptation guarantees that the assembly will *not* hear the text *this* time!

The balance will probably be achieved best by those who are truly involved with the thought and images of the passage. If you are truly thinking of the difference between being hungry and full, happy or mournful, well or poorly treated, then you will probably communicate the feeling of the text and enable the formulaic pattern to accomplish its intended effect.

7TH SUNDAY IN ORDINARY TIME

Lectionary #81

READING I 1 Samuel 26:2, 7–9, 12–13, 22–23

A reading from the first Book of Samuel

An abridged short story. Read it with gusto.
Ziph = zif

In *those* days, *Saul* went down to the desert of *Ziph*
with three thousand *picked* men of *Israel*,
to search for *David* in the *desert* of Ziph.

Abishai = uh-BĪ-shay-ī, uh-BĪ-shī

So David and *Abishai* went among Saul's *soldiers* by *night*
and *found* Saul lying *asleep* within the *barricade*,
with his *spear* thrust into the *ground* at his *head*
and *Abner* and his men sleeping *around* him.

Abner = AB-ner
The details of the scene make it vivid. We can sense David and Abishai tiptoeing around the camp.

Abishai *whispered* to David:
"God has *delivered* your *enemy* into your *grasp* this day.
Let me *nail* him to the *ground* with one *thrust* of the *spear*;
I will not need a *second* thrust!"

The point is made here: "Do not harm the Lord's anointed."

But *David* said to *Abishai*, "Do not *harm* him,
for who can lay *hands* on the LORD'S *anointed*
and remain *unpunished*?"

So David *took* the spear and the *water* jug from their place
at Saul's *head*,
and they got *away* without anyone's *seeing* or *knowing*
or *awakening*.
All remained *asleep*,
because the *LORD* had put them into a deep *slumber*.

Going across to an *opposite* slope,
David stood on a remote *hilltop*
at a great *distance* from Abner, son of Ner, and the *troops*.

Ner = ner

READING I **To understand this reading, we need to know that Saul (in an insane rage) is seeking to kill David, who is a threat to Saul's kingship. David will be king of Israel after Saul, and Saul cannot bear the thought. This is not the first time David has triumphed over Saul's meanness, demonstrating that he could have had the upper hand but refused to harm the Lord's anointed one.**

The entire story is much more complicated than today's snippets from it reveal. The reason this much of the tale forms the first reading is that it complements the message of Jesus in the gospel: "Love your enemies." It may also remind us that Jesus is a descendant of the house of David and the fullest realization of all the prophecies concerning David as the ideal king. David's virtues of mercy and justice are perfected in Jesus' teaching on love.

David's elaborate ruse should be read for the contrast it shows between David's respect for the king (appointed by the Lord) and Saul's inability to show like respect. The extent to which David goes to demonstrate his superiority and yet refuse to harm the king is almost humorous. Indeed, in an earlier encounter, it is downright comical. David sneaks up behind Saul and cuts off a piece of his cloak while Saul is attending to the call of nature in a cave. Though remorseful, David nevertheless must let Saul know that more than once he has had him in his power and yet did not harm him.

Saul responds each time with regret that he has pursued David in hate. And yet each time he returns to his former ways. In short, David is a model of tolerance and

He said: "Here is the king's *spear*.
Let an *attendant* come over to *get* it.
The LORD will *reward* each man for his *justice* and *faithfulness*.
Today, though the LORD *delivered* you into my *grasp*,
I would not *harm* the LORD'S *anointed*."

The point is made again in this paragraph.

READING II 1 Corinthians 15:45–49

A reading from the first Letter of Saint Paul to the Corinthians

Brothers and sisters:
It is *written*, The *first* man, *Adam*, became a living *being*,
the *last* Adam a life-giving *spirit*.
But the *spiritual* was not *first*;
rather the *natural* and *then* the spiritual.

Take this brief dissertation slowly. It's packed.

The *first* man was from the *earth*, *earthly*;
the *second* man, from *heaven*.
As was the *earthly* one, so also are the *earthly*,
and as is the *heavenly* one, so also are the *heavenly*.

"Man" here refers to Adam or Christ. Do not change it.

Here, as above, the force of this text lies in the contrasts between first and second, earthly and heavenly. Vocal variety and contrasting emphasis is the secret.

Just as we have borne the image of the *earthly* one,
we shall *also* bear the image of the *heavenly* one.

respect. Saul is an example of the opposite, though our harsh evaluation of his behavior should be mitigated by the realization that he was probably insane.

READING II This is a difficult reading. Paul is concerned with yet another mistaken notion of the Christians at Corinth. And the history of the argument is complex. They felt that a spiritual existence (which all had possessed in the beginning but was now trapped inside a corruptible body) had been regained in baptism and sustained in the other sacraments. In other words, the feeling was that participation in the divine life was already more or less complete.

Paul seeks to show otherwise—that our participation in divinity is indeed a reality, but that it is not complete, and will not be complete until we have been raised from the dead as Christ was and reunited with him in glory. And the other concern is to show that the divine life we now share was not something we regained, but something that became possible only through Jesus' death and resurrection.

Adam figures in this reading because the Corinthians had inherited a notion that began with the philosopher Philo, who justified the two variant accounts of creation in Genesis by asserting the existence of two Adams: the first an ideal spiritual being, the second a corruptible being. Paul reverses the entire argument. The first being, he says, is corruptible and that is Adam (the

GOSPEL Luke 6:27–38

A reading from the holy Gospel according to Luke

"To you who *hear,*" implies a great deal beyond the literal sense of hearing. It means rather, "you who are willing to understand and heed what you hear."

A series of epigrams or sayings follows. This is the first. Do not rush from one to the next.

Jesus said to his *disciples*:
"To you who *hear* I say,
love your *enemies*, do *good* to those who *hate* you,
bless those who *curse* you, *pray* for those who *mistreat* you.
To the person who strikes you on *one* cheek,
offer the *other* one as well,
and from the person who takes your *cloak*,
do not withhold even your *tunic*.

The second saying.

Give to everyone who *asks* of you,
and from the one who *takes* what is yours do not demand it *back*.
Do to *others* as you would have *them* do to *you*.

"For if you *love* those who love *you*,
what credit is *that* to you?
Even *sinners* love those who *love* them.
And if you do *good* to those who do good to *you*,
what credit is *that* to you?
Even *sinners* do the same.

The third saying. And it is explicated at some length.

If you lend *money* to those from whom you expect *repayment*,
what credit is *that* to you?
Even *sinners* lend to *sinners*,
and get back the same *amount*.

one and only, from earth). The second being is spiritual and that is Christ (the one and only, from heaven). Once we were like Adam, corruptible—and we still have Adam-like qualities, even as we share in the divine life. But the day is coming, though not yet, when we will be completely like Christ, incorruptible, our bodies raised in glory like his.

The best your proclamation can do is remind us that, just as now we share an earthly existence, so we will one day share a heavenly life with Christ.

GOSPEL There are two important things to keep in mind as you prepare this section of Jesus' great Sermon on the Plain. First, a literal interpretation will miss the point entirely. Jesus is not asking us to endure physical abuse passively. He is not asking us to place our health or our lives in jeopardy through some romantic notion about martyrdom. Second, the final section about judging and giving is in no way meant to represent God as some kind of pawnbroker. Christianity does not involve tit-for-tat. To assert such a notion is to put ourselves on equal terms with God—as though we had a right to bargain, or to claim rights to deserved rewards. Though Christian behavior sometimes seems to be based on such notions, nothing could be farther from the truth. Our relationship with God is never based on our earnings. God is love. God moves toward us in love. God forgives in love. God's grace is free—and even to put it that way is redundant. After all, the word "grace" means "free."

But *rather*, *love* your enemies and do *good* to them,
and *lend* expecting nothing *back*;
then your *reward* will be *great*
and you will be *children* of the Most *High*,
for he *himself* is kind to the *ungrateful* and the *wicked*.

The fourth saying, and in an "if . . . then" construction.

Be *merciful*, just as your *Father* is merciful.

"Stop *judging* and you will not *be* judged.
Stop *condemning* and you will not *be* condemned.

This fifth saying sums up all the rest.

Forgive and you will be *forgiven*.

Finally, an exhilarating promise.

Give and gifts will be *given* to you;
a good *measure*, packed *together*, shaken *down*,
and *overflowing*,
will be poured into your *lap*.
For the *measure* with which you *measure*
will in *return* be measured *out* to you."

So what is this radical text all about? It's about being radical: radically loving, radically forgiving, radically generous, radically God-like. All the kinds of behavior that Luke records here are summed up in one kind of behavior: God-like behavior. To what extent can we behave like God? To a far greater extent than most of us do. That's the point.

The bottom line may be put this way: If there is no difference between how Christians behave and how non-Christians behave, where's the evidence that Christianity is different? If we use the same measurement of fairness and generosity as the world uses, where is the influence of Jesus' example of total self-giving? If Christians feel they have a right to judge and condemn, where is the evidence that God has forgiven and redeemed them? Christ-like behavior is its own reward. Can you imagine wanting more than that?

ASH WEDNESDAY

Lectionary #219

READING I Joel 2:12–18

A reading from the Book of the Prophet Joel

Begin with an exalted tone. This is poetry, recognizable as such from the first words of the passage. And the feeling is upbeat because the Lord is forgiving, merciful, and gracious.

Even *now*, says the LORD,
 return to me with your whole *heart*,
 with *fasting*, and *weeping*, and *mourning*;
Rend your *hearts*, not your *garments*,
 and return to the *LORD*, your *God*.
For *gracious* and *merciful* is he,
 slow to anger, *rich* in kindness,
 and *relenting* in punishment.
Perhaps he will *again* relent
 and leave behind him a *blessing*,
Offerings and *libations*
 for the LORD, your *God*.

This is a new section; pause before it. Then about ten short directives follow. Don't rush through them. Let each image sink in.

Blow the *trumpet* in *Zion*!
 proclaim a *fast*,
 call an *assembly*;
Gather the people,
 notify the congregation;
Assemble the *elders*,
 gather the *children*
 and the *infants* at the *breast*;
Let the *bridegroom quit* his room,
 and the bride her *chamber*.

READING I Though we may not look forward to Lent's abstinence and severity, we know it is important to acknowledge our sinfulness, the sober truth of our mortality, and the need to take stock of our lives. We come to church for ashes and prepare ourselves for an honest appraisal.

The members of the assembly are in a receptive mood, expecting a message that will help them live up to their lenten resolutions. You, the reader, have a wonderful opportunity to fulfill their expectations. Notice first of all that the first reading is poetry. The prophet is calling the people to conversion, and he does so in exalted and beautiful language. When you proclaim these words with exaltation and communicate their beauty, you ennoble your listeners and their good intentions. You create the effect Joel intended.

The opening words "Even now . . ." imply "Even with things as bad as they are . . ." Joel is describing a bad situation; it is clear that the people's only recourse is to God. We know, of course, that our only reliable recourse is to God, but Lent reminds us that we need to concentrate on that fundamental truth once again. Lent is a time for getting back to basics. It is a time for examining and reevaluating our priorities.

The trumpet call is a summons to come together and rally ourselves for action. Notice that the call is to the community as a whole. We are not entering the lenten season to engage in a lonely struggle all by ourselves. The entire church is called to this challenge. This makes our efforts not only

Between the *porch* and the *altar*
let the *priests*, the *ministers* of the LORD, *weep*,
And say, "*Spare*, O LORD, your *people*,
and make not your *heritage* a *reproach*,
with the nations *ruling* over them!
Why should they say among the *peoples*,
'Where is their *God*?'"

Pause again here, then read the last sentence with a sense of peaceful resolution.

Then the LORD was stirred to *concern* for his land
and took pity on his people.

READING II 2 Corinthians 5:20—6:2

A reading from the second Letter of Saint Paul to the Corinthians

This is a brief reading with two sections, and the prose is dense with meaning. The assembly will need time to absorb it.

Brothers and sisters:
We are *ambassadors* for *Christ*,
as if *God* were *appealing* through *us*.
We *implore* you on behalf of Christ,
be *reconciled* to God.
For *our* sake he made him to *be* sin
who did not *know* sin,
so that we might become the *righteousness*
of *God* in *him*.

easier but more gratifying. Because of our human tendency to get wrapped up in ourselves, especially when it comes to awareness of sin, the communal aspect of Lent reminds us that we are one in the body of Christ. Each one's sins affect all the rest, and the good works of each member reflect on the entire church.

READING II Notice first of all in this reading the plentiful plural pronouns: we, us, our, you, your. The use of these words creates an immediacy that can make the reading more forceful, easier to listen to, more applicable to each hearer. It also creates a feeling of community, bringing us together. Make the most of it in your proclamation.

The first reading called us together and directed us to examine our lives as individuals and as a community. The second reading turns us outward as a community, reminding us that we, like Paul, are ambassadors for Christ in the world. A dimension of Lent involves an assessment of ourselves as a church. How well are we doing as ambassadors for Christ? Is the church more attractive to outsiders this year than it was last year? What kind of image does the church present? Is it welcoming and inclusive? We hope so, but we know there is room for improvement in each of us as individual ambassadors and in the church as a whole.

Every time is an acceptable time; every day is a day of salvation. But we need to set aside special times and days to call ourselves back to the simplicity of our belief and mission. Paul begs us not to receive the

The second section begins here. Renew the plea.

Working together, then,
we *appeal* to you not to receive the *grace*
of God in *vain*.
For he says:

In an *acceptable* time I *heard* you,
and on the day of *salvation* I *helped* you.

There is a sense of urgency in "Now! Now!"

Behold, *now* is a very acceptable time;
behold, *now* is the day of *salvation*.

GOSPEL Matthew 6:1–6, 16–18

A reading from the holy Gospel according to Matthew

Be aware from the beginning that you are reading a carefully structured text (see the commentary). The first couple of lines state the principle. Three examples follow, stated with an easy-to-remember formula.

This is the first example. Experiment with emphasis on "you" to imply contrast with the hypocrites.

Jesus said to his *disciples*:
"Take *care* not to perform righteous *deeds*
in order that people may *see* them;
otherwise, you will have no *recompense*
from your heavenly *Father*.
When *you* give alms,
do not blow a *trumpet* before you,
as the *hypocrites* do in the synagogues
and in the streets
to win the *praise* of others.
Amen, I say to you,
they have *received* their reward.
But when *you* give alms,
do not let your *left* hand know what your *right* is *doing*,
so that *your* almsgiving may be *secret*.
And your *Father* who *sees* in *secret* will *repay* you.

grace of God in vain. By this statement he reminds us of what the Good News is, namely, that we have received the grace of God. Think of the implications of receiving that grace: divine acceptance, infinite love, total forgiveness, the assurance of eternal life. All of them are given for one reason only: God loves us. How terrible to think we could receive such wonders in vain!

GOSPEL To understand Jesus' words here it is absolutely essential that we understand one thing clearly: The good works we do, the sacrifices we make, the alms we give are simply a matter of justice. It is difficult for me to write a check for a needy cause without feeling like I have done something special. In one sense I have, of course, because I've recognized a need. But I must keep reminding myself that what I have given away always belonged to the needy person who received it. The extra prayers I say are simply what is appropriate. The fasting I do, the abstinence, is simply deciding not to eat or drink something that really belongs to anyone who needs it more than I do.

Looking at our good lenten works this way shows how ridiculous it is to blow our horn, to brag about our piety, or be an exhibitionist in our self-denial. We give things up because someone needs them more than we do. Rather than brag about our generosity, we might be embarrassed that we were keeping for ourselves what belonged to someone else. This is the kind of revolutionary Christianity we get when we take

The second example begins here: "When you pray . . ."

"When *you* pray,
do not be like the *hypocrites*,
who love to stand and pray in the *synagogues*
and on *street* corners
so that others may *see* them.
Amen, I say to you,
they have *received* their reward.
But when *you* pray, go to your inner *room*,
close the *door*, and pray to your Father in *secret*.
And your Father who *sees* in *secret* will *repay* you.

The third example begins here: "When you fast . . ."

"When *you* fast,
do not look *gloomy* like the *hypocrites*.
They *neglect* their appearance,
so that they may *appear* to others to be fasting.
Amen, I say to you, they have *received* their reward.
But when *you* fast,
anoint your head and *wash* your face,
so that you may *not* appear to be fasting,
except to your *Father* who is *hidden*.
And your Father who *sees* what is *hidden*
will *repay* you."

Jesus at his word. How long will it take us to realize that as long as there is one hungry person in the world, we're not doing our job?

With all this in mind, you will be able to proclaim this reading in a bright tone of voice. Your purpose is to strengthen the members of the assembly in their lenten resolutions by reminding them of the noblest way of carrying them out. The reading is not about hypocrites; it's about us.

There are three sections to the passage, each composed of three parts: "When you give alms . . . When you pray . . . When you fast." Then, for each good work, Jesus admonishes us to avoid hypocrisy and to do our fasting, prayer, and almsgiving secretly. This kind of formulaic teaching is common in scripture. It is probably a reflection of the oral tradition that existed long before these words were written down. The threefold pattern and the repeated phrases make the instruction easier to memorize.

Your proclamation can communicate something of this structure. The pattern should be discernible and even predictable. In this way, your listeners should be able to see how the reading builds upon itself so that the lesson becomes clearer and clearer. Allow the familiarity of the text to assist you. Enable the assembly to welcome these words of Jesus both in their familiarity and their challenge.

1ST SUNDAY OF LENT

Lectionary #24

READING I Deuteronomy 26:4–10

A solemn liturgical scene is depicted here. The basket is the first fruits of the harvest.

The next section is a narrative, the story of Israel's oppression and liberation. It is our story, too.

Aramean = air-uh-MEE-uhn

A reading from the Book of Deuteronomy

Moses spoke to the *people*, saying:
"The *priest* shall receive the *basket* from you
and shall set it in front of the *altar* of the LORD, your *God*.

"Then you shall *declare* before the LORD, your God,
'My *father* was a wandering *Aramean*
who went down to *Egypt* with a small *household*
and *lived* there as an *alien*.
But *there* he became a *nation*
great, *strong* and *numerous*.
When the Egyptians *maltreated* and *oppressed* us,
imposing hard *labor* upon us,
we cried to the *LORD*, the God of our *fathers*,
and he *heard* our cry
and saw our *affliction*, our *toil* and our *oppression*.

"'He brought us *out* of Egypt
with his strong *hand* and outstretched *arm*,
with terrifying *power*, with *signs* and *wonders*;
and bringing us into *this* country,
he gave us *this* land flowing with *milk* and *honey*.

READING I At the beginning of the season of Lent we find ourselves in the context of an ancient liturgical rite: the offering of the first fruits of the harvest. Gifts are offered for the sacrifice, the history of God's intervention on behalf of the people is recounted, God's promises of deliverance and restoration are recalled, and the people respond in humble and grateful worship. Finally, in the verse that follows the lectionary's selection, the entire people, including the strangers among them, celebrate the Lord's bounty.

In a broad way, we imitate during the lenten season all that is described in this reading. We offer the very best of our praise, together with penance—knowing that we have fallen short. We hear again the history of God's plan of salvation for us and the fidelity of God's intervention on behalf of our ancestors in the faith. In Jesus we see the fulfillment of God's promises of deliverance through a suffering Messiah who ultimately conquers death and opens an eternal kingdom for us. Our response to this forty-day liturgy is the joyful celebration of Easter, when we, like the Israelites in this reading, will "make merry over all these good things" (v. 11).

Lent has been described as a time for getting back to basics. In this first reading we do just that. We return to the earliest events in our history as God's people and remind ourselves of the constancy of God's

This is a rubric for worship—in thanksgiving.

Therefore, I have now brought you the *firstfruits*
of the products of the *soil*
which *you,* O LORD, have *given* me.'

Predicts the gospel: "God alone shall you worship."

"And having *set* them before the LORD, your *God,*
you shall bow *down* in his *presence."*

READING II Romans 10:8–13

A reading from the Letter of Saint Paul to the Romans

The initial question is rhetorical. A good attention-getter.

Brothers and sisters:
What does *Scripture* say?

The word "faith" must be emphasized here, to communicate Paul's distinction.

"The word is *near* you,
in your *mouth* and in your *heart"*
—that is, the word of *faith* that we *preach*—
for, if you *confess* with your *mouth* that *Jesus* is *Lord*
and *believe* in your *heart* that God *raised* him from the *dead,*
you will be *saved.*

The meaning here is not "this one" and "another one," but "everyone believes and everyone confesses."

For one *believes* with the *heart* and so is *justified,*
and one *confesses* with the *mouth* and so is *saved.*

For the *Scripture* says,
"No one who *believes* in him will be put to *shame."*
For there is no *distinction* between *Jew* and *Greek*;
the *same* Lord is Lord of *all,*
enriching all who *call* upon him.

This is a powerful statement. Make it ring out.

For "*everyone* who calls on the name of the *Lord* will be *saved."*

loving plan to save us. Our exodus, our deliverance, our land of milk and honey, are achieved through the Easter mystery.

READING II We are certainly back to basics in this joyous passage. Those who proclaim aloud that Jesus is Lord and believe that God raised him from the dead will be saved! It doesn't get much simpler than this.

It is not as though we ignore the complexities of everyday life when we formulate our beliefs in such simple terms. Rather, the effect is to put those complexities into perspective. We remind ourselves that the creed by which Christian life is measured is, after all, a simple one. Christians proclaim by their lives that Jesus is Lord of all, and they believe that he has conquered every earthly trial, including death. Our lives are a response this good news.

And the good news is for everyone. In your proclamation of this reading, take special note of the words "no one," "all," and "everyone." "*No one* who believes will be put to shame." "*Everyone* who calls on the name of the Lord will be saved." "*All* who call upon him will be enriched." Perhaps during this Lent we can take a significant step toward the day when these words are taken to heart by all who hear them.

GOSPEL Luke 4:1–13

A reading from the holy Gospel according to Luke

For Luke it is important that the Spirit of God lead Jesus toward the trial of his temptation. The point is that Jesus does everything under the guidance of the Spirit.
Temptation comes when we are weakened by hunger or need.

Filled with the Holy *Spirit*, Jesus *returned* from the *Jordan*
and was *led* by the Spirit into the *desert* for forty *days*,
to be *tempted* by the *devil.*
He ate *nothing* during those days,
and when they were *over* he was *hungry.*

Do not rush through the dialogue. Pause between sections—and before each of Jesus' responses.

The devil said to him,
"*If* you are the Son of *God*,
command this *stone* to become *bread.*"
Jesus answered him,
"It is *written*, 'One does not *live* on bread *alone.*' "

Each temptation is more complex and dramatic than the last. There must be a sense of build throughout the reading.

Then he took him up and showed him
all the *kingdoms* of the *world* in a single *instant.*
The devil said to him,
"I shall *give* to you all this *power* and *glory*;
for it has been handed *over* to me,
and I may *give* it to whomever I *wish.*
All this will be *yours*, if you *worship* me."
Jesus said to him in *reply*,
"It is *written*:
'You shall worship the *Lord*, your *God*,
and him *alone* shall you serve.' "

GOSPEL We always hear the story of Jesus' temptation in the desert on the 1st Sunday of Lent. In Year A, Matthew's account is read and it is the most familiar version. Mark's account, in Year B, is very brief, excluding even the dialogue between Jesus and the devil and the three temptations. Each gospel writer has his own point to make or lesson to teach in telling his story a certain way. Matthew wants us to see Jesus as the new Moses, so the details in his story emphasize the parallels between Jesus' experience in the desert and a similar testing undergone by Moses. Clearly there are associations between Jesus' 40 days in the desert and Israel's 40 years of exile. Mark's intent is similar: Both emphasize that Jesus had to undergo a test before beginning his public ministry.

Luke's primary intention, it seems, is to provide Jesus' followers with an example of stalwart obedience and complete reliance on God. Notice that Luke implies that Satan will return at an opportune time to continue testing Jesus. In fact, we see Jesus contending with the devil elsewhere in Luke. In other words, temptation is a lifelong experience for Jesus, as it is for us.

Then he led him to *Jerusalem*,
made him *stand* on the parapet of the *temple*, and said to him,
"*If* you are the Son of *God*,
throw yourself *down* from here, for it is *written*:
'He will command his *angels* concerning you, to *guard* you,'
and:
'With their *hands* they will *support* you,
lest you dash your *foot* against a *stone*.' "
Jesus said to him in reply,
"It *also* says,
'You shall not put the Lord, your *God*, to the *test*.' "

Pause slightly before the words "for a time." The battle has just begun.

When the devil had *finished* every temptation,
he *departed* from him for a *time*.

The connection between fasting and being filled with the Spirit is not apparent to most contemporary Christians. We tend to connect fasting with penance and sacrifice. We fast as a form of mild self-inflicted suffering in reparation for our sins. The concept and the practice should be much fuller (and more positive) than that! The true purpose of our lenten fast is to encourage us toward fullness of the Spirit. The point is—and human experience bears it out—you can't be full of roast beef and alert to the Spirit at the same time. Fasting makes us alert and attentive, ready to detect the thousand signs of the Spirit's movement in our lives.

The fast that Jesus takes upon himself is to show that true sustenance comes from God. Jesus' hunger is for the will of God. Yes, it is physical hunger too, but that hunger is a symbol of spiritual hunger. The kind of bread the devil offers is insufficient.

Likewise, the power the devil offers will inevitably enslave the one who accepts it. The power that comes from serving God is liberating. The test of God's love and provident care that the devil urges on Jesus is ludicrous. It betrays either a complete lack of faith or a total misunderstanding of who God is. Because this final test is the most important in Luke's mind, he places it last.

2ND SUNDAY OF LENT

Lectionary #27

READING I Genesis 15:5–12, 17–18

A reading from the Book of Genesis

Be careful to note the difference between Abram and Abraham. The name change comes later.

The Lord *GOD* took *Abram outside* and said,
"Look up at the *sky* and count the *stars*, if you can.
Just *so*," he added, "shall your *descendants* be."
Abram put his *faith* in the LORD,
who *credited* it to him as an act of *righteousness*.

The Lord offers identification here. Moses recognizes it.

Ur = er

Chaldeans = kal-DEE-uhns

He *then* said to him,
"I am the *LORD* who brought you from *Ur* of the *Chaldeans*
to *give* you this *land* as a *possession*."

Emphasize the word "know." Abram has a right to ask this question. The Lord's response is actually, "So that I may show you, bring me . . ."

"O Lord *GOD*," he asked,
"how am I to *know* that I shall possess it?"

He answered him,
"Bring me a three-year-old *heifer*, a three-year-old *she-goat*,
a three-year-old *ram*, a *turtledove* and a young *pigeon*."
Abram *brought* him all these, split them in *two*,
and placed each half *opposite* the *other*;
but the *birds* he did *not* cut up.
Birds of *prey* swooped down on the *carcasses*,
but Abram *stayed* with them.
As the *sun* was about to *set*, a *trance* fell upon Abram,
and a *deep*, terrifying *darkness enveloped* him.

READING I **As Abraham is our father in faith and the covenant God made with him is the beginning of salvation history for the chosen people, so Jesus in the gospel today is revealed as the ultimate fulfillment of that covenant, the culmination and summation of a long history of God's self-revelation through the law and the prophets. In Jesus, the law and the prophets are confirmed and brought to perfection.**

Abraham (his name is Abram until God changes it) is called "our father in faith" in Eucharistic Prayer I. It is a title we do well to recall frequently, for it reminds us that the history of our redemption has its roots in the earliest Hebrew scriptures. In this first reading today we hear the great promise God makes to Abram—whose descendants we are, together with Jews and Muslims, and by later extension the entire world. Pope John XXIII said it beautifully: "Spiritually, we are all Semites."

Notice that Abram asks for a guarantee: "How will I know that the land promised me will be mine?" There is no arrogance implied. The literary tradition employed here always involves a dialogue and the give-and-take that is part of making a covenant or bargain.

The ritual involved seems very strange to us, but is firmly grounded in ancient practice. The sacrificial animals are cut in two and those making the covenant walk

A new section begins here: signs of God's presence.

When the sun had *set* and it was *dark*,
there appeared a smoking *fire pot* and a flaming *torch*,
which passed *between* those pieces.

It was on *that* occasion that the LORD made a *covenant* with Abram,
saying: "To your *descendants* I give this *land*,
from the Wadi of *Egypt* to the *Great* River, the *Euphrates*."

READING II Philippians 3:17—4:1

A reading from the Letter of Saint Paul to the Philippians

The feeling is upbeat, encouraging.

Join with *others* in being *imitators* of *me*, brothers and sisters,
and *observe* those who thus *conduct* themselves
according to the *model* you have in *us*.
For *many*, as I have often *told* you
and *now* tell you even in *tears*,
conduct themselves as *enemies* of the cross of Christ.

A change of mood; but more sorrow than anger.

Their end is *destruction*.
Their *God* is their *stomach*;
their *glory* is in their "*shame*."
Their *minds* are occupied with *earthly* things.

Strong contrast; upbeat again—indeed, exaltation!

But *our* citizenship is in *heaven*,
and *from* it we also await a *savior*, the Lord Jesus *Christ*.
He will *change* our *lowly* body
to *conform* with his *glorified* body
by the *power* that enables him *also*
to bring *all* things into *subjection* to *himself*.

between the separated halves, vowing that any breech of the covenant will bring the same kind of death on the participant who proves unfaithful.

The birds of prey that swoop down are potential threats to the covenant, perhaps bad omens. Abram's persistence is confirmation of his resolve and fidelity. The trance that overcomes him and the darkness that surrounds him are traditional ways of preparing for divine revelation. The fire and the torch are symbols of God, who passes between the carcasses to confirm the divine side of the bargain.

READING II Paul had a special love for the Philippians. They always compare well with less cooperative and charitable communities. Like a parent rejoicing over a particularly loyal and obedient child, Paul ends this passage with affection.

In fact, the entire reading is filled with strong emotions. It is "in tears" that Paul remembers those who act like enemies of Christ. Their problem seems to be complete absorption in the things of this world and the corresponding inability to behave like people who know where their true home is. To say that one's god is one's stomach is about as vivid an image as we can imagine. And it strikes home with special force during the lenten season when we are reminded that we do not live "on bread alone."

Paul at his most affectionate and tender.

Therefore, my brothers and sisters,
whom I *love* and *long for*, my *joy* and *crown*,
in *this* way stand *firm* in the *Lord*.

[Shorter: Philippians 3:20—4:1]

GOSPEL Luke 9:28b–36

A reading from the holy Gospel according to Luke

The literary form is narrative, like a short story.

Jesus took *Peter*, *John* and *James*
and went up the *mountain* to *pray*.
While he was praying, his *face* changed in *appearance*
and his *clothing* became dazzling *white*.

Jesus' departure, or exodus, is his approaching passing over from life to death . . . to life!

And *behold*, two *men* were *conversing* with him, *Moses*
and *Elijah*,
who appeared in *glory* and spoke of his *exodus*
that he was going to *accomplish* in *Jerusalem*.

Peter and his *companions* had been overcome by *sleep*,
but becoming fully *awake*,
they *saw* his glory and the two men *standing* with him.

Peter's confusion is understandable, but Luke's purpose is to show that full understanding won't come until later.

As they were about to *part* from him, Peter said to *Jesus*,
"*Master*, it is *good* that we are *here*;
let us make three *tents*,
one for *you*, one for *Moses*, and one for *Elijah*."
But he did not know *what* he was saying.

The tragedy for those whose sights are set so low (on their midsection) is that the transformation we are to undergo in Christ escapes them. It is not possible to live in anticipation of our true home (heaven) when we are so tied to this present existence. The virtue of detachment is counseled here—not the kind of detachment that makes us unconcerned about this life and its sufferings (or its riches), but the kind of detachment that keeps our priorities straight.

Paul is content with nothing less than transfiguration in Jesus (see today's gospel). In other words, we have already been radically changed in baptism, and our great joy and duty is to allow that change to show. There is no arrogance in Paul's recommendation that the Philippians use him as a model. There is only the conviction that the transformation he has undergone through his belief in Christ is real, and will one day be complete.

GOSPEL **The 2nd Sunday of Lent always brings us the awesome story of the transfiguration. It is a strange and wonderful narrative, rich in symbol, recalling the ancient tradition that is so integral to our contemporary faith.**

To understand the transfiguration we must realize the context in which Luke presents it. Only a few verses earlier Jesus extracted from his disciples (particularly Peter) the truth about who he is. "Who do you say that I am?" he asked. "The Messiah

While he was still *speaking*,
a *cloud* came and cast a *shadow* over them,
and they became *frightened* when they *entered* the cloud.

These are the same words we heard at Jesus' baptism; a kind of final confirmation.

Then from the cloud came a *voice* that said,
"This is my *chosen Son*; *listen* to him."
After the voice had *spoken*, Jesus was found *alone*.

Pause before this quiet conclusion. A sense of awe remains.

They fell *silent* and did not at that *time*
tell *anyone* what they had *seen*.

of God," Peter responded. And then Jesus tells the Twelve these shocking words: "The Son of Man must undergo great suffering . . . and be killed . . . and be raised." Such a horrible change from his earlier preaching demands some kind of proof. Is this the same Jesus who has proved himself master of demons and ruler of the laws of nature? The transfiguration in the presence of Peter, James, and John is offered as that proof, for in that experience we hear once again the divine stamp of approval: "This is my Son," the same approval we heard at his baptism.

And we see Jesus in the company of Moses and Elijah, two of the greatest figures of salvation history, both of whom underwent persecution. These three are in conversation about the "exodus" that Jesus is to undergo in Jerusalem. As Israel passed through the Red Sea and out of the land of exile, so Jesus will pass through death and into resurrection.

The response of the three disciples is not what we might expect. They are, in effect, struck dumb. Though they have heard and seen wondrous things that demonstrate God's approval of Jesus' dire predictions concerning himself, it is still too early for them to understand or accept such things. They will see clearly with the eyes of faith only after the resurrection.

3RD SUNDAY OF LENT

Lectionary #30

READING I Exodus 3:1–8a, 13–15

A reading from the Book of Exodus

The story of Moses and the burning bush is a favorite. Tell it carefully.
Jethro = JETH-roh
Midian = MID-ee-uhn
Horeb = HOHR-eb
It's difficult to read familiar texts with freshness. Vocal variety is the key.

Moses was tending the *flock* of his father-in-law *Jethro*,
the priest of *Midian*.
Leading the flock across the *desert*, he came to *Horeb*,
the mountain of *God*.
There an *angel* of the LORD *appeared* to Moses in *fire*
flaming out of a *bush*.
As he looked *on*, he was *surprised* to see that the *bush*,
though on *fire*, was not *consumed*.

So Moses decided,
"I must go over to *look* at this remarkable *sight*,
and see *why* the bush is not *burned*."

Do not adopt a "God voice" when calling Moses' name. You are proclaiming the text, not re-enacting it.

When the LORD *saw* him coming over to look at it more *closely*,
God called *out* to him from the bush, "*Moses*! *Moses*!"
He answered, "Here I *am*."
God said, "Come no *nearer*!
Remove the *sandals* from your *feet*,
for the *place* where you *stand* is *holy* ground.

Move through the dialogue with a solid, warm tone of voice. It is a solemn encounter.

"I am the God of your *fathers*," he continued,
"the God of *Abraham*, the God of *Isaac*, the God of *Jacob*."
Moses hid his *face*, for he was *afraid* to look at God.

But the *LORD* said,
"I have witnessed the *affliction* of my people in *Egypt*

READING I Moses is a classic example of our tradition's truth that the call creates the prophet. It is never a matter of a simple invitation from God and acceptance by the one who is called. Much needs to be asked and much needs to be explained. For a look at Moses' reluctance to take on the role God assigns him, read the entire account of his exchange with the divine prophet-maker! Moses has many reasons not to accept this duty. But he soon learns what we all learn. When the call comes it shapes us for the role to which we are called and supplies us with all we need to fulfill it.

We can look at all three readings today as having a central concern: God calls us through chosen individuals as a community, as a people. The idea of Moses' election is that God wills to rescue the Israelites from their affliction and renew with them the special relationship of old—as a people. This reading reminds us again that, from the very beginning of salvation history right up to our present day, God calls us in community, redeems us in community, and expects our service to take place in community. While it is certainly true that we can pray to God on Sunday morning from our armchair, it is not the place where we practice forming the body of believers to whom and for whom we are responsible. That can only be accomplished in the messy joy of community!

God takes the initiative in our regard; therein lies the great mystery and our joy. We are recipients of divine favor. How is it that we find this so easy to forget? There are always signs that religious people feel

and have heard their cry of *complaint* against their
slave drivers,
so I know *well* what they are *suffering*.
Therefore I have come down to *rescue* them
from the hands of the *Egyptians*
and lead them *out* of that land into a *good* and *spacious* land,
a land *flowing* with *milk* and *honey*."
Moses said to God, "But when I *go* to the Israelites
and *say* to them, 'The God of your *fathers* has *sent* me to you,'
if they *ask* me, 'What is his *name*?' what am I to *tell* them?"

Moses is given several signs as proof that his mission will succeed. The great "I AM" is the final guarantee.

It is not easy to read "I AM" as a proper name; be bold about it.

God replied, "I *am* who *am*."
Then he added, "*This* is what you shall tell the Israelites:
I *AM* sent me to you."

God spoke *further* to Moses, "*Thus* shall you say
to the *Israelites*:
The *LORD*, the God of your *fathers*,
the God of *Abraham*, the God of *Isaac*, the God of *Jacob*,
has *sent* me to you.

The final line has a natural sense of closure. Keep the voice strong.

"This is my *name forever*;
thus am I to be *remembered* through all *generations*."

READING II 1 Corinthians 10:1–6, 10–12

A reading from the first Letter of Saint Paul to the Corinthians

The opening sentence employs the negative form for emphasis. "I do not want you to be unaware" is stronger than "I want you to be aware."

I do not want you to be *unaware*, brothers and sisters,
that our *ancestors* were all under the *cloud*
and all *passed* through the *sea*,

called to save the world, or at least themselves. God has already done that; it is our vocation to spread the news—it is already accomplished by the great "I AM," the God who brings into being everything that is.

The God of Abraham, Isaac, and Jacob is the same God who has approached us in Jesus and who continues to intervene in history through the communities of humankind throughout the world. Our tendency to limit this God to certain times, places, and peoples will be lessened to the degree that we understand the absolute sovereignty revealed in this reading. Our response in love will be increased to the degree that we realize how consistently and urgently God continues to call out to us.

READING II Paul reminds us that opportunities to respond to God's call have been missed in the past. He recalls the events of the Exodus, when the Israelites all shared the great opportunity to be delivered. Yet not all seized that opportunity. We must learn from the mistakes and the triumphs of our ancestors.

The cloud, the sea, the food, the rock are all images from the Exodus event. The cloud was the sign of God's presence that followed the Israelites on their journey. The sea is the Red Sea, across which the Israelites marched on dry land and in which Pharaoh and his army were drowned. The spiritual food was the manna that fell from heaven and enabled the people to survive the long pilgrimage. And the rock was the one struck by Moses to bring forth water when the people grumbled against him. Paul says the

The two matched lists of three phrases have a natural building-up effect.

and all of them were *baptized* into *Moses*
in the *cloud* and in the *sea*.
All *ate* the same spiritual *food*,
and all *drank* the same spiritual *drink*,
for they drank from a spiritual *rock* that *followed* them,
and the *rock* was the *Christ*.

And here is the climax of the build.

Yet God was not *pleased* with *most* of them,
for they were struck *down* in the *desert*.

The rest of the reading is an application of the "history lesson."

These things *happened* as *examples* for us,
so that we might not desire *evil* things, as *they* did.
Do not *grumble* as some of *them* did,
and suffered *death* by the *destroyer*.

These things *happened* to them as an *example*,
and they have been written *down* as a *warning* to us,
upon whom the end of the *ages* has come.
Therefore, whoever thinks he is standing *secure*
should take *care* not to *fall*.

GOSPEL Luke 13:1–9

A reading from the holy Gospel according to Luke

The long sentence is a difficult beginning. Take a deep breath.
Galileans = gal-ih-LEE-uhnz

Some people told *Jesus* about the *Galileans*
whose *blood Pilate* had *mingled* with the blood
of their *sacrifices*.

Jesus said to them in *reply*,
"Do you think that because these Galileans *suffered*
in this way
they were greater *sinners* than all *other* Galileans?

Jesus answers with rhetorical questions. Let them sound rhetorical, not literal.

rock "followed them," indicating an ancient legend to that effect.

Since Paul interprets all of the images and events in the light of Jesus, he attributes Christian significance to them and speaks of the crossing of the Red Sea, for example, as a baptism. The spiritual food (manna) he sees as a foreshadowing of the eucharist. And the rock, he says, was Christ himself. The effect is to make his readers realize that their ancestors had all the same opportunities as they do to follow God and yet many perished. With such a warning before them, how could they possibly repeat the mistakes of the past? Just because the "end of the ages" has come upon us (in Christ), we cannot risk the sin of presumption.

People in relationship know that they must keep the relationship alive and strong by nurturing it, reaffirming it, expressing it, and learning from it. They do not presume that love will continue to burn bright without careful tending.

GOSPEL The events related here do not appear elsewhere in the gospels, only in Luke, whose purpose in using them is to provide a context for Jesus' call to repentance. Notice the refrain that appears twice as the response to his own question: "By no means! But I tell you, if you do not repent, you will all perish as they did!" When bad things happen to good people, we naturally wonder why. Those who told Jesus about the murdered Galileans may have wondered if the Galileans died as a punishment for their sins. Such questions

By no *means*!
But I tell *you*, if you do not *repent*,
you will all *perish* as *they* did!
Or those eighteen people who were *killed*
when the tower at *Siloam* fell on them—
do you think *they* were more *guilty*
than everyone *else* who lived in Jerusalem?
By no *means*!
But I tell *you*, if you do not *repent*,
you will all *perish* as *they* did!"

Siloam = sih-LOH-uhm (not SIL-oh-ahm)

The refrain Jesus employs is a strong warning. Be sure it comes across as a refrain. The words are identical each time.

Pause significantly before the parable.

And he told them this *parable*:
"There once was a person who had a *fig* tree planted
in his *orchard*,
and when he came in search of *fruit* on it but *found* none,
he said to the *gardener*,
'For three *years* now I have come in search of *fruit*
on this fig tree
but have *found* none.
So cut it *down*.
Why should it exhaust the *soil*?'
"He said to him in *reply*,
'*Sir*, leave it for *this* year also,
and I shall *cultivate* the ground around it and *fertilize* it;
it may bear *fruit* in the *future*.
If *not* you can cut it *down*.'"

Pause after the question and be deliberate with the next clause. Otherwise it can be difficult for your hearers to understand easily to whom the pronouns relate. "He" refers to the gardener.

The gardener reasons with the vineyard owner calmly. There is no hint of begging, simply a sensible suggestion to improve the tree's chances with some extra care.

The ending is somewhat abrupt, so ease into it for a sense of closure.

are idle; they can never be answered. More important, they are misleading. They distract us from the business of seeing that we are prepared for death whenever and however it comes.

This reading is a powerful reminder of what we are concerned with during this season of Lent. Jesus' words here are some of his strongest. The warning is clear: Conversion of life through penance is an ongoing necessity if we wish to be disciples.

The parable that forms the second half of the reading echoes the opportunity theme we spoke of in the commentary on the second reading. God returns again and again to offer us the chance to be productive, to bear fruit. And even when we do not, mercy prevails to give us yet another chance—even to the extent of making it easier for us to be productive. Nevertheless, there is such a thing as the *last* chance. And if it is not accepted, the fig tree will be uprooted and thrown into the fire.

Luke is revealing that Jesus himself is the final opportunity, the culmination of God's long history of opportunities. Don't miss it! Now is the time of salvation. Now is the time for the church to renew itself and continue the cycle inward, toward deeper and deeper conversion, and outward, toward greater and greater productiveness.

3RD SUNDAY OF LENT, YEAR A

Lectionary #28

READING I Exodus 17:3–7

There are several voices here: the people, Moses, God, the narrator. Though appropriate vocal variety is important, do not adopt character voices. Liturgical proclamation is different from dramatic interpretation.

A reading from the Book of Exodus

In those days, in their thirst for *water*,
the people *grumbled* against Moses,
saying, "Why did you ever make us leave *Egypt*?
Was it just to have us *die* here of *thirst*
with our *children* and our *livestock*?"
So *Moses* cried out to the *LORD*,
"What shall I *do* with this people?
A little *more* and they will *stone* me!"

Pause slightly before the Lord's response to Moses.

The LORD *answered* Moses,
"Go over there in front of the *people*,
along with some of the *elders* of Israel,
holding in your *hand*, as you go,
the *staff* with which you struck the *river*.

Horeb = HOHR-eb

I will be standing there in *front* of you on the *rock* in *Horeb*.
Strike the rock, and the *water* will flow from it
for the people to *drink*."
This Moses *did*, in the presence of the *elders* of Israel.

Pause before the final comment at the end of the narrative.
Massah = MAH-sah
Meribah = MAIR-ih-bah

The final question is abrupt. This is a rare kind of ending, but an effective one. Do not soften it, and do not rush on to "The word of the Lord." Let the question hang there a moment.

The place was called *Massah* and *Meribah*,
because the Israelites *quarreled* there
and *tested* the LORD, saying,
"Is the LORD in our *midst* or *not*?"

The readings for the 3rd, 4th, and 5th Sundays of Lent during Year A are so filled with basic images of our faith—water, light, death to life—that they may be read on those Sundays in Years B and C in place of the readings proper to Years B and C. It is particularly fitting to exercise this option if the assembly is preparing to celebrate the reception of catechumens into the church at the Easter Vigil.

READING I Today's readings are saturated with water imagery, especially this first reading and the gospel. Water is one of our most basic needs; life as we know it is impossible without water. How natural, then, that water initiates us into Christian life. It is through the water of baptism that we became who we are: members of the body of Christ and heirs of the reign of God.

It may be difficult for us today to appreciate the image of water, perhaps because for many of us water is taken for granted. It was not so with the Israelites during their sojourn in the desert, as indeed it is not for many people today, for whom water is a precious commodity. If we lived in one of the more arid parts of the world, like Palestine, we might be able to appreciate the readings today at a more elemental level.

In this first reading we witness a serious confrontation between Moses and the unruly people he is leading through the desert. They are panicky with thirst; Moses is frightened for his life. The real problem, of course, is that the people doubt that God

READING II Romans 5:1–2, 5–8

A reading from the Letter of Saint Paul to the Romans

There is a hint of disbelief in the goodness of this news, as if to say, "Can you believe it?"

Brothers and sisters:
Since we have been *justified* by *faith*,
we have *peace* with *God* through our Lord Jesus *Christ*,
through whom we have gained *access* by faith
to this *grace* in which we *stand*,
and we boast in *hope* of the glory of *God*.

The text is dense, though the thought will be clear if you proclaim it with great care and understanding.

And *hope* does not *disappoint*,
because the *love* of *God* has been *poured out* into our hearts
through the Holy *Spirit* who has been *given* to us.
For *Christ*, while we were still *helpless*,
died at the appointed time for the *ungodly*.
Indeed, only with *difficulty* does one die for a *just* person,
though perhaps for a *good* person one *might* even
find courage to *die*.

Christ died for us "while we were still sinners"! Give due emphasis to this good news.

But *God proves* his love for us
in that while we were still *sinners* Christ *died* for us.

will be with them in their need. Thus they ask a question that echoes in the heart of every believer who has undergone severe temptation or suffering: "Is the Lord with us or not?"

The words Massah and Meribah mean "quarrel" and "testing," as the text makes clear. You can indicate this by reading them with parallel emphasis. And don't shy away from the chilling question that ends the reading. It's a fact of life that we doubt and question, especially during difficult times. This reading acknowledges our weakness and then demonstrates that the Lord does appear among us. Doubting is not a sin; it is part of the struggle inherent in a life of faith. We have a lot in common with the grumbling Israelites—our ancestors in faith—and we need not be ashamed of it.

READING II Christianity is not about what we are supposed to do. It is about what has already been done for us by a loving God. As obvious as this, it is difficult to live out in the practice of our faith. We have been justified by faith; we have been reconciled with God; we have been granted access to grace. Notice how all this is in the past tense. It has happened. It's a given. "Have you been saved?" we are sometimes asked. Yes, we have. Have we accepted the salvation granted us out of pure love? Do we believe God loves us infinitely and without reserve? Well, there's the challenge. But the more we come to believe it, the more spontaneous and joyous

GOSPEL John 4:5–42

A reading from the holy Gospel according to John

Begin slowly and quietly (but audibly!) to set the scene.
Samaria = suh-MAIR-ee-uh
Sychar = SĪ-kahr

Jesus came to a town of *Samaria* called *Sychar*,
near the plot of land that *Jacob* had given to his son *Joseph*.
Jacob's *well* was there.
Jesus, *tired* from his *journey*, sat down there at the *well*.
It was about *noon*.

Be careful with "Give me a drink." It should not sound hard or demanding. Perhaps there can be a note of pleading or even the hint of a question or request.

A *woman* of *Samaria* came to draw *water*.
Jesus *said* to her,
"Give me a drink."
His *disciples* had gone into the *town* to buy *food*.

The woman is neither shy nor rude but honest and straightforward.

The Samaritan woman said to him,
"How can *you*, a *Jew*, ask *me*, a *Samaritan* woman,
for a *drink*?"
—For *Jews* use *nothing* in common with *Samaritans*.—
Jesus answered and said to her,
"If you knew the *gift* of God
and *who* is saying to you, 'Give me a drink,'
you would have asked *him*
and he would have given *you living* water."

The following exchanges should not be too solemn. There is every indication here that a kind of gentle banter is going on. On the other hand, a frivolous or joking tone would be completely out of place.

The woman said to him,
"Sir, you do not even have a *bucket* and the cistern is *deep*;
where then can you *get* this living water?
Are you greater than our father *Jacob*,
who *gave* us this cistern and drank from it *himself*
with his *children* and his *flocks*?"

our response to love will be. Good works are done not in the hope of earning God's favor—we already have that. Rather, good works express our gratitude.

To demonstrate his point, Paul illustrates the difference between human and divine love. Yes, on rare occasions we hear of one person giving up life itself out of love for another. Parents may sacrifice their own lives to save an endangered child, and they do so out of love for the child.

God's love for us in Christ is something like that, only greater. Christ died for us whether we deserved it or not. He died for us regardless of whether we care or not. He died for us whether or not we even hear about it until we meet him in glory! Perhaps most amazing is that in dying for us, he made us deserving. But he chose to leave us free to believe this good news or not. That, too, is a sign of his love and respect.

GOSPEL Today we see the Israelites thirsting for water in the desert. Today we hear Paul tell us that the love of God has been "poured out" into our hearts. And today we hear the story of the "woman at the well," a gospel story so popular and well known it has acquired this special title.

Taking the shorter form of this gospel weakens its impact, so avoid that if at all possible. If you are concerned about the

The point is that Jesus is greater than Jacob. Great leaders were often noted for the good wells they dug to provide for their people. Jesus surpasses them all.

Jesus answered and said to her,
"Everyone who drinks *this* water will be thirsty *again*;
but whoever drinks the water *I* shall give will *never* thirst;
the water *I* shall give will become in him
a *spring* of water welling up to eternal *life*."

The woman said to him,
"Sir, *give* me this water, so that *I* may not be thirsty
or have to keep coming here to *draw* water."

Jesus seems to set a trap here, but there is no hint of condemnation. It's more like a setup so he can reveal who he really is.

Jesus said to her,
"*Go* call your *husband* and come *back*."
The woman answered and said to him,
"I do not *have* a husband."
Jesus answered her,
"You are *right* in saying, 'I do not have a husband.'
For you have had *five* husbands,
and the one you have *now* is *not* your husband.
What you have said is *true*."

The woman said to him,
"Sir, I can see that you are a *prophet*.
Our *ancestors* worshiped on this *mountain*;
but *you* people say that the place to worship is in *Jerusalem*."
Jesus said to her,
"*Believe* me, woman, the hour is coming
when you will worship the Father
neither on this mountain *nor* in Jerusalem.

There is no need for this challenge to sound condemnatory. It is a statement of fact, and the woman is clearly not offended by it. She already knows she is speaking with a prophet.

"*You* people worship what you do not *understand*;
we worship what we *understand*,
because *salvation* is from the *Jews*.

celebration taking too long, consider other legitimate ways to abbreviate the liturgy. If you are worried that the assembly will find such a long reading boring, use your most accomplished deacon or priest to proclaim this text.

Begin your study of this gospel by reminding yourself that, in the words of the gospel writer, "Jews use nothing in common with Samaritans." Then notice as you approach the end of the story that the Samaritans come to Jesus and beg him to stay with them awhile. While these startling expressions of reconciliation between groups known for their mutual hatred are not the central point of John's account, they color it from start to finish. You might recall as well that Jesus is breaking another taboo by speaking with a woman in public, and a Samaritan woman at that. It's not a bad thing to keep in mind the reconciling power of Jesus' presence as we hear him, tired from his journey, ask for a drink of water and then reveal himself as the Messiah. Only one other time do we hear Jesus speak of his thirst—when he was lifted up on the cross and drew all the world to himself.

Though the story centers on water and its many associations, there are many other instances that urge us to look for the deeper meaning in the several topics raised in this encounter between Jesus and the Samaritan woman. The woman speaks of water, and

But the hour is *coming*, and is now *here*,
when *true* worshipers will worship the Father
in *Spirit* and *truth*;
and indeed the Father seeks such people to worship him.
God is Spirit, and those who worship him
must worship in Spirit and truth."

The woman said to him,
"I know that the *Messiah* is coming, the one called the *Christ*;
when he *comes*, he will tell us *everything*."
Jesus said to her,
"*I* am he, the one *speaking* with you."

This is a thunderclap of truth. We can only imagine the woman's reaction. It is clearly an allusion to God's "I AM" in Exodus and would have been recognized by John's readers. Let it be followed by a significant pause.

At that moment his *disciples* returned,
and were *amazed* that he was talking with a *woman*,
but still no one said, "What are you *looking* for?"
or "Why are you *talking* with her?"
The woman *left* her water jar
and went into the *town* and said to the people,
"Come see a man who told me *everything* I have *done*.
Could he possibly be the *Christ*?"
They went out of the town and *came* to him.
Meanwhile, the disciples *urged* him, "Rabbi, *eat*."
But he said to them,
"*I* have food to eat of which you do not *know*."
So the disciples said to one another,
"Could someone have *brought* him something to eat?"

John mentions the fact that "the woman left her water jar" for a reason; give it some emphasis.

The entrance of the disciples provides another opportunity for teaching.

Jesus said to them,
"*My* food is to do the will of the one who *sent* me
and to finish *his* work.
Do you not say, 'In four months the *harvest* will be here'?
I tell you, look *up* and *see* the fields *ripe* for the harvest.

Jesus turns the conversation to living water. The woman refers to Jacob, giver of the well, the source of the water, and Jesus makes it clear that indeed he is greater than Jacob. Jesus has a different kind of water to offer. The woman brings up the disagreement about where one should worship God, and Jesus explains that God is Spirit and can be worshiped anywhere by one with a truthful heart.

Even the disciples provide Jesus with an opportunity to speak of deeper matters. They urge him to eat something. He speaks of bringing the Father's work to completion as the food that sustains him. Finally, Jesus speaks of the gratuitous gift of God, Jesus himself. There is no need to sow, for the harvest is provided. God has done the work, and we reap the grain without labor. God has become one with us: "Sower and reaper may rejoice together."

A sensitive proclamation should concentrate on revealing as much of the richness here as possible. The vivid imagery, the rich dialogue, the underlying issues of race and gender, the questions of the disciples, and the conversion of the Samaritans make this gospel story one of the most formative, educational, and inspiring of the New Testament.

The *reaper* is already receiving *payment*
and gathering crops for eternal *life*,
so that the *sower* and *reaper* can *rejoice* together.
For *here* the saying is verified that '*One* sows and *another* reaps.'
I sent you to *reap* what you have not *worked* for;
others have done the *work*,
and *you* are sharing the *fruits* of their work."

Many of the *Samaritans* of that town began to *believe* in him
because of the word of the *woman* who testified,
"He told me *everything* I have *done*."
When the Samaritans *came* to him,
they invited him to *stay* with them;
and he *stayed* there two *days*.
Many *more* began to believe in him because of his *word*,
and they said to the *woman*,
"We no longer believe because of *your* word;
for we have heard for *ourselves*,
and we know that this is *truly* the savior of the *world*."

[Shorter: John 4:5–15, 19b–26, 39a, 40–42]

Here is the ultimate payoff. The woman spreads the good news, the Samaritans come to hear Jesus, and then they move from hearsay belief to personal faith. John has made the striking point that Jesus' mission is universal. This really is the Savior of the whole world!

4TH SUNDAY OF LENT

Lectionary #33

READING I Joshua 5:9a, 10–12

A reading from the Book of Joshua

Joshua = JOSH-oo-uh

A very strong opening. Today! This is the day!

Gilgal = GIL-gal

Jericho = JAIR-ih-ko

The *LORD* said to *Joshua,*
"*Today* I have removed the *reproach* of *Egypt* from you."

While the *Israelites* were encamped at *Gilgal* on the plains of *Jericho,*
they celebrated the *Passover*
on the evening of the *fourteenth* of the *month.*

"Produce of the land" deserves emphasis. This is the point. They are no longer nomads.

On the day *after* the Passover,
they ate of the *produce* of the *land*
in the form of unleavened *cakes* and parched *grain.*
On that *same day* after the Passover,
on which they ate of the *produce* of the *land,* the *manna ceased.*

"No longer"–a solemn announcement.

Canaan = KAY-nun

No *longer* was there *manna* for the Israelites,
who *that* year ate of the *yield* of the *land* of *Canaan.*

READING II 2 Corinthians 5:17–21

A reading from the second Letter of Saint Paul to the Corinthians

A hymn of exaltation. Great joy is sustained throughout.

Brothers and sisters:
Whoever is in *Christ* is a new *creation*:
the *old* things have passed *away*;
behold, new things have come.

READING I The Israelites have arrived in the land promised them. They have crossed over the Jordan, just as they crossed through the Red Sea, and are once again able to live off the produce of the land. Their journey has ended. In this reading the writer is making special note of the celebration of Passover/Unleavened Bread to mark the end of their journeys. Remember that the pilgrimage in exile also began, forty years previously, on the feast of Passover. The cessation of the manna marks this historic day—and at the same time reminds us that the Lord God saw Israel safely through the desert by providing their needs.

The importance of this text for us today is that it bespeaks a time of dramatic change, a time of coming home and being in a newly established right relationship with God. This, of course, is the central concern of the lenten observance. The same theme appears in today's second reading and gospel.

One of the important aims of the Second Vatican Council (1962–1965) was to "open the Scriptures" to our liturgical assemblies. Over the years since then we have experienced a deeper and deeper awareness of our roots in the Old Testament. The history of Israel is *our* history, not merely as a foreshadowing of the Christian era but as a long and consistent continuum of God's loving intervention on our behalf.

READING II The theme of reconciliation that Paul develops here is the lenten observance in a nutshell. In fact, it is salvation history in a nutshell—for the story of God's intervention in human history from Genesis to the Book of Revelation is

This long sentence is easier if seen as poetic. Let each assertion stand out.

And *all* this is from *God*,
who has *reconciled* us to himself through *Christ*
and given us the *ministry* of reconciliation,
namely, God was reconciling the *world* to himself in *Christ*,
not *counting* their *trespasses* against them
and entrusting *to* us the *message* of reconciliation.

So we are *ambassadors* for Christ,
as if *God* were *appealing* through *us*.
We *implore* you on *behalf* of Christ,
be *reconciled* to God.
For *our* sake he made him to *be* sin who did not *know* sin,
so that *we* might become the *righteousness* of God in *him*.

"To *be* sin who did not *know* sin." The point is that Jesus became something (sin), so that we may become its opposite (righteousness).

GOSPEL Luke 15:1–3, 11–32

A reading from the holy Gospel according to Luke

The setting in which Jesus tells this parable is important. See the commentary.

Tax collectors and *sinners* were all drawing near to *listen* to *Jesus*,
but the *Pharisees* and *scribes* began to *complain*, saying,
"*This* man welcomes *sinners* and *eats* with them."

Tell the familiar story with full animation, so that it will be fresh.

So to *them* Jesus addressed this *parable*:
"A man had two *sons*, and the *younger* son said to his father,
'*Father* give me the *share* of your estate that should *come*
to me.'
So the father *divided* the property *between* them.
"After a few *days*, the younger son *collected* all his belongings
and set *off* to a distant *country*
where he *squandered* his inheritance on a life of *dissipation*.

one long account of God's will to reconcile the human with the divine. It's a sure thing!

Paul reminds us that our cooperation in the plan is crucial—because the work of reconciliation has been accomplished but not fully realized. This is the classic Christian understanding: "already but not yet." And although this sounds like a conundrum, it is not. The wedding has taken place and the reception banquet is about to be served. The guests are being seated, the air is full of anticipation, the kitchen is a bustle of last minute preparations. The bride and groom are wed; the reason for the celebration is a done deed. But the feast has not been served and much remains to be done.

We are a new creation, says Paul. God has reconciled the world; now the world must reconcile itself with God. And how did all this happen? Well, since reconciliation means (in part) forgiveness of sin, God made Christ—who never sinned—become sin. That is, Christ became what we are so that we may become what Christ is. The reconciliation has taken place; what remains is that we respond to it and make it complete.

GOSPEL The word "prodigal" has two meanings. As an adjective it describes someone who is excessive, extravagant, immoderate and wasteful. The opposite of "prodigal" is "frugal." As a noun it is a synonym for the profligate, the spendthrift, the squanderer, the wastrel. We can see, then, why this familiar and much-loved story has been called the parable of the prodigal son. The boy was certainly wasteful of his inheritance and squandered his father's money. He was the opposite of frugal and moderate.

A new section begins here. Pause.

"When he had freely spent *everything*,
a severe *famine* struck that country,
and he *found* himself in dire *need*.
So he hired himself *out* to one of the local *citizens*
who sent him to his *farm* to tend the *swine*.
And he longed to eat his *fill* of the *pods* on which the *swine* fed,
but nobody *gave* him any.

"Coming to his *senses* he thought,
'How many of my *father's* hired *workers*
have more than *enough* food to eat,
but here am *I*, dying from *hunger*.
I shall get *up* and go to my *father* and I shall *say* to him,
"*Father*, I have sinned against *heaven* and against *you*.
I no longer *deserve* to be called your *son*;
treat me as you would treat one of your *hired* workers."'

Communicate the father's eagerness. It is amazing that the father's compassion is so great even while the son is "a long way off." Jesus' hearers would see the father's running as undignified—and sense more of his abandonment to mercy.

"So he got *up* and went *back* to his father.
While he was still a *long* way *off*,
his *father* caught *sight* of him, and was filled with *compassion*.
He *ran* to his son, *embraced* him and *kissed* him.

"His son *said* to him,
'*Father*, I have *sinned* against *heaven* and against *you*;
I no longer *deserve* to be *called* your *son*.'

The son's remorse is not directly acknowledged. No need for long apologies here. It is almost irrelevant in the light of the father's joy.

But his *father* ordered his *servants*,
'*Quickly* bring the finest *robe* and put it *on* him;
put a *ring* on his *finger* and *sandals* on his *feet*.
Take the fattened *calf* and *slaughter* it.
Then let us *celebrate* with a *feast*,
because this *son* of mine was *dead*, and has come to *life* again;
he was *lost*, and has been *found*.'
Then the celebration *began*.

The "lost and found" image is one of Luke's favorites.

I agree with those who feel that the story would be more appropriately called the parable of the prodigal father. Clearly, the point that Jesus makes in this story is not how bad the boy (or his elder brother) is but how good the father is. It is the father who is excessive and extravagant and immoderate, anything but frugal with his forgiveness and mercy. It is the father who squanders love and reconciliation on the son. The father is the true spendthrift here, sparing no cost or labor to celebrate the homecoming of his wayward son. The reluctance of the elder brother to forgive with similar prodigality makes the father seem all the more generous.

And so God deals with us. While we are "still a long way off," still covered with the mire of the pig pen, God rushes toward us with compassion, giving orders to prepare the feast before we can even get the words of remorse out of our mouths.

Above all, notice that Jesus tells this parable in response to personal criticism. He has scandalized the Pharisees and scribes by consorting with sinners. It is absolutely necessary for him to show his identity with just this kind of person, even eating with them—which for the people in this historical context meant identification with them. This parable is a forecast of Jesus' ultimate identification with sinners: his death on the cross. So the bottom line here is that Jesus is the prodigal, the spendthrift, the profligate, the one who squanders his love on those who need it most.

This much-loved parable exudes the essence of Christianity at its purest and best. It is also so carefully constructed that it reveals the greatest challenge Christians

"Now the *older* son had been out in the *field*
and, on his way *back*, as he neared the *house*,
he heard the sound of *music* and *dancing*.
He called one of the *servants* and asked what this might *mean*.
The *servant* said to him,
'Your *brother* has *returned*
and your *father* has slaughtered the fattened *calf*
because he has him back *safe* and *sound*.'

The older son is jealous; but he is hurt as well. Don't be too hard on him.

"He became *angry*,
and when he refused to enter the *house*,
his *father* came out and *pleaded* with him.
He said to his father in *reply*,
'*Look*, all these *years* I *served* you
and not *once* did I disobey your *orders*;
yet you never gave *me* even a young *goat*
to feast on with my *friends*.
But when your *son* returns
who *swallowed up* your property with *prostitutes*,
for *him* you slaughter the fattened *calf*.'

The father is the soul of kindness, even toward the mean-spirited elder son.

"He said to him,
'My *son*, you are *here* with me *always*;
everything I *have* is *yours*.
But *now* we *must* celebrate and rejoice,
because your *brother* was *dead* and has come to *life* again;
he was *lost* and has been *found*.'"

face: to believe that God's love and forgiveness and acceptance and welcome are so available and so . . . well, prodigal! We simply do not forgive each other in the way the parable teaches us to. We hold grudges, we presume recidivism, we hang on to cynical views of weak human nature, and perhaps most tragically, we don't trust that God's prodigal forgiveness and love extends to ourselves in any personal way. We do better than this to some extent, of course, but it's a matter of degree that this parable teaches us.

The parable says: Don't let the sinners back in and then make them sit in the corner to atone for their sins. Don't give them warnings ("If ever again!") and finger-wagging scoldings, and snippy assurances that they are lesser creatures because of their mistakes. And above all, don't let the fear of scandal provide you with an excuse for keeping them hidden from public view—lest someone find out they have returned, retell their misdeeds and cause problems for you. We find it difficult to live the parable because we don't really believe in the repentance of the prodigal son or the prodigious love of the prodigal father. We do these things because we have resigned ourselves to suffer contentedly with elder-brother syndrome. (Thank heaven, the prodigal father is loving toward him as well, though one does get the impression he is not the happiest member of the household.)

No, there is only one way to deal with sinners. Put a ring on their finger, invite them to dinner, or at the very least run to greet them with a hug and kiss while they are still far off.

4TH SUNDAY OF LENT, YEAR A

Lectionary #31

READING I 1 Samuel 16:1b, 6–7, 10–13a

A reading from the first Book of Samuel

The *LORD* said to *Samuel*:
"Fill your *horn* with *oil*, and be on your *way*.
I am sending you to *Jesse* of *Bethlehem*,
for I have chosen my *king* from among his *sons*."

Some verses have been omitted here, so there is no context for the words "to the sacrifice."
Eliab = ee-LĪ-uhb

As Jesse and his sons came to the *sacrifice*,
Samuel looked at *Eliab* and thought,
"Surely the LORD's *anointed* is here *before* him."
But the *LORD* said to *Samuel*:
"Do not judge from his *appearance* or from his lofty *stature*,
because I have *rejected* him.
Not as *man* sees does *God* see,
because *man* sees the *appearance*
but the *LORD* looks into the *heart*."

The predictability is intentional here. The literary form used to tell this story is formulaic.

In the same way Jesse presented *seven sons* before Samuel,
but Samuel said to Jesse,
"The LORD has not chosen *any one* of these."
Then Samuel asked Jesse,
"Are these *all* the sons you *have*?"
Jesse replied,
"There is still the *youngest*, who is tending the *sheep*."
Samuel said to Jesse,
"*Send* for him;
we will not begin the sacrificial *banquet* until he *arrives* here."

Again, the "sacrificial banquet" appears with no context.

The readings for the 3rd, 4th, and 5th Sundays of Lent during Year A are so filled with basic images of our faith—water, light, death to life—that they may be read on those Sundays in Years B and C in place of the readings proper to Years B and C. It is particularly fitting to exercise this option if the assembly is preparing to celebrate the reception of catechumens into the church at the Easter Vigil.

READING I **Not as we see does God see! While we see only the outer appearance, God sees into the heart. All of today's readings are about light and darkness, blindness and sight, seeing without really seeing, and the inability to see one's own blindness. We are reminded of the old truth, "There are none so blind as those who will not see."**

The point of this reading is that God's ways and choices are different from our own, and God's choices are not to be questioned even when they seem unlikely. The presumption is that God sees the ultimate outcome of any choice, while we do not. This lesson is taught in the formulaic procession of Jesse's seven sons before the prophet Samuel, each one being rejected by the Lord despite Samuel's inclination to choose the eldest, the next eldest, and so on.

Not surprisingly, considering the literary formula being followed here, it is David, Jesse's youngest son, that the Lord chooses, the one who seemed so unlikely a choice that his father had not even thought to present him. David comes on the scene and makes a good impression: young, handsome, ruddy. These are the kind of features that might

Jesse *sent* and had the young man *brought* to them.
He was *ruddy*, a youth *handsome* to behold
and making a *splendid* appearance.
The LORD said,
"*There*—anoint *him*, for *this* is the one!"

Then Samuel, with the horn of *oil* in hand,
anointed David in the presence of his *brothers*;
and from *that* day *on*, the *spirit* of the LORD
rushed upon David.

The last sentence, stating the proof of the validity of God's choice, deserves special emphasis.

READING II Ephesians 5:8–14

A reading from the Letter of Saint Paul to the Ephesians

Brothers and sisters:
You were once *darkness*,
but *now* you are *light* in the *Lord*.
Live as children of *light*,
for *light* produces every kind of *goodness*
and *righteousness* and *truth*.

Try to learn what is *pleasing* to the Lord.
Take no part in the *fruitless* works of *darkness*;
rather *expose* them, for it is shameful even to *mention*
the things *done* by them in *secret*;
but everything exposed by the *light* becomes *visible*,
for everything that becomes visible *is* light.
Therefore, it says:
"*Awake*, O sleeper,
and *arise* from the *dead*,
and *Christ* will give you *light*."

This is not a particularly easy text, for Paul's images tumble over one another. Nevertheless, the metaphor is clear: Those who are "light" do good deeds; those who are "darkness" do shameful deeds. Be what you are: light!

The final lines are a fragment from an ancient baptismal hymn. Read them boldly as the summons they clearly are.

draw us to choose David as a leader—and the very kind of external appearance by which God does not judge. Is there a contradiction here? Is God choosing by outward appearance? The point is that God sees into David's heart and knows he will be a good king, aside from his youth, physical appearance, and the fact that Jesse never thought he had a chance.

God's choice is confirmed immediately as the spirit of the Lord rushes upon David. All the messianic promises associated with David's lineage (which culminate in Jesus) are thereby given credibility. Had the choice been left to human vision and perception, the outcome might have been very different. Not as we see does God see.

READING II **Father Hugh Tasch, a monk of Conception Abbey, has penned some of the loveliest lyrics ever inspired by sacred scripture. This passage from Ephesians prompted him 40 years ago to write:**

**Once you were darkness, Pharaoh's
prison band.
Now you are sunlight, dwelling
in the Land.
Walk then in sunlight, high
upon the shore.
Rise from the waters, dying now
no more.**

The strength of Paul's imagery here is the bluntness of his metaphors. He doesn't say we were *in* darkness; he says we *were* darkness itself. He does not say we are *in* the sunlight (of Christ); he says we *are* sunlight itself. This is how Paul shows us the dramatic change that takes place at baptism. As we prepare for Easter and the renewal

GOSPEL John 9:1–41

A reading from the holy Gospel according to John

The opening line, "As Jesus passed by," is distracting. Passed by what? Pause after these words to make their meaning clearer.

"Blind from birth" is an important phrase. There is no other instance in the gospels of a person afflicted from birth. This is different from restoring sight; it is giving sight!

As Jesus passed by he saw a man *blind* from *birth*.
His *disciples* asked him,
"Rabbi, who *sinned*, this *man* or his *parents*,
that he was born *blind*?"

Jesus answered,
"Neither *he nor* his parents sinned;
it is so that the works of *God* might be made *visible*
through him.
We have to *do* the works of the one who sent me while it is *day*.
Night is coming when *no one* can work.
While I am in the *world*, I am the *light* of the world."
When he had said this, he *spat* on the *ground*
and made *clay* with the saliva,
and *smeared* the clay on his *eyes*, and said to him,
"Go *wash* in the Pool of *Siloam*"—which means *Sent*.
So he *went* and *washed*, and came back able to *see*.

There are clear divisions in this story. Precede each one with a pause and begin in a fresh tone.

His *neighbors* and those who had seen him *earlier*
as a *beggar* said,
"Isn't *this* the one who used to *sit* and *beg*?"
Some said, "It *is*,"
but others said, "*No*, he just *looks* like him."

The dialogue is tight here. Take it slowly and deliberately.

He said, "I *am*."
So they said to him, "How were your eyes *opened*?"
He replied,
"The man called *Jesus* made *clay* and *anointed* my eyes
and told me, 'Go to *Siloam* and *wash*.'
So I *went* there and *washed* and was able to *see*."

of our baptismal vows, it is good to be reminded of the difference between what we used to be and what we are now.

The text is particularly important for those preparing for baptism. So closely is light associated with baptism that the early church referred to the newly baptized as "those who have been illumined." This theme of light continues and is brought to fullness in the gospel narrative. Jesus proclaims publicly, "I am the light of the world," which is all the more reason to proclaim this brief passage carefully and clearly. It prepares us to hear Jesus' words with greater understanding.

GOSPEL If this gospel narrative seems to you like a long reading, think of it instead as a short story! It has all the elements of that literary genre: situation, conflict, resolution, and so on. It is, literally and figuratively, about not seeing the light, being afraid to see the light, seeing the light, and refusing to see the light because we are convinced we already do!

This is another gospel passage that lends itself to effective proclamation with multiple readers. With careful preparation, three or four readers could proclaim this story in the assembly in a new and refreshing way. One reader could take the words of Jesus, another those of the man born blind, and another those of the neighbors, the disciples, the parents of the blind man and the Pharisees. Needless to say, the passage must be proclaimed extremely well, which means that such a proclamation would require a great deal of preparation and rehearsal.

And they said to him, "Where *is* he?"
He said, "I don't *know*."

Here's the problem for the Pharisees: Jesus healed on the sabbath, which was forbidden except when death threatened.

They brought the one who was once blind to the *Pharisees*.
Now Jesus had made *clay* and opened his eyes on a *sabbath*.
So then the *Pharisees also* asked him how he was able to see.
He said to them,
"He put *clay* on my eyes, and I *washed*, and now I can *see*."
So some of the Pharisees said,
"This man is *not* from *God*,
because he does not keep the *sabbath*."
But *others* said,
"How can a *sinful* man do such *signs*?"
And there was a *division* among them.
So they said to the blind man *again*,
"What do you have to *say* about him,
since he opened your eyes?"
He said, "He is a *prophet*."

Now the Jews did not *believe*
that he had been *blind* and gained his *sight*
until they summoned the *parents* of the one
who had gained his sight.
They asked *them*,
"Is this your *son*, who you say was born *blind*?
How does he now *see*?"
His parents answered and said,
"We *know* that this is our *son* and that he was *born blind*.
We do *not* know how he *sees* now,
nor do we know *who* opened his eyes.
Ask *him*, he is of age;
he can speak for *himself*."

The man born blind could not see the light until Jesus, the light of the world, covered his eyes with mud, sent him to the pool to wash and restored his sight. A treasure chest of lenten, baptismal, and messianic images tumble out before us in the story. Even the mudpack Jesus uses as a salve reminds us of the dust we are made of and to which we shall return. The pool of Siloam (meaning "one who is sent") reminds us of both the waters of baptism and Christ himself, who has been sent from God and who sends us forth through our baptismal commission to be light in the world's darkness.

But there are several kinds of blindness depicted here. Some characters even remain blind at the end of the story, choosing not to see because they are convinced their vision is not impaired. The Pharisees are downright annoying in their reluctance to believe the simple story of this simple man. He tells the story of his cure over and over to no avail: "I was blind. I did what this Jesus told me to do. Now I see. It's as simple as that." The Pharisees refuse to believe it, and the bystanders refuse to believe the man was blind in the first place.

The parents of the blind man are blinded by fear, and our hearts go out to them. They are afraid to acknowledge what Jesus did, afraid to get involved because the Pharisees can cause them real trouble. Here we have an example of an age-old evil: unjust and self-serving authorities who oppress people and, with threats of reprisal, keep them afraid to speak the truth. Whether such evil is blatant or subtle, it is still very much with us today. We are struck in this story by the degree of resistance to something wonderful. How many find the good news too good to be true or even a threat to their own position?

His parents said this because they were *afraid*
of the Jews, for the Jews had already *agreed*
that if anyone *acknowledged* him as the *Christ*,
he would be *expelled* from the *synagogue*.
For *this* reason his parents said,
"*He* is of age; question *him*."

Here again the dialogue is tight. Take it slowly.

So a *second* time they called the man who had been blind
and said to him, "Give *God* the praise!
We know that *this* man is a *sinner*."
He replied,
"If he is a *sinner*, I do not *know*.
One thing I *do* know is that I was *blind* and now I *see*."
So they said to him,
"What did he *do* to you?
How did he open your eyes?"
He answered them,
"I told you *already* and you did not *listen*.
Why do you want to hear it *again*?
Do *you* want to become his disciples, *too*?"
They *ridiculed* him and said,
"*You* are *that* man's disciple;
we are disciples of *Moses*!
We *know* that God spoke to *Moses*,
but we do not know where *this* one is *from*."

The man answered and said to them,
"This is what is so *amazing*,
that you do not know where he is *from*,
yet he opened my *eyes*.
We *know* that God does not listen to *sinners*,
but if one is *devout* and does his *will*, he *listens* to him.

Perhaps the most exciting development in the story is that the beggar, blind from birth, became an ambassador for Jesus, insisting that Jesus must be from God or he could not have performed such wonders. For this brave act of apostleship the blind man is excommunicated. But Jesus seeks him out and takes his belief one step further into ultimate sight: faith in the Son of God.

The story ends on a sad note. Perhaps the old expression "There are none so blind as those who will not see" is wrong. There are apparently some who are even more blind than willful blindness can make them. They are the ones who are convinced, even in their blindness, that they see clearly. However, one often gets the feeling that people in this last group protest too much. They know better, but panic in the face of what the truth might mean renders them helpless.

The consequences of becoming children of the light are quite profound. "Now you are sunlight, dwelling in the Land." That "Land" is the promised land into which Christ leads us through baptism. It is a land filled with new meaning and new brightness for those with eyes to see it. But it is a land whose promise is not yet fully realized. In the meantime, there is danger of compromise that could snuff out the light, keep it hidden, or force it behind a cloud of fear. We are desperately in need of Christ the Light but are often desperately fearful of the consequences of being illumined.

It is *unheard* of that anyone ever opened the eyes
of a person *born* blind.
If this man were not from *God*,
he would not be able to do *anything*."
They answered and said to him,
"You were born *totally* in *sin*,
and are *you* trying to teach *us*?"
Then they *threw* him *out*.

Don't miss the compassion here. Jesus seeks out the excommunicated man!

When Jesus *heard* that they had thrown him out,
he *found* him and said, "Do you *believe* in the Son of *Man*?"
He answered and said,
"Who *is* he, sir, that I *may* believe in him?"
Jesus said to him,
"You have *seen* him,
the one *speaking* with you is *he*."
He said,
"I *do* believe, Lord," and he *worshiped* him.

The real tragedy is that the religious leaders had the obligation to point out the Messiah when at last he came. Now here he is, and yet they do not see him.

Then Jesus said,
"I *came* into this world for *judgment*,
so that those who do *not* see *might* see,
and those who *do* see might become *blind*."
Some of the *Pharisees* who were with him *heard* this
and said to him, "Surely *we* are not also blind, *are* we?"
Jesus said to them,
"If you *were* blind, you would have no *sin*;
but *now* you are saying, 'We *see*,' so your sin *remains*."

[Shorter: John 9:1, 6–9, 13–17, 34–38]

5TH SUNDAY OF LENT

Lectionary #36

READING I Isaiah 43:16–21

A reading from the Book of the Prophet Isaiah

"Thus says the Lord" is a formula that precedes the most solemn announcements. This text is a brilliant piece of poetry. Proclaim it with high dignity.

Thus says the LORD,
who opens a *way* in the *sea*
and a *path* in the mighty *waters*,
who leads out *chariots* and *horsemen*,
a powerful *army*,
till they lie *prostrate* together, never to *rise*,
snuffed *out* and *quenched* like a *wick*.

Everything that follows the word "wick" is what the Lord says; all the relative clauses that precede it summarize God's saving attributes and deeds.

Remember *not* the events of the *past*,
the things of long *ago* consider *not*;
see, I am doing something *new*!

Now it springs *forth*, do you not *perceive* it?

These are vivid concrete images.

In the *desert* I make a *way*;
in the *wasteland*, *rivers*.

Wild *beasts honor* me,
jackals and *ostriches*,
for I put *water* in the *desert*
and *rivers* in the *wasteland*
for my chosen *people* to *drink*,

The greatest evidence of God's holiness is the extent of divine love.

the people whom I *formed* for *myself*,
that they might *announce* my *praise*.

READING I We have seen in previous lenten Sunday readings that the Exodus (Israel's flight from Egypt) is a classic theme for this season. Here in this reading we see a beautifully poetic recounting of that great event. The writer clearly presumes that his audience will know the details, for he chooses words for their effect, not their historical precision.

The Lord who "opens a way in the sea" is the great Yahweh who parted the waters of the Red Sea to let the Israelites pass over on dry land. The chariots and horsemen are Pharaoh's armies in hot pursuit—until the waters flooded back over them. (We will hear the original account of the exodus at the Easter Vigil.)

This text is more than a poetic history lesson, of course. In fact, it tells the reader to forget the events of the past, because the Lord has exceeded all expectations. The Lord is more than a powerful deliverer; the Lord is a provider, supplying in adversity (the desert) the life-giving water without which no life is possible. Even the beasts honor this provident God. Above all else, the Lord is holy. But, contrary to expectation, that holiness does not create an unbridgeable chasm between the divine and the human. No, this God is immanent, close by, on the lookout for Israel's welfare, perpetually intervening in their lives to demonstrate a love beyond all imagining.

As we have seen, and will see again, the Christian tradition proclaims its own "exodus" in Jesus' crossing over from death to life. As we draw nearer the great paschal mystery we become more and more aware of the sweep of salvation history.

READING II Philippians 3:8–14

A reading from the Letter of Saint Paul to the Philippians

Brothers and sisters:

A powerful statement about priorities.

I consider *everything* as a *loss*
because of the supreme *good* of knowing Christ *Jesus* my *Lord.*
For *his* sake I have *accepted* the loss of *all* things

A long, complex sentence. Take it slowly and let each sense line sink in. Grammatical precision is not necessary for understanding.

and I *consider* them so much *rubbish,*
that I may gain *Christ* and be found in *him,*
not having any righteousness of my *own* based on the *law*
but that which comes through *faith* in *Christ,*
the righteousness from God,
depending on faith to know him and the power
of his resurrection
and the sharing of his sufferings by being conformed
to his death,
if somehow I may attain the resurrection from the dead.

Here Paul denies a mistaken notion on the part of some of his hearers.

It is not that I have already taken hold of it
or have already attained perfect maturity,
but I continue my pursuit in hope that I may possess it,
since I have indeed been taken possession of by Christ Jesus.

Brothers and sisters, I for my part
do not consider myself to have taken possession.

The remainder of the text is good advice for getting on with one's life after mistakes or difficult times.

Just one thing: forgetting what lies behind
but straining forward to what lies ahead,
I continue my pursuit toward the goal,
the prize of God's upward calling, in Christ Jesus.

READING II Although we celebrate resurrection through baptism and rejoice in the triumph over sin and death that Jesus achieved, we all know full well that we do not yet possess that new life in all its fullness. The experience of being saved is ongoing, not absolute, not finished, not perfected.

Throughout the history of Christianity there have always been groups who felt the need to proclaim themselves as having arrived, that is, having been made perfect through baptism and the sacraments. To a lesser extent we all are tempted at times to think of ourselves as being "in" with God through our religious affiliations. Paul is addressing such a group in this reading. He is reminding them that the prize of salvation is ours for the taking, but the "taking" involves an ongoing pursuit of it. To the question "Have you been saved?" the best response might well be: "Yes, and every day I try to behave accordingly. Some days are better than others!"

The Lord Jesus has taken possession of us. Now we strive to live like possessed people! Possessed with the joy of pursuing the goal of eternal happiness. And the way to that goal (as it was for Jesus) is through the cross. For as Paul makes clear, we have to be conformed to Christ's death in order to be conformed to his resurrection from the dead. There is no other way.

There is something in human nature which tends to long for the prize but dread the pursuit. But this is not cause for lamentation. Knowing human nature enables us to recognize our lack of realism. Being closely in touch with the sufferings of earthly life enables us to recognize the truth of what Paul tells us in this reading: "forgetting

GOSPEL John 8:1–11

A reading from the holy Gospel according to John

Jesus went to the Mount of *Olives*.
But early in the *morning* he arrived again in the *temple* area,
and all the *people* started *coming* to him,
and he sat *down* and *taught* them.

The context is crucial. The scribes and Pharisees are trying to trap Jesus. You can communicate something of their trickery.

Then the *scribes* and the *Pharisees* brought a *woman*
who had been caught in *adultery*
and made her stand in the *middle*.
They said to him,

They think they have an airtight case: "the *very act* of adultery!"

"*Teacher*, this *woman* was caught
in the very *act* of committing *adultery*.
Now in the *law*, *Moses* commanded us to *stone* such women.
So what do *you* say?"
They said this to *test* him,
so that they could have some *charge* to bring against him.

Jesus' initial silence and the mysterious writing on the ground are an effective contrast to the agitated malice of his opponents.

Pause before this section. Jesus' response is a thunderclap, silencing his enemies.

Jesus bent *down* and began to *write* on the *ground* with his *finger*.
But when they *continued* asking him,
he straightened *up* and said to them,
"Let the one among you who is *without* sin
be the *first* to throw a *stone* at her."
Again he bent down and wrote on the *ground*.

And in *response*, they went *away* one by *one*,
beginning with the *elders*.
So he was left *alone* with the woman *before* him.

what lies behind" we push forward toward the goal that has been placed within our reach, but as yet exceeds our grasp.

GOSPEL **The radical nature of divine forgiveness, seen in both the Hebrew scriptures and in the Christian tradition, seems to be one of the most difficult to take seriously. We are perhaps a little closer to the heart of the matter today than in previous centuries. Elaborate codifications of sin and its various degrees of seriousness don't plague us as much as they used to. But there will always be something in the less attractive part of fallen human nature that finds unreserved forgiveness difficult. All the more reason for us to proclaim the good news in gospel stories like today's with special ardor.**

This gospel story of the woman taken in adultery—a favorite with many—has a complex history. It did not appear in the earliest manuscripts of the gospel, and many feel it was perhaps suppressed by the early church because the degree of mercy shown here was too much to believe—or at least too much for the common person to understand correctly. Indeed, it seemed to threaten the sanctity of marriage. Remember that the law of Moses imposed a death sentence on the crime of adultery, yet Jesus suspends the woman's sentence and puts her merely on probation.

Nevertheless, the story has survived to become one of the most frequently quoted and dearly loved. It demonstrates in a dramatic way the quality and extent of divine forgiveness and a good reminder of the difference between the sin and the sinner.

Absolute tenderness characterizes Jesus' question.

Then Jesus straightened *up* and *said* to her,
"*Woman*, where *are* they?
Has no one *condemned* you?"
She replied, "*No one*, sir."
Then Jesus said, "Neither do *I* condemn you.
Go, and from now *on* do not *sin* any *more*."

The final words combine forgiveness with encouragement.

Though the sin may be grievous, the sinner is always loved.

However, the reason for the story's appearance at this point in the liturgical year has a great deal to do with its context. That is, we see Jesus becoming more and more embroiled in a contest with the local authorities, more and more a thorn in their sides, more and more a threat to their authority. Next Sunday we will see where the struggle ends: on the cross.

There is probably no event in Jesus' life that more clearly demonstrates the triumph of mercy over justice. The parable of the prodigal son, which we heard just last Sunday, is another example of the prodigality of God's loving forgiveness.

Today's story is a classic demonstration of why we are counseled over and over not to judge others. Not because we *shouldn't* so much as because we *can't*. It is impossible to know the heart, the motive, the pain, the weakness, the struggle of another human being. How can we possibly pass judgment without knowing these things? Legal systems have to judge criminals, of course, for the protection of society at large. But even the best system is flawed. We visit prisoners because they are not summed up by their crimes. Regarding personal evaluations of each other, Jesus' incisive solution is flawless: "If you are without sin, you may cast stones." That pretty much excludes all stone throwing, doesn't it?

5TH SUNDAY OF LENT, YEAR A

Lectionary #34

READING I   Ezekiel 37:12–14

A reading from the Book of the Prophet Ezekiel

Any text that begins with "Thus says the Lord God" is a solemn proclamation. Such words are meant to catch our attention so that we will listen with special care. Speak the words with great conviction.

The repetition of "O my people" is meant to reassure us. Don't be reluctant to give the phrase the force and feeling it is clearly meant to convey.

Thus says the Lord *GOD*:
O my *people*, I will *open* your *graves*
  and have you *rise* from them,
  and bring you *back* to the land of *Israel*.
Then you shall *know* that *I* am the *LORD*,
  when I open your *graves* and have you *rise* from them,
  O my *people*!

I will put my *spirit* in you that you may *live*,
  and I will *settle* you upon your *land*;
  thus you shall *know* that *I* am the LORD.
I have *promised*, and I will *do* it, says the LORD.

The readings for the 3rd, 4th, and 5th Sundays of Lent during Year A are so filled with basic images of our faith—water, light, death to life—that they may be read on those Sundays in Years B and C in place of the readings proper to Years B and C. It is particularly fitting to exercise this option if the assembly is preparing to celebrate the reception of catechumens into the church at the Easter Vigil.

READING I **The first reading is brief but packed with good news. It must be proclaimed slowly, deliberately, and with great care. Every line contains a promise that we rejoice to hear. The words are strangely beautiful, too. "Bring you back to the land of Israel" is loaded with meaning and nuance. "Open your graves" is slightly horrifying, but we know it is a promise of life beyond death. When God says, "I will put my spirit in you," we know God is promising something both tremendous and beyond our understanding.**

All of these wonderful occurrences will convince us once and for all that God is truly the Lord of life and death. And to comfort us further, God promises to *keep* these awesome promises. The same theme of death and resurrection appears in all of today's readings. And there is a progression in the quality of our belief in the good things God wills for us.

The words you are reading come from a unique context, different from our own. Ezekiel is in the famous "valley of dry bones," looking forward to a day when Israel's exile will be ended and their suffering vindicated.

READING II Romans 8:8–11

A reading from the Letter of Saint Paul to the Romans

Brothers and sisters:
Those who are in the *flesh cannot* please *God*.
But *you* are *not* in the flesh;
on the *contrary*, *you* are in the *spirit*,
if only the *Spirit* of God *dwells* in you.
Whoever does *not* have the Spirit of Christ
does not *belong* to him.

Begin quite slowly; give yourself and the assembly time and space to relish the contrast between being "in the flesh" and being "in the spirit."

But if Christ *is* in you,
although the *body* is *dead* because of *sin*,
the *spirit* is *alive* because of *righteousness*.

If the *Spirit* of the one who raised *Jesus* from the dead
dwells in you,
the one who raised Christ from the dead
will give life to *your* mortal bodies *also*,
through his *Spirit* dwelling in you.

The last sentence is long and begins with a long conditional "if." Take a deep breath and proceed with care so that you can tie it all together.

GOSPEL John 11:1–45

A reading from the holy Gospel according to John

Now a man was *ill*, *Lazarus* from *Bethany*,
the village of *Mary* and her sister *Martha*.
Mary was the one who had *anointed* the Lord with perfumed *oil*
and dried his *feet* with her *hair*;
it was her *brother* Lazarus who was ill.

Being restored to the land that is their birthright would be very much like being raised from the dead for the people of Israel. Anything approaching our modern belief about the resurrection of the body came much later in Jewish thought. Nevertheless, the loving care God exhibits for the chosen people is seen as extending beyond destruction and death. In the end (whatever that end may be), the love of God (and the startling reality that God's spirit lives in us) will enable us to triumph.

READING II **Easter is two weeks away. The catechumens who hear today's readings will be given a preview of the great truth of Easter resurrection. In this second reading and in the gospel we are inundated with words about death and life, flesh and spirit, grave and resurrection. Paul is at pains to explain to us that the Spirit of God dwelling in us is our guarantee that life does not end; it merely changes.**

The evidence for the truth of our belief, Paul says, is the resurrection of Jesus. Most challenging for the reader here is a deft handling of the paradox that Paul presents. Our bodies are dead to sin because our spirits are alive in God. And our mortal bodies, which carry in them many signs of death (illness, pain, sin), are nonetheless enlivened by the spirit we received at baptism. Unfortunately, this text has led many to believe and preach that we must despise the body because it is mortal.

Nothing could be further from Paul's meaning. The physical body is, after all, the only instrument we have for doing the good works of the Spirit that lives in us. It is possible to love and respect the body without

"The one you love is ill" is a striking way of naming a dear friend; the name isn't necessary.

John begins to insert his teaching about Jesus into the story. Lazarus' illness will be an opportunity for the glory of God to shine and the conversion of many.

When Jesus waits two more days to go to Lazarus, he makes it clear that he is confident of his mastery over death. The more obstacles placed in his way, the more dramatic his victory will be.

This is an elusive passage, but it surely indicates that the disciples would understand why Jesus has to go back to Judea if they could see more clearly what his ultimate mission is to be. It has the feeling of a proverb: "Let us do it now, for now is the right time."

The "sleep versus death" discussion is simply John's way of emphasizing that Lazarus is really dead and that Jesus will do far more than wake him from slumber.

So the sisters sent *word* to Jesus saying,
"*Master*, the one you *love* is *ill*."
When Jesus *heard* this he said,
"*This* illness is *not* to end in *death*,
but is for the glory of *God*,
that the *Son* of God may be *glorified* through it."

Now Jesus *loved* Martha and her sister and Lazarus.
So when he heard that he was *ill*,
he *remained* for two *days* in the place where he *was*.
Then *after* this he said to his *disciples*,
"Let us go back to *Judea*."
The disciples said to him,
"*Rabbi*, the Jews were just trying to *stone* you,
and you want to go *back* there?"
Jesus answered,
"Are there not twelve *hours* in a *day*?
If one walks during the *day*, he does not *stumble*,
because he sees the *light* of this world.
But if one walks at *night*, he *stumbles*,
because the light is not *in* him."

He said this, and then told them,
"Our friend *Lazarus* is *asleep*,
but I am going to *awaken* him."
So the disciples said to him,
"*Master*, if he is *asleep*, he will be *saved*."
But Jesus was talking about his *death*,
while *they* thought that he meant ordinary *sleep*.
So then Jesus said to them *clearly*,
"*Lazarus* has *died*.
And I am *glad* for you that I was not *there*,
that you may *believe*.

being a slave to it. There is a great deal of difference between being "in the flesh" and being flesh. We don't have much choice on this side of heaven with regard to being flesh. But we certainly can choose not to be "in the flesh" rather than "in the spirit," that is, guided by the spirit and not by the flesh.

The evidence that we have the Spirit of God in us is found in the way we lead our lives even now: not putting our trust in fallible and corruptible flesh, for the flesh is subject to weakness and sin. No, we lead lives of holiness because we are "in the Spirit" and the Spirit is in us, a power that both enlivens and surpasses our mortal nature.

GOSPEL **If today's gospel narrative seems to you like a long reading, think of it instead as a short story. Like the gospel stories we have heard for the last two Sundays, the story of Lazarus has all the elements of the literary genre we call short story: situation, conflict, characters, point of view, and resolution. It is, literally and figuratively, about death, victory over death, and the promise of resurrection for all of us in Jesus, who proclaims, "I myself am the resurrection and the life."**

Although it is not especially lengthy, this is another gospel narrative that lends itself to effective proclamation with multiple readers. With careful preparation, three readers could proclaim this story in the assembly in a new and refreshing way. One reader could take the words of Jesus, another those of the disciples and Mary and Martha, and a third the words of the narration. Needless to say, the passage must be proclaimed extremely well, and so such a

Didymus = DID-ih-muhs

Let us *go* to him."
So *Thomas*, called Didymus, said to his fellow disciples,
"Let us *also* go to *die* with him."

When Jesus *arrived*, he found that Lazarus
had already been in the *tomb* for four *days*.
Now *Bethany* was *near* Jerusalem, only about two miles *away*.
And many of the *Jews* had come to Martha and Mary
to *comfort* them about their brother.
When Martha heard that *Jesus* was coming,
she went to *meet* him;
but *Mary* sat at *home*.
Martha said to Jesus,
"Lord, if you had *been* here,
my brother would not have *died*.
But even *now* I know that whatever *you* ask of God,
God will *give* you."
Jesus said to her,
"Your *brother* will *rise*."

Martha said to him,
"I *know* he will rise,
in the *resurrection* on the last *day*."
Jesus told her,

Here is the heart of John's account. Notice that it falls precisely in the center of the narrative. These words must be proclaimed with special (and memorable) conviction.

"*I* am the resurrection *and* the *life*;
whoever believes in *me*, even if he *dies*, will *live*,
and everyone who lives and believes in *me* will *never* die.
Do you *believe* this?"
She said to him, "*Yes*, Lord.
I have come to believe that you are the *Christ*, the Son of *God*,
the one who is *coming* into the *world*."

proclamation would require a great deal of preparation and rehearsal.

John's strange and wonderful story about the raising of Lazarus is filled with strong emotions, dramatic scenes, and profound teaching about the person of Jesus. The combination of narrative with discussion is explained by the fact that John has taken a preexisting account of Lazarus being brought back to life and has overlaid it with his own special brand of teaching.

The Lazarus story appears in John's gospel shortly before Jesus is captured, tried, and crucified. It is the event that most directly results in his condemnation by those who were seeking to kill him. In the other gospels, it is another event that turns the officials against Jesus: the cleansing of the temple. The effect of John's arrangement is striking, since Jesus proclaims immediately before his death and resurrection the words that form the heart of today's story: "I am the resurrection and the life." All the elements of the story point toward these words and put them in bold relief.

We learn first that Lazarus is a special friend, so we might think that Jesus would hasten to his side in his sickness. But his delay gives the author of the story the opportunity to point out that time is irrelevant. The degree of Lazarus' illness is also irrelevant. Jesus is the master of life and death. The entire event, as Jesus says, is an opportunity for the Son of Man (Jesus himself) to be glorified.

When the disciples protest Jesus' decision to go back to Judea (where he is in trouble with the authorities), the author has the opportunity to show that this too is irrelevant. What does the master of life and death have to fear from such dangers?

When she had said this,
she went and called her sister Mary *secretly*, saying,
"The *teacher* is here and is *asking* for you."
As soon as she *heard* this,
she rose *quickly* and *went* to him.
For Jesus had not yet come into the *village*,
but was still where Martha had *met* him.
So when the Jews who were *with* her in the house *comforting* her
saw Mary get up quickly and go *out*,
they *followed* her,
presuming that she was going to the *tomb* to *weep* there.

When Mary came to where *Jesus* was and *saw* him,
she fell at his *feet* and said to him,
"Lord, if *you* had been here,
my *brother* would not have *died*."

Emotions run high in this section. Even Jesus is "perturbed and deeply troubled." In the shortest verse in the Bible (John 11:35), the Lord of Life is in tears. In both the Latin Vulgate and the King James version of the Bible, two words are used: *"Jesus flevit"*; "Jesus wept." The very brevity of the verse makes it strong. Pause briefly here.

When Jesus saw her *weeping* and the Jews who had come
with her weeping,
he became *perturbed* and deeply *troubled*, and said,
"Where have you *laid* him?"
They said to him, "Sir, come and *see*."
And *Jesus wept*.
So the Jews said, "See how he *loved* him."
But some of them said,
"Could not the one who opened the eyes of the *blind* man
have done something so that *this* man would not have *died*?"

The drama of the scene reaches its climax. Nothing could make the reality of death more vivid than the "stench." In a masterful literary and theological stroke, John juxtaposes the horror of bodily corruption with the glory of victory over it. The final command, "Lazarus, come out," is preceded by a prayer by which Jesus reminds us of his relationship with the Author of life.

So *Jesus*, perturbed *again*, came to the *tomb*.
It was a *cave*, and a *stone* lay across it.
Jesus said, "Take away the *stone*."
Martha, the dead man's *sister*, said to him,
"Lord, by *now* there will be a *stench*;
he has been *dead* for *four days*."

The strange poetic response of Jesus to the apostles' protest is difficult to understand. It certainly means that Jesus sees the outcome of the situation more clearly than his followers do. And he also seems to be saying, "Open your eyes and see what I have been trying to teach you: You have been enlightened by belief in me; you have nothing to fear from anyone. If you still feel unequal to the risk and challenge of being my follower, believe more strongly and the light within you will increase."

But the proverbial feeling of the saying indicates something more like, "Strike while the iron is hot," or "For everything there is an appointed time." In other words, Jesus is saying there is a time for doing what must be done, and there is a time for delaying what must be done until a more propitious time arrives. The daylight hours are a good time for walking; when night comes, it's best to postpone the walk until you can see the road. It's possible that this proverb or saying has been inserted into John's Lazarus story, because it seems appropriate to the disciples' hesitancy to take the risk of returning to Judea. It could be as simple as "It's now or never!"

Thomas the Twin responds either with real courage or impulsive enthusiasm—or perhaps with an "Oh, what the heck!" resignation. Whatever the motive behind his response, it is obviously a decision to accept the consequences of being a disciple.

The discussion about the difference between sleep and death is John's way of impressing upon us even further that Jesus is actually going to raise the dead, not merely revive the seriously ill. And the fact

Jesus said to her,
"Did I not *tell* you that if you *believe*
you will see the glory of *God*?"

So they took away the *stone*.
And Jesus raised his *eyes* and said,
"*Father*, I *thank* you for *hearing* me.
I know that you *always* hear me;
but because of the *crowd* here I have said this,
that they may *believe* that you *sent* me."

And when he had said this,
he *cried out* in a loud *voice*,
"*Lazarus*, come *out*!"
The dead man came *out*,
tied hand and foot with *burial* bands,
and his *face* was wrapped in a *cloth*.
So Jesus said to them,
"*Untie* him and let him *go*."

The purpose of the event is fulfilled. Those who witnessed it put their faith in Jesus.

Now *many* of the Jews who had come to *Mary*
and *seen* what he had done began to *believe* in him.

[Shorter: John 11:3–7, 17, 20–27, 33b–45]

that Lazarus has been dead for four days impresses the witnesses of the miracle even more. Custom and law required burial within 24 hours since modern-day means of preserving a corpse were not available. The central point is further stressed: Nothing can hinder the master of life and death.

It is also John's intent in this story to prefigure the imminent suffering of Jesus himself. The personal grief and emotional stress that Jesus expresses at the loss of his friend is a prediction of his own passion and death. But that suffering and death, too, will be overcome when God raises Jesus from the dead.

Finally, John points out to us in the last sentence of this reading that all the signs had their intended effect: "This caused many of the Jews . . . to put their faith in him." In your proclamation of John's account of this wonderful occurrence, realize that it is packed with instruction for the assembly. Some of that instruction is direct: "I am the resurrection and the life. Believe in me and you will rise from the dead." Some of the instruction is indirect: Jesus' emotional involvement here is unusually dramatic. If the Lord Jesus seems far away from our experience at times, here is a poignant glimpse into the tenderness of his vulnerable humanity. There may be no more vivid illustration of the fact that Jesus "shared completely in our weakness." The historical facts are important, but they are primarily the framework to support the fundamental doctrine of Christ's mastery over sin and its ultimate consequence: death.

PALM SUNDAY OF THE LORD'S PASSION

Lectionary #37

GOSPEL AT THE PROCESSION Luke 19:28–40

A reading from the holy Gospel according to Luke

The reading begins rather quietly, with preparations. There should be a sense that all of these details have a purpose: to set us up for the paradox of "humble royalty."
Bethphage = BETH-fuh-jee

Jesus proceeded on his *journey* up to *Jerusalem*.
As he drew near to *Bethphage* and *Bethany*
at the place called the Mount of *Olives*,
he sent two of his *disciples*.
He said, "Go into the *village* opposite you,
and as you *enter* it you will find a *colt* tethered
on which no one has ever *sat*.
Untie it and bring it *here*.
And if anyone should *ask* you,
'*Why* are you untying it?'
you will *answer*,
'The *Master* has need of it.'"

So those who had been *sent* went *off*
and found *everything* just as he had *told* them.
And as they were *untying* the colt, its *owners* said to them,
"Why are you untying this *colt*?"
They answered,
"The *Master* has need of it."

So they *brought* it to Jesus,
threw their *cloaks* over the colt,
and helped Jesus to *mount*.

PROCESSION GOSPEL In popular piety this day will probably continue to be called Palm Sunday for a good many years. But the intention of the liturgical reform that calls today "Palm Sunday of the Lord's Passion" is to restore an ancient view of the Sunday before Easter, namely, an anticipation of Good Friday. The idea was never completely lost, simply because we have always heard the proclamation of the Passion of Jesus on this day. Sometimes, however, the procession with palms, recalling Jesus' triumphant entry into Jerusalem, overshadows the day's true character. We should do our best to observe today's celebration in such a way that the "Hosannahs" are an ironic preparation for the cries of "Crucify him!" For that is what they were in Jesus' experience.

The procession gospel from Luke makes it easy for us to keep things in perspective. Luke constructs his gospel in such a way that he keeps reminding us that Jesus is on his way to Jerusalem where he will complete his work on the cross. Remember the text from the 2nd Sunday of Lent, the account of the transfiguration: Moses and Elijah discuss with Jesus the exodus he was about to fulfill in Jerusalem. Today's text begins with the same point: Jesus continued his ascent to Jerusalem. The triumphal entry into the city is merely another step toward the cross—by means of which he will journey back to the Father.

Notice that there are no palm branches mentioned in Luke's account of the procession. He tells us, instead, that the people threw their cloaks in his path. Nothing is too good for the master, and one's cloak was the most expensive garment one had. Notice,

Paint a picture with these details. The assembly is about to engage in a faint liturgical copy of them.

As he rode *along*,
the *people* were spreading their *cloaks* on the *road*;
and *now* as he was approaching the *slope* of the Mount of *Olives*,
the whole *multitude* of his *disciples*
began to praise God *aloud* with *joy*
for all the mighty *deeds* they had seen.
They proclaimed:
"*Blessed* is the *king* who comes
in the *name* of the *Lord*.
Peace in *heaven*
and *glory* in the *highest*."

Here, as elsewhere, the reader in no way tries to imitate the shouts of a jubilant crowd. To do so is ridiculous in a liturgical context. We are not re-creating the scene; we are commemorating it and celebrating its deeper significance. The reader's voice merely suggests the historical scene; the hearts of the assembled faithful do the rest.

Some of the *Pharisees* in the crowd said to him,
"*Teacher*, *rebuke* your disciples."
He said in reply,
"I *tell* you, if *they* keep silent,
the *stones* will cry out!"

Lectionary #38

READING I Isaiah 50:4–7

A reading from the Book of the Prophet Isaiah

The lector's creed! Your tongue has been most effectively trained by your own faith experience of joy and pain.

The Lord GOD has *given* me
a *well*-trained *tongue*,
that I might *know* how to *speak* to the *weary*
a *word* that will *rouse* them.
Morning after *morning*
he opens my *ear* that I may *hear*;
and I have not *rebelled*,
have not turned *back*.

Every day, every moment, is an opportunity to hear more clearly.

too, that Luke does not use the word "hosannah." Instead he recalls his own story of the angels' song at Jesus' birth: Peace in heaven, glory in the highest! In a special way for Luke, Jesus is the bringer of peace.

READING I The poetry we hear from Isaiah today comes from one of the great songs of the suffering servant. Who is speaking in this first-person narrative—a brief section of Isaiah's poetic depiction of the suffering servant, the one who is persecuted for doing the Lord's work? As Christians, we see Jesus in the role described, especially today when we hear the record of his suffering at the hands of his persecutors. But the voice also belongs to the God of heaven and earth, revealed to be a God of compassion, intimately involved with creation.

It is also the voice of those who spoke on God's behalf throughout history: Jeremiah, the prophet who was called to live out in his person the suffering of his people; Israel, God's chosen people who have suffered so much because of that election; and, indeed, the men and women of every time and place who have borne the pain of the suffering poor and carried the burden of straying sinners.

You speak for all these as you proclaim this text. The desired response of the members of the assembly is that they hear themselves speaking these words—and experience a renewal of their oneness with, and responsibility for, a pain-ridden world. There are perhaps no stronger words in scripture than these to describe those faithful servants who "set their faces like flint"

The poetry demands an exalted delivery. The meaning is bigger than the actual words.

I *gave* my back to those who *beat* me,
my *cheeks* to those who plucked my *beard*;
my *face* I did not *shield*
from *buffets* and *spitting*.

The Lord *GOD* is my *help*,
therefore I am not *disgraced*;
I have set my *face* like *flint*,
knowing that I shall *not* be put to *shame*.

READING II Philippians 2:6–11

The text is neatly divided into two sections: (1) empty, slave, human, humbled, obedient, death, and (2) exalted, name above every other, knees bend, tongues confess, glory, Lord!

A reading from the Letter of Saint Paul to the Philippians

Christ *Jesus*, though he was in the *form* of *God*,
did *not* regard *equality* with God
something to be *grasped*.
Rather, he *emptied* himself,
taking the form of a *slave*,
coming in *human* likeness;
and found *human* in *appearance*,
he *humbled* himself,
becoming *obedient* to the point of *death*,
even death on a *cross*.

Any notion that the second half of the reading ends in a shout is mistaken. A whisper would be a more sensitive human response—and yet this too is inappropriate in the liturgical context. Strive for all the confidence, joy, and strength you can muster, but be awed by your realization of the consequences of the message.

Because of this, God greatly *exalted* him
and *bestowed* on him the *name*
which is above *every* name,
that at the name of *Jesus*
every *knee* should *bend*,
of those in *heaven* and on *earth* and *under* the earth,
and every *tongue confess* that
Jesus *Christ* is *Lord*,
to the glory of *God* the *Father*.

toward the difficulties they must encounter to be true to a God of righteousness while living in a world marred by injustice.

READING II The second chapter of Paul's letter to the Philippians contains one of the most moving and beautiful sketches of Christ's mission and person. Your purpose here is to move your hearers to live lives in imitation of their noble model: selfless, humble, obedient, confident of ultimate victory through the name that has been bestowed on them—the name "Christian."

Most striking of all is that the model placed before us is God, who is just as much God in suffering as in glory. Suffering is not merely something endured for a time because it leads to glory. Rather, suffering and glory are the natural mix that defines God and us as disciples.

When we proclaim that "Jesus Christ is Lord, to the glory of God the Father," we are accepting the apparent contradiction of a Christian life. Since Jesus is the perfect model of perfect acceptance of the paradox, "every knee should bend" to acknowledge and to imitate that perfection.

Here is the Easter mystery in a nutshell. And it surely is a mystery! How well can any of us live up to Paul's challenge to make Christ's attitude our own? Why do our hearts rise to the challenge and sink in the face of it at the same moment? Have we come face to face with the reason why this observation has been made so often: "We don't know whether Christianity will work or not because it's never been tried"? As you read this amazing passage, try to assist the assembly in asking themselves such questions.

PASSION Luke 22:14—23:56

The word "hour" here is crucial. The emphasis must communicate that it (the hour of Jesus' death) has been coming for a long time and now, dramatically, has arrived: "When the hour [finally] *came* . . ."

The words of the Last Supper are precious to every Christian. Read them with great care and tenderness.

There is no more horrendous betrayal than by someone who shares your table.

The debate about who is the greatest arises out of the discussion of who could be the traitor.

The Passion of our Lord Jesus Christ according to Luke

(1) When the *hour* came,
Jesus took his *place* at *table* with the *apostles.*
He said to them,
"I have *eagerly* desired to eat this *Passover* with you
before I *suffer,*
for, I *tell* you, I shall not eat it *again*
until there is *fulfillment* in the kingdom of *God.*"

Then he took a *cup,* gave *thanks,* and said,
"*Take* this and *share* it among yourselves;
for I *tell* you that from this time *on*
I shall not *drink* of the fruit of the *vine*
until the kingdom of God *comes.*"

Then he took the *bread,* said the *blessing,*
broke it, and *gave* it to them, saying,
"This is my *body,* which will be *given* for you;
do this in *memory* of me."
And likewise the *cup* after they had *eaten,* saying,
"This *cup* is the new *covenant* in my *blood,*
which will be *shed* for you.

(2) "And yet *behold,* the *hand* of the one who is to *betray* me
is *with* me on the *table;*
for the Son of Man *indeed goes* as it has been *determined;*
but *woe* to that man by *whom* he is *betrayed.*"
And they began to *debate* among themselves
who among them would *do* such a deed.

(3) Then an *argument* broke out among them
about *which* of them should be regarded as the *greatest.*

PASSION It is not inconceivable that the entire passion narrative can be effectively read by one well-prepared person. Liturgical practice through the ages, however, has preferred a group—not only because it adds variety, but because it adds dynamism and power. Sometimes the members of the assembly speak certain lines, although this unfortunately requires them to read along throughout the proclamation. Perhaps an antiphon might be used at predetermined intervals, indicating the natural shifts in the narrative. However your community proclaims the passion, proper preparation is essential.

If several readers share the responsibility, they should be chosen for their ability to make the reading come alive. This involves reading the entire passion alone or in a group, discussing it and praying about it, allowing the tension and the drama to sink into your bones. Remember that in proclaiming this important reading, you are helping your entire community to participate in the events described.

All of the readers should have strong voices and clear diction. Although Jesus' words are few and his tone sometimes subdued, his speech is central; whoever reads them should have an especially strong voice. Determine in advance who will read what sections, and then practice together in the church. Know when you will move and where you will stand; become comfortable with the text and with the microphone. At least one person who is not reading should be present during the practices to listen from various parts of the church to offer feedback regarding clarity and volume.

He said to them,
"The kings of the *Gentiles lord* it over them
and those in *authority* over them are addressed as
'*Benefactors*';
but among *you* it shall not *be* so.
Rather, let the *greatest* among you be as the *youngest*,
and the *leader* as the *servant*.
For who is *greater*:
the one seated at *table* or the one who *serves*?
Is it not the one seated at *table*?
I am among you as the one who *serves*.
"It is *you* who have *stood* by me in my *trials*;
and I confer a *kingdom* on you,
just as my *Father* has conferred one on *me*,
that you may *eat* and *drink* at my *table* in my *kingdom*;
and you will sit on *thrones*
judging the twelve tribes of *Israel*.

The rhetorical questions are strikingly resolved in those wonderful words of self-definition: "I am among you as the one who serves." They deserve special emphasis.

(4) "*Simon*, *Simon*, behold *Satan* has demanded
to *sift* all of you like *wheat*,
but I have *prayed* that your own *faith* may not *fail*;
and once you have turned *back*,
you must strengthen your *brothers*."
He said to him,
"*Lord*, I am prepared to go to *prison* and to *die* with you."
But he replied,
"I *tell* you, Peter, before the *cock* crows this day,
you will deny *three times* that you *know* me."

The repetition of Simon's name makes it a calling for attention. On the other hand, it can carry a feeling of warning (or lament), preparing for the sad prediction of Peter's denial. In any case, a significant pause should follow Jesus' prediction—to let the horror of it sink in.

(5) He said to them,
"When I sent you *forth* without a *money* bag or a *sack*
or *sandals*,
were you in *need* of anything?"

This is a very mysterious question. What has changed to make what once was unnecessary now a requirement? It is possible that those who represent Jesus in the future will not be met with a welcome or hospitality. Jesus is warning his friends of trials that lie ahead.

When the details are settled in advance, all involved will be able to concentrate on the important ministry of proclaiming this central story of salvation history.

The story of Christ's passion and death is told by all four evangelists. Over the three-year cycle of the lectionary we read Matthew, Mark, and Luke on Passion Sunday. John's version is read every year on Good Friday. It is very important to realize that each of the four writers had more in mind than a literal telling of the events. Each had a particular point of view and a particular purpose. Thus the accounts differ. Thus the importance of choosing a mode of proclamation that serves the faith-building insight offered rather than the events related. To this end, we should not be timid in our experimentation, but we do need to be sensitive. Above all, we need to remember that liturgical proclamation is very different from dramatic (theatrical) re-enactment (granting the obvious similarities). To ignore this difference is to reduce the word of God to a history lesson, and the assembled worshipers to an emotionally manipulated audience.

In Luke's narrative of the passion, as throughout his gospel, several themes stand out. The most obvious of these we might call, after the hymn title, "There's a Wideness in God's Mercy." The outcast, the neglected, the socially inferior (especially women)—all these receive special treatment from Luke's Jesus. The universal love that God has for the world is most vividly presented, and it is paralleled by the degree and quality of God's mercy—offered again and again even in the face of repeated rejection. That rejection comes most often, in Luke's view, not from the people, but from their leaders.

"No, nothing," they replied.
He said to them,
"But *now* one who *has* a money bag should *take* it,
and likewise a *sack*,
and one who does *not* have a *sword*
should sell his *cloak* and *buy* one.
For I tell you that this *Scripture* must be *fulfilled* in me,
namely, 'He was counted among the *wicked*';
and *indeed* what is *written* about me is coming to *fulfillment*."

This is a difficult passage. Jesus is not speaking of a literal sword, though the disciples seem to think so. He is warning them about ultimate persecution to come. His words, "It is enough," do not convey this clearly. In fact, they could be interpreted by some hearers to mean "two swords are sufficient," and that is clearly not his meaning. The meaning is more like "Enough!", intending to convey that the topic of conversation has ended.

Then they said,
"Lord, *look*, there are two swords *here*."
But he replied, "It is *enough*!"

(6) Then going out, he *went*, as was his *custom*, to the Mount of *Olives*,
and the disciples *followed* him.
When he *arrived* at the place he said to them,
"*Pray* that you may not undergo the *test*."

The natural transition here must be indicated by a pause, followed by a renewed briskness in the narrative tone.

After withdrawing about a stone's *throw* from them and *kneeling*,
he *prayed*, saying, "*Father*, if you are *willing*,
take this cup *away* from me;
still, not *my* will but *yours* be done."

And to *strengthen* him an angel from *heaven* appeared to him.
He was in such *agony* and he prayed so *fervently*
that his *sweat* became like drops of *blood*
falling on the *ground*.
When he *rose* from prayer and returned to his *disciples*,
he found them *sleeping* from *grief*.
He said to them, "Why are you *sleeping*?
Get *up* and *pray* that you may not undergo the *test*."

Jesus is much more vulnerable in Luke's passion narrative. He is the most rejected of all, completely identified with the poor and the weak, at the mercy of those with evil intentions. Thus he is more martyr than messiah, more victim than victor. He fulfills in a wrenching and pathetic way the role of suffering servant—whom God will ultimately vindicate, but for now is "counted among the lawless."

Another Lucan theme is that of the New Israel. The clearest parallel is the group of Twelve that Jesus gathers about himself and to whom he gives the commission to preach the good news throughout the world. The twelve tribes of Israel are formed anew in Luke. And the temple in Jerusalem, where Luke begins his gospel, is the origin of this new creation as well as the center from which it goes forth through all the earth. Luke's second book, The Acts of the Apostles, continues this theme.

The historical situation in which Luke wrote explains in part the themes he chose to emphasize. His audience is largely Gentile. They need to understand how Jewish history applies to them—if this Jesus was so strongly rejected by it. Luke demonstrates that God's promises to Israel were completely fulfilled in Jesus, but in a way far different from what was expected. Those who follow Jesus—the poor, the repentant sinners, society's outcasts—are the New Israel, through whom God's uninterrupted plan of salvation continues to be worked out. Thus, there is continuity with the historical chosen people, though it is different from, and much broader, than anyone could have realized.

In your proclamation of Luke's passion narrative, try to draw special attention to

The traitor's kiss is an image so powerful that it stuns us. A tone of incredulity is appropriate. "Is it possible that you are betraying me with a gesture of intimate affection?"

"But this is *your* hour . . . ." When evil reigns. *Jesus'* hour (his death) will conquer evil and usher in light.

(7) While he was still speaking, a *crowd* approached
and in *front* was one of the *Twelve*, a man named *Judas*.
He went up to Jesus to *kiss* him.
Jesus said to him,
"*Judas*, are you *betraying* the Son of *Man* with a *kiss*?"

His disciples *realized* what was about to *happen*, and they asked,
"*Lord*, shall we *strike* with a *sword*?"
And *one* of them struck the high priest's *servant*
and cut off his right *ear*.
But *Jesus* said in *reply*,
"*Stop*, no *more* of this!"
Then he *touched* the servant's ear and *healed* him.

And Jesus said to the chief *priests* and *temple* guards
and *elders* who had come for him,
"Have you come out as against a *robber*, with *swords*
and *clubs*?
Day after *day* I was *with* you in the *temple* area,
and you did not *seize* me;
but this is *your* hour, the time for the power of *darkness*."

(8) After *arresting* him they led him *away*
and took him into the house of the *high* priest;
Peter was following at a *distance*.

They lit a *fire* in the middle of the *courtyard* and *sat* around it,
and Peter sat down *with* them.
When a maid *saw* him seated in the *light*,
she looked *intently* at him and said,
"*This* man *too* was with him."

But he *denied* it saying,
"Woman, I do not *know* him."

those sections that emphasize particularly Lucan themes. The commentary will do the same. For ease of reference, the passion and the commentary are divided into matching numbered sections.

(1) The hour mentioned here is not the time for the meal but the hour of Jesus' death—the fulfillment of his mission on earth. The fact that the climax begins in the context of a meal reminds us of several similar contexts presented in Luke. Jesus was often criticized for eating with sinners. This meal is no different in that sense, for the apostles show themselves to be weak and quarrelsome and unfaithful. More broadly, the context shows us again that Jesus has come to save those who are lost.

There is a deep poignancy in Jesus' words, "I have eagerly desired." The Latin, still remembered by some, was even stronger: *"Cum desidero desideravi"*: "With great desire have I desired" to eat this Passover meal with you. It bespeaks Jesus' realization that his long and arduous mission is about to be accomplished.

The celebration of Passover for the Jews commemorated their liberation from slavery, and God's promise to restore Israel in a wonderful way. The Last Supper thus reveals the *new* covenant in Jesus whereby these promises have been fulfilled. Jesus passes over from death to life, and paves the way for us to do the same.

When Luke record the words of Jesus, "This is *my body,*" he uses a word that could just as easily be translated "my self," for it includes both body and soul—the entire person. And "my blood" could be understood as "my life," for blood is seen as the life force. Thus, the "new covenant in my blood" makes

Galilean = gal-ih-LEE-uhn

There is something quite startling in the look that Jesus gives Peter. The moment is profoundly moving.

A new day has come. Signal the transition with a pause and a renewed briskness in the narration.

A short while *later* someone *else* saw him and said,
"You *too* are one of them";
but Peter answered, "My *friend*, I am *not*."
About an hour *later*, still *another* insisted,
"*Assuredly*, *this* man too was *with* him,
for he *also* is a *Galilean*."
But Peter said,
"My *friend*, I do not know what you are *talking* about."
Just as he was *saying* this, the *cock* crowed,
and the Lord *turned* and *looked* at Peter;
and Peter remembered the *word* of the Lord,
how he had *said* to him,
"Before the *cock* crows today, you will *deny* me three *times*."
He went *out* and began to *weep bitterly*.

(9) The men who held Jesus in *custody* were *ridiculing* and *beating* him.
They *blindfolded* him and *questioned* him, saying,
"*Prophesy*! Who is it that *struck* you?"
And they *reviled* him in saying many *other* things against him.

(10) When *day* came the council of *elders* of the people *met*,
both chief *priests* and *scribes*,
and they brought him before their *Sanhedrin*.
They said, "If you are the *Christ*, *tell* us,"
but he *replied* to them, "If I *tell* you, you will not *believe*,
and if I *question*, you will not *respond*.
But from this time *on* the Son of *Man* will be seated
at the *right* hand of the power of *God*."
They all asked, "*Are* you then the Son of *God*?"
He replied to them, "You *say* that I am."
Then they said, "What further *need* have we for *testimony*?
We have *heard* it from his own *mouth*."

it clear that the bloody sacrifices of the old covenant have been replaced.

(2) The worst kind of betrayal is by a friend. And to the Middle Eastern mind, the greatest sign and expression of friendship is to share a meal together. This betrayal, then, is all the more painful because it is committed by one of those most close to Jesus. Notice, however, that Judas' name is not mentioned here in Luke's account. This is probably because Luke means to generalize the situation and imply that any one of us is capable of such terrible treachery.

(3) Jesus' response to the disciples' squabbles is more an opportunity to teach than an occasion to scold. Nevertheless, the context does bring this important teaching of Jesus into bold relief. There can be no doubt about Jesus' revolutionary view of genuine leadership in the church. Unfortunately, it seems to be a difficult lesson to learn. Christian churches are often where we see examples of the dictum: "Power corrupts; absolute power corrupts absolutely." And this is true despite the wonderful promise of reward for truly dedicated leaders. The reference to the restored Israel ("the twelve tribes") immediately precedes the special address to Simon, implying that he will be given a special position of leadership—as indeed he is later on.

(4) There is no guarantee for any of us, not even with a special prayer of Jesus, that we will stand firm in the face of trial. There is no better illustration of this than Peter's denial, foreseen by Jesus, but also immediately followed by the strongest kind of conversion ("turned back") that enables him to strengthen others. Sometimes a more romantic notion of leadership forgets that

(11) Then the whole *assembly* of them *arose* and brought him
before *Pilate*.
They brought *charges* against him, saying,
"We found this man *misleading* our *people*;
he *opposes* the payment of *taxes* to *Caesar*
and maintains that he is the *Christ*, a *king*."

All the charges are false. Jesus' cryptic responses neither affirm nor deny them. The point is that everything is proceeding according to God's will, and nothing can stop it. There is a sense of futility in these proceedings.

Pilate asked him, "*Are* you the *king* of the *Jews*?"
He said to him in reply, "You *say* so."
Pilate then addressed the chief *priests* and the *crowds*,
"*I* find this man *not guilty*."
But they were *adamant* and said,
"He is *inciting* the people with his *teaching*
throughout all *Judea*,
from *Galilee* where he *began* even to *here*."
(12) On hearing *this* Pilate asked if the man was a *Galilean*;
and upon learning that he was under *Herod's* jurisdiction,
he *sent* him to Herod, who was in *Jerusalem* at that time.

Herod was very *glad* to see Jesus;
he had been *wanting* to see him for a long *time*,
for he had *heard* about him
and had been *hoping* to see him perform some *sign*.
He *questioned* him at *length*,
but he gave him no *answer*.

The chief *priests* and *scribes*, meanwhile,
stood by *accusing* him *harshly*.
Herod and his *soldiers* treated him *contemptuously*
and *mocked* him,
and after *clothing* him in resplendent *garb*,
he sent him back to *Pilate*.
Herod and Pilate became *friends* that very *day*,
even though they had been *enemies formerly*.

Notice how this passage is an aside, a comment on the events. The reader can indicate this with a shift in tone. There is irony in the "friendship" between Herod and Pilate. It arises from their cooperation in evil. Though they do not find Jesus guilty, neither do they resist those who do. Political expediency takes priority over justice.

the best teachers are those who have known personal failure.

(5) The meaning of this passage is subtle and elusive. It is not to be taken literally, as though Jesus were telling his disciples to take up arms. His response to violence just a few verses later is enough to show us that he is not advocating warfare. Some scholars interpret the sense of the passage this way: "The time of trouble has arrived, and it will plague my followers everywhere. As they persecute me, so will they persecute you." The disciples (and we ourselves) take Jesus' words literally: "Here are two swords!" And Jesus must say, in effect, "No, no, that's not what I mean." Here, as elsewhere, we see Luke's particular view of the passion: Jesus is undergoing a martyrdom, and his followers will suffer in like manner.

(6) There are two responses to fear and suffering here. Jesus fights the battle in obedience and is victorious. His agony is great, but he comes through the struggle. The disciples are crippled by fear and succumb to it "sleeping from grief." A translation that makes Jesus' victory even clearer and suggests Luke's intended reference to the resurrection uses the words, "When he rose from prayer."

(7) Again we are confronted with violence: the violence of Judas' hypocrisy in a treacherous kiss, and the wound inflicted on the high priest's servant. Jesus' response is immediate and strong. Luke is the only gospel writer who records the healing of the high priest's servant, and thus in a striking way demonstrates love of one's enemies. Jesus makes his role as martyr even clearer by contrasting his non-resistance with the weapons carried by those who apprehend him.

(13) *Pilate* then summoned the chief *priests*, the *rulers* and the *people*
and said to them, "You *brought* this man to me
and *accused* him of inciting the people to *revolt*.
I have *conducted* my investigation in your *presence*
and have *not* found this man *guilty*
of the charges you have *brought* against him,
nor did *Herod*, for *he* sent him back to *us*.
So no *capital* crime has been *committed* by him.
Therefore I shall have him *flogged* and then *release* him."

But all *together* they shouted *out*,
"*Away* with this man!
Release *Barabbas* to us."
—Now *Barabbas* had been imprisoned for a *rebellion*
that had taken place in the city and for *murder*.—
Again Pilate addressed them, still wishing to *release* Jesus,
but they *continued* their shouting,
"*Crucify* him! *Crucify* him!"
Pilate addressed them a *third* time,
"What *evil* has this man done?
I found him guilty of *no* capital *crime*.
Therefore I shall have him *flogged* and then *release* him."

With loud *shouts*, however,
they *persisted* in calling for his *crucifixion*,
and their voices *prevailed*.
The verdict of *Pilate* was that their *demand* should be *granted*.
So he *released* the man who had been imprisoned
for *rebellion* and *murder*, for whom they *asked*,
and he handed *Jesus* over to them to deal with as they *wished*.

Barabbas = buh-RAB-uhs

The shouts of "Crucify him!" should be proclaimed with energy, but not shouted or in any way suggesting a re-enactment.

(8) The story of Peter's denial and repentance is one of the most affecting in the passion narrative. It is all the more poignant because of the narrative detail, "the Lord turned and looked at Peter." It is a look of compassion and forgiveness at the very instant the predicted denial is expressed. And it has its intended effect: Peter repents with a profound remorse and we realize that Jesus' prayer on his behalf has been answered.

(9) This section of Luke's passion narrative differs greatly from that of Mark, Matthew, and John. And that is because has a particular teaching about Jesus in mind. Jesus is shown here to be the archetypal rejected prophet, renounced by the whole leadership of Israel, ironically acknowledged as (a false) Messiah and the Son of God. In other words, Jesus is put to death for telling the truth—just as all the old prophecies foretold—by the very people who claim to have the fullest understanding of those prophecies. The irony for us readers is all the more bitter because Jesus is accused of being a false prophet immediately after proving himself a good prophet in the matter of Peter's denial.

(10) The encounter with Pilate is thick with deceit and irony! Each one of the charges brought against Jesus is patently false. He misled nobody (the opposite is true), he recommended paying the civil tax, and he never said he was a Messiah-king (he revealed himself as Messiah-servant). Thus, ironically, Pilate finds him innocent. But political exigencies prevail, and the one who finds Jesus innocent passes the buck.

(11) Herod has several reasons for wanting to see Jesus, and they are all the

A significant pause here, to signal the next stage of the narrative.
Cyrenian = sī-REE-nee-uhn

(14) As they led him *away*
they took hold of a certain *Simon*, a *Cyrenian*,
who was coming in from the *country*;
and after laying the *cross* on him,
they made him *carry* it behind *Jesus*.

A large crowd of *people* followed Jesus,
including many *women* who *mourned* and *lamented* him.
Jesus *turned* to them and said,

Jesus' words are probably best read as though they were filled with gentle sadness and resignation, even his prediction of cataclysm.

"Daughters of *Jerusalem*, do not weep for *me*;
weep *instead* for *yourselves* and for your *children*
for *indeed*, the days are *coming* when people will say,
'*Blessed* are the *barren*,
the *wombs* that never *bore*
and the *breasts* that never *nursed*.'

"At *that* time people will say to the *mountains*,
'*Fall* upon us!'
and to the *hills*, '*Cover* us!'
for if these things are done when the wood is *green*,
what will happen when it is *dry*?"

Now two *others*, both *criminals*,
were led *away* with him to be *executed*.
(15) When they came to the place called the *Skull*,
they *crucified* him and the *criminals* there,
one on his *right*, the other on his *left*.

After the labored feeling of the trial and condemnation, the actual crucifixion proceeds with contrasting expediency. Jesus' words ("Father, forgive them . . .) sound calm and strong in the midst of chaotic sneering and jeering.

Then Jesus said,
"Father, *forgive* them, they *know* not what they *do*."
They divided his *garments* by casting *lots*.

wrong reasons. Thus when he does see Jesus, he is unable to see him for who he truly is. Luke makes much of the kind of sight it take to see things truly.

(12) Pontius Pilate could be the patron of self-serving politicians. His decisions are based not on truth (though he makes an initial effort) but on the whim and sway of his loudest and least informed constituency—which has its own agenda. In other words, when it came to the bottom line, Pilate's governance of the situation was carried out in such a way that his own job security took top priority. Luke shows us a devastating kind of blindness—inflicted by fear. No one notices that the prisoner who is released has a name that translates "son of the father" (*Bar* = son; *abba* = father). The prisoner who is unjustly condemned is, in fact, "Son of the Father."

(13) Though it seems straightforward, this section of the story is fraught with deeper meaning. Simon is apprehended. The word translated here also means to "lay hands on" in a positive way, for example, to heal or to single out for praise. The deeper significance of Luke's words here reveal his beliefs about discipleship. Simon finds himself in the position of a true disciple: carrying the cross and following Jesus. And the same is true for the women, so dear to Luke. Marginal in their own society, they now share the dignity Jesus bestows in a special way on outcasts. His words to them are a dire prediction of suffering to be visited on those who reject God's prophet.

(14) Luke places Jesus among sinners throughout his gospel narrative—and most dramatically here at the end of it. The irony

The *people* stood by and *watched*;
the *rulers*, meanwhile, *sneered* at him and said,
"He saved *others*, let him save *himself*
if he is the *chosen* one, the Christ of *God.*"

Even the *soldiers* jeered at him.
As they approached to offer him *wine* they called *out*,
"If you are *King* of the *Jews*, *save* yourself."
Above him there was an *inscription* that read,
"*This* is the *King* of the *Jews.*"

Even moments before death, Jesus finds himself in the midst of controversy. The quarreling thieves being crucified with him demonstrate that the presence of Jesus forces us to choose. The thief who chooses rightly receives a promise that rings through the centuries.

(16) Now one of the *criminals* hanging there *reviled* Jesus, saying,
"Are you not the *Christ*?
Save yourself and us."
The *other*, however, *rebuking* him, said in reply,
"Have you no fear of *God*,
for you are *subject* to the *same* condemnation?
And *indeed*, we have been condemned *justly*,
for the sentence *we* received corresponds to our *crimes*,
but *this* man has done *nothing* criminal."
Then he said,
"*Jesus*, *remember* me when you come into your *kingdom*."
He replied to him,
"*Amen*, I *say* to you,
today you will *be* with me in *Paradise*."

Take this short passage slowly and broadly—to prepare for the finality of Jesus' cry and the liturgical observance of silence that follows it.

(17) It was now about *noon* and *darkness* came
over the whole *land*
until three in the *afternoon*
because of an *eclipse* of the *sun*.
Then the *veil* of the *temple* was *torn* down the *middle*.
Jesus cried *out* in a loud *voice*,
"*Father*, into your *hands* I commend my *spirit*";
and when he had *said* this he breathed his *last*.

of it all is that this is precisely where Jesus chooses to be: sinless among sinners. The religious leaders scoff, and the soldiers jeer, but the common folk merely stand and watch. Later they will beat their breasts in remorse. The contrast between the reactions to Jesus' misery is made most personal and concrete in the two thieves. One ridicules bitterly; the other seeks forgiveness. The two thieves are at war in the heart of every Christian. But the last word goes to Jesus, in which he gathers all of salvation history, from Eden to Calvary, into one. Paradise is once again accessible.

(15) The awesome signs that accompany Jesus' final hours allow Luke to show us what has been accomplished: God's judgment has come upon the earth, and it comes in clouds of darkness as it had throughout Israel's history; and the temple veil or curtain that stood between the people and God's holy place is torn away. There is nothing now that separates God from the people chosen so long ago. Jesus has removed every obstacle. Finally, the response of both Jew and Gentile allow Luke to assert again the universality of Jesus' accomplishment. The Gentile centurion glorifies God and the Jewish people return home filled with remorse. Those closest to Jesus in life now remain near him in death, including the faithful women who show us what discipleship means.

(16) Joseph of Arimathea shows us that not even among the religious leadership was the condemnation of Jesus unanimous.

The centurion's declaration and the people's remorse, as well as the faithful vigilance of Jesus' acquaintances, create a new mood of utter resignation.

The tone becomes more brisk as the necessary burial arrangements are made—and must be completed before the beginning of the sabbath.

Arimathea = air-ih-muh-THEE-uh

The drama ends on a tender note. The faithful love of the women follows Jesus even in death.

He provides for the Messiah the kind of burial he deserved—wrapped in linen, a symbol of immortality, and laid in a tomb that had not been used before. Thus, finally, when he is completely powerless, Jesus is treated with the respect that is rightfully his. He has come among us not to reign but to serve. Having served to the last measure of devotion, he now shows us the final irony: those who serve thus in fact reign.

[Here all kneel and pause for a short time.]

(18) The *centurion* who *witnessed* what had happened glorified
God and said,
"*This* man was *innocent* beyond *doubt*."
When all the *people* who had *gathered* for this spectacle saw
what had *happened*,
they returned *home* beating their *breasts*;
but all his *acquaintances* stood at a *distance*,
including the *women* who had *followed* him from *Galilee*
and *saw* these events.

(19) Now there was a *virtuous* and *righteous* man
named *Joseph*, who,
though he was a member of the *council*,
had not *consented* to their plan of *action*.
He came from the *Jewish* town of *Arimathea*
and was *awaiting* the kingdom of *God*.
He went to *Pilate* and asked for the *body* of Jesus.
After he had taken the body *down*,
he *wrapped* it in a linen *cloth*
and *laid* him in a rock-hewn *tomb*
in which *no one* had yet been *buried*.

It was the day of *preparation*,
and the *sabbath* was about to *begin*.
The *women* who had come from *Galilee* with him
followed *behind*,
and when they had *seen* the tomb
and the *way* in which his *body* was *laid* in it,
they *returned* and prepared *spices* and perfumed *oils*.
Then they rested on the *sabbath* according to the *commandment*.

[Shorter: Luke 23:1–49]

HOLY THURSDAY: MASS OF THE LORD'S SUPPER

Lectionary #39

READING I Exodus 12:1–8, 11–14

A solemn proclamation from the Lord God begins this evening's liturgy of the word and the great Paschal Triduum. The solemnity of solemnities has begun. From the original celebration of Passover, when the Lord liberated Israel from captivity, we progress over the next three days to the fulfillment of Passover, when the risen Christ liberates us from sin and death. Let the weight of this reading shine through your proclamation.

A reading from the Book of Exodus

The *LORD* said to *Moses* and *Aaron* in the land of *Egypt*,
"*This* month shall stand at the *head* of your *calendar*;
you shall *reckon* it the *first* month of the *year*.
Tell the whole *community* of *Israel*:
On the *tenth* of this month every *one* of your *families*
must *procure* for itself a *lamb*, one *apiece* for each *household*.
If a family is too *small* for a *whole* lamb,
it shall *join* the *nearest* household in procuring one
and shall *share* in the lamb
in *proportion* to the number of *persons* who *partake* of it.

"The *lamb* must be a year-old *male* and without *blemish*.
You may take it from either the *sheep* or the *goats*.
You shall *keep* it until the *fourteenth* day of this month,
and *then*, with the whole *assembly* of Israel *present*,
it shall be *slaughtered* during the evening *twilight*.
They shall take some of its *blood*
and *apply* it to the two *doorposts* and the *lintel*
of every *house* in which they *partake* of the lamb.
That *same night* they shall *eat* its roasted *flesh*
with unleavened *bread* and bitter *herbs*.

READING I The holiest days of the liturgical year begin with this evening's celebration of the eucharist. And the three days we call the Triduum (Holy Thursday evening through Easter Sunday evening) are not three celebrations but one: the Passover of the Lord. Notice that all three readings this evening describe a communal gathering around a supper table. The image of a banquet leads us from Holy Thursday to the wedding banquet of the risen Lamb in heaven, the eternal Easter. For Christians, the experience of the shared meal is always sacred.

The first reading is a detailed description of the ritual Passover seder meal commemorating Israel's escape from slavery in Egypt. Notice that it is a family meal. So important is the family dimension of the seder that smaller families who cannot afford or consume a whole lamb are to join with their neighbors for the feast. What began in an earlier age as a simple sacrifice takes on the important dimension of participation, signified by eating the sacrificial offering in a communal setting. It is not too great a leap from the Passover seder to the eucharistic meal that is the summit and source of our life.

The intricate details of the reading are not as important as the significance of the overall event. It is obviously a form of the meal that Jesus shared with his disciples on the night before he died and should allow us to experience a gratifying link with our ancient past.

The details of how the Passover meal is eaten reveal the urgency of the situation. The pilgrim people have to be ready for travel. Having one's "loins girt" means being dressed for physical labor. We are not passive observers; we participate in these marvelous deeds.

"*This* is how you are to *eat* it:
with your *loins girt*, *sandals* on your *feet* and your *staff* in *hand*,
you shall *eat* like those who are in *flight*.
It is the *Passover* of the LORD.

"For on this *same* night I will go through *Egypt*,
striking *down* every *firstborn* of the *land*, both *man* and *beast*,
and executing *judgment* on all the *gods* of Egypt—*I*, the LORD!

"But the *blood* will mark the *houses* where *you* are.
Seeing the blood, I will pass *over* you;
thus, when I *strike* the land of *Egypt*,
no destructive *blow* will come upon *you*.

"This *day* shall be a *memorial* feast for you,
which all your *generations* shall *celebrate*
with *pilgrimage* to the LORD, as a perpetual *institution*."

READING II 1 Corinthians 11:23–26

A reading from the first Letter of Saint Paul to the Corinthians

Some of the most important pieces of our history and tradition are expressed in brief statements. This reading is one of them, and so it must be proclaimed with great deliberation.

Brothers and sisters:
I *received* from the *Lord* what I *also* handed on to *you*,
that the Lord *Jesus*, on the night he was handed *over*,
took *bread*, and, after he had given *thanks*,
broke it and said, "*This* is my *body* that is for *you*.
Do this in *remembrance* of *me*."

In the same *way* also the *cup*, after *supper*, saying,
"This *cup* is the new *covenant* in my *blood*.

In proclaiming this text, strive to create an atmosphere of solemn significance. Ceremonies made holy by time and devout practice almost compel our attention as we prepare to carry out the Lord's command to celebrate the eucharistic meal as a perpetual memorial of his sacrificial love for us.

READING II Here we have the eucharistic tradition in Paul's words. How rich is this word "tradition," from the Latin *tradere*. It means "to hand on" or "to hand over"; Paul uses it in both senses here. Paul hands on to us the tradition of what Jesus did at the Last Supper. Jesus used the ancient ceremony that was "handed on" through his Jewish tradition, and he did all this on the night that he was "handed over" by Judas. A good lector ought to be aware of how the reading turns on the meaning and intricate use of "tradition."

Paul's emphasis is not on what Jesus did, but on what the assembled community of the church does when it gathers in his memory. Difficulties among the Corinthians Paul addressed had led to rival factions and the exclusion of the poor from the eucharistic meal in that place. Paul is reminding the church at Corinth that the purpose of this holy meal is to proclaim the Lord's death until the end of time, a duty that must never exclude others or be confused with gatherings of lesser significance.

In this brief reading you use Paul's words to remind the members of your assembly what they are about to do in the Holy Thursday celebration. You remind them of its solemnity and its meaning. Whenever we

Emphasize this final sentence. Consider its meaning so that your proclamation will impress its significance upon the assembly.

Do this, as often as you *drink* it, in *remembrance* of *me*."
For as often as you *eat* this *bread* and *drink* the *cup*,
you proclaim the *death* of the *Lord* until he *comes*.

GOSPEL John 13:1–15

A reading from the holy Gospel according to John

On the feast of Passover, the Lord Jesus passes over from death to life. Let the assembly hear John's play on the word.

Before the feast of *Passover*,
Jesus *knew* that his *hour* had *come*
to pass from *this* world to the *Father*.
He *loved* his *own* in the world and he *loved* them to the *end*.

There is another play on words here: Judas hands Jesus over to betrayal, and Jesus hands over his life so that he can hand everything back to the Father, who handed everything over to him. Iscariot = is-KAIR-ee-uht

The *devil* had already induced *Judas*, son of Simon the *Iscariot*,
to hand him *over*.
So, during *supper*,
fully *aware* that the *Father* had put *everything* into his *power*
and that he had *come* from God and was *returning* to God,
he *rose* from supper and took off his outer *garments*.
He took a *towel* and tied it around his *waist*.
Then he poured *water* into a *basin*
and began to *wash* the disciples' *feet*
and *dry* them with the *towel* around his *waist*.

Let the dialogue be a narrative, not a reenactment.

He came to Simon *Peter*, who said to him,
"*Master*, are you going to *wash* my *feet*?"
Jesus *answered* and said to him,
"What I am *doing*, you do not *understand now*,
but you *will* understand *later*."
Peter said to him, "You will *never* wash my feet."

gather for the eucharist we proclaim the Lord's death until he comes again in glory.

GOSPEL It may strike us as strange that our celebration of Holy Thursday does not include a gospel account of Jesus' words "Take and eat; take and drink." Matthew, Mark, and Luke all record these words. But today we read from the gospel of John, which does not record the "words of institution," although the events described here clearly occur within the context of the Passover seder.

John's account of the Last Supper, however, gives us something just as precious as Jesus' words. The evangelist records the dramatic and moving scene of Jesus washing the feet of his disciples. In doing so, John gives us profound insight into the meaning and consequence of the eucharist. We can put it quite plainly: Our celebration of the eucharist requires that we wash one another's feet, serve one another, revere Christ present in one another. It means that we become great only by serving all the rest. To refuse to serve is to refuse salvation. In the second reading, Paul gave us the words of Christ's sacrificial love. In John's gospel we hear the words that tell us what it means to accept that love.

The washing of the feet is made all the more striking by the presence of Judas, the betrayer. He is not excluded from the washing, even though Jesus refers to him as unclean. And since the washing of feet symbolizes the ultimate act of service, it reveals an even deeper level of the meaning of the eucharist: No one—not even a traitor—is undeserving of our loving service.

Jesus answered him,
"Unless I *wash* you, you will have no *inheritance* with me."
Simon Peter said to him,
"*Master*, then not *only* my *feet*, but my *hands*
and *head* as *well*."
Jesus said to him,
"Whoever has *bathed* has no *need*
except to have his *feet* washed,
for he is clean all *over*;
so you are *clean*, but not *all*."
For he *knew* who would *betray* him;
for *this* reason, he said, "Not *all* of you are clean."

So when he had washed their *feet*
and put his *garments* back on and reclined at *table* again,
he *said* to them, "Do you *realize* what I have *done* for you?
You call me '*teacher*' and '*master*,' and rightly *so*, for indeed I *am*.
If *I*, therefore, the *master* and *teacher*, have washed *your* feet,
you ought to wash one *another's* feet.
I have given you a *model* to follow,
so that as *I* have done for *you*, you should *also* do.

The secret of effective proclamation here is to get the right emphasis on the pronouns. Practice diligently so that Jesus' definition of authentic ministry makes an impression on your hearers.

Peter's refusal to allow Jesus to wash his feet indicates two things: Peter still does not fully understand the kind of Messiah Jesus is, nor does he understand the full implication of the meal he is sharing with Jesus. And how could he? That understanding will come fully only with the resurrection. Note well, though, that Peter understands enough to know that he wants to be part of Jesus' mission and plan. He may not understand it fully, but he trusts Jesus enough to submit his doubts and questions to the will of his master. How beautifully Peter shows us our own faith experience: We do not fully understand either, but faith in the person of Jesus enables us to follow his example and submit to his teaching.

GOOD FRIDAY: CELEBRATION OF THE LORD'S PASSION

Lectionary #40

READING I Isaiah 52:13—53:12

A reading from the Book of the Prophet Isaiah

The reading begins on a bright note, despite the images of suffering that follow.

See, my *servant* shall *prosper*,
he shall be raised *high* and greatly *exalted*.
Even as *many* were *amazed* at him—
so *marred* was his *look* beyond human *semblance*
and his *appearance* beyond that of the sons of *man*—
so shall he *startle* many *nations*,
because of him *kings* shall stand *speechless*;
for those who have not been *told* shall *see*,
those who have not heard shall *ponder* it.

Rhetorical questions are powerful. They help the assembly "tune in" again. Make the most of them.

Who would *believe* what we have *heard*?
To *whom* has the *arm* of the LORD been *revealed*?
He grew *up* like a *sapling* before him,
like a *shoot* from the parched *earth*;
there *was* in him no *stately* bearing to make us *look* at him,
nor *appearance* that would *attract* us to him.
He was *spurned* and *avoided* by people,
a man of *suffering*, accustomed to *infirmity*,
one of those from whom people hide their *faces*,
spurned, and we *held* him in no *esteem*.

At this point we move from simple narrative to an examination of the meaning underlying it. You are explaining the suffering servant's mission.

Yet it was *our* infirmities that he *bore*,
our sufferings that he *endured*,
while *we* thought of him as *stricken*,
as one smitten by *God* and *afflicted*.

READING I This is the fourth and most significant of the four suffering servant songs from the book of Isaiah. The liturgy applies the text and the term "suffering servant" to Jesus and his redemptive mission. Originally, of course, the application of the term was to the whole people of Israel. The servant is really God's servants, and the language of poetry has collected the people of God into one figure. Even the most basic awareness of the history (both ancient and modern) of the Jewish people enables us to hear the heartrending poignancy of the suffering servant songs.

It is not certain whether Jesus actually applied this text to himself, but it has been applied to him in the liturgy since the earliest Christian writers began to interpret his life, mission, passion and death. He is seen as the culmination of the suffering servant theme, fulfilling the Isaian prophecy in every detail. No other scriptural text is more suitable for the Good Friday liturgy.

One implicit idea must be communicated in the proclamation: Obedience is the suffering servant's greatest virtue and the ultimate reason why the servant triumphs and wins salvation. It is obedience to God that ennobles the servant's agony and wins the allegiance and contrition of all who witness the servant's pain. The second reading today makes this point clearly: Even though Jesus was God's own Son, he became obedient because of what he suffered. The idea that the servant became obedient unto death already makes the servant a heroic figure. The idea that the servant's death gives life to others makes the servant even more than a hero: The servant becomes a personification of God's creative and redemptive love, which is precisely who Jesus is, of course.

But he was *pierced* for *our offenses*,
 crushed for *our sins*;
upon him was the *chastisement* that makes us *whole*,
 by his *stripes* we were *healed*.

We had all gone *astray* like *sheep*,
 each following his *own way*;
but the *LORD* laid upon *him*
 the *guilt* of us *all*.

Though he was *harshly* treated, he *submitted*
 and opened not his *mouth*;
like a *lamb* led to the *slaughter*
 or a *sheep* before the *shearers*,
 he was *silent* and opened not his *mouth*.

Patience and quiet endurance are not the same as submissiveness. This should sound strong, not pitiful or weak.

Oppressed and *condemned*, he was taken *away*,
 and who would have thought any *more* of his *destiny*?
When he was cut *off* from the land of the *living*,
 and *smitten* for the sin of his *people*,
a *grave* was assigned him among the *wicked*
 and a *burial* place with *evildoers*,
though he had done no *wrong*
 nor *spoken* any *falsehood*.
But the LORD was *pleased*
 to crush him in *infirmity*.

There must be a significant pause here. Let the horror of it sink in.

Begin anew with a fresh tone of voice, for this is the good news.

If he gives his *life* as an offering for *sin*,
 he shall see his *descendants* in a long *life*,
 and the will of the *LORD* shall be *accomplished* through him.

Because of his *affliction*
 he shall see the *light*
 in fullness of *days*;

This is a lengthy reading, or, more properly, a lengthy poem. The rich images build throughout the passage until we are caught up in a morass of mixed emotions. We are filled with admiration for the servant's humility and meekness. We are suffused with guilt and gratitude for the servant's willingness to suffer so that we could be freed from sin and justified in the sight of God. We are reminded of countless thousands of martyrs who have suffered for their beliefs, been persecuted for their skin color, race, creed, sex, sexual orientation, or social status. And, sadly, we are reminded that such persecution continues even in our own day, which makes the text as appropriate today as it was when it was written. The suffering and death of those whom the world persecutes is precious in God's sight and will be vindicated.

Jesus, the suffering servant, can suffer no more, having triumphed over death. But his kingdom on earth has not yet come to perfection, and he is still put to death in the suffering members of his mystical body. That tells us two things. First, our suffering has meaning and significance; we are not merely victims of cruel fate. Second, we know that the ultimate victory is ours, won for us by a loving redeemer. Nothing can separate us from the love of Christ.

A worthy proclamation of this moving text requires exceptional skill, careful preparation, and a heart full of compassion.

READING II **The author of the letter to the Hebrews is writing to comfort Jewish Christians who have been alienated from the Jewish tradition because of their faith in Jesus. This part of the letter assures them that Jesus is the perfect high**

through his *suffering*, my *servant* shall justify *many*,
and their *guilt* he shall *bear*.

Utter confidence should fill these final lines. Allow for a significant pause before saying "The word of the Lord."

Therefore I will give him his *portion* among the *great*,
and he shall divide the *spoils* with the *mighty*,
because he *surrendered* himself to *death*
and was *counted* among the *wicked*;
and he shall take *away* the sins of *many*,
and win *pardon* for their *offenses*.

READING II Hebrews 4:14–16; 5:7–9

A reading from the Letter to the Hebrews

There is more than a hint of pleading here: "Don't be afraid; approach God with bold confidence!"

Brothers and sisters:
Since we have a great *high* priest who has passed
through the *heavens*,
Jesus, the Son of *God*,
let us hold *fast* to our *confession*.
For we do not have a high priest
who is *unable* to *sympathize* with our *weaknesses*,
but one who has *similarly* been *tested* in every *way*,
yet without *sin*.
So let us *confidently* approach the *throne* of *grace*
to receive *mercy* and to find *grace* for timely *help*.

Now you explain how Jesus accomplished what he did. It is a model for us.

In the days when Christ was in the *flesh*,
he offered *prayers* and *supplications* with loud *cries* and *tears*
to the one who was able to *save* him from *death*,
and he was *heard* because of his *reverence*.

priest, whose unique sacrifice has brought all others to fulfillment. There is no further need for sacrificial victims to take away our sins and justify us in the sight of God. Jesus has done that once and for all. The eucharist we celebrate continues Christ's sacrifice, a perfect sacrifice offered by a high priest who identifies completely with our weakness.

The effect of hearing this text on Good Friday is that we understand more clearly the way Jesus functions as the source of eternal salvation. Jesus is both divine and human, and is therefore the perfect mediator. He shares our humanity and shares with us his divinity. As God and human, Jesus has made us one with himself in reconciling love.

Jesus knows our temptations—he underwent them. He knows our suffering—he taught us obedience by enduring them. This is why we can approach the throne of grace with utter confidence. We know we will be heard and understood by the one who has experienced all that we have. This is the great good news: God is revealed to us in Jesus, whom we know intimately. There is no longer any need to appease God. Our sacrificial offerings express our loving gratitude.

Oddly, we have a hard time believing that the good news is that simple or that wonderful. And yet it is. We have a great high priest who has passed through the heavens: Jesus, the Son of God, who has shown us that God is love.

PASSION **It is very rare these days that the accounts of the passion on Palm Sunday and Good Friday are proclaimed by one reader. Everyone seems to sense the efficacy of employing several readers (at least three), not only because the text is long but because the narrative seems**

Son though he *was*, he learned *obedience* from what he *suffered*;
and when he was made *perfect*,
he became the *source* of eternal *salvation* for all who *obey* him.

PASSION John 18:1—19:42

The Passion of our Lord Jesus Christ according to John

Kidron = KID-ruhn

John's narrative moves from place to place, progressing inexorably from the garden to Golgotha. In each location there is an important revelation, a dynamic interplay of characters, and a kind of resolution. Then the action moves on. Many commentators have made mention of the dramatic action in John's narrative. The various stages of this action must be set off by clear transitions (pauses, tones of voice, a different proclaimer, and so on).

Nazorean = naz-uh-REE-uhn

(1) *Jesus* went out with his *disciples* across the Kidron *valley*
to where there was a *garden*,
into which *he* and his *disciples entered*.
Judas his *betrayer also* knew the place,
because Jesus had *often* met there with his disciples.
So *Judas* got a band of *soldiers* and *guards*
from the chief *priests* and the *Pharisees*
and *went* there with *lanterns*, *torches*, and *weapons*.

Jesus, knowing *everything* that was going to *happen* to him,
went out and said to them, "*Whom* are you *looking* for?"
They *answered* him, "*Jesus* the *Nazorean*."
He said to them, "*I AM*."
Judas his *betrayer* was *also* with them.
When he said to them, "*I AM*,"
they turned *away* and fell to the *ground*.
So he *again* asked them,
"Whom are you *looking* for?"
They said, "*Jesus* the *Nazorean*."
Jesus answered,
"I *told* you that *I AM*.

to demand such a proclamation to bring it to life. This is not to say, however, that a full-scale reenactment or a dramatic interpretation of the passion is to be preferred over a proclamation. The liturgy does not lend itself to anything approaching theatrical presentation, which can be quite effective on stage (if superbly done). No, the liturgy is ritual behavior and requires the kind of restraint and dignity that respects the solemnity and weight of its content and purpose. The liturgy never reenacts its subject matter. It memorializes, commemorates and recalls the paschal mystery. It does not re-create what has already been accomplished once and for all. Those who take creative approaches to the proclamation of the passion narratives must keep in mind that they are presenting precisely that, a narrative, not a script. In an age awash in cinematic realism, the kind of heightened solemnity demanded by the liturgy may seem less immediate and more formal. Nevertheless, it must be maintained if we are to avoid trivializing its subject matter.

Perhaps the form of proclamation most true to liturgical tradition is the singing or chanting of the passion by three cantors, one taking the voice of the gospel writer, one the voice of all speakers except Jesus, and one the voice of Jesus. The solemnization of the passion achieved with this kind of proclamation can be quite moving.

In recent years the members of the assembly have been provided copies of the text of the passion to allow them to read aloud the words of the crowds. While this practice may seem to accomplish a higher degree of participation, it also requires the members of the assembly to follow along with the proclaimers (to be ready for their

So if you are looking for *me*, let *these* men *go*."
This was to *fulfill* what he had said,
"I have not lost *any* of those you *gave* me."

(2) Then Simon *Peter*, who had a *sword*, *drew it*,
struck the high priest's *slave*, and cut off his right *ear*.

Malchus = MAL-kuhs

The slave's *name* was *Malchus*.
Jesus said to Peter,
"Put your *sword* into its *scabbard*.
Shall I not drink the *cup* that the Father *gave* me?"

The action moves to the residence of Annas, then on to a meeting with the high priest, Caiaphas.
Annas = AN-uhs
Caiaphas = KAY-uh-fuhs

So the band of *soldiers*, the *tribune*, and the Jewish *guards* *seized* Jesus,
bound him, and brought him to *Annas* first.
He was the *father-in-law* of *Caiaphas*,
who was *high* priest that year.
It was *Caiaphas* who had counseled the *Jews*
that it was *better* that *one* man should die
rather than the *people*.

(3) Simon *Peter* and *another* disciple *followed* Jesus.
Now the *other* disciple was *known* to the *high* priest,
and he entered the *courtyard* of the high priest with *Jesus*.
But *Peter* stood at the gate *outside*.
So the *other* disciple, the acquaintance of the *high* priest,
went out and spoke to the *gatekeeper* and brought Peter in.
Then the *maid* who was the *gatekeeper* said to Peter,
"You are not one of this man's *disciples*, are you?"

Notice that the denials of Peter are separated by the interrogation of Jesus by the high priest. Peter is in the shadows listening to Jesus testify to his public teaching. The irony is compelling.

He said, "I am *not*."
Now the *slaves* and the *guards* were standing
around a charcoal *fire*
that they had made, because it was *cold*,
and were *warming* themselves.
Peter was *also* standing there keeping warm.

part), which prevents them from fully attending to the proclamation. The benefits of this practice should not be presumed but carefully evaluated in the light of fundamental liturgical and pastoral principles.

Whatever practice is observed in your community, it should try to meet the challenge of a long proclamation (potentially tedious if not done well) and avoid the excesses of a presentation so elaborate or literal that the assembly is preoccupied with the manner of proclamation at the expense of the message.

The story of Christ's passion and death is told in more or less straightforward narrative by all four evangelists. Over the course of the three years of the Sunday lectionary, we read Matthew, Mark, and Luke on Passion Sunday. John's account is read every year on Good Friday. It is important to realize that each of the four writers had more in mind than a literal account of the events. Each had a particular point of view and purpose, and so the accounts differ from each other. For this reason, it is important to choose a mode of proclamation that serves the faith-building insight offered rather than the events related.

John's passion narrative portrays Jesus as the eternal Word, the divine creator of the universe, who appeared in the flesh to redeem us in love. John clearly plays down the physical sufferings of Jesus in order to emphasize his divine nature, origin, and purpose. The entire gospel of John is preoccupied with Jesus as king and priest, which sets it apart from the other three gospels.

There is a danger here of making Jesus sound defensive. He makes no defense; he simply tells the truth, quietly, strongly, gently.

(4) The *high* priest *questioned* Jesus
about his *disciples* and about his *doctrine.*
Jesus *answered* him,
"I have spoken *publicly* to the *world.*
I have always *taught* in a *synagogue*
or in the *temple* area where all the Jews *gather,*
and in *secret* I have said *nothing.* Why ask *me?*
Ask those who *heard* me what I said to them.
They know what I said."

When he had said *this,*
one of the temple *guards* standing there *struck* Jesus and said,
"Is *this* the way you answer the *high* priest?"
Jesus answered him,
"If I have spoken *wrongly, testify* to the wrong;
but if I have spoken *rightly,* why do you *strike* me?"
Then *Annas* sent him bound to *Caiaphas* the *high* priest.

Now Simon *Peter* was standing there keeping *warm.*
And they said to him,
"You are not one of his *disciples,* are you?"
He *denied* it and said,
"I am *not.*"
One of the *slaves* of the high priest,
a *relative* of the one whose *ear* Peter had cut *off,* said,
"Didn't I *see* you in the *garden* with him?"
Again Peter denied it.
And *immediately* the *cock* crowed.

Now the action moves to the praetorium and thus into the world of the Gentiles. Here John reveals the prediction and fulfillment of the kind of death Jesus will die.

(5) *Then* they brought Jesus from *Caiaphas* to the *praetorium.*
It was *morning.*
And they *themselves* did not *enter* the praetorium,
in order not to be *defiled* so that they could eat the *Passover.*

You will notice as you read John's account that Jesus is much more in control of the situation than in the other three passion narratives, even (and perhaps especially) when he would seem by human estimation to be most vulnerable. Within the first few sentences of John's passion narrative we are reminded that *Jesus is aware of all that will happen to him.* There are no surprises, and, indeed, Jesus directly or indirectly guides the course of events from his arrest to his crucifixion. Let this awareness guide you as you proclaim the text.

To some, Jesus seems less accessible, more distant, in John than in Matthew, Mark, or Luke. And yet it is John who reveals more directly than the others that Jesus is the Father's love made flesh, a love that is noble and ennobling, exalted but intimate, eternal but expressed with deep human emotion.

(1) It is remarkable that such an impressive contingent appears to arrest Jesus. There is a cohort of soldiers as well as temple police, armed with weapons and carrying lanterns and torches. Why is such an army necessary to apprehend an itinerant preacher who has no history of violence and no band of fighters to protect him? At least one answer is that John intends to show that no force, however great, can prevail against the Son of God. The inequity of the situation is almost ridiculous but for the larger point being made. One word from Jesus and the assembled forces retreat and fall to the ground. The words Jesus speaks clearly echo the great "I AM" from Exodus, God's response to Moses' question "Who should I say has sent me?" The army that has come to arrest a troublemaker finds itself

So *Pilate* came *out* to them and said,
"What *charge* do you *bring* against this man?"
They answered and said to him,
"If he were not a *criminal*,
we would not have handed him *over* to you."
At *this*, Pilate said to them,
"Take him *yourselves*, and *judge* him according to *your* law."
The Jews *answered* him,
"We do not have the *right* to *execute* anyone, "
in order that the *word* of Jesus might be *fulfilled*
that he said *indicating* the kind of *death* he would die.

So *Pilate* went back into the *praetorium*
and *summoned* Jesus and said to him,
"*Are* you the *King* of the *Jews*?"
Jesus answered,
"Do you say this on your *own*
or have others *told* you about me?"
Pilate answered,
"*I* am not a Jew, *am* I?
Your own *nation* and the chief *priests* handed you *over* to me.
What have you *done*?"
Jesus answered,
"*My* kingdom does not *belong* to *this* world.
If my kingdom *did* belong to this world,
my *attendants* would be *fighting*
to keep me from being handed *over* to the *Jews*.
But as it *is*, my *kingdom* is not *here*."
So Pilate said to him,
"Then you *are* a king?"
Jesus answered,
"You *say* I am a king.

The questioning of Jesus by Pilate must be handled with great care. Presume that Pilate is genuinely curious and that Jesus is sincerely trying to explain the sense in which he is, indeed, a king. If a blatant contest of wills is communicated, Pilate's later discomfort will not seem believable.

face to face with divinity. Their response testifies to Jesus' true identity.

Notice, too, that Jesus is in charge, as he will be throughout his trial. He has the first and the last words, indeed the only words, except for the responses to his questions. And the scene of his arrest ends with the order he gives: "Let these men go." The order is obeyed, as it must be, to fulfill his own prophecy: "I have not lost any of those you gave me." In John's gospel the figure of Jesus is authoritative. He is not only the central figure, he is the one who directs all that happens to him. That calmly assertive authority must be communicated in the proclamation of John's passion narrative.

(2) Peter's impulsive move to protect Jesus gets a response that reminds us of another time when Peter acts without understanding. Earlier in the gospel, Peter reproaches Jesus after hearing him speak of his approaching suffering and death. "Lord," he says, "do not say this; such a thing must not be." And Jesus responds, "Away from me! You are thinking in human terms rather than God's." Here, too, Jesus must remind Peter that God's plan is different from what anyone expected. And why is there no retaliation from the arresting cohort? Because Jesus, not the soldiers, is directing matters here.

Another point is being made here: By severing the ear of the high priest's servant, Peter has symbolically rendered the high priest himself unfit for office according to ancient Jewish law. The evangelist is saying in effect that the old law is passing away, and a new order is being established.

(3) It is a mistake to oversimplify Peter's denial as presented by John. He does deny

For this I was *born* and for this I *came* into the *world*,
to *testify* to the *truth*.
Everyone who belongs to the truth *listens* to my *voice*."
Pilate said to him, "What is *truth*?"

(6) When he had said this,
he *again* went out to the *Jews* and said to them,
"*I* find no *guilt* in him.
But you have a *custom* that I release one *prisoner*
to you at *Passover*.
Do you want me to release to you the *King* of the *Jews*?"
They cried out again,
"Not *this* one but *Barabbas*!"
Now *Barabbas* was a *revolutionary*.

Pilate finds no reason to put Jesus to death. We must remember that, for it is a statement of his innocence. Pilate tries to placate the crowd by having Jesus scourged, but it is not enough.

Barabbas = buh-RAB-uhs

(7) Then Pilate took Jesus and had him *scourged*.
And the *soldiers* wove a *crown* out of *thorns*
and placed it on his *head*,
and *clothed* him in a purple *cloak*,
and they came to him and said,
"*Hail*, King of the *Jews*!"
And they *struck* him *repeatedly*.

Once *more* Pilate went out and said to them,
"*Look*, I am bringing him *out* to you,
so that you may *know* that I find no *guilt* in him."
So Jesus came *out*,
wearing the crown of *thorns* and the purple *cloak*.
And he said to them, "*Behold*, the man!"

When the chief *priests* and the *guards saw* him they cried *out*,
"*Crucify* him, *crucify* him!"
Pilate said to them,
"Take him *yourselves* and crucify him.

the Lord, just as Jesus predicted he would. But John points out that Peter (in company with another disciple) followed Jesus closely when he was taken to trial. Later in the narrative we are reminded that Simon Peter is present throughout the questioning in the high priest's courtyard. Why is he there, so dangerously close? And why does he deny knowing Jesus when he is asked? Is it fear for his own safety, or simple expediency so that he can continue to remain close to the proceedings? For that matter, what kind of courage did it take for Peter to raise his sword against the large arresting cohort? It is only when the cock crows that Peter disappears from the scene, presumably shaken by the fulfillment of Jesus' prediction, but also perhaps because he has finally seen clearly Jesus' resolve to carry out a divine plan that included the necessity of his death. Peter's denial can be seen as far more than simple infidelity to a promise or a cowardly betrayal of a friend. It is much more likely that his struggle presents us with a model for our own struggle to come to accept a Messiah who brings salvation in a way different from what we expect or hope or even like. Peter's life after the resurrection shows us the empowerment that comes with that acceptance, regardless of past failures during the struggle that precedes it.

The way John interweaves Peter's denials with Jesus' bold defense of the truth during his trial is striking. As truth and falsehood are thus played out, each puts the other in bold relief. Truth appears to lose; Jesus is condemned to death. Falsehood appears to win; Peter escapes being identified with a criminal. The dramatic irony is palpable: We know even as we hear the account that appearances are not reality.

I find no *guilt* in him."
The Jews answered,
"We have a *law*, and *according* to that law he ought to *die*,
because he *made* himself the Son of *God*."

Now when Pilate heard *this* statement,
he became even *more* afraid,
and went back into the *praetorium* and said to Jesus,
"Where are you *from*?"
Jesus did not *answer* him.

The questioning continues. Pilate comes across as a man genuinely seeking to do the right thing. The Jewish leaders seem blindly bent on killing Jesus at any cost. This passage reveals John's strong anti-Jewish sentiment. It cannot be concealed in the proclamation.

So Pilate said to him,
"Do you not *speak* to me?
Do you not *know* that I have *power* to *release* you
and I have *power* to *crucify* you?"
Jesus answered him,
"You would have *no* power over me
if it had not been *given* to you from *above*.
For this *reason* the one who handed me *over* to you
has the greater *sin*."
Consequently, Pilate *tried* to *release* him; but the *Jews* cried out,
"If you *release* him, you are not a Friend of *Caesar*.
Everyone who makes himself a *king* opposes *Caesar*."

When Pilate heard *these* words he brought Jesus *out*
and *seated* him on the *judge's* bench
in the place called *Stone Pavement*, in *Hebrew*, *Gabbatha*.

Gabbatha = GAB-uh-thuh

It was *preparation* day for *Passover*, and it was about *noon*.
And he said to the *Jews*,
"*Behold*, your *king*!"
They cried out,
"Take him *away*, take him *away*! *Crucify* him!"

(4) Jesus' bold dialogue with the high priest Annas makes John's emphasis clear: The real authority here lies with the one charged with the crime, not with the one who brings the charge. Notice that the high priest is given no words at all. Only Jesus' words are recorded. Furthermore, Jesus questions and directs the questioner, indicating not only that his authority is from above but that the high priest is not even following proper procedure. According to Jewish law, the high priest should not be questioning the defendant or forcing him to incriminate himself; he should be questioning witnesses both for and against him. For this impudence Jesus is physically abused, a common enough response to someone who points out injustice. How often does it happen that those in high position regard themselves as being above the law? Annas wanted to get rid of this nuisance and was willing to do anything to do so. Jesus nevertheless has the last word, a resounding indictment of the whole process: "Why do you hit me for telling the truth?"

(5) In the exchange between Pilate and Jesus, John most clearly reveals the divine kingship of Jesus that is the writer's real interest. Jesus speaks at length of his dominion, which does not belong to this world, and boldly asserts his true purpose and mission. Later, Pilate is frightened when Jesus reminds him of the true source of all power. Pilate's discomfort reveals John's desire to show us the convincing power of Jesus' words.

Pilate was in a vulnerable position, caught between Rome and Palestine, and he responds to the situation as those who have sold themselves to the systems of

Pilate again tries to resist but ultimately surrenders his will to that of the mob.

Pilate said to them,
"Shall I crucify your *king*?"
The chief *priests* answered,
"We have no *king* but *Caesar*."
Then he handed him *over* to them to be *crucified*.

Golgotha = GOL-guh-thuh

The action now moves toward Golgotha. Jesus carries his cross by himself. There is no one to help him in John's account because Jesus is in charge here and needs no help.

(8) So they *took* Jesus, and, carrying the *cross himself*,
he went out to what is called the Place of the *Skull*,
in *Hebrew*, *Golgotha*.
There they *crucified* him, and with him two *others*,
one on either *side*, with Jesus in the *middle*.

Pilate also had an *inscription* written and put on the *cross*.
It read,
"*Jesus* the *Nazorean*, the *King* of the *Jews*."
Now *many* of the Jews *read* this inscription,
because the *place* where Jesus was *crucified* was near the *city*;
and it was written in *Hebrew*, *Latin*, and *Greek*.

So the chief *priests* of the Jews said to *Pilate*,
"Do not write 'The *King* of the *Jews*,'
but that he *said*, 'I am the King of the Jews'."
Pilate answered,
"What I have *written*, I have *written*."

There is a significant transition here. After Pilate's famous words, "What I have written, I have written," let there be a dramatic pause. The deed has been done.

The details that follow all prove that Jesus is the long-awaited Messiah-king.

When the soldiers had *crucified* Jesus,
they took his *clothes* and *divided* them into four *shares*,
a share for each *soldier*.
They *also* took his *tunic*, but the tunic was *seamless*,
woven in one *piece* from the top *down*.
So they *said* to one another,
"Let's not *tear* it, but cast *lots* for it to see whose it will *be*,"

power often do. He tries to wash his hands of the situation and avoid responsibility for what happens.

As we watch this scene unfold, the sense of irony increases with every exchange between these two rulers: one who rules heaven and earth but needs no trappings of royalty to prove it; and another who has all the outward signs of power but is unable even to help the innocent man before him. Pilate is one of the saddest figures in history. He put himself in the terrible position of not being able to do the right thing even when he knows what to do.

(6) Barabbas means "son of the father" or "the father's son" (*bar* corresponds to "son," *abbas* to "father"). In the other gospels we learn that the man's full name was Jesus Barabbas. So we have two figures here with the same name: Jesus, son of the father. And, from the point of view of the author, the crowd chooses the wrong one, although the people's choice allows the true Son of the Father to complete his mission. Furthermore, Barabbas is described by John as an insurrectionist or revolutionary.

And, of course, Jesus is also a revolutionary, but on an entirely different plane.

(7) The Roman soldiers at the crucifixion see Jesus as just another in a long line of puny revolutionaries from an inferior race. The fact that he has claimed to be a king makes him all the more ridiculous in their eyes. In our eyes, blessed with hindsight, Jesus becomes an even more tragic figure when we see him being abused by those who had no idea who he was.

The food for thoughtful meditation here is plentiful. John presents a drama so fraught with irony, contradiction, and paradox that

in order that the passage of *Scripture* might be *fulfilled*
that says:
"They divided my *garments* among them,
and for my *vesture* they cast *lots*."
This is what the soldiers *did*.

Clopas = KLOH-puhs

Standing by the *cross* of Jesus were his *mother*
and his mother's *sister*, *Mary* the wife of *Clopas*,
and Mary of *Magdala*.

When Jesus saw his *mother* and the *disciple* there whom he *loved*
he said to his *mother*, "*Woman*, *behold*, your *son*."
Then he said to the *disciple*,
"*Behold*, your *mother*."
And from that *hour* the disciple took her into his *home*.

After *this*, aware that everything was now *finished*,
in order that the *Scripture* might be *fulfilled*,
Jesus said, "I *thirst*."
There was a *vessel* filled with common *wine*.

hyssop = HIS-uhp

So they put a *sponge* soaked in wine on a sprig of *hyssop*
and put it up to his *mouth*.
When Jesus had taken the *wine*, he said,
"It is *finished*."
And bowing his *head*, he handed *over* the *spirit*.
[Here all kneel and pause for a short time.]

After Jesus utters his final words and gives up his spirit, all kneel for a short time. Allow a significant period of silence (no less than 15 seconds, and 30 would be better). When all rise, wait until all noise ceases before continuing. The calm that follows the storm characterizes the closing paragraphs. Let them move slowly, confidently, to the simple conclusion of the story. After the proclamation, all should be seated and, with no rush, the homily begins. It is a somber moment.

Now since it was *preparation* day,
in order that the *bodies* might not remain
on the *cross* on the *sabbath*,
for the *sabbath* day of that week was a *solemn* one,
the *Jews* asked *Pilate* that their *legs* be broken
and that they be taken *down*.

we cannot exhaust the richness of its implication and application. It is the experience of faith painted in brutal strokes. Believing in what we cannot see, we see the person in whom we believe being ridiculed. The divine creator of heaven and earth wills to subject himself to earthly power in order to redeem the earth and reunite it with heaven.

Three kings appear in this passage: the King of the Jews, rejected by those whose name he bears; a king of shreds and patches, ridiculed and mocked by those he came to save in love; and the king of the universe, recognized only by a faithful remnant that will proclaim his sovereignty throughout the world. When the mob cries, "We have no king but Caesar," they utter the most grotesque blasphemy. But in that same breath they prepare the way for their own redemption by unknowingly becoming participants in God's plan to save the world.

(8) There is no Simon of Cyrene in John's gospel to help Jesus carry the cross. The sovereignty of Jesus is thus asserted again in John's account of the passion. In many other details of the narrative, John carries out his purpose. The seamless garment for which the soldiers cast lots, the thirst quenched by sour wine and the fact that Jesus' legs are not broken all provide John the opportunity to show the scriptures being fulfilled in Jesus. John, the eyewitness, is gathering testimony in defense of this Messiah-king, for whom the world had waited so long but whom it failed recognize when he appeared.

Notice, too, that there are no jeering crowds at the foot of the cross. Instead Jesus' mother and the writer himself along with a few others stand by his side. Jesus is

So the *soldiers* came and broke the legs of the *first*
and then of the *other* one who was crucified with Jesus.
But when they came to *Jesus* and saw that he was already *dead*,
they did not *break* his legs,
but *one* soldier thrust his *lance* into his *side*,
and *immediately blood* and *water* flowed out.

An *eyewitness* has testified, and his *testimony* is *true*;
he *knows* that he is speaking the *truth*,
so that you *also* may come to *believe*.

For this *happened* so that the *Scripture* passage might be *fulfilled*:
"Not a *bone* of it will be *broken*."
And again *another* passage says:
"They will *look* upon him whom they have *pierced*."

Arimathea = air-ih-muh-THEE-uh

After *this*, *Joseph* of *Arimathea*,
secretly a *disciple* of Jesus for fear of the *Jews*,
asked *Pilate* if he could remove the *body* of Jesus.
And Pilate *permitted* it.
So he came and *took* his body.

aloes = AL-ohz

Nicodemus, the one who had first *come* to him at *night*,
also came bringing a mixture of *myrrh* and *aloes*
weighing about one hundred *pounds*.
They took the *body* of Jesus
and *bound* it with *burial* cloths along with the *spices*,
according to the Jewish *burial* custom.
Now in the *place* where he had been *crucified* there was a *garden*,
and in the garden a new *tomb*, in which no one
had *yet* been *buried*.
So they laid Jesus *there* because of the Jewish *preparation* day;
for the *tomb* was close *by*.

not totally abandoned, as he is in the other gospel accounts. And although he is subjected to the most horrible indignities, Jesus' dignity is palpable throughout. Those who mock Jesus in John's passion narrative sink lower with every attempt to raise themselves above the object of their hatred.

As we look at Jesus in John's passion narrative, we see a much more voluble and assertive victim than we saw in Matthew's account last Sunday. Jesus responds differently to his situation in John. He is treated differently, too. The inscription on the cross ("Jesus the Nazorean, the King of the Jews") appears in three languages, an indication that this king's reign is universal. Even the demand to change the inscription cannot get it altered, for Jesus *is* king of the Hebrews, as well as king of the Romans and the Greeks. He is king of the entire universe. When Pilate utters those unforgettable words, "What I have written, I have written," he becomes an unwitting ambassador for Christ the King.

In John, Jesus *reigns* from his cross. In a final decree he sends out the proclamation "It is finished." His spirit is not taken from him; he commends it and the world into the hands of the Father. Even after his death, the signs of his reign continue. The enormous quantity and richness of the materials Nicodemus provides for Jesus' burial are more appropriate for a king than a crucified criminal. Our proclamation of John's view of the suffering and dying Jesus must always strive to assert the royal dignity he retains at every moment.

EASTER VIGIL

Lectionary #41

READING I Genesis 1:1—2:2

The Vigil began in darkness and silence, as does this reading. Do not begin until absolute stillness settles over the assembly. Then let your proclamation of Genesis start quietly, for you need to build through to the end.

Do not rush from one section to the next. Refresh your tone of voice with each "Then God said."

Each "Let . . ." must be authoritative. God creates the world with a word!

A reading from the Book of Genesis

In the *beginning*, when *God* created the *heavens* and the *earth*,
the earth was a formless *wasteland*, and *darkness*
covered the *abyss*,
while a mighty *wind* swept over the *waters*.

Then God said,
"Let there be *light*," and there *was* light.
God saw how *good* the light was.
God then *separated* the light from the *darkness*.
God called the light "*day*" and the darkness he called "*night*."
Thus *evening* came, and morning *followed*—the *first* day.

Then God said,
"Let there be a *dome* in the middle of the *waters*,
to separate *one* body of water from the *other*."
And so it *happened*:
God made the *dome*,
and it separated the water *above* the dome
from the water *below* it.
God called the dome "the *sky*."
Evening came, and morning *followed*—the *second* day.

Then God said,
"Let the *water* under the sky be *gathered* into a single *basin*,
so that the dry *land* may appear."

READING I Genesis, the "book of beginnings," was the source of our first reading on the 1st Sunday of Lent. Now, as the celebration of the paschal mystery reaches its highest point, we read from it again to include all of creation in the great work Jesus is about to accomplish on our behalf.

There is one controlling idea that runs throughout this wonderful story of creation: God the Almighty is the source of all life, the cause and the ultimate goal of every living thing, and the one who sustains everything in existence. But to put it that way renders this awesome truth colorless and dull. The author of this creation account knows by instinct that great truths must be told in memorable ways. And what is more memorable than the first chapter of Genesis?

The reading before you is immense, profound, laden with centuries of tradition and countless generations of use. Because

And so it *happened*:
the water under the *sky* was gathered into its *basin*,
and the dry *land* appeared.
God called the dry land "the *earth*,"
and the basin of the *water* he called "the *sea*."
God saw how *good* it was.
Then God said,
"Let the *earth* bring forth *vegetation*:
every kind of *plant* that bears *seed*
and every kind of *fruit tree* on earth
that bears fruit with its *seed* in it."
And so it *happened*:
the earth brought forth every *kind* of plant that bears *seed*
and every kind of *fruit tree* on earth
that bears *fruit* with its *seed* in it.
God saw how *good* it was.
Evening came, and morning *followed*—the *third* day.

Remember that you are continuing to build. A significant jump should be detected as you proclaim the creation of the lights of heaven.

Then God said:
"Let there be *lights* in the dome of the *sky*,
to separate *day* from *night*.
Let them mark the fixed *times*, the *days* and the *years*,
and serve as *luminaries* in the dome of the *sky*,
to shed *light* upon the earth."
And so it *happened*:
God made the two great *lights*,
the *greater* one to govern the *day*,
and the *lesser* one to govern the *night*;
and he made the *stars*.
God *set* them in the dome of the *sky*,
to shed *light* upon the earth,
to *govern* the day and the night,
and to separate the *light* from the *darkness*.

it is so familiar, however, there is some risk that its words will be "tuned out" if you, the proclaimer, exert less than your finest skill. Strive for a mode of proclamation that reveres the text, loves the message, and makes it fresh. This does not mean that you exaggerate in any way; rather, it means you prepare and proclaim carefully and sensitively, so that the way you read the text asserts its importance. It is a ringing proclamation of cosmic significance and deserves all the nobility and sincerity you can muster.

You cannot help but notice the refrain-like repetition of several phrases. There is a repetitive kind of rhythm that is part of the author's intention. For one thing, before we had the ease of printed text, the refrains would make the passage easier to memorize. But there is another reason for these refrains: They produce an almost hypnotic effect, giving the story more of the feeling of a long-revered fable, even a formula. It marches through the seven days with gratifying predictability, relying precisely on the

"Let the water *teem* . . ." Let the power of the words do their job. Something of the prodigality of nature is asserted here. The water isn't just filled with abundant life, it *teems* with it.

God saw how *good* it was.
Evening came, and morning *followed*—the *fourth* day.

Then God said,
"Let the water *teem* with an *abundance* of living *creatures*,
and on the *earth* let *birds* fly beneath the dome of the *sky*."
And so it *happened*:
God created the great *sea* monsters
and all kinds of *swimming* creatures with which
the water *teems*,
and all kinds of winged *birds*.
God saw how *good* it was, and God *blessed* them, saying,
"Be *fertile*, *multiply*, and *fill* the water of the seas;
and let the *birds* multiply on the *earth*."
Evening came, and morning *followed*—the *fifth* day.

Then God said,
"Let the *earth* bring forth all kinds of living *creatures*:
cattle, *creeping* things, and wild *animals* of all *kinds*."
And so it *happened*:
God made all kinds of wild *animals*, all kinds of *cattle*,
and all kinds of *creeping* things of the earth.
God saw how *good* it was.

Then God said:
"Let us make *man* in our *image*, after our *likeness*.
Let them have *dominion* over the fish of the *sea*,
the birds of the *air*, and the *cattle*,
and over all the wild *animals*
and all the creatures that *crawl* on the *ground*."
God *created* man in his *image*;
in the image of *God* he created him;
male and *female* he created them.

familiarity that makes for enjoyable listening. Each time you proclaim the refrains "God saw how good it was," or "And so it happened," you assert the sovereignty of God's creative love. Don't rush these refrains in the fear that the assembly will be bored by them. Relish each occurrence, realizing that the power of the refrains lies precisely in the assembly's awareness that they come with soothing regularity.

Let your proclamation be guided by your own awareness that one simple truth underlies this account of creation: All that is comes from the heart of a loving God, and all of it is good! "Rejoice, O earth, in shining splendor, radiant in the brightness of your King."

God *blessed* them, saying:
"Be *fertile* and *multiply;*
fill the earth and *subdue* it.
Have *dominion* over the fish of the *sea*, the birds of the *air*,
and all the *living* things that *move* on the earth."

God *also* said:
"*See,* I give you every seed-bearing *plant* all over the *earth*
and every *tree* that has seed-bearing *fruit* on it to be your *food;*
and to all the *animals* of the land, all the birds of the *air*,
and all the living *creatures* that crawl on the *ground*,
I give all the green *plants* for *food*."
And so it *happened*.

God *looked* at everything he had made, and he found it
very *good*.
Evening came, and morning *followed*—the *sixth* day.

After the sixth day, begin to reduce the intensity and close on the same quiet note with which you began. A significant pause must precede "The word of the Lord" (which is never thrown away as an afterthought).

Thus the *heavens* and the *earth* and all their *array*
were *completed*.
Since on the *seventh* day God was *finished*
with the work he had been doing,
he *rested* on the seventh day from all the *work*
he had *undertaken*.

[Shorter: Genesis 1:1, 26–31a]

READING II Genesis 22:1–18

A reading from the Book of Genesis

The purpose (to test Abraham) is stated abruptly in the opening words. Follow them with a pause. Then be careful with "Here I am." Try emphasizing "am" rather than "here" to avoid a childish sound.

God put *Abraham* to the *test*.
He *called* to him, "*Abraham!*"
"Here I *am*," he replied.

READING II For the Christian, the story of Abraham and Isaac has long been a compelling symbol or prefiguring of the sacrifice of God's Son for the redemption of the world. Abraham is perfectly obedient; Isaac is perfectly innocent. Isaac even bears the wood for his sacrifice upon his own shoulders. In Eucharistic Prayer I, we proclaim Abraham to be "our father in faith," and so he is, because of the beautiful blessing and promise he receives at the end of the reading.

Our first response to this story may be horror at God's demand of such a sacrifice. But we need to remind ourselves of the purpose of the story and what the writer wants us to take from it. This is always the case with scripture: The message is always more than the mere historical details. By the time the Abraham and Isaac story was written, human sacrifice was no longer practiced

Then God said:
"Take your son *Isaac*, your only *one*, whom you *love*,
and *go* to the land of *Moriah*.
There you shall offer him *up* as a *holocaust*
on a *height* that I will point *out* to you."

Moriah = moh-RĪ-uh
holocaust = HOL-uh-kawst

Early the next *morning* Abraham saddled his *donkey*,
took with him his son *Isaac* and two of his *servants* as *well*,
and with the *wood* that he had cut for the *holocaust*,
set out for the *place* of which God had *told* him.

Note the immediacy of Abraham's response to this horrific command. This is not because he is heartless but because he has total faith in God's goodness.

On the *third day* Abraham got *sight* of the place from *afar*.
Then he said to his *servants*:
"Both of you stay *here* with the *donkey*,
while the *boy* and I go on over *yonder*.
We will *worship* and then come *back* to you."
Thereupon Abraham took the *wood* for the *holocaust*
and laid it on his son *Isaac's shoulders*,
while he *himself* carried the *fire* and the *knife*.

As the two walked on *together*, Isaac *spoke*
to his father Abraham:
"*Father*!" Isaac said.
"*Yes*, son," he replied.
Isaac *continued*, "Here are the *fire* and the *wood*,
but where is the *sheep* for the holocaust?"
"*Son*," Abraham answered,
"God *himself* will provide the *sheep* for the *holocaust*."
Then the two *continued* going *forward*.

Abraham's trust ("God will provide") is also a prediction of the outcome of the story.

When they came to the *place* of which God had *told* him,
Abraham built an *altar* there and arranged the *wood* on it.
Next he *tied up* his son Isaac,
and put him on *top* of the wood on the *altar*.

among the Israelites. That's part of the point of the story. As a way of proclaiming God's sovereignty, the firstborn of every creature belonged to God. And each firstborn human child was "redeemed" by the substitute of an animal sacrifice.

The focus throughout the reading is Abraham's willingness to relinquish what he loves most to God's sovereignty. It is the ultimate test for all believers to arrive at the kind of faith that relinquishes control and affirms God to be in charge of life as a provident guardian. Indeed, this is the meaning of the name that Abraham bestows on the site where the sacrifice took place. The translation of "Yahweh-yireh" is complex, but it means God will see that the covenant and promise will be kept. As God provided the ram for sacrifice in place of Isaac, so God will see to the redemption of the people of the covenant.

Let the messenger's voice be strong and calm, not urgent.

Because of this outcome, the firstborn that belongs to God is redeemed by the substitution of an animal sacrifice. We cannot help but think here of the Lamb of God, sacrificed to redeem us.
Yahweh-yireh = Yah-way-YEER-ay

This is the great blessing explaining why we call Abraham "our father in faith." Note that all the nations of the earth, not just Abraham's people, shall be blessed.

Then he *reached out* and took the *knife* to *slaughter* his *son*.
But the LORD's *messenger* called to him from *heaven*,
"Abraham, Abraham!"
"Here I *am*," he answered.
"Do not lay your *hand* on the boy," said the messenger.
"Do not do the least *thing* to him.
I *know* now how *devoted* you are to God,
since you did not *withhold* from me your own beloved *son*."
As Abraham looked *about*,
he spied a *ram* caught by its *horns* in the *thicket*.
So he went and took the *ram*
and offered *it* up as a holocaust in place of his *son*.
Abraham *named* the site *Yahweh-yireh*;
hence people *now* say, "On the *mountain* the LORD will *see*."

Again the LORD's messenger called to Abraham from *heaven*
and said:
"I *swear* by *myself*, declares the LORD,
that because you *acted* as you *did*
in not *withholding* from me your beloved *son*,
I will *bless* you *abundantly*
and make your *descendants* as countless
as the *stars* of the *sky* and the *sands* of the *seashore*;
your *descendants* shall take *possession*
of the gates of their *enemies*,
and in your *descendants* all the *nations* of the *earth*
shall find *blessing*—
all *this* because you *obeyed* my *command*."

[Shorter: Genesis 22:1–2, 9a, 10–13, 15–18]

The reward for Abraham's obedience and service is the beautiful blessing that concludes the passage. It should be read with breadth and conviction. The assembly will instinctively draw the parallels between Abraham and Isaac, and God the Father and Jesus. A revered foreshadowing of Jesus' sacrifice in obedience to his Father's will takes on special meaning for us as we celebrate the paschal mystery on this holiest of nights.

"Father, how wonderful your care for us! How boundless your merciful love! To ransom a slave you gave away your Son."

READING III The story of the crossing of the Red Sea—surely one of the most beloved in Jewish and Christian traditions—recounts a central event in salvation history. It is the classic image of a people being delivered from captivity. As the Israelites pass through the waters and arrive

READING III Exodus 14:15—15:1

A reading from the Book of Exodus

We see a people cowering in fright, afraid to move forward until their leader instructs them in no uncertain terms to put their trust in God. Then the feeling of resolve and courage begins to build as God manifests divine power on their behalf.

The LORD said to *Moses*, "*Why* are you crying *out* to me?
Tell the *Israelites* to go *forward*.
And *you*, lift up your *staff* and, with hand *outstretched*
over the *sea*,
split the sea in *two*,
that the *Israelites* may pass *through* it on *dry land*.
But I will make the *Egyptians* so *obstinate*
that they will go in *after* them.
Then I will receive *glory* through *Pharaoh* and all his *army*,
his *chariots* and *charioteers*.

The important words are "I am the Lord." Both sides must learn this lesson, just as we learn it sometimes when we make the mistake of siding with Pharaoh!

The Egyptians shall *know* that *I* am the LORD,
when I receive *glory* through *Pharaoh*
and his *chariots* and *charioteers*."

The *angel* of God, who had been *leading* Israel's *camp*,
now *moved* and went around *behind* them.
The column of *cloud* also, leaving the *front*,
took up its place *behind* them,
so that it came *between* the camp of the *Egyptians*
and that of *Israel*.

These are strong images! Let your proclamation match them.

But the cloud *now* became *dark*, and thus the night *passed*
without the rival camps coming any closer *together*
all night *long*.

Then *Moses* stretched out his *hand* over the *sea*,
and the LORD *swept* the sea
with a strong east *wind* throughout the *night*
and so *turned* it into *dry land*.

safely on the other shore, leaving their pursuers behind, so we pass through the waters of baptism and are admitted into the fellowship of the Body of Christ, leaving sin and death behind.

The imagery of these parallel events has been beautifully captured in a song by Father Hugh Tasch, OSB, of Conception Abbey, Conception, Missouri:

Once you were darkness, Pharaoh's
prison band.
Now you are sunlight dwelling
in the Land.
Walk, then, in sunlight, high
upon the shore.
Rise from the waters, dying now
no more.

So important is the Red Sea crossing in our Christian tradition that this reading is obligatory tonight even if others are omitted for pastoral reasons. In your community there may be catechumens awaiting baptism at this very moment. Let your proclamation be for them in a special way. Let it echo what we heard in the Exsultet at the beginning of this holy night: "This is the night

When the water was thus *divided*,
the *Israelites* marched into the *midst* of the sea on dry *land*,
with the *water* like a *wall* to their *right* and to their *left*.

This is a vivid story, like an action movie. We must sense the energy here but not lose ourselves in the details. God's solid and uncontestable power is the point.

The *Egyptians* followed in *pursuit*;
all Pharaoh's *horses* and *chariots* and *charioteers*
went *after* them
right into the *midst* of the *sea*.
In the night *watch* just before *dawn*
the LORD *cast* through the *column* of the fiery *cloud*
upon the Egyptian *force* a *glance* that threw it into a *panic*;
and he so *clogged* their *chariot* wheels
that they could hardly *drive*.
With *that* the Egyptians sounded the *retreat* before Israel,
because the *LORD* was fighting for them *against* the Egyptians.

Then the LORD told Moses, "Stretch out your *hand* over the *sea*,
that the water may flow *back* upon the *Egyptians*,
upon their *chariots* and their *charioteers*."
So Moses *stretched* out his hand over the *sea*,
and at *dawn* the sea flowed *back* to its normal *depth*.
The Egyptians were fleeing *head on* toward the sea,
when the LORD *hurled* them into its *midst*.
As the water flowed *back*,
it *covered* the *chariots* and the *charioteers*
of Pharaoh's whole *army*
which had followed the *Israelites* into the *sea*.
Not a single *one* of them *escaped*.

But the *Israelites* had marched on dry *land*
through the *midst* of the sea,
with the water like a *wall* to their *right* and to their *left*.

The conclusion should not be anticlimactic. Keep the energy level up.

Thus the LORD *saved* Israel on that day
from the *power* of the *Egyptians*.

when first you saved our ancestors: you freed the people of Israel from their slavery and led them dry-shod through the sea."

READING IV After hearing of the exercise of divine power on behalf of the chosen people, we now hear a gentle proclamation of God's love for them. It would be difficult to find a more moving expression of devotion than this one. It is a poem of intimacy between God and the holy city, Jerusalem. It refers first to Jerusalem's people, the race God has chosen, but is ultimately addressed to all humankind.

In this love song we see evidence of a stormy relationship, which should not surprise us. Any relationship that strives for genuine union between two independent hearts will have its turbulent times. But in this reading, as in our experience, the difficulties encountered in honest love serve only to make that love stronger.

The theme of Israel's exile is clear in the image of the abandoned wife. The promise of deliverance and prosperity is just as clear in the *shalom* or "peace" of the next generation. The image of the marital bond is often

When Israel *saw* the Egyptians lying *dead* on the *seashore*
and beheld the great *power* that the LORD
had *shown* against the Egyptians,
they *feared* the LORD and *believed* in him
and in his servant *Moses*.

Then *Moses* and the *Israelites* sang this *song* to the *LORD*:
I will sing to the LORD, for he is gloriously triumphant;
horse and chariot he has cast into the sea.

READING IV Isaiah 54:5–14

A reading from the Book of the Prophet Isaiah

How can the all-powerful God of hosts also be a loving spouse? Let the exhilarating paradox exert its power!

The One who has become your *husband* is your *Maker*;
his *name* is the LORD of *hosts*;
your *redeemer* is the *Holy* One of *Israel*,
called *God* of all the *earth*.
The LORD calls you *back*,
like a *wife forsaken* and grieved in *spirit*,
a *wife* married in *youth* and then cast *off*,
says your God.

The prophet gives God a human voice, speaking in the frailty of human language. Thus the desire for intimacy prevails over struggle and infidelity.

For a brief *moment* I *abandoned* you,
but with great *tenderness* I will take you *back*.
In an outburst of *wrath*, for a *moment*
I hid my *face* from you;
but with enduring *love* I take *pity* on you,
says the *LORD*, your *redeemer*.

employed in scripture as the only one intimate enough to describe God's love for Israel.

The same bond describes the love between Christ and the church. Christ is the bridegroom who has rescued his beloved from every danger and given his life for her happiness. Conjugal bliss is an appropriate image as we celebrate this holiest of nights. As we heard in the Exsultet: "O night truly blessed, when heaven is wedded to earth and we are reconciled with God."

READING V **Scripture scholars believe that the author of this passage of poetry lived and struggled in a poor community. It's not surprising, then, that we find here images of a sumptuous banquet and the encouraging message that the riches promised come at no cost from the hand of a loving provider. The prophet appeals to his audience in images his hearers can understand.**

Beyond the local circumstances that gave birth to Isaiah's poetry, this reading shows us the kind of sustenance that comes

This is for me like the days of *Noah*,
when I swore that the *waters* of Noah
should never *again deluge* the earth;
so I have *sworn* not to be *angry* with you,
or to *rebuke* you.

The combination of strength and tenderness here is moving.

Though the *mountains* leave their *place*
and the *hills* be *shaken*,
my *love* shall never *leave* you
nor my covenant of *peace* be *shaken*,
says the *LORD*, who has *mercy* on you.

carnelians = kahr-NEEL-yuhnz

carbuncles = KAHR-bung-k*lz

O *afflicted* one, *storm-battered* and *unconsoled*,
I lay your pavements in carnelians,
and your foundations in sapphires;
I will make your *battlements* of *rubies*,
your *gates* of *carbuncles*,
and all your *walls* of precious *stones*.

The repetition of the word "children" means you must emphasize other words in the sentence. See the emphasis markings.

Utter confidence and peace bring the reading to a close.

All your *children* shall be taught by the *LORD*,
and *great* shall be the *peace* of your children.
In *justice* shall you be *established*,
far from the fear of *oppression*,
where *destruction* cannot come *near* you.

READING V Isaiah 55:1–11

A reading from the Book of the Prophet Isaiah

Another message of consolation is solemnly presented here. Let your proclamation concentrate on the strength of the message, avoiding a softness that would be inappropriate.

Thus says the *LORD*:
All you who are *thirsty*,
come to the *water*!
You who have no *money*,
come, receive grain and eat;

from trust in a God who is a provident Father. Isaiah's prophecy predicts a future time of peace and prosperity. Again we are presented with a vision of the end times (heaven), and we are encouraged to see the signs that indicate the imminent arrival of those times: the mercy and redemptive love of God, symbolized here in the image of a banquet.

The great challenge to faith, of course, is to see the signs of God's perfect love in an imperfect world. It takes genuine, profound and ongoing conversion. It means acknowledging deep down that God's ways are different from our own and then aligning our ways with those of the divine: mercy over vengeance, persons over things, love over security. In fervent prayer for such insight, we do not change God's will; we change ourselves.

Finally, we are reminded here that God's word is irrevocable and will accomplish the purpose for which you proclaim it.

"Bread" is a symbolic term here, signifying the nourishment of wisdom. Recall Jesus' words: "My food and drink is to do the will of God who sent me."

"So shall you summon . . ." This is a tongue-twister. Take it slowly.

come, without *paying* and without *cost*,
drink *wine* and *milk*!
Why spend your *money* for what is not *bread*,
your *wages* for what fails to *satisfy*?
Heed me, and you shall eat *well*,
you shall *delight* in rich *fare*.
Come to me *heedfully*,
listen, that you may have *life*.
I will *renew* with you the everlasting *covenant*,
the *benefits* assured to *David*.

As I made him a *witness* to the *peoples*,
a *leader* and *commander* of *nations*,
so shall you *summon* a nation you knew *not*,
and nations that knew *you* not shall *run* to you,
because of the *LORD*, your *God*,
the *Holy* One of *Israel*, who has *glorified* you.

Seek the LORD while he may be *found*,
call him while he is *near*.
Let the *scoundrel* forsake his *way*,
and the *wicked* man his *thoughts*;
let him turn to the *LORD* for *mercy*;
to our *God*, who is *generous* in *forgiving*.

For *my* thoughts are not *your* thoughts,
nor are *your* ways *my* ways, says the LORD.
As high as the *heavens* are above the *earth*,
so *high* are *my* ways above *your* ways
and *my* thoughts above *your* thoughts.

For just as from the *heavens*
the *rain* and *snow* come down

The paschal mystery we are celebrating is our best evidence that God's word has been accomplished: "This is the night when Jesus Christ broke the chains of death and rose triumphant from the grave."

READING VI **The sixth and seventh readings of the Vigil remind us that without the intervention of God's love we would still be slaves to sin and death. The governing image is Israel's exile and unfaithfulness. As Israel was rescued from exile and restored to God's favor, so it is with us this night. "This is the night when first you saved our ancestors: you freed the people of Israel from their slavery and led them dry-shod through the sea."**

The poetry of Baruch is a call to awareness. The cosmic imagery creates a sense of the immensity and universality of God's

This is a powerful image of how God's word does its work. For you who proclaim it, know that you are enabling the word to achieve its purpose, despite your weakness or strength. Take courage.

and do not *return* there
till they have *watered* the earth,
making it *fertile* and *fruitful*,
giving *seed* to the one who *sows*
and *bread* to the one who *eats*,
so shall my *word* be
that goes *forth* from my *mouth*;

In the paschal mystery we celebrate tonight, we see that God's word has indeed achieved its purpose in the resurrection of Jesus Christ.

my word shall not *return* to me *void*,
but shall *do* my *will*,
achieving the *end* for which I *sent* it.

READING VI Baruch 3:9–15, 32—4:4

Baruch = buh-ROOK

A reading from the Book of the Prophet Baruch

Anytime you encounter the words "Hear, O Israel," you have come upon a solemn pronouncement. The most fundamental of Jewish prayers, the Shema, begins with these words: "Hear, O Israel, the Lord our God is One!"

Hear, O Israel, the *commandments* of *life*:
listen, and know *prudence*!
How *is it*, Israel,
that you are in the *land* of your *foes*,
grown *old* in a *foreign* land,
defiled with the *dead*,
accounted with those *destined* for the *netherworld*?

These are harsh words, but we need to hear how much we need God's loving redemption.

You have *forsaken* the fountain of *wisdom*!
Had you *walked* in the way of *God*,
you would have *dwelt* in enduring *peace*.

Learn where *prudence* is,
where *strength*, where *understanding*;
that you may know *also*
where are length of *days*, and *life*,
where light of the *eyes*, and *peace*.

domain. Above all, it is a call to seek wisdom, that most insightful of virtues that enables us to see how different our ways are from God's and to reorient ourselves to God's way of dealing with the world. Wisdom is a gift from God and a manifestation of God. It is withheld from none, not reserved to the intelligent or denied to the simple. It enables us to see God revealed in every aspect of creation, from the four-footed beasts to the stars in heaven. To find wisdom we must resist our tendency to shortsightedness and raise our eyes to the universe.

In his historical context the prophet is calling out to Israel, dispersed as its people are throughout the pagan world. If they are concerned that they cannot serve God well in the midst of foreigners, they must be reminded that their exile is the result of failing to serve God well in their homeland. The prophet's indictment may seem harsh, but he is more eager to point out that wisdom is available wherever we are because God has revealed the word by which we can guide our behavior and our devotion. It is discernible in nature but even more so in the hearts of the just, who have loved the

The rhetorical questions center on God as creator and sustainer of all that is. Wisdom begins when we realize, as we heard in the last reading, that God's ways are different from our own.

Who has found the place of *wisdom*,
who has *entered* into her *treasuries*?

The One who knows *all* things knows *her*;
he has *probed* her by his *knowledge*—
the One who established the *earth* for all *time*,
and *filled* it with four-footed *beasts*;
he who dismisses the *light*, and it *departs*,
calls it, and it *obeys* him *trembling*;
before whom the *stars* at their *posts*
shine and *rejoice*;
when he *calls* them, they answer, "Here we *are*!"
shining with *joy* for their *Maker*.

Such is our *God*;
no *other* is to be *compared* to him:
He has traced out the whole *way* of *understanding*,
and has given her to *Jacob*, his *servant*,
to *Israel*, his beloved *son*.

Wisdom appeared on earth in the love God has for us. If we can learn and believe that we are loved, we will become truly wise.

Since then she has *appeared* on earth,
and *moved* among *people*.
She is the *book* of the *precepts* of God,
the *law* that endures *forever*;
all who *cling* to her will *live*,
but those will *die* who *forsake* her.

Here the prophet sounds arrogant and xenophobic. You must not. The point is that there is justifiable pride in being the chosen people. Only later will Israel learn that all the nations of the earth are chosen for redemption.

Turn, O Jacob, and *receive* her:
walk by her *light* toward *splendor*.
Give not your *glory* to *another*,
your *privileges* to an *alien* race.
Blessed are we, O Israel;
for what *pleases* God is *known* to us!

law and whose lives make the goodness of God visible.

In a dramatic way, Baruch is discouraging us from seeking tidy answers to specific questions. Serving God well means seeing the world in a certain way and behaving accordingly. There is no rule book or catechism that can instill such vision or guarantee that we have aligned our ways with God's. Only wisdom can do that. But Baruch tells us not to be discouraged. Even when we merely search for wisdom we already serve God well.

READING VII **Israel's exile and return to the land of their ancestors is central to their faith, which is why so much of the Hebrew scriptures dwell on the subject. The prophet Ezekiel is a colorful writer. His images range from the harshest condemnations (as we find in this reading) to the most tender expressions of God's redeeming power. When the facts of the case are harsh, Ezekiel pulls no punches.**

Bad as it is, however, Israel's infidelity is no worse than human infidelity at any age. What is most distressing is that the chosen people have profaned the name of the God who chose them. It is no different with us.

READING VII Ezekiel 36:16–17a, 18–28

Ezekiel = ee-ZEE-kee-uhl

These are tough words to proclaim and to hear. But our sins do bring evil upon the earth, and we need to be reminded of the consequences of our actions. The amazing thing is that God can bring good even out of evil. God will love Israel back into favor.

A reading from the Book of the Prophet Ezekiel

The word of the LORD came to me, saying:
Son of *man*, when the house of *Israel* lived in their *land*,
they *defiled* it by their *conduct* and *deeds*.
Therefore I poured out my *fury* upon them
because of the *blood* that they poured out on the *ground*,
and because they *defiled* it with *idols*.
I *scattered* them among the *nations*,
dispersing them over *foreign* lands;
according to their *conduct* and *deeds* I *judged* them.

But when they came among the *nations wherever* they came,
they served to *profane* my holy *name*,
because it was *said* of them: "*These* are the people of the LORD,
yet they had to *leave* their *land*."

So I have *relented* because of my holy *name*
which the house of *Israel profaned*
among the *nations* where they *came*.
Therefore say to the house of Israel: *Thus* says the Lord GOD:
Not for *your* sakes do I *act*, house of Israel,
but for the *sake* of my holy *name*,
which you *profaned* among the *nations* to which you *came*.

I will prove the *holiness* of my great name,
profaned among the *nations*,
in whose *midst* you have *profaned* it.
Thus the nations shall *know* that *I* am the LORD,
says the Lord GOD,
when in their *sight* I prove my *holiness* through *you*.

Chosen as we are by a merciful and loving God, our refusal to be merciful and loving is all the more terrible.

But again God relents, as we have come to expect, since mercy always triumphs over justice where God is concerned. Although our homecoming is said to be for the sake of the holiness of God's great name among the foreign nations—and not because God pities us—we are nevertheless to be reestablished as the people of the covenant.

Ezekiel's point is that neither our good deeds nor our bad ones nor our repentance *earn* the love of God. That love is gratuitous, always a gift freely given by God, for it is God's nature. God *makes* us holy in spite of ourselves. Again, as we heard in the Exsultet: "This is the night when Christians everywhere, washed clean of sin and freed from all defilement, are restored to grace and grow together in holiness."

On this night of all nights, we need to be reminded that the sacrificial love demonstrated in Christ's death and resurrection is a totally free act of love. We can accept it with grateful hearts, or we can reject it with stony ones; there is no way we can *earn* it. We can, however, heed the voice of the prophet and respond to love with the new hearts of flesh God has given us. "What good would life have been to us, had Christ not come as our Redeemer?"

EPISTLE **Finally we come to the reading that ties all the others together in the Christian tradition. It adds**

For I will take you *away* from among the nations,
gather you from all the foreign *lands*,
and bring you *back* to your *own* land.

The image of hearts of flesh versus hearts of stone is powerful. A heart of stone may be hard for many reasons: sinfulness, sorrow, resentment, suffering. Appeal to the stony hearts without scolding.

I will sprinkle clean *water* upon you
to *cleanse* you from all your *impurities*,
and from all your *idols* I will *cleanse* you.
I will give you a *new heart* and place a *new spirit* within you,
taking from your bodies your *stony* hearts
and giving you *natural* hearts.
I will put my *spirit* within you and make you live by my *statutes*,
careful to observe my *decrees*.
You shall *live* in the land I gave your *fathers*;
you shall be *my people*, and I will be *your God*.

Pay attention to the words "my people" and "your God." Lovers always have the sense of belonging to each other. How wonderful to be claimed as God's own!

EPISTLE Romans 6:3–11

A reading from the Letter of Saint Paul to the Romans

The opening rhetorical question is always effective. Make the most of it.

Brothers and sisters:
Are you *unaware* that we who were *baptized* into Christ *Jesus*
were *baptized* into his *death*?
We were indeed *buried* with him through *baptism* into *death*,
so that, just as Christ was *raised* from the dead
by the glory of the *Father*,
we *too* might live in newness of *life*.

This is a difficult text. It follows its own logic (as Paul so often does) not in syllogistic form but by unfolding the basic premise that we have died and risen with Christ. Here are the implications of that fact. Proceed slowly and let Paul's meditation unfold.

For if we have grown into *union* with him
through a *death* like his,
we shall *also* be united with him in the *resurrection*.

them all up and shows us that the resurrection of Christ is the culmination of God's intervention in the world since its creation. It begins with a powerful rhetorical question: "It's not possible, is it," Paul asks, "that you don't understand the consequences of your baptism?" The question must be proclaimed so that the members of the assembly will spontaneously cry out in their hearts: "We do understand! Our old selves have died with Christ; our new selves have risen with him."

Thus begins a masterful comparison between baptism and death, and between Jesus' bodily resurrection and our spiritual resurrection. But it's more complex than that. Paul's argument is not tidy, nor was it meant to be. He draws together images of life, death, baptism, resurrection and sin in order to emerge with the clear conviction that baptism has transformed us, just as the resurrection has transformed Jesus.

We know by experience that in many ways we appear to be the same as we were before baptism. But the spiritual insight we must capture here is that, appearances notwithstanding, we are totally changed by baptism.

Baptism is union with Christ in his death and resurrection. It is a death to our old selves and a new life in Christ. Sin no longer has any power over us because Christ's death put an end to death, which is the ultimate consequence of sin. Obviously, a dead

We know that our *old* self was *crucified* with him,
so that our *sinful* body might be done *away* with,
that we might no *longer* be in slavery to *sin*.
For a *dead* person has been *absolved* from sin.
If, then, we have *died* with Christ,
we believe that we shall also *live* with him.

We know that *Christ*, *raised* from the dead, dies no *more*;
death no longer has *power* over him.
As to his *death*, he died to sin *once* and for *all*;
as to his *life*, he lives for *God*.

The last sentence is the practical consequence of all that precedes it. It tells us how to behave because of what we believe.

Consequently, you *too* must think of *yourselves*
as being *dead* to sin
and *living* for *God* in Christ *Jesus*.

GOSPEL Luke 24:1–12

A reading from the holy Gospel according to Luke

Be aware of the heightened solemnity of the moment as you begin. We've been waiting a long time to hear this good news!

At *daybreak* on the *first* day of the *week*
the *women* who had come from *Galilee* with Jesus
took the *spices* they had prepared
and went to the *tomb*.
They found the *stone* rolled *away* from the tomb;
but when they *entered*,
they did *not* find the *body* of the Lord *Jesus*.

In contrast to the fright of the women, the voice of the messengers is full of confidence, peace, and warmth. Their words must sound gentle and comforting.

While they were *puzzling* over this, *behold*,
two *men* in dazzling *garments appeared* to them.
They were *terrified* and bowed their *faces* to the *ground*.

person cannot sin. The dead are outside the power of sin. This is true of us as well because our union with Christ's death has killed that part of us that was subject to sin.

The bottom line, and the great good news, is that we are also united with Christ in his resurrection. The age-old promise of victory over death and sin has come to fruition in the paschal mystery we have gathered to celebrate this very night. "The power of this holy night dispels all evil, washes guilt away, restores lost innocence, brings mourners joy; it casts out hatred, brings us peace and humbles earthly pride."

GOSPEL **When the Easter Vigil is celebrated in all its fullness (all the readings, all the responses), the proclamation of the gospel will have an effect on us that is unmatched throughout the liturgical year. In the announcement of the resurrection, we hear the culmination of all that has gone before—every promise fulfilled, every believing heart gratified! The Easter gospel deserves nothing less than our finest effort.**

Luke makes it easy for us. Recall that Luke is the author of two accounts of the Christian saga: his gospel narrative and his record of the missionary efforts of the early church, the Acts of the Apostles. In them are two rhetorical questions posed by Luke that can serve as a poetic summary of all he wrote. Today we hear the messengers from God challenge the grieving women with the first question: "Why do you seek the living

They said to them,
"Why do you seek the *living* one among the *dead*?
He is not *here*, but he has been *raised*.
Remember what he *said* to you while he was still in *Galilee*,
that the Son of *Man* must be handed over to *sinners*
and be *crucified*, and *rise* on the third *day*."
And they *remembered* his words.

Pause after the messengers' words. The statement that the women then remembered Jesus' words should be isolated and given special emphasis.

Then they *returned* from the tomb
and *announced* all these things to the *eleven*
and to all the *others*.
The women were *Mary Magdalene*, *Joanna*,
and *Mary* the mother of *James*;
the *others* who *accompanied* them *also* told this
to the *apostles*,
but their *story* seemed like *nonsense*
and they did not *believe* them.

Indeed, who would not think such news nonsense—until they remembered Jesus' words!

But *Peter* got up and ran to the *tomb*,
bent *down*, and saw the *burial* cloths *alone*;
then he went home *amazed* at what had *happened*.

Peter's amazement is our own. He had been told by Jesus that death would have not power over him, but for Peter seeing is believing.

one among the dead?" On the Feast of the Ascension, forty days hence, we will hear a second question: "Men of Galilee, why do you stand looking up at the skies?"

Rhetorical questions call for no response; they work their effect by assuming that the hearers know the answer. The implied answer this morning is clear: "Your search for Jesus in a tomb is misguided. You will find no evidence of death's victory here, for God has raised him up—as promised—and the Kingdom he came to establish on earth is fully inaugurated." The messengers then go on to remind the women of Jesus' promise that all would take place in this way. Once reminded, they see for the first time what they could not possibly have seen or believed until this morning. Their experience is the prototype of every Christian's journey toward belief. Until we see the empty tomb, we cannot believe with the strength necessary for life's struggle. Until we are struck with the question, "Why look for the living among the dead?" we can expect only an intellectual faith, a kind of understanding and appreciation, but no real ardor.

The Ascension question, too, must be heard in all its power: "Why gaze upward in grief after the ascended Lord? Has he not promised that he will come again? Go now, and prepare the way for his return."

Ironically, what brings the Christian to full maturity—and full strength—are two experiences of emptiness: an empty tomb and an empty sky. They are two spaces once occupied by God in human form. Now they are mute assurances that every divine promise will be fulfilled.

EASTER SUNDAY

Lectionary #42

READING I Acts 10:34a, 37–43

A reading from the Acts of the Apostles

This reading is packed with information. It must be taken slowly, meditatively, and in a natural conversational tone. You are not Peter, but you are telling the story in his words.

Peter proceeded to *speak* and said:
"You *know* what has happened all over *Judea*,
beginning in *Galilee* after the *baptism*
that *John* preached,
how *God* anointed *Jesus* of *Nazareth*
with the Holy *Spirit* and *power*.
He went about doing *good*
and *healing* all those oppressed by the *devil*,
for *God* was with him.

Notice the "we" and "us," which give your proclamation immediacy and a kind of intimacy with the assembly.

"We are *witnesses* of all that he *did*
both in the country of the *Jews* and in *Jerusalem*.
They put him to *death* by hanging him on a *tree*.
This man God *raised* on the third day and granted
that he be *visible*,
not to *all* the people, but to *us*,
the witnesses *chosen* by God in *advance*,
who *ate* and *drank* with him after he *rose* from the *dead*.

The dramatic simplicity of the final sentence deserves special emphasis. The most important word, perhaps, is "everyone."

"He *commissioned* us to *preach* to the people
and *testify* that *he* is the one appointed by *God*
as *judge* of the *living* and the *dead*.
To *him* all the *prophets* bear *witness*,
that everyone who *believes* in him
will receive forgiveness of *sins* through his *name*."

READING I Today is the solemnity of solemnities, the greatest feast on the liturgical calendar. The paschal celebration peaked during last night's Vigil, and now we bask in the glory of the resurrected Lord for the 50-day season of Easter, which culminates in the celebration of the coming of the Holy Spirit on Pentecost. During the rest of the liturgical year, the first reading is taken from the Old Testament. But during Easter the first reading comes from the Acts of the Apostles, the wonderful account of the early Christian community's struggles and triumphs.

We begin today with Peter's summary of the life, work, death, and resurrection of Jesus. It is a reminder that Jesus is Lord and lives in our midst. The recurrent theme here is that Peter and the others who received their commission from the risen Lord were eyewitnesses of his glory. Of particular note is that they proclaim Christ to be the judge of the living and the dead. The concern about the "last days" and the end of time reminds us that the risen Christ is now with God the Father, having completed the work for which he was sent. The words of the creed take on a startling immediacy today: "He will come again in glory to judge the living and the dead."

Now we hear Peter teaching what Jesus said so often about himself during his earthly ministry: All the prophets have testified to the coming of the Messiah, and their expectations have been fulfilled in Jesus. Furthermore, although our sins brought Jesus to the cross, his suffering and death have healed us. What is the appropriate response to this good news? All that we have to do is believe in Christ crucified and risen.

READING II Colossians 3:1–4

A reading from the Letter of Saint Paul to the Colossians

Notice the elevating effect of this text. Encourage those in the assembly to raise their sights.

The contrast between being hidden and being revealed must be emphasized.

Brothers and sisters:
If then you were *raised* with Christ, *seek* what is *above,*
where Christ is *seated* at the right hand of *God.*
Think of what is *above,* not of what is on *earth.*
For you have *died,* and your life is *hidden* with Christ in *God.*
When Christ your life *appears,*
then you *too* will appear with him in *glory.*

Or:

READING II 1 Corinthians 5:6b–8

A reading from the first Letter of Saint Paul to the Corinthians

One image (yeast) controls this reading. Be sure you understand it (see the commentary) and enable the assembly to understand it. The shorter the reading, the more careful and deliberate the proclamation must be!

Brothers and sisters:
Do you not *know* that a little *yeast* leavens *all* the dough?
Clear out the *old* yeast,
so that you may become a *fresh* batch of dough,
inasmuch as you are *unleavened.*
For our paschal *lamb, Christ,* has been *sacrificed.*
Therefore, let us *celebrate* the feast,
not with the *old* yeast, the yeast of *malice* and *wickedness,*
but with the *unleavened* bread of *sincerity* and *truth.*

There is a choice of second readings today. Speak with the liturgy coordinator or the homilist to find out which reading will be used.

READING II **COLOSSIANS. Notice how brief some readings, such as this one, are. As complicated as it may sometimes seem, the good news of Jesus Christ can be summarized in a few words. It is the simplest of messages: Christ has died, Christ is risen, Christ will come again. Sometimes we need to remind ourselves how beautifully simple our faith can be.**

Paul's words make it clear that we are living an entirely new life as a result of our baptism, which we renew at today's Mass. When Paul says that our life is hidden now with Christ, he means there is more to come and that the work of salvation is not complete until the end of time. Scholars speak of "partially realized eschatology," a formidable phrase meaning that the reign of God is established on earth but has not yet reached perfection. Another way of putting it is "already, but not yet!" Christ's reign is already victorious, but it is not yet fully visible to us. It will no longer be hidden when Christ returns in glory. When he appears, we will also appear as we really are—completely transformed through the waters of baptism.

Living in faith is a matter of realizing who we really are in spite of who we sometimes seem to be. It is a matter of living out our true identity in Christ rather than the false identity of sinfulness. By faith we know that we are "already" raised up to eternal life with Christ. By setting our hearts

It is early Sunday morning; it is not the sabbath, the seventh day, the day of rest, but the first day of a new week. The Christian observance of Sunday rather than the Jewish sabbath begins here.

Mary presumes the body has been stolen, but the disciples see evidence to the contrary (see the commentary).

These details can be proclaimed in a tone of voice that offers them as evidence of the resurrection. That is their purpose. Experiment.

GOSPEL John 20:1–9

A reading from the holy Gospel according to John

On the *first* day of the *week*,
Mary of *Magdala* came to the *tomb* early in the *morning*,
while it was still *dark*,
and saw the *stone removed* from the tomb.
So she *ran* and went to Simon *Peter*
and to the *other* disciple whom Jesus *loved*, and *told* them,
"They have taken the *Lord* from the *tomb*,
and we don't know *where* they *put* him."

So *Peter* and the *other* disciple went *out* and came to the *tomb*.
They both *ran*, but the *other* disciple ran *faster* than Peter
and arrived at the tomb *first*;
he bent *down* and saw the *burial* cloths there, but did
not go *in*.

When Simon *Peter* arrived *after* him,
he went *into* the tomb and saw the *burial* cloths there,
and the cloth that had covered his *head*,
not with the *burial* cloths but rolled up in a separate *place*.
Then the *other* disciple *also* went in,
the one who had arrived at the tomb *first*,
and he *saw* and *believed*.
For they did not yet *understand* the Scripture
that he had to *rise* from the *dead*.

on this higher realm we can lessen the evidence that it has "not yet" appeared!

1 CORINTHIANS. Paul's words here were prompted by the presence in the Corinthian community of a person of evil influence. Paul is reminding the community that one bad apple can spoil the whole barrel. But he uses an image common in his day: yeast, which leavens all the dough. With its fermentation process, yeast is an effective simile for evil. It works its effect subtly but with obvious results.

When Paul refers to Christ as "our paschal lamb," unleavened bread immediately comes to mind. Unleavened bread (made without yeast) is still eaten at Jewish Passover meals, along with the Passover lamb, in memory of God's command to Israel to be ready for a speedy escape from Egypt. There was no time to wait for the dough to rise.

For all of us, in the context of the Easter celebration, the image reminds us of the need to restore our baptismal innocence. The overall effect of the reading is to make a good case for the need to purify ourselves of wickedness, restore our baptismal innocence, and lead renewed lives of simple sincerity and truthfulness.

The gospel from the Easter Vigil may be read at any Mass on Easter Sunday, at any time of the day. Luke 24:13–35 may be used at an afternoon or evening Mass.

GOSPEL Last night at the Vigil we heard Luke's account of the resurrection, or rather his description of events that followed the resurrection. The gospel

Lectionary #46

AFTERNOON GOSPEL Luke 24:13–35

A reading from the holy Gospel according to Luke

That very *day*, the *first* day of the *week*,
two of Jesus' *disciples* were going
to a *village* seven *miles* from Jerusalem called *Emmaus*,
and they were *conversing* about all the things
that had *occurred*.
And it *happened* that while they were *conversing* and *debating*,
Jesus *himself* drew near and *walked* with them,
but their *eyes* were *prevented* from *recognizing* him.

Emmaus = eh-MAY-uhs

He *asked* them,
"What are you *discussing* as you walk along?"
They *stopped*, looking *downcast*.
One of them, named *Cleopas*, said to him in *reply*,
"Are you the *only* visitor to *Jerusalem*
who does not *know* of the things
that have taken *place* there in these days?"

Proclaim this wonderful story with all the dignity and feeling you can. It deserves to be "heard again for the first time."

Cleopas = KLEE-oh-puhs

Note the dramatic effect Jesus' question has. They are incredulous.

And he replied to them, "What *sort* of things?"
They said to him,
"The things that happened to *Jesus* the *Nazarene*,
who was a *prophet mighty* in *deed* and *word*
before *God* and all the *people*,
how our chief *priests* and *rulers* both handed him *over*
to a sentence of *death* and *crucified* him.
But *we* were hoping that he would be the one to *redeem* Israel;
and *besides* all *this*,
it is now the *third day* since this took place.

There is much dialogue here with very little intervening text. Be sure it's clear when the speaker changes.

writers offer evidence of Jesus' resurrection, not proof of a scientific kind. Such proof was not available to them, nor is it to us. The overall purpose in the way John describes the scene is to testify to the disciples' response of faith when they saw the empty tomb. No further proof was necessary for him. The same is true of us. No amount of physical evidence can force us into believing. Faith is always a gift from God that we are free to accept or refuse.

John's account contains some unique features. For example, the race between John and Peter has John arriving at the tomb first. The meaning of this detail is more than an observation that John is the younger and swifter of the two. It is a statement about John's special position as "the disciple whom Jesus loved." The same point is made when John enters the empty tomb and makes his act of faith: "He saw and believed." This is the powerful testimony of an eyewitness who has the clarity of vision unique to those who love deeply and are likewise loved.

The almost tedious description of the burial cloth and the head cloth folded up neatly by itself offers evidence that the body of Jesus had not been stolen, as was feared by the authorities and presumed here by Mary. The scene is orderly rather than chaotic; the disorder one would expect to be left by grave robbers is absent. It corrects Mary's presumption and refutes any similar claim.

The passage includes an almost contradictory parenthetical remark by the writer. Immediately following John's profession of faith ("he saw and believed"), we are reminded that the disciples did not yet understand that Jesus had to rise from the

The disciples seem to move back and forth between high hopes and bitter disappointment.

Some *women* from our group, however, have *astounded* us:
they were at the *tomb* early in the *morning*
and did not find his *body*;
they came *back* and reported
that they had indeed seen a *vision* of *angels*
who announced that he was *alive*.

"Then some of those *with* us went to the tomb
and *found* things just as the women had *described*,
but *him* they did not *see*."

Let there be no hint of rebuke in Jesus' words here. Clearly the disciples take no offense.

And he said to them, "Oh, how *foolish* you are!
How *slow* of heart to *believe* all that the prophets *spoke*!
Was it not *necessary* that the Christ should *suffer* these things
and enter into his *glory*?"

The word is opened.

Then beginning with *Moses* and all the *prophets*,
he *interpreted* to them what *referred* to him
in all the *Scriptures*.
As they approached the *village* to which they were *going*,
he gave the impression that he was going on *farther*.
But they *urged* him, "*Stay* with us,
for it is nearly *evening* and the day is almost *over*."
So he went in to *stay* with them.

The bread is broken.

And it *happened* that, while he was with them at *table*,
he took *bread*, said the *blessing*,
broke it, and *gave* it to them.

The disciples recognize the Lord.

With *that* their eyes were *opened* and they *recognized* him,
but he *vanished* from their *sight*.

dead. Notice that what they did not understand was the *scripture* testifying to the resurrection. This they will understand only when the risen Lord appears to them, opens their minds to the scripture's meaning, and then ascends to resume his place in glory at the Father's side.

The process implied here reflects our own religious experience during the 50 days of Easter. We also have our understanding stretched and fleshed out by the risen Lord's teaching before he ascends to the Father and sends the Holy Spirit to teach all of us the truth.

AFTERNOON GOSPEL **Whenever you have the opportunity to proclaim a gospel narrative from Luke, consider yourself empowered in a special way. Well proclaimed, Luke can stir faith to new heights. He tells his stories with such warmth and immediacy that many of the events in Jesus' life are remembered in Luke's version above that of the other gospel writers. This is one of his most memorable and poignant narratives. Before the reform of the lectionary mandated by the Second Vatican Council, the day on which this gospel was read was called "Emmaus Day." (By the way, it is pronounced "eh-MAY-us," "not EE-mouse"!)**

The story of the disciples on the road to Emmaus is filled with the kind of vivid detail and human emotion that make the story both moving and unforgettable. The scene is tranquil, even sad, as the disciples make their way along the seven-mile journey, discussing the tragic result of their hope that Jesus would be the Messiah to set Israel free. But they are also marveling at news of a resurrection brought to them by some of their group.

Then they *said* to each other,
"Were not our *hearts burning* within us
while he *spoke* to us on the way and opened the *Scriptures* to us?"

So they set out at *once* and returned to *Jerusalem*
where they found gathered *together*
the *eleven* and those with them who were saying,
"The Lord has *truly* been *raised* and has *appeared* to *Simon*!"

Then the two *recounted*
what had taken place on the *way*
and how he was made *known* to them in the *breaking* of *bread*.

We do not know precisely why they do not recognize Jesus when he joins them on their trek, but, as is customary for this gospel, the author is probably saving the recognition until the trio breaks bread together. Luke could also be saying that none of us can recognize Jesus unless we look with the eyes of faith and listen with the heart. In any event, the disciples are stopped in their tracks by Jesus' feigned ignorance of the events they are discussing. "What things?" he asks, setting the scene for the gratifying and gentle revelation.

We may be startled by what sounds like a rebuke on the lips of Jesus: "Oh, how foolish you are!" But there is no need for this to sound reproachful. After all, Jesus has strung them along to prepare for this moment. When you read his words, imagine him reaching out to place his hand on the arm of his companions and shaking his head in mock scorn. There is no dignity lost in such an image, and the words take on the sound of an encouraging teacher nudging a young student toward deeper insight.

Finally, notice what leads up to the disciples' recognition of Jesus and the meaning of his explanation. It is not until after the scriptures have been opened and the bread broken that they see him for who he is. In what other context do we gather to open the scriptures and break bread together? Luke has provided us with the essentials of a Christian eucharistic liturgy, as he so often does in the gospel. When word and action are joined, the eyes of the disciples are opened, and they recognize Jesus. And they respond to this recognition in the only way a Christian can: They rush out to share the good news.

2ND SUNDAY OF EASTER

Lectionary #45

READING I Acts 5:12–16

A reading from the Acts of the Apostles

Many *signs* and *wonders* were done among the people
at the hands of the *apostles.*
They were all *together* in Solomon's *portico.*
None of the *others* dared to *join* them, but the *people*
esteemed them.

Yet more than *ever,* believers in the *Lord,*
great *numbers* of men and women, were *added* to them.
Thus they even carried the *sick* out into the *streets*
and laid them on *cots* and *mats*
so that when *Peter* came by,
at least his *shadow* might fall on one or another of them.

A large number of people from the towns
in the vicinity of *Jerusalem also* gathered,
bringing the *sick* and those disturbed by unclean *spirits,*
and they were *all cured.*

Solomon's portico: a special gathering place. Jesus had taught there.

See the commentary on this cryptic line, why others dared not join them.

You can marvel at the faith exhibited here.

The ending is joyful, even amazing!

READING I For the seven Sundays of the Easter season, the first reading—usually taken from the Old Testament—is a selection from the Acts of the Apostles, giving us an extended view of the risen Christ moving among the early believers. During Year C, when we take the gospel readings from Luke, we have a special situation: Luke wrote both the gospel and Acts. Scripture scholars have shown us that each book is most profitably read in light of the other. Many of the themes we have heard in Luke's gospel so far this year will be heard in Acts as well. During Eastertime, the gospel readings are from John, but when Ordinary Time arrives again, we will return to Luke.

* * * * *

In the brilliance of the resurrection, the apostles' missionary effort bears fruit in thrilling ways. They enjoy the esteem of the people and their leadership is recognized. More dramatically, their faith enables them to minister the Lord's healing love in the very "signs and wonders" he had promised would accompany their work. The church is growing as the Lord adds more and more to its number.

This selection has one difficult passage: "None of the others dared to join them, but the people esteemed them." The difficulty is resolved by context. Just before this passage is the terrifying story of a man and his wife who make a gift to the new church—but lie to the apostles in the process. They say they are giving all the proceeds from the sale of a piece of land, but they have held some of the money back. They were free to give or not to give, Peter

READING II Revelation 1:9–11a, 12–13, 17–19

A reading from the Book of Revelation

The opening sentence is long and complex. The sentence demands careful delivery and vocal variety that signals the subordinate elements.

I, *John*, your *brother*, who *share* with you
the *distress*, the *kingdom*, and the *endurance* we have
in *Jesus*,
found myself on the *island* called *Patmos*
because I proclaimed God's *word* and gave *testimony* to Jesus.

Here the narrative begins. You are narrating a vision!

I was caught up in *spirit* on the *Lord's* day
and heard *behind* me a *voice* as loud as a *trumpet*, which said,
"Write on a *scroll* what you *see*."

"Son of man" here means simply "in human form," but also recalls the heavenly visions in the book of Daniel in the Hebrew scriptures.

Then I turned to see *whose* voice it *was* that spoke to me,
and *when* I turned, I saw seven gold *lampstands*
and in the *midst* of the lampstands one like a son of *man*,
wearing an ankle-length *robe*, with a gold *sash*
around his *chest*.

The tone of the long quotation is solemn and peaceful, mighty but serene.

"I was dead, but now I live," clearly identifies the Risen Christ.

When I caught *sight* of him, I fell down at his *feet* as though *dead*.
He *touched* me with his right *hand* and said, "Do *not* be afraid.
I am the *first* and the *last*, the one who *lives*.
Once I was *dead*, but now I am *alive* forever and *ever*.
I hold the keys to death and the *netherworld*.
Write *down*, therefore, what you have *seen*,
and what is *happening*, and what *will* happen *afterwards*."

points out, but they sinned grievously in misrepresenting their gift. They have lied to the Holy Spirit. As a result, they fall down dead on the spot. Peter's prescience and the general aura of God's presence explains why "none of the others dared to join them." As reader you cannot supply this context, but perhaps your tone can convey with such expressions as "signs and wonders" something of the awe that permeates this text.

READING II The second reading is filled with even more reverential awe than the first. Here we see a vision of the resurrected Christ in glory revealing to John messages for the Christian communities. Though we tend to separate the Christ we see in the book of Revelation from the Christ we see in his post-resurrection appearances on earth, it is the same risen Lord. In fact, there are those who hold that the appearances in the book of Revelation are a continuation of the appearances immediately after the resurrection.

One of the most striking things about this text is the juxtaposition of John's situation (exiled and under persecution) with the heavenly glory of the vision he sees. It seems so often to be the case throughout Christian history that the clearest visions, the most startling revelations, come to those who are suffering for their faith. We have all heard that the church seems to thrive and grow most when it is being persecuted. But why does this surprise us? Surely we see in this the pattern set for us by Jesus himself. At the moment when his persecutors seemed most to triumph, Jesus accomplished the salvation of the world.

All the imagery of this text recalls similar scenes in Hebrew literature, especially

GOSPEL John 20:19–31

A reading from the holy Gospel according to John

This is an amazing story. Proclaim it with joy and wonder.

On the evening of that *first* day of the *week*,
when the *doors* were locked, where the *disciples* were,
for fear of the *Jews*,
Jesus came and stood in their *midst*
and said to them, "*Peace* be with you."

Emphasize the word "peace" (not "with") each time Jesus says "Peace be with you."

When he had *said* this, he showed them his *hands* and his *side*.
The disciples *rejoiced* when they saw the Lord.

Jesus said to them *again*, "*Peace* be with you.
As the *Father* has sent *me*, so *I* send *you*."

And when he had said this, he *breathed* on them and said to them,
"Receive the Holy *Spirit*.
Whose *sins* you forgive are *forgiven* them,
and whose sins you *retain* are *retained*."

The power to forgive sins is conferred almost casually.

Pause before the new section begins. Into this scene of wonder and joy is introduced the struggle involved in believing. "Didymus" means "twin."

Thomas, called *Didymus*, one of the *Twelve*,
was not *with* them when Jesus came.
So the *other* disciples said to him, "We have seen the *Lord*."
But he said to them,
"Unless I see the mark of the *nails* in his *hands*
and put my *finger* into the *nailmarks*
and put my *hand* into his *side*, I will not *believe*."

Now a week *later* his disciples were *again* inside
and Thomas was *with* them.
Jesus *came*, although the *doors* were locked,
and stood in their *midst* and said, "*Peace* be with you."

the book of Daniel. The seven lamp stands symbolize the seven churches—which are about to receive special messages. The long robe and the gold sash (and other imagery omitted from the passage) emphasize the divine nature of the one who speaks. The passage must be proclaimed with a sensitive ear for its poetic elements.

GOSPEL **This wonderful gospel story is such a favorite that it is read on this Sunday in all three years of the lectionary cycle (A, B, and C). It records the first post-resurrection appearance of Jesus and provides us with an archetypal experience of doubt, struggle, and final assent in faith. It is every Christian's experience: to believe without having seen.**

We are presented with a conflict-filled situation that is resolved. In fact, we have a story within a story here: the appearance of Jesus to encourage the fearful disciples, and the resolution of Thomas' doubts. Thomas believes only when he hears the Lord's call to belief. It is not so much his eyes as his ears that call him to faith. For all but a few of the earliest Christians, faith comes through hearing.

Paint the scene for your hearers so they get a clear, fresh picture of the situation. We are about to witness the first public appearance of Jesus since the resurrection and the bestowing of the Holy Spirit on the apostles. It is a thrilling experience.

Thomas is often made to sound like a stubborn unbeliever (by hitting the word "not" too hard: "I will *not* believe!"). But Thomas' problem is doubt—as the phrase

Then he said to *Thomas*, "Put your finger *here* and *see* my hands,
and bring your *hand* and put it into my *side*,
and do not be *unbelieving*, but *believe*."

And now the climax! Thomas' act of faith ("My Lord and my God!") is the victory cry of anyone who has doubted.

Thomas *answered* and said to him, "My *Lord* and my *God*!"

Jesus said to him, "Have you come to believe
because you have *seen* me?

There is no hint of rebuke here.

Blessed are those who have *not* seen and have *believed*."

The last two sentences are commentary on what has happened. A pause and a change of tone should communicate this.

Now Jesus did many *other* signs in the presence of his disciples
that are not *written* in this *book*.
But *these* are written that you may come to *believe*
that *Jesus* is the *Christ*, the Son of *God*,
and that through this *belief* you may have *life* in his *name*.

"doubting Thomas" makes clear. Read this passage with more emphasis on "believe"—implying "I want to, but I *can't* believe without some physical evidence."

"I'll never *believe* it without . . ."

When Jesus appears again a week later, Thomas gets the evidence he needs. There is no sense of rebuke in Jesus' reply to Thomas' affirmation of faith. Rather, the reply is for all succeeding generations of Christians (like the ones you are reading to!) who are challenged to believe without having seen.

The final paragraph is a tag—John's application of this story to our lives. The tone changes to that of commentator rather than narrator. Here again, direct address is used: "that *you* may come to believe . . ." and "*you* may have life . . ."

3RD SUNDAY OF EASTER

Lectionary #48

READING I Acts 5:27b–32, 40b–41

A reading from the Acts of the Apostles

Sanhedrin = san-HEE-druhn

The interrogation scene gives Peter an opportunity to review fundamental Christian belief.

When the *captain* and the court *officers* had brought
the *apostles* in
and made them stand before the *Sanhedrin,*
the *high* priest *questioned* them,
"We gave you strict *orders,* did we not,
to stop *teaching* in that *name?*
Yet you have filled *Jerusalem* with your teaching
and want to bring this man's *blood* upon us."

Pause before continuing; now comes the substance of the reading.

But *Peter* and the *apostles* said in reply,
"We must obey *God* rather than *men.*
The God of our ancestors *raised* Jesus,
though you had him *killed* by hanging him on a *tree.*
God *exalted* him at his right *hand* as *leader* and *savior*
to grant *Israel repentance* and forgiveness of *sins.*
We are *witnesses* of these things,
as is the Holy *Spirit* whom God has *given* to those who
obey him."

The resolution is striking. The apostles are not relieved that they got off with a rebuke; no, they are rejoicing for the privilege of suffering for Christ's name.

The *Sanhedrin* ordered the apostles
to *stop* speaking in the name of Jesus, and *dismissed* them.
So they *left* the presence of the Sanhedrin,
rejoicing that they had been found *worthy*
to suffer *dishonor* for the sake of the *name.*

READING I No doubt about it—without the point of view offered by faith, we Christians are an odd lot! Take the final sentence of this reading, for example. The apostles are full of joy at suffering dishonor for the sake of Jesus. Only faith can understand such a response to persecution. Only strong belief and a clear view of the difference between obedience to God and obedience to human authority brings such confidence. And the joy we feel when we identify with the suffering of the world is not the kind of joy the world gives us.

Peter's response to the high priest's reprimand is the Luke's way of giving us another glimpse into the earliest Christian convictions about Jesus. Notice how tightly packed Peter's words are with the elements of Christian belief: "the God of our ancestors [Abraham, Isaac, Jacob] raised Jesus"—so we see continuity with Israel's past. "Though you had him killed"—God's word and will are inexorable. "God exalted him"—the promised Messiah, come to grant redemption. The Holy Spirit is witness to these things—assuring the proclamation of this good news in all times until the end of the world.

This brief reading contains a thumbnail sketch of the plan and purpose of Jesus' sojourn on earth and his return to God in glory. Why the strong objections from the Sanhedrin? Because the apostles are preaching a message that runs counter to expectations. It is not easy to hear that God's ways are not our own. And yet we must always be open to new understanding, for the Spirit that witnessed to the events that Peter related is still witnessing today. Jesus is

READING II Revelation 5:11–14

A reading from the Book of Revelation

The exalted vision deserves exalted prose.

I, *John*, looked and heard the voices of many *angels*
who surrounded the *throne*
and the living *creatures* and the *elders*.

The "loud voice" belongs to the living creatures and elders, not to you, the reader. Proclamation is not re-enactment, not literal interpretation.

They were *countless* in number, and they cried out
in a loud *voice*:
"*Worthy* is the *Lamb* that was *slain*
to receive *power* and *riches*, *wisdom* and *strength*,
honor and *glory* and *blessing*."

Then I heard every creature in *heaven* and on *earth*
and *under* the earth and in the *sea*,
everything in the *universe*, cry out:

Let your voice be big and broad and noble. Volume is less important (though you must be heard clearly) than pitch and vocal variety.

"To the one who sits on the *throne* and to the *Lamb*
be *blessing* and *honor*, *glory* and *might*,
forever and *ever*."
The four living *creatures* answered, "*Amen*,"
and the *elders* fell down and *worshiped*.

GOSPEL John 21:1–19

A reading from the holy Gospel according to John

The narrative has four major sections: the opening scene, the appearance of Jesus, the breakfast meal, and the dialogue with Peter. Be sure to signal the divisions with appropriate pauses.
Didymus = DID-ee-muhs
Nathanael = nuh-THAN-ee-uhl
Zebedee's = ZEB-uh-deez

At that time, Jesus *revealed* himself *again* to his *disciples*
at the Sea of *Tiberias*.
He revealed himself in this *way*.
Together were Simon *Peter*, *Thomas* called Didymus,
Nathanael from Cana in Galilee,
Zebedee's sons, and two *others* of his disciples.

alive and active in our midst. Old expectations must be open to scrutiny—and the possibility of new and wonderful insights in our own time.

READING II John's visions of the heavenly court fill the Sundays of Easter (in Year C) with a sense of exaltation and triumph that contrasts with the severity of the Sundays of Lent. His view of the "Lamb that was slain" (Jesus) is that of the Lamb "Worthy to receive power and riches, honor and glory." The overall theme here is reflected in the words of a hymn sung frequently during Eastertime: "The strife is o'er, the victory won." It is intended to be an encouragement for all who remain faithful, for one day our strife will be over and we will have won the victory.

It may be that we have here a glimpse of part of the earliest Christian liturgy. The shouts of praise certainly are heard in every modern liturgy in the preface of the eucharistic prayer and in the "Holy, holy, holy." And we call out to the "Lamb of God" in every liturgy as well. Jesus the paschal lamb is the central character in John's vision as he is in every celebration of the eucharist. He is the Lamb that was slain but rose from the dead and now receives the praise of all living creatures.

Though the language in this reading is exalted, and the images are awesome, the scene is very like the one witnessed in every worshiping congregation today. Though our worship may be more subdued than what John describes here, the shouts of praise in our hearts and on our lips are no less fervent.

GOSPEL There are four major things to consider in this gospel

Close the first section quietly. Begin the second section with intensity. The word "children" may strike you as odd. It is a word used frequently by John and is full of tenderness as well as authority.

Simon *Peter* said to them, "I am going *fishing*."
They said to him, "We also will come *with* you."
So they went *out* and got into the *boat*,
but that night they caught *nothing*.

When it was already *dawn*, *Jesus* was standing on the *shore*;
but the disciples did not *realize* that it was Jesus.
Jesus said to them, "*Children*, have you *caught* anything to *eat*?"
They answered him, "*No*."
So he said to them, "Cast the net over the *right* side of the boat
and you will *find* something."
So they *cast* it, and were not able to pull it *in*
because of the number of *fish*.

"It is the Lord!" is the climax, a sudden and striking revelation. It changes the color of the remainder of the reading.

So the disciple whom Jesus *loved* said to Peter, "It is the *Lord*."
When Simon Peter heard that it was the *Lord*,
he tucked in his *garment*, for he was *lightly* clad,
and *jumped* into the *sea*.
The *other* disciples came in the *boat*,
for they were not far from *shore*, only about a hundred *yards*,
dragging the *net* with the *fish*.

The third section begins here. Pause, then begin with fresh intonation.

When they climbed out on *shore*,
they saw a charcoal *fire* with *fish* on it and *bread*.
Jesus said to them, "Bring some of the *fish* you just caught."
So Simon *Peter* went over and dragged the net *ashore*
full of one *hundred fifty-three* large *fish*.
Even though there were so *many*, the *net* was not *torn*.
Jesus said to them, "*Come*, have *breakfast*."
And none of the disciples dared to *ask* him, "Who *are* you?"
because they *realized* it was the *Lord*.
Jesus came over and took the *bread* and *gave* it to them,
and in like *manner* the *fish*.

The echoes of eucharist are very clear in these words. And the final sentence in this section reaffirms the realness of the resurrected Jesus.

story: the appearance of Jesus, the large catch of fish, the meal shared with the risen Lord, and the poignant dialogue between Jesus and Peter.

It seems clear that this final section of John's gospel was a later addition. It brings together a number of separate occurrences and interprets them—one in the light of the other. The narrative begins calmly, with a hint of bleakness. Peter's decision to go fishing has a feeling of resignation about it—hinting at the depression he and the disciples must have experienced after the death of Jesus. Note, too, that Peter is returning to his old profession. It is necessary, then, for the Lord to remind Peter that he has been commissioned to fish for men and women—members of the newly inaugurated reign of God!

The appearance of Jesus is shrouded in mystery, the familiar atmosphere of "not knowing who he was" that we see so often in the gospels, especially in Mark. The experience of surprised recognition is very much a part of everyone's faith.

Also, the appearance takes place in the context of the extraordinary, the "miraculous draught of fishes," as it was named for many years. The Lord's presence turns a failing fishing expedition into an especially successful one. John goes so far as to number the catch, and although we do not know the precise symbolic meaning of this number, it likely refers to the future missionary work of the apostles and its universal character. "The net was not torn"—that is, the Christian community will not be divided, despite the great number and variety of the catch.

It is the beloved disciple who recognizes the Lord first. Clearly, love has its own kind of vision, more acute than mere human

This was now the *third* time Jesus was revealed to his disciples after being *raised* from the *dead*.

When they had finished *breakfast*, Jesus said to Simon *Peter*, "*Simon*, son of *John*, do you *love* me more than *these*?"

The formulaic nature of this dialogue (three questions, three responses) must not be avoided. The more familiar the formula the more delight we take in hearing it again.

Simon Peter *answered* him, "*Yes*, Lord, you *know* that I love you."
Jesus said to him, "*Feed* my *lambs*."

He then said to Simon Peter a *second* time, "*Simon*, son of *John*, do you *love* me?"
Simon Peter answered him, "*Yes*, Lord, you *know* that I love you."
Jesus said to him, "Tend my *sheep*."

Jesus said to him the *third* time, "*Simon*, son of *John*, do you *love* me?"

Peter's pain here is deeply moving. But Jesus does not doubt Peter's love; he is showing Peter just how much the shepherd must love in order to tend the flock.

Peter was *distressed* that Jesus had said to him a *third* time, "Do you *love* me?" and he said to him, "Lord, you know *everything*; you *know* that I love you."
Jesus said to him, "*Feed* my *sheep*.

Jesus employs an old proverb here and applies it to Peter in a special way. Old age brings helplessness. Peter's martyrdom will bring a special kind of helplessness. The words "Follow me" hint that Peter's death will come about in much the same way as the death of Jesus.

"*Amen, amen*, I say to you, when you were *younger*,
you used to dress *yourself* and go where you *wanted*;
but when you grow *old*, you will stretch out your *hands*,
and someone *else* will dress you
and *lead* you where you do *not* want to go."
He said this signifying by what kind of *death* he would glorify *God*.
And when he had said this, he said to him, "*Follow* me."

[Shorter: John 21:1–14]

understanding. And it is Love who sets the meal alluding to the eucharistic: "Jesus took the bread and gave it to them." The apostles know it is the Lord in the context of this meal. They recognize him in the breaking of the bread—just as we do at every eucharistic celebration.

The second part of the reading is a commission, and a poignant one at that! Peter's threefold denial of Jesus during the trial and crucifixion is not canceled out by the threefold declaration of love. And each declaration is followed by a command to do what true love compels us to do: "Feed my sheep." Peter's distress is understandable. It is not easy to have one's declaration of love challenged. But every Christian knows full well that genuine love is put to the test over and over again.

Finally, the description of Peter's death. Before betraying his Lord through denial, Peter had protested his fidelity at the Last Supper: "I will lay down my life for you." Ironically, he was predicting his own martyrdom, but from the perspective of a one who has not yet been tested and known failure. Indeed, Peter does lay down his life for the Lord, but in a way far different from what he expected in the full flush of over-confidence. The proverbial saying about the helplessness of old age is adapted by Jesus to show that Peter will be martyred. And the final words, "Follow me," have a striking impact in the light of early tradition that Peter was crucified.

4TH SUNDAY OF EASTER

Lectionary #51

READING I Acts 13:14, 43–52

A reading from the Acts of the Apostles

Perga = PER-guh
Antioch = AN-tee-ahk
Pisidia = pih-SID-ee-uh

Paul and *Barnabas* continued on from *Perga*
and reached *Antioch* in *Pisidia*.
On the *sabbath* they entered the *synagogue* and took their *seats*.

Many *Jews* and worshipers who were *converts* to Judaism
followed Paul and Barnabas, who *spoke* to them
and *urged* them to remain *faithful* to the grace of *God*.

On the *following* sabbath almost the whole *city* gathered
to hear the word of the Lord.

Notice the contrast. One week earlier, Paul and Barnabas got a positive reception. Now the situation is quite different.

When the Jews *saw* the crowds, they were filled with *jealousy*
and with violent *abuse contradicted* what Paul *said*.

Harsh words. Paul's tone, however, seems matter-of-fact. The rejection of the word by some leads to acceptance of it by others: Both are part of God's plan.

Both Paul and Barnabas spoke out *boldly* and said,
"It was *necessary* that the word of God be spoken to you *first*,
but since you *reject* it
and *condemn* yourselves as *unworthy* of eternal *life*,
we *now* turn to the *Gentiles*.
For so the *Lord* has *commanded* us,
I have *made* you a *light* to the *Gentiles*,
that you may be an *instrument* of *salvation*
to the ends of the *earth*."

The *Gentiles* were *delighted* when they heard this
and *glorified* the word of the Lord.

READING I In both of Luke's works, the gospel and Acts, we see heavy emphasis on the universal mission of Christianity—that is, the goal to bring the good news of Jesus to the Gentiles. It is difficult for us to realize just how amazing such a mission was. To think that the God of the Hebrews would now reach beyond the chosen people and embrace the Gentiles—which means all non-Jews—would be difficult for Luke's contemporaries. The idea was not entirely unknown in the pre-Christian era, but it now emerges with startling clarity. The dark side of the idea is explicitly stated in today's first reading: The Jews have rejected the word of God, so now it is offered to the Gentiles.

An overly simple understanding of texts such as these is common. The point to be made (by Paul, by you, and by the homilist) is not that those who reject the word of God are condemned. The point is that the word *must* be preached throughout the world, and it *will* take root and bear fruit among all who receive it. Those who reject the word, whether Jew or Gentile, will never be able to keep it from going forth to the farthest reaches of the earth. The will of God guarantees that nothing will prevent the good news from being offered to the entire world. That's the point of this reading. And it is a point made often throughout the missionary activity recorded in the Acts of the Apostles.

A secondary point is clearly made in the last third of the reading. There will always be resistance to the spread of the word. There will always be those who refuse to accept the good news. They can not be coerced. History is replete with mistaken notions about forced conversions, but the paradoxical truth remains the same.

Here's the main point: "The word of the Lord continued to spread."

All who were destined for eternal *life* came to *believe*,
and the word of the Lord continued to *spread*
through the whole *region*.
The *Jews*, however, incited the women of *prominence*
who were *worshipers*
and the leading *men* of the city,

Here's the other side of the coin: "[They] stirred up a persecution."

stirred up a *persecution* against Paul and Barnabas,
and *expelled* them from their *territory*.
So they shook the *dust* from their feet in *protest* against them,
and went to *Iconium*.
The *disciples* were filled with *joy* and the Holy *Spirit*.

READING II Revelation 7:9, 14b–17

A reading from the Book of Revelation

The visionary's tone is exultant yet solemn.

I, *John*, had a *vision* of a great *multitude*,
which *no* one could *count*,
from every *nation*, *race*, *people* and *tongue*.
They stood before the *throne* and before the *Lamb*,
wearing white *robes* and holding *palm* branches
in their hands.
Then one of the *elders* said to me,

The elder explains, and the explanation is both promise and fulfilled promise. The proclamation here is stronger because more clearly poetic.

"*These* are the ones who have *survived* the time
of great *distress*;
they have washed their *robes*
and made them *white* in the *blood* of the *Lamb*.
"For this *reason* they stand before God's *throne*
and *worship* him day and *night* in his *temple*.

Nothing can force men and women to accept the good news. And nothing can stop the good news from being accepted by men and women who freely choose to believe.

READING II There is great comfort and joy in this scripture passage. It records a vision of the evidence that those who endure the trials and sufferings that inevitably afflict the faithful will one day know the triumph of their faith. Notice that these words continue a central theme in the first reading and the implicit promise in Jesus' words in the gospel.

In contemporary Christianity, the sense that persecution is inevitable and suffering for the faith is integral to the Christian experience may not be easy to appreciate. It is safe to say that the vast majority of us who read this commentary do not experience obvious threats to the practice of our religion. The zealot may say that this is because we do not practice our religion with sufficient radical dynamism. "If we were truly Christian, the world would persecute us." There is a grain of truth in this position.

However, the distinction between faith and religion can go a long way to place such a debate in perspective. That part of us where genuine faith resides is always something of a battleground. Believing completely in Jesus and the values of the reign of God immediately puts us at odds with many values of the world in which we live. We may be blessed with guarantees that we can practice our *religion* without interference. But we are mistaken if we believe that sincere practice of our *faith* will go unchallenged.

The one who sits on the *throne* will *shelter* them.
They will not *hunger* or *thirst* anymore,
nor will the *sun* or any *heat strike* them.
For the Lamb who is in the *center* of the throne
will *shepherd* them
and *lead* them to springs of life-giving *water*,
and God will wipe *away* every *tear* from their *eyes*."

It is the presence of the Lamb (the Risen Christ) that guarantees assurance and the end of tears.

GOSPEL John 10:27–30

A reading from the holy Gospel according to John

Jesus said:
"*My* sheep *hear* my *voice*;
I *know* them, and they *follow* me.
I give them eternal *life*, and they shall never *perish*.
No one can take them out of my *hand*.
My *Father*, who has *given* them to me, is greater than *all*,
and *no* one can take them out of the *Father's* hand.
The Father and I are *one*."

This brief reading is entirely in Jesus' words. Realize how powerful this text is because of the use of first-person pronouns (I, my, me). Allow yourself to communicate both the intimacy and the majesty.

Pause before the final brief line. It is the ultimate statement of love.

Therefore, since we can be certain that struggle will be part of our faith experience, we need the comfort of the promise: "God will wipe away every tear from their eyes."

GOSPEL Jesus the Good Shepherd relies on one of his favorite metaphors to assure us that we can place our confidence in him. During the season of Easter, these words ring out with special emphasis. Though spoken by Jesus during his earthly life, this promise of our solidarity with him and the Father now has the stamp of the resurrection upon it.

The unity of the Father and the Son referred to here is an assertion that Jesus is in perfect accord with the Father's will to save us. And the foundation of that oneness is love. Jesus is saying that he and the Father are in perfect loving harmony. The statement is not about Jesus' identity, but about his relationship with the Father. He loves the Father. The Father loves him. And the demonstration of that oneness in love is Jesus' obedience. In perfect loving obedience to God's will, Jesus has not only *shown* us the way to salvation; he has also *become* the way of salvation.

Finally, notice that Jesus' promise continues an idea found in all of today's readings. In assuring us that "no one can take [us] out of the Father's hand," he implies that there will be those who will try to do so. In promising that "[we] will never perish," Jesus implies that without the gift of eternal life that he brought to us, we would be in danger of perishing. For the Christian, faith and struggle are inextricably interwoven into the fabric of life.

5TH SUNDAY OF EASTER

Lectionary #54

READING I Acts 14:21–27

A reading from the Acts of the Apostles

Barnabas = BAHR-nuh-bus
Derbe = DER-bee
Lystra = LĪS-truh
Iconium = ī-KOH-nee-uhm
Antioch = AN-tee-ahk

It is very important that you master these (and all) pronunciations—not so much for correctness as to avoid distracting stumbling and struggling. Strange scriptural names are a problem for the assembly only when they seem to be problematic for the reader.

After *Paul* and *Barnabas* had proclaimed the good *news*
to that city
and made a *considerable* number of *disciples*,
they returned to *Lystra* and to *Iconium* and to *Antioch*.
They strengthened the *spirits* of the *disciples*
and *exhorted* them to *persevere* in the *faith*, saying,
"It is *necessary* for us to undergo many *hardships*
to enter the kingdom of *God*."
They appointed *elders* for them in each *church* and,
with *prayer* and *fasting*, *commended* them to the *Lord*
in whom they had put their *faith*.

The geographical information is context for important articles of belief. Do not be tempted to toss off what appears to be merely factual information.
Pisidia = pih-SID-ee-uh
Pamphylia = pam-FIL-ee-uh
Perga = PER-guh
Attalia = uh-TAHL-ee-uh

God has accomplished these wonders!

Then they traveled through *Pisidia* and reached *Pamphylia*.
After proclaiming the word at *Perga* they went down to *Attalia*.
From *there* they sailed to *Antioch*,
where they had been *commended* to the grace of *God*
for the *work* they had now *accomplished*.

And when they *arrived*, they called the church *together*
and *reported* what God had *done* with them
and how he had opened the door of *faith* to the *Gentiles*.

READING I There is a great deal of history in this reading. It gives us geographical information about the travels of Paul and Barnabas, and it describes their appointment of overseers in the new Christian communities. It also includes a brief bit of catechism and testimony to the activity of God in their ministry.

The challenge here is to proclaim the reading for what it truly is: not a history lesson, but evidence that the church is growing and that God's word is having its promised effect. The Christian communities are becoming more and more established in the faith of Jesus and confirmed in the spirit of the apostolic preaching.

The final sentence contains a pure act of faith. Paul and Barnabas gather the community to proclaim to them that it is God who is responsible for their successes, and it is God who has opened the door of faith to the Gentiles. What an inspiration for men and women who work in the Christian ministry (including readers)! Their efforts are a channel through which God's loving plan of salvation is brought to fulfillment—and to God belongs all the glory.

When the writers of sacred scripture chronicle events, there is always a larger purpose than history in their words. The events of *salvation* history always include a touch of eternity.

READING II The richness of this brief reading is not immediately apparent. If we read it as a vision of the world to come, we can appreciate the promise of a future where all that our faith teaches us about God's love has been fulfilled. In a way, it sounds like our modern

READING II Revelation 21:1–5a

Bring out the contrast strongly between the new heaven and earth and what has passed away.

Let the "bride/husband" imagery ring fresh.

"Behold!" This is the new reality: God's home is in our midst!

A triumphant conclusion! Nothing will ever be the same.

A reading from the Book of Revelation

Then I, *John*, saw a *new* heaven and a *new* earth.
The *former* heaven and the *former* earth had passed *away*,
and the *sea* was no *more*.

I also saw the holy *city*, a *new* Jerusalem,
coming down out of *heaven* from *God*,
prepared as a *bride* adorned for her *husband*.

I heard a loud *voice* from the *throne* saying,
"*Behold*, God's *dwelling* is with the human *race*.
He will *dwell* with them and they will be his *people*
and God *himself* will *always* be with them as their *God*.
He will wipe every *tear* from their *eyes*,
and there shall be no more *death* or *mourning*, *wailing* or *pain*,
for the *old* order has passed *away*."

The One who sat on the *throne* said,
"*Behold*, I make *all* things *new*."

notions of heaven. But the vision is founded on ancient expectations that arose long before the dawn of the Christian era with Jesus. The restoration of divided Israel, symbolized by the reconstruction of the temple and the renewed city of Jerusalem, is clearly part of John's vision. The imagery of bride and husband to describe the relationship between God and Israel is found in the ancient prophets. So the vast sweep of this vision takes in all of Judeo-Christian salvation history.

A completely new reality is envisioned here. Nothing of the old remains. Created order has completely destroyed chaos ("the sea was no more"), and the new Jerusalem is of divine origin ("coming down out of heaven"), not merely the old city with a new dress. Though not mentioned in this brief passage, it is the Lamb who was slain who presides over this new creation, the risen Lord Jesus, whose reign covers heaven and earth and "makes all things new."

Although the vision is dream-like, it is very much in touch with reality. The promise that there will be no more death or mourning, that every tear will be wiped away, contains the recognition that death, mourning, and tears are present now. Our sufferings make us long for the new heaven and earth; the sure promise of comfort enables us not only to endure our sufferings but to embrace them.

GOSPEL Perhaps it seems strange to return to the scene of the Last Supper for a gospel selection during Eastertime. But neither the liturgy nor the writers whose words we read at liturgy are concerned with chronology. Today's text

GOSPEL John 13:31–33a, 34–35

See the commentary for hints on how to proclaim this poetic and elusive text.

Pause. What follows is a dramatic switch from grandeur to intimacy.

The final sentence is for all Christians in every age. It is ultimate challenge and ultimate comfort.

A reading from the holy Gospel according to John

When *Judas* had left them, *Jesus* said,
"*Now* is the Son of Man *glorified*, and *God* is glorified *in* him.
If God is *glorified* in him,
God will *also* glorify him in *himself*,
and God will glorify him at *once*.

"My *children*, I will be with you only a *little* while *longer*.
I give you a *new* commandment: *love* one another.
As *I* have loved *you*, so you *also* should love one *another*.
This is how all will *know* that you are my *disciples*,
if you have *love* for one another."

makes that point clear. It seems that, in the first half of this reading, John has taken the words of a Christian hymn and altered them to fit the circumstances of the meal Jesus took with his disciples before he died. The technical word for this practice in writing is anachronism—reading contemporary reality back into an earlier historical situation. It usually has negative connotations in literary criticism, but such is not the case in the Bible. The scriptural writers use the present to interpret the past and look into the future—as, indeed, we all do, though usually with less free association.

The effect of the meditation on the mutual glorification of God and the Son is to enable us to look at Jesus from two perspectives during Eastertime. First, the Son of Man is glorified in his obedience to God—obedience unto death, death on a cross. And God is glorified in the fulfillment of the divine will. And then God glorifies the Son in the splendor of the resurrection, wherein death is overcome by life. God raised Jesus from the dead, thereby glorifying the Son. The Son's victory over death—the guarantee of our redemption—gives glory to God the Father.

The second half of the reading shows us John's particular theology. "My children" is an expression highly favored in the fourth gospel. It is both a term of affection and an assertion of our dependence upon God. And the new commandment to love one another reveals the trait by which true followers of Christ can be recognized.

6TH SUNDAY OF EASTER

Lectionary #57

READING I Acts 15:1–2, 22–29

A reading from the Acts of the Apostles

Some who had come down from *Judea* were *instructing*
the brothers,
"Unless you are *circumcised* according to the Mosaic *practice*,
you *cannot* be *saved*."
Because there arose no little *dissension* and *debate*
by *Paul* and *Barnabas* with them,
it was *decided* that Paul, Barnabas and some of the *others*
should go up to *Jerusalem* to the *apostles* and *elders*
about this question.

The *apostles* and *elders*, in agreement with the whole *church*,
decided to choose *representatives*
and to *send* them to *Antioch* with *Paul* and *Barnabas*.
The ones *chosen* were *Judas*, who was called *Barsabbas*,
and *Silas*, *leaders* among the brothers.
This is the *letter* delivered by them:

"The *apostles* and the *elders*, your *brothers*,
to the brothers in *Antioch*, *Syria* and *Cilicia*
of *Gentile* origin: *Greetings*.
Since we have heard that *some* of our number
who went out without any *mandate* from us
have *upset* you with their *teachings*
and *disturbed* your peace of *mind*,
we have with one *accord* decided to choose *representatives*

Mosaic = moh-ZAY-ik

Barnabas = BAHR-nuh-buhs

Antioch = AN-tee-ahk
Barsabbas = bahr-SAH-buhs
Silas = SĪ-luhs

Syria = SEER-ee-uh
Cilicia = sih-LISH-ee-uh

The narrative is filled with conflict and struggle. The proclamation that resolves the conflict is calm.

READING I **In this dramatic picture of the early church in debate, we see clearly that controversies and the need for discussion and resolution are a natural part of the Christian community. If our picture of the church is idyllic, we will be troubled by debate. The remedy for an unrealistically idealized notion of church is to remember our theme song: "The kingdom has already come, but it is not yet completed."**

More important than the differing points of view related in this reading is the compromise arrived at after discussion. Throughout Christian history there have always been zealous people who insist on a point of doctrine or tradition that is really not essential to Christian belief. We all have a right to be misguided in our fervor from time to time. But we all have the obligation to humility as well—the obligation to listen and learn and discover that a personal conviction we hold dear may not be required of all. During the Second Vatican Council (1962–1965), there were church leaders who agreed that the liturgy needed to be updated, but insisted that not one word of the eucharistic prayer of the Mass could ever be changed. Shortly thereafter, Pope John XXIII inserted the name of Saint Joseph, husband of Mary, into the prayer. A minor change. Who could object to the inclusion of Joseph, patron of the universal church? And who could then maintain that not one word of the prayer could be changed?

and to *send* them to you along with our beloved *Barnabas*
and *Paul*,
who have dedicated their *lives* to the name of our
Lord Jesus *Christ*.

"So we are sending *Judas* and *Silas*
who will *also* convey this same *message* by word of *mouth*:
'It is the *decision* of the Holy *Spirit* and of *us*
not to *place* on you any *burden* beyond these *necessities*,
namely, to abstain from *meat* sacrificed to *idols*,
from *blood*, from meats of *strangled* animals,
and from unlawful *marriage*.
If you keep free of *these*,
you will be doing what is *right*. *Farewell*.'"

The final sentence is full of assurance and comfort.

READING II Revelation 21:10–14, 22–23

A reading from the Book of Revelation

The *angel* took me in *spirit* to a great, high *mountain*
and showed me the holy *city Jerusalem*
coming down out of *heaven* from *God*.
It *gleamed* with the *splendor* of God.
Its *radiance* was like that of a precious *stone*,
like *jasper*, clear as *crystal*.

It had a massive, high *wall*,
with twelve *gates* where twelve *angels* were stationed
and on which *names* were inscribed,
the names of the twelve *tribes* of the *Israelites*.

This is exalted prose, full of symbol and metaphor. Relish each image. Nothing here is matter-of-fact!

Israelites = IZ-ray-uh-līts (four syllables, not three) In this image we see the long-awaited restoration of Israel. Nothing could be more gratifying to John's contemporaries.

It was a far greater challenge to the early Jewish Christians to give up the ancient practice of circumcision as their particular sign of covenant with God. And yet they did, seeing it as an unnecessary burden and realizing that there were far more important practices to uphold: abstaining from idolatry (in all its forms) and from unlawful marriage (incest).

The Christian creed is simple. This reading reminds us that it is the quality of our belief, not the quantity of our beliefs, that is most important.

In places where the Ascension of the Lord is celebrated next Sunday, May 23, the second reading and the gospel of the 7th Sunday of Easter (lectionary #61) may be read today. Check with the liturgy coordinator or homilist to find out which readings will be used today.

READING II **As we continue to read John's heavenly vision during these Sundays of Eastertime, we continue to remind ourselves of the tension that characterizes Christian life. In this vision of the heavenly kingdom, the new Jerusalem, we see the church triumphant and at rest. It is a view of the kingdom that is not yet part of our experience, and yet the Lamb who reigns there (the risen Lord) has already inaugurated his kingdom on earth. We are perhaps more aware of the distinctions than the similarities between the kingdoms to which we belong. Our participation in the life of God has already begun; we simply long for—and work for—its fulfillment.**

There were *three* gates facing *east*,
three *north*, three *south*, and three *west*.
The *wall* of the city had twelve courses of *stones*
as its *foundation*,
on which were inscribed the twelve *names*
of the twelve *apostles* of the *Lamb*.

A truly beautiful image. No temple, no sun, no moon. There is no need for created light in the presence of the creator of light.

I saw no *temple* in the city
for *its* temple is the Lord God *almighty* and the *Lamb*.
The city had no *need* of *sun* or *moon* to *shine* on it,
for the glory of *God* gave it light,
and its *lamp* was the *Lamb*.

GOSPEL John 14:23–29

A reading from the holy Gospel according to John

The entire text is made up of the words of Jesus, speaking in the first person. The solemnity is tempered with intimacy.

Jesus said to his *disciples*:
"Whoever *loves* me will keep my *word*,
and my *Father* will love *him*,
and we will *come* to him and make our *dwelling* with him.
Whoever does *not* love me does *not* keep my words;
yet the *word* you hear is not *mine*
but that of the *Father* who *sent* me.

The sense here is: "I am telling you these things now even though you will not completely understand them; the Holy Spirit will enable you to understand fully."

"I have *told* you this while I am *with* you.
The *Advocate*, the Holy *Spirit*,
whom the *Father* will send in my *name*,
will teach you *everything*
and *remind* you of all that I *told* you.

Notice that John's vision encompasses all of salvation history. The twelve tribes of Israel are the gates into the city. Salvation comes from the Jews. Abraham is our father in faith. Jesus came not to abolish the law and the prophets, but to bring them to perfection. The foundation stones of the city are the apostles of the Lamb, the twelve to whom Jesus entrusted his word and his mission. The church to which we belong is apostolic, that is, founded on the apostolic tradition.

The absence of the temple is particularly instructive. Though the Lord chooses to meet us in word and sacrament now, such is not the case in the eternal city. There is no temple there because the Lord himself is the temple. In other words, though we encounter the Lord through the veil of word and sacrament now, in that new heaven we will see Christ face to face.

GOSPEL **Once again we return to the words Jesus spoke at the Last Supper. They are particularly appropriate now, for we read them in the light of all we have celebrated since Holy Thursday—and they are imbued with greater meaning. Jesus looks ahead to his suffering and death, then beyond it to his resurrection, and further still to the coming of the Holy Spirit, who guarantees that his words will remain and bear fruit.**

"*Peace* I leave with you; my *peace* I give to you.
Not as the *world* gives do I give it to you.
Do not let your hearts be *troubled* or *afraid*.

"You heard me *tell* you,
'I am going *away* and I will come *back* to you.'
If you *loved* me,
you would *rejoice* that I am going to the *Father*;
for the Father is *greater* than I.
And now I have *told* you this before it *happens*,
so that *when* it happens you may *believe*."

There is no question that the disciples love Jesus. The meaning is "If you understood enough to love me for who I really am (which you cannot possibly know until after the resurrection), then you would rejoice that I return to the Father."

This reading is part of the farewell discourse of Jesus, and so prepares us for the celebration of his ascension. The risen Christ returns to the Father from whom he was sent, and in his stead the Holy Spirit now becomes God's way of dwelling among us. Filled with that Spirit, the apostles can continue to carry on Christ's work with confidence and peace, knowing that they are accompanied and guided by the divine presence. The Holy Spirit brings no new teaching; it reminds the apostles (enables them to keep in mind) the teachings and deeds of Jesus.

The peace that Jesus leaves with his apostles (and with us) is not the peace that the world gives. Here is a distinction that sometimes eludes us. What is the difference between the peace Jesus gives and the peace of the world? First of all, we know that peace is more than the absence of war or controversy. The peace that Jesus gives is more profound and fundamental than that. It brings the assurance that nothing can separate us from the love of Christ. When our faith truly believes that ultimate victory over suffering is inevitable, then we can be full of peace in a way that a worldly view of suffering cannot know. This is the peace that enables us to live optimistically, to withstand the blows life brings, to be courageous in the face of fear and sorrow, and to live our lives with the healthiest form of detachment.

MAY 20, 2004

ASCENSION OF THE LORD

Lectionary #58

READING I Acts 1:1–11

A reading from the beginning of the Acts of the Apostles

Luke, the great storyteller, is the author here. The first book he refers to is his gospel. Theophilus (Greek for "one who loves God") may not be a specific person, but any reader of good will.

In the *first* book, Theophilus,
I dealt with all that Jesus *did* and *taught*
until the day he was taken *up*,
after giving *instructions* through the Holy *Spirit*
to the *apostles* whom he had *chosen*.
He presented himself *alive* to them
by many *proofs* after he had *suffered*,
appearing to them during forty *days*
and *speaking* about the kingdom of *God*.

The story of the ascension begins here. The text clearly demands a pause before beginning this section.

While *meeting* with them,
he *enjoined* them not to depart from *Jerusalem*,
but to *wait* for "the promise of the *Father*
about which you have heard me *speak*;
for *John* baptized with *water*,
but in a few *days you* will be baptized with the Holy *Spirit*."

Pause slightly after the apostles' question. This will give weight to Jesus' response—as well as hint at the difference between what they want to hear and what Jesus tells them.

When they had gathered *together* they *asked* him,
"Lord, are you at this time going to *restore*
the kingdom to *Israel*?"
He answered them, "It is not for *you* to know the *times*
or *seasons*
that the Father has *established* by his own *authority*.

If the Ascension of the Lord is celebrated on Sunday, May 23, today's readings are to be used then, not those for the 7th Sunday of Easter.

READING I **The point of this first section of the book of Acts is to show that God's plan to save us continues in one great sweep from the time of Jesus' ministry on earth, through his suffering and resurrection and ascension, and beyond. "Yes," Jesus says, "you will be my witnesses even to the ends of the earth." The good news of Jesus' victory on our behalf will spiral out from Jerusalem to Samaria and around the world.**

And when will the rule of Israel be restored? The gentle answer is that only the Father knows. The question is asked in sincerity, but Jesus must point out that it is outmoded. The rule or kingdom of Israel, as conceived by Israel (that is, a temporal triumph over all the nations of the world, wrought by a miraculous divine stroke) was not to be. Although this was a cherished notion, Jesus spent his life demonstrating a different kind of kingdom—universal, characterized by fidelity to God's law of love. These two kingdoms have much in common. In both, peace and justice triumph over discord and greed. But the way in which the two kingdoms were to be established was radically different.

We must appreciate the eagerness of Jesus' oppressed Jewish contemporaries for the establishment of the kingdom, even as we see how differently Jesus established it. Their lives were difficult, their dignity compromised, their autonomy squashed by Roman domination, and their awareness of the difference between present conditions

But you will receive *power* when the Holy *Spirit* comes upon you,
and you will be my *witnesses* in *Jerusalem*,
throughout *Judea* and *Samaria*,
and to the ends of the *earth*."

At the end of Jesus' words, pause slightly. A dramatic scene follows.

When he had *said* this, as they were *looking on*,
he was lifted *up*, and a *cloud* took him from their *sight*.

Isolate this sentence. A slight pause precedes and follows it.

While they were looking *intently* at the *sky* as he was *going*,
suddenly two *men* dressed in white *garments*
stood *beside* them.

They said, "Men of *Galilee*,
why are you *standing* there looking at the *sky*?

Do not make the angels' question sound like ridicule. Make it gentle and comforting.

This *Jesus* who has been taken *up* from you into *heaven*
will *return* in the same way as you have *seen* him
going into heaven."

READING II Hebrews 9:24–28; 10:19–23

A reading from the Letter to the Hebrews

Hebrews is an *apologia*—an effort to explain how Christ's sacrifice fulfilled all others. You are a teacher as you proclaim this message of assurance that sin has been conquered once for all.

Christ did not enter into a *sanctuary* made by *hands*,
a *copy* of the true one, but heaven *itself*,
that he might *now* appear before *God* on our *behalf*.
Not that he might offer himself *repeatedly*,
as the *high* priest enters each *year* into the sanctuary
with *blood* that is not his *own*;
if *that* were so, he would have had to *suffer* repeatedly
from the *foundation* of the *world*.

The words "once for all" are crucial. Make the most of them.

But *now* once for *all* he has *appeared* at the *end* of the *ages*
to take away *sin* by his *sacrifice*.

and the promises of the prophets acutely painful. Their longing for the rule of Israel is far more poignant than power-hungry. But the business at hand is to get the word out that Jesus is truly the Messiah, and that the Kingdom of God upon earth has begun. When it will come to completion no one knows—and no one who understands it really cares about when. The concern must be with how. And Jesus made the how very clear.

The angels' question brings the point home. "Why stand here looking up at the skies? Go now and tell the world all that Jesus did and taught."

There is a choice of second readings today. Speak with the liturgy coordinator or the homilist to find out which reading will be used.

READING II **HEBREWS. The author of the letter to the Hebrews is writing to comfort Jewish Christians who have been alienated from the Jewish tradition they had combined with their faith in Jesus. The point of this part of the letter is to assure them that Jesus is the perfect high priest whose perfect and unique sacrifice has brought all others to fulfillment. There is no further need for sacrificial victims to take away our sins and to justify us in the sight of God. Jesus has done that once and for all. The eucharistic sacrifice we celebrate is a continuing proclamation of the one sacrifice of Christ. And that sacrifice was perfected by a high priest who identified completely with our weakness.**

The effect of hearing this text on Ascension is that we understand more clearly the way in which Jesus' mission began in eternity and now continues there.

Pause. Then explain the consequences of Jesus' sacrifice: He opened the way to glory for us!

Just as it is *appointed* that men and women die *once*,
and *after* this the *judgment*, so also *Christ*,
offered *once* to take away the sins of *many*,
will appear a *second* time, not to take away *sin*
but to bring *salvation* to those who eagerly *await* him.

And since this is the case, how should we approach the throne of grace? With sincerity and trust.

Therefore, brothers and sisters, since through the *blood* of *Jesus*
we have *confidence* of entrance into the *sanctuary*
by the *new* and *living* way he *opened* for us
through the *veil*, that is, his *flesh*,
and since we have "a *great* priest over the house of *God*,"
let us *approach* with a sincere *heart* and in absolute *trust*,
with our *hearts* sprinkled *clean* from an evil *conscience*
and our *bodies* washed in pure *water*.

Encouragement! Our hope is anchored in one who is trustworthy.

Let us hold *unwaveringly* to our *confession* that gives us *hope*,
for he who made the *promise* is *trustworthy*.

Or:

READING II Ephesians 1:17–23

The reading is three sentences grammatically. The middle sentence is too long and complex to be read as a unit. Let each sense line guide you. Read these faith assertions slowly.

The first sentence is straightforward and simple.

The sentence is poetic in form. It must be read with great care and sensitivity, keeping the initial idea alive throughout: "that you may know."

A reading from the Letter of Saint Paul to the Ephesians

Brothers and sisters:
May the *God* of our *Lord* Jesus *Christ*, the Father of *glory*,
give you a Spirit of *wisdom* and *revelation*
resulting in *knowledge* of him.

May the eyes of your hearts be enlightened,
that you may *know* what is the *hope* that belongs to his *call*,
what are the riches of *glory*
in his *inheritance* among the *holy* ones,

Jesus is both God and human being and therefore the perfect priest. He has shared our identity as human and has shared with us his identity as God. The mediation is perfect and complete. As God, he has made us one with himself in reconciling love. Having accomplished the purpose for which the Father sent him, Jesus now returns to glory—and his risen presence abides with the believers until we all join him in eternity.

EPHESIANS. This reading is an exultant hymn celebrating the role of Christ in God's plan to save. It should be proclaimed with energy and joy. The first paragraph is a greeting and a blessing and a prayer for all who hear it. It prays that all may receive understanding and wisdom regarding what God has accomplished for the salvation of the world through Jesus the Christ. And then it proceeds to recount that accomplishment.

In the second paragraph we hear the writer celebrate the completion of Christ's earthly ministry and his return to the glory of the Father's right hand, surely explaining why the text was chosen for today's feast.

In the final paragraph we see Christ as ruler of the world, head of the church (his body), and the fullness of the believers who fill every corner of the universe. It is a victory hymn as we approach the end of the Easter season. "The battle is over, the victory won."

Count the blessings this prayer includes: (1) knowledge of God through insightful wisdom, (2) enlightenment in hope that guides us through difficult times, (3) awareness of the inheritance that is ours, (4) understanding of how powerful our faith is. The power that raised Jesus from the dead is in our hands for the doing of good. And finally, we

and what is the surpassing *greatness* of his *power*
for us who *believe*,
in accord with the *exercise* of his great *might*,
which he worked in *Christ*,
raising him from the *dead*
and *seating* him at his right *hand* in the *heavens*,
far *above* every *principality*, *authority*, *power*, and *dominion*,
and every *name* that is *named*
not only in *this* age but *also* in the one to *come*.

The final sentence is simple, though the thought contained in it is not. The pronouns can be confusing unless you understand the text: "And *the Father* put all things beneath *Christ's* feet . . ."

And he put *all* things beneath his *feet*
and gave him as *head* over all things to the *church*,
which is his *body*,
the *fullness* of the one who fills *all* things in every *way*.

GOSPEL Luke 24:46–53

A reading from the holy Gospel according to Luke

Jesus said to his *disciples*:

It is the risen Christ who speaks these words of victory over sin and the coming of the Spirit (the promise of the Father).

"Thus it is *written* that the *Christ* would *suffer*
and *rise* from the dead on the third *day*
and that *repentance*, for the forgiveness of *sins*,
would be *preached* in his *name*
to *all* the nations, *beginning* from *Jerusalem*.

The witnesses here include the assembly, yourself, and all Christians.

You are *witnesses* of these things.

are defined as the body of Christ, with Christ as the head. We are the fullness of Christ that fills the universe. Can we ever think small again after realizing what we are?

Anything less than a powerful, intelligent, sensitive, and spirited proclamation of this beautiful text will not do it justice. You will have to practice diligently to make certain every element of this powerful prayer is grasped by the assembly. It is meant to empower them and that is your task and privilege.

GOSPEL **Luke's gospel ends where it began: in the temple. Luke opens his gospel with the story of Zachary, the father of John the Baptist, fulfilling his priestly duty in the temple. And that is where Luke ends his gospel as well, as we hear today. The apostles, having witnessed the ascension of the risen Lord, returned to Jerusalem with great joy, where they were continually in the temple praising God.**

It is useless to argue about when the ascension occurred or whether it took place in a dramatic, literal way. It is possible that the resurrection and ascension of Jesus occurred in the twinkling of an eye. The Eastern mentality confuses us Westerners again! We tend to look for a literal record of historical events in biblical literature. But the authors of that literature sought rather to write interpretations of such events in their efforts to describe the indescribable. Even the forty days between the resurrection and the ascension (mentioned in the Acts of the Apostles) is a symbolic number of perfection or fullness.

And *behold* I am sending the *promise* of my *Father* upon you;
but stay in the *city*
until you are clothed with *power* from on *high*."

Pause here. The reading is clearly in two parts. You move from quoting Jesus' exalted words to a simple narrative of events.

Then he led them *out* as far as *Bethany*,
raised his *hands*, and *blessed* them.
As he *blessed* them he *parted* from them
and was taken up to *heaven*.
They did him *homage*
and then returned to *Jerusalem* with great *joy*,
and they were *continually* in the *temple* praising *God*.

What prompted the Eleven to prostrate themselves in reverence? Surely there is something awesome in this scene. The Lord has gone and yet they are filled with joy! Much is implied in this simple statement about the faith of the Eleven. And their spontaneous response was to gather in the temple for prayer.

The ascension means that Christians have always believed that Jesus, having completed his earthly mission, returned to God, from whom he was sent, and now takes up his continuing role as priest, prophet, and king. That is the meaning of the words "took his seat at God's right hand." There is no implication that Christ is no longer present in the world or is inactive. Christ has not gone to a specific place any more than God can be said to be in a particular place; rather, Christ has taken on the role of intermediary in a new and entirely spiritual way.

The emphasis on the mission of the Eleven further demonstrates the continuing activity of the risen Christ. There is comfort and confirmation in the evidence that the Lord manifests himself through the work of the apostles, filled with power from on high—that is, filled with the Holy Spirit on Pentecost. The mission of the Eleven extends through the ages and is shared by all the baptized.

We are approaching the end of the Easter season and are reaching the fullness of Pentecost. Ten days hence we will celebrate the coming of the Holy Spirit—the ultimate and enduring manifestation of the risen Lord's presence in the world. We should not think of the feast of the ascension as the church's farewell to Jesus until the end of time. Rather, we celebrate today the risen Lord's appearance among us in a new and wonderful way, far beyond the power of the human eye, but well within the loving grasp of the believing heart.

MAY 23, 2004

7TH SUNDAY OF EASTER

Lectionary #61

READING I Acts 7:55–60

This reading presents us with the end of a story in which Stephen professes the belief for which he is now about to die.

A reading from the Acts of the Apostles

Stephen, filled with the Holy *Spirit*,
looked up intently to *heaven* and saw the glory of *God*
and *Jesus* standing at the right *hand* of God,
and Stephen said, "*Behold*, I see the heavens *opened*
and the Son of *Man* standing at the right hand of *God*."

The ears are covered to block out what sounds like blasphemy to the hearers.

But *they* cried out in a loud *voice*,
covered their *ears*, and *rushed* upon him *together*.
They *threw* him out of the *city*, and began to *stone* him.
The *witnesses* laid down their *cloaks*
at the feet of a young *man* named *Saul*.

This Saul is soon to become Paul.

As they were *stoning* Stephen, he called out,
"Lord *Jesus*, receive my *spirit*."
Then he fell to his *knees* and cried out in a loud *voice*,
"*Lord*, do not hold this sin *against* them";
and when he *said* this, he fell *asleep*.

Only a man of strong faith can pray like this. Communicate the nobility of Stephen's words.

If the feast of the Ascension of the Lord is celebrated today, please see the previous section for the appropriate readings.

READING I Luke produced a two-volume work: his gospel account of the life and deeds of Jesus, and his account of the early history of the newly established Christian community. Luke's gospel and his Acts of the Apostles should be studied together, for each reveals something about the other. In the first reading today, we hear Luke's story of the church's first martyr, Stephen.

The parallels Luke draws between Stephen and Jesus are strikingly apparent in three places. When Stephen refers to Jesus as "the Son of Man" he uses a title heretofore used only by Jesus himself. The title always carries a note of final judgment, and was indeed used by Jesus in Luke's account of Jesus' trial before the Jewish authorities. Luke places a close copy of the words used by Jesus ("The Son of Man will be seated at the right hand of the power of God") on Stephen's lips.

Secondly, Stephen's words "Lord Jesus, receive my spirit" are a clear echo of Jesus' cry at the moment of his death, "Father, into your hands I commend my spirit." Stephen's vision beholds the risen Jesus at the right hand of God. In a long self-defense immediately before his death, the martyr has proclaimed the resurrection, ascension and enthronement of Jesus. His vision corroborates the testimony for which he is being killed.

Finally, Luke has Stephen imitate Jesus in praying for his persecutors. In the gospel we hear Jesus pray, "Father, forgive them

READING II Revelation 22:12–14, 16–17, 20

There is such finality and assurance in this text. Proclaim it boldly. The cosmic dimensions of these words demand great solemnity and broadness.

A reading from the Book of Revelation

I, *John*, heard a *voice* saying to me:
"*Behold*, I am coming *soon*.
I *bring* with me the *recompense* I will give to *each*
according to his *deeds*.
I am the *Alpha* and the *Omega*, the *first* and the *last*,
the *beginning* and the *end*."

This is praise for the martyrs.

Blessed are they who wash their *robes*
so as to have the *right* to the tree of *life*
and enter the *city* through its *gates*.

"I, *Jesus*, sent my *angel* to give you this *testimony*
for the *churches*.
I am the *root* and *offspring* of *David*,
the bright *morning* star."

There is certainty here for those who may have doubted.

The *Spirit* and the *bride* say, "*Come*."
Let the *hearer* say, "Come."
Let the one who *thirsts* come *forward*,
and the one who *wants* it receive the *gift* of life-giving *water*.

The final "Come, Lord Jesus," is a cry of the heart, filled with poignancy.

The one who *gives* this testimony says, "*Yes*, I am coming *soon*."
Amen! *Come*, Lord Jesus!

for they know not what they do." Stephen, too, prays that the sin of his persecutors will not be held against them.

READING II Today, on the seventh and last Sunday of Easter, we hear the final words of the last book of the Bible. And such words they are! Full of glory and exaltation, and yet quiet, tender and reassuring. The combined feelings of longing and fulfillment bring together the entire liturgical season. As in Advent we cried out again and again, "Come, Lord Jesus!" so now in Easter we repeat the cry and hear in response, "Yes, I am coming soon."

The Lord does come to us in word and in sacrament, and still we cry, "Come!" For until we see Christ face to face, we have not experienced the fullness of the kingdom. There are signs of Christ's coming everywhere, yet his coming is not yet complete. The "bright morning star" that signals the dawn can be seen, yet the dawn has not yet fully broken. There are pleas for Christ's coming in every age. Those who have "washed their robes" are those who have died for the faith and with their very lifeblood cried, "Come!" The Spirit and the bride—both are voices of the divine—call out to the world to come to salvation. And we who thirst are invited to drink the water of eternal life.

The cries echo across the chasm that still divides us from John's vision. From both sides, the cry is sent forth. On both sides it is heard and responded to. "Come!" we cry out in our longing for the Lord. "Come!" the Spirit and the bride cry out to us. "Come back to the garden, for you have a right to the tree of life."

GOSPEL John 17:20–26

A reading from the holy Gospel according to John

Again this week, all the words of the gospel are in the first person. Jesus alone speaks here. The fervor of his prayer is clear.

Lifting up his eyes to *heaven*, Jesus *prayed* saying:
"Holy *Father*, I pray not only for *them*,
but *also* for those who will *believe* in me through their *word*,
so that they may *all* be *one*,
as *you*, Father, are in *me* and *I* in *you*,
that they *also* may be in *us*,
that the *world* may *believe* that you *sent* me.

Take it slowly. The words are not easy to grasp. The meditative spirit of the prayer is not tightly constructed.

And I have *given* them the *glory* you gave *me*,
so that they may be *one*, as *we* are one,
I in *them* and you in *me*,
that they may be brought to *perfection* as one,
that the *world* may *know* that you *sent* me,
and that you loved *them* even as you loved *me*.

"Father, they are your *gift* to me.
I wish that where *I* am they *also* may be *with* me,
that they may see my *glory* that you *gave* me,
because you *loved* me before the foundation of the *world*.

Strive for a feeling of urgency rather than for tidiness of thought. This will require careful placement of emphasis. For example: "I made *known* to them your *name* and I *will* make it known, that the *love* with which you loved *me* may *be* in them and *I* in them." These are not the only possible choices.

"Righteous *Father*, the *world* also does *not* know you,
but *I* know you, and *they* know that you *sent* me.
I made *known* to them your *name* and I *will* make it known,
that the *love* with which you loved *me*
may *be* in them and *I* in them."

GOSPEL The prayer "that they may all be one" has cosmic and eternal significance. The unity upon which this prayer of Jesus is based is, first, the unity that Jesus has with the Father. In perfect obedience, Jesus has made himself one with God. And the prayer is based, secondly, on the oneness Jesus has achieved with his followers—the disciples and all whom they bring to faith through their preaching. It is a prayer for solidarity of belief and the continuation of the message and mission inaugurated by Jesus during his time on earth.

All who believe in Jesus are affected by this fervent prayer—whether Catholic or Protestant or Orthodox or the tiniest and most unknown group who looks upon Jesus as Savior. We should avoid interpreting this prayer as a call for perfect uniformity of belief among all the Christians of the world. It is far greater than an ecumenical ideal. When we hear Jesus' words about unity in their cosmic profundity, we will move further and further away from judgments about Christians whose beliefs and practices are different from our own. Instead, we will emphasize our oneness—that we all call upon the name of the Lord Jesus and place our hopes for salvation in him.

There is a kind of perversity in human beings that makes us need to be right, and judge those who do not agree with us as wrong. We seem to feel more in control when we have divided reality into neat categories. Unfortunately, reality is never neat and we are fooling ourselves. The more thoroughly we shed our tendency to categorize, the more thoroughly we will appreciate the Lord's counsel that we not judge one another.

The more we look for unity, the more we find it—and the more we create it.

PENTECOST VIGIL

Lectionary #62

READING I Genesis 11:1–9

A reading from the Book of Genesis

This is a simple story with a clear lesson. Tell it straightforwardly but with all the energy it contains.

Shinar = SHĪ-nahr

bitumen = bih-TOO-m*n

God uses the royal plural: "Let us then go down . . ."

The whole *world* spoke the same *language*, using the
same *words*.
While the people were *migrating* in the *east*,
they came upon a *valley* in the land of *Shinar* and *settled* there.
They said to one another,
"*Come*, let us mold *bricks* and *harden* them with *fire*."
They used bricks for *stone*, and bitumen for *mortar*.

Then they said, "*Come*, let us build ourselves a *city*
and a *tower* with its *top* in the *sky*,
and so make a *name* for ourselves;
otherwise we shall be *scattered* all over the *earth*."

The LORD came down to *see* the city and the tower
that the people had built.
Then the LORD said: "If now, while they are *one* people,
all speaking the same *language*,
they have started to do *this*,
nothing will later *stop* them from doing
whatever they *presume* to do.
Let us then go *down* there and *confuse* their *language*,
so that one will not *understand* what another *says*."

Thus the LORD *scattered* them from there all over the *earth*,
and they stopped *building* the city.

There is a choice of first readings today. Speak with the liturgy coordinator or homilist to find out which reading will be used.

READING I GENESIS. The story of the Tower of Babel is one of several options for the vigil celebration because tomorrow's first reading (Acts 2:1–11) alludes to it. While God punishes those who build the tower because of their pride by dividing their one language into many, the linguistic divisions among peoples are bridged by the unifying power of the Holy Spirit on Pentecost. The effect of juxtaposing these readings is twofold. First, it shows us that our understanding of God has grown and changed over the centuries, becoming clearest in the person of Jesus. Secondly, it emphasizes Luke's controlling theme about the universality of God's saving plan for the world. All the nations have become the chosen people.

In this delightful story from Genesis we see a traditional explanation for the many diverse tongues spoken by the peoples of the earth. In the story from Acts we see a traditional explanation for the rapid spread of the gospel. God's jealousy in the Genesis reading makes more sense when we realize that the people were defying God's command to settle in their respective homelands. Their disobedience brings punishment

Babel = BAB-*l (Notice the similarity to "babble.")

That is why it was called *Babel,*
because *there* the LORD confused the *speech* of all the *world.*
It was from that place that he *scattered* them all over the *earth.*

Or:

READING I Exodus 19:3–8a, 16–20b

A reading from the Book of Exodus

Notice that this story has two parts. First, God reminds the people (through Moses) of their deliverance from Egypt and secures their promise of obedience. Then comes a display of divine power.

Moses went up the mountain to *God.*
Then the LORD *called* to him and said,
"*Thus* shall you say to the house of *Jacob;*
tell the Israelites:
You have *seen* for *yourselves* how I *treated* the *Egyptians*
and how I *bore you up* on eagle *wings*
and *brought* you here to *myself.*

"*Therefore,* if you hearken to my *voice* and keep my *covenant,*
you shall be my *special possession,*
dearer to me than all *other* people,
though all the *earth* is mine.
You shall *be* to me a kingdom of *priests,* a *holy* nation.
That is what you must tell the *Israelites.*"

So Moses *went* and *summoned* the *elders* of the people.
When he set before them
all that the LORD had *ordered* him to tell them,
the people all answered *together,*
"Everything the LORD has *said,* we will *do.*"

upon them; willful pride creates division among them, as it does to this day.

This is a classic fable, one of many in Genesis that make the point that God is the creator and cause of everything that is. Proclaim the story with all the skill you have as a storyteller. There is a timeless moral lesson here, perhaps all the more relevant in a world that continues to shrink, as we become more and more aware of ourselves as a global village.

EXODUS. The second option for the first reading shows us the traditional signs of God's powerful intervention in Israel's history: smoke, cloud, fire, and a thunderous roar. With the coming of the Holy Spirit, fire reveals God's presence, a brilliant image of the all-consuming nature of God's love and the fervor of those who are filled with it.

In this reading we encounter the awesome occasion when God gives the law to Israel through Moses. The chapter following this one in Genesis lists the ten commandments. The parallels between the giving of the law and the coming of the Spirit are easy to see, as are the differences between the two events.

In both events the people are brought into a covenant relationship with God, and

Read the signs of God's power as a narrative, not a reenactment.

On the morning of the *third* day
there were peals of *thunder* and *lightning*,
and a heavy *cloud* over the mountain,
and a very loud *trumpet* blast,
so that all the people in the camp *trembled*.
But *Moses* led the people *out* of the camp to meet *God*,
and they *stationed* themselves at the *foot* of the mountain.
Mount *Sinai* was all wrapped in *smoke*,
for the *LORD* came down upon it in *fire*.
The smoke *rose* from it as though from a *furnace*,
and the whole *mountain* trembled *violently*.

There is a dialogue between God and Moses; it is not a one-sided decree.

The *trumpet* blast grew *louder* and *louder*,
while Moses was *speaking*,
and God *answering* him with *thunder*.

When the LORD came *down* to the top of Mount *Sinai*,
he summoned *Moses* to the *top* of the mountain.

Or:

READING I Ezekiel 37:1–14

Ezekiel = ee-ZEE-kee-uhl

This wonderful story is vivid and has always captured the imagination. You are speaking for Ezekiel in the first person ("I"), which makes the scene more immediate.

A reading from the Book of the Prophet Ezekiel

The hand of the *LORD* came upon me,
and he led me *out* in the *spirit* of the LORD
and set me in the center of the *plain*,
which was now filled with *bones*.
He made me *walk* among the bones in every *direction*
so that I *saw* how *many* they were on the surface of the plain.
How *dry* they were!

both events are characterized by theophanies (dramatic signs of God's presence). In the first, God entrusts to Israel the fundamental law by which all succeeding generations will live. In the second, the presence of the Holy Spirit confers the power to preach the gospel on an assembly made up of peoples from many parts of the world.

Clearly we are beginning to understand that God's redemptive love is intended for all the nations of the earth. Empowered by the divine Spirit, we are able to spread the Good News of this new covenant—revealed to us in Jesus, God's love made visible.

EZEKIEL. The third option for today's first reading is the story of the valley of the dry bones, made justly famous by the wonderful African American spiritual: "Dem bones, dem bones, dem dry bones!" It is the story of a faithful and loving God restoring his beloved Israel to new life. Ezekiel foresees the revival of a destitute people, who reclaim their rightful place through the mercy of a God who is not hindered by death or the grave.

Take the changes in the dialogue slowly. God asks several rhetorical questions here. It's part of the narrative style.

He asked me:
Son of man, can these bones come to *life*?
I answered, "Lord *GOD*, you *alone* know that."

Then he said to me:
Prophesy over these bones, and *say* to them:
Dry *bones*, hear the *word* of the *LORD*!
Thus says the Lord *GOD* to these bones:
See! I will bring *spirit* into you, that you may come to *life*.
I will put *sinews* upon you, make *flesh* grow over you,
cover you with *skin*, and put *spirit* in you
so that you may come to *life* and know that *I* am the *LORD*.

prophesy = PROF-uh-sī

sinews = SIN-yooz

This reminds us of the "spirit of life" God blew into the nostrils of Adam.

prophesied = PROF-uh-sīd

I, Ezekiel, prophesied as I had been *told*,
and even as I was *prophesying* I heard a *noise*;
it was a *rattling* as the bones came *together*, *bone* joining *bone*.
I saw the *sinews* and the *flesh* come upon them,
and the skin *cover* them, but there was no *spirit* in them.

Then the LORD said to me:
Prophesy to the *spirit*, *prophesy*, son of man,
and *say* to the spirit: Thus says the Lord *GOD*:
From the four winds *come*, O spirit,
and *breathe* into these *slain* that they may come to *life*.
I prophesied as he *told* me, and the spirit *came* into them;
they came *alive* and stood *upright*, a vast *army*.

Then he said to me:
Son of man, these *bones* are the whole house of *Israel*.
They have been saying,
"Our bones are *dried up*,
our *hope* is *lost*, and we are *cut off*."

The day of restoration comes in a new way on Pentecost. God's promise to place a new spirit within the people, giving them hearts of flesh to replace their stony ones, takes on a whole new meaning in the light of Pentecost fire.

Ezekiel foretold the fulfillment of God's promises at the end of time. The Pentecost event in Acts recounts the fulfillment of that promise and the inauguration of that end-time even now.

The familiarity of this wonderful story is part of its charm. Your proclamation should convey suspense, awe, wonder, and power so that the assembly will hear the passage in a fresh way.

JOEL. In this fourth option for the first reading, we see the signs of God's power in smoke and fire as the spirit of God is poured out on all living flesh. No longer are the gifts of prophecy reserved for a chosen few. Instead, the whole people, from youngest to oldest and from least to greatest, will prophesy in the Lord's name.

The horrific images of blood, smoke, fire, and darkness are necessary to impress us with the vastness of God's power and our total dependence on divine mercy. The Day of the Lord will be terrible only if we rebel against the goodness of God. Everyone who

The poignancy of God's solemn promise ("O my people, O my people") should be felt in your proclamation.

Therefore, *prophesy* and say to them:
Thus says the Lord GOD:
O my *people*, I will open your *graves*
and have you *rise* from them,
and bring you *back* to the land of *Israel*.

Then you shall *know* that *I* am the LORD,
when I open your *graves* and have you *rise* from them,
O my *people*!
I will put my *spirit* in you that you may *live*,
and I will *settle* you upon your *land*;
thus you shall *know* that *I* am the LORD.
I have *promised*, and I will *do* it, says the LORD.

Or:

READING I Joel 3:1–5

A reading from the Book of the Prophet Joel

Here we have a solemn proclamation from the mouth of God. This is exalted poetry.

prophesy = PROF-uh-sī

Thus says the *Lord*:
I will pour out my *spirit* upon all *flesh*.
Your *sons* and *daughters* shall *prophesy*,
your *old* men shall dream *dreams*,
your *young* men shall see *visions*;
even upon the *servants* and the *handmaids*,
in those days, I will pour out my *spirit*.
And I will work *wonders* in the *heavens* and on the *earth*,
blood, *fire*, and columns of *smoke*;
the *sun* will be turned to *darkness*,
and the *moon* to *blood*,

calls upon the name of the Lord will be rescued from it. They are the remnant that will remain.

The image of the faithful remnant is a favorite in Hebrew scriptures. It is a positive image rather than a negative one. It does not mean that only a few shall be saved; rather, it makes the point that, no matter how bad things seem, God never abandons the faithful.

It is difficult for us to appreciate fully the richness of God's spirit and how it transforms those upon whom it rests. It is the breath and life and substance of God, not merely a ghostly phantasm. The spirit of God is real and enables those who receive it to see things as God sees them, to reorient their lives to right relationship with God, to live their full dignity as God's creatures and to proclaim God's goodness to the world around them. To receive a portion of God's spirit is to receive a portion of God's life.

This is what happens on Pentecost. All the world, people of every race and tongue, receive that spirit and speak of the marvels God has accomplished in a language that all can understand: the language of love, justice, respect, and humility.

Notice that the narrative changes from first person ("I") to third person ("the Lord"), but it is still God speaking. Despite the terrifying images, the reading ends with a comforting promise.

at the coming of the *day* of the LORD,
the *great* and *terrible* day.

Then everyone shall be *rescued*
who *calls* on the name of the LORD;
for on Mount *Zion* there shall be a *remnant*,
as the LORD has said,
and in *Jerusalem survivors*
whom the LORD shall *call*.

READING II Romans 8:22–27

A reading from the Letter of Saint Paul to the Romans

The use of "we," "our," and "us" gives you an immediate rapport with the assembly. Make use of it.

Brothers and sisters:
We *know* that all *creation* is *groaning* in *labor* pains
even until *now*;
and not only *that*, but we *ourselves*,
who have the *firstfruits* of the Spirit,
we *also* groan within ourselves
as we wait for *adoption*, the redemption of our *bodies*.

Let the rhetorical question be a real question. Pause slightly after it.

For in *hope* we were *saved*.
Now *hope* that *sees* is *not* hope.
For who *hopes* for what one *sees*?
But if we hope for what we do *not* see, we wait with *endurance*.

Notice throughout that Paul presents a problematic condition followed by "But . . ." Let the contrast ring out.

In the same *way*, the Spirit *too* comes to the *aid* of our weakness;
for we do not *know* how to pray as we *ought*,
but the Spirit *himself* intercedes with inexpressible *groanings*.

READING II Though the thought here is clear and simple, its expression is complex. It is a vivid portrayal of our present spiritual condition. We rejoice in the assurance that faith gives us at the same moment we long for its promise to be complete. We long fervently for the peace that comes from union with God even as we struggle to maintain that relationship through prayer. We should take great comfort in hearing that the Spirit helps us in our weakness. Even wanting to pray is itself a prayer, for the Spirit is at prayer within our very desire. Perhaps we really begin to pray when we grow tired of "saying prayers" and let the Spirit take over.

This most striking thing about this text is the enormous dignity Paul accords hopeful believers. The Spirit, dwelling within us, gives our efforts, our suffering, and our weakness the same nobility we see in the struggles of Jesus.

We should not regret that we must live in hope, subject to all the miseries of the flesh. How could it be otherwise? Is it possible to hope for something we already have? Indeed, we hope for what we cannot see and do not yet have. And we do so in patient endurance, the same patient endurance we see in Jesus at Gethsemane, before Pilate, and on the cross. We keep that cross before us daily precisely because we know what lies beyond it. Life itself presents us with the cross; Spirit-filled hope draws us on toward the resurrection.

The final paragraph is complex in structure. Take it deliberately.

And the one who searches *hearts*
knows what is the *intention* of the *Spirit,*
because he *intercedes* for the *holy* ones
according to God's *will.*

GOSPEL John 7:37–39

A reading from the holy Gospel according to John

This is a brief gospel text that makes up in power what it lacks in length.

On the *last* and *greatest* day of the feast,
Jesus stood up and *exclaimed,*
"Let anyone who *thirsts* come to *me* and *drink.*
As *Scripture* says:
'Rivers of *living* water will *flow* from *within* him
who *believes* in *me.*'"

Clearly the second half of the reading is John's commentary on Jesus' outcry. Make this clear in your proclamation.

He *said* this in reference to the *Spirit*
that those who came to *believe* in him were to *receive.*
There *was,* of course, no Spirit *yet,*
because *Jesus* had not yet been *glorified.*

GOSPEL **The festival the gospel passage refers to is the Jewish feast of Tabernacles, which included scripture readings and the ceremonial drawing of water to celebrate the great day of Israel's restoration, when "You will draw water joyfully from the springs of salvation" (Isaiah 12:3). We sang this song at the Easter Vigil.**

Jesus announces that those who thirst for living water must find it in him. He is the spring of salvation Isaiah had foretold. The parenthetical commentary by John equates the "living water" with the outpouring of the Holy Spirit at Pentecost, following Jesus' resurrection and ascension. His point, written with the benefit of hindsight, is that the sacrificial death of Jesus made the Spirit's coming possible.

Notice that Jesus is not speaking of himself as being the source of living water but instead says that all those who drink of him shall have the spring of salvation flow from within them. Clearly, we are recipients of the water and the Spirit so that we can become sources of living water in the world. To drink from the fountain is to *become* a fountain.

PENTECOST

Lectionary #63

READING I Acts 2:1–11

A dramatic and wonder-filled narrative. It will require your best efforts to convey the awe and delight of those who witnessed this great event.

All these signs of God's power appear in the Hebrew scriptures. They are familiar, but never fail to startle us.

A reading from the Acts of the Apostles

When the time for *Pentecost* was fulfilled,
they were all in one place *together*.
And *suddenly* there came from the *sky*
a *noise* like a strong driving *wind*,
and it filled the entire *house* in which they were.
Then there appeared to them *tongues* as of *fire*,
which *parted* and came to *rest* on each *one* of them.
And they were all *filled* with the Holy *Spirit*
and began to speak in different *tongues*,
as the Spirit *enabled* them to *proclaim*.

Almost parenthetical, this paragraph makes the point that the Spirit's aim is to reach "every nation under heaven."
Galileans = gal-ih-LEE-uhnz
Parthians = PAHR-thee-uhnz
Medes = meedz
Elamites = EE-luh-mīts
Mesopotamia = mes-uh-poh-TAY-mee-uh
Judea = joo-DEE-uh
Cappadocia = kap-uh-DOH-shee-uh

Now there were devout *Jews* from every nation under *heaven*
staying in Jerusalem.
At this *sound*, they gathered in a large *crowd*,
but they were *confused*
because *each one* heard them speaking in his own *language*.
They were *astounded*, and in *amazement* they asked,
"Are not all these people who are speaking *Galileans*?
Then how does each of us *hear* them in his *native language*?
We are *Parthians*, *Medes*, and *Elamites*,
inhabitants of *Mesopotamia*, *Judea* and *Cappadocia*,

READING I Remember the story of the Tower of Babel in the book of Genesis? Today's reading from Acts reverses the situation. Whereas the people who built the Tower (in prideful disobedience) had their one language split into many, the people who experience the coming of the Spirit see their many languages made intelligible to all. The point is clear: The coming of the Holy Spirit is a unifying force that binds all peoples together.

When did this marvelous event take place? According to Luke in this reading, it is on the Jewish feast of Pentecost (when Jewish practice at the time commemorated the giving of the Law on Mount Sinai—an event also accompanied by wind and fire). In the gospel of John, the coming of the Holy Spirit occurs when the risen Christ first appears to the disciples sequestered in the upper room. The writers of scripture have their reasons for situating the occurrence at different times. Luke wants to associate the new Pentecost with the old, and to show the new Pentecost to be the fulfillment of the ancient prophecies. John associates the gift of the Spirit with teaching (John 14) the commission to forgive sins (John 20). In any case, the coming of the Spirit cannot be limited to any particular moment in history. It is a constant and dynamic reality.

And most important are the consequences of that reality. The God who gave the Law now gives far more—the Divine Spirit itself, the very "self" of God. And that Spirit is given not to a chosen few—it fills the entire world.

There is a choice of second readings today. Speak with the liturgy coordinator or the homilist to find out which reading will be used.

Pontus = PON-tuhs
Phrygia = FRIJ-ee-uh
Pamphylia = pam-FIL-ee-uh
Libya = LIB-ee-uh
Cyrene = sī-REE-nee
Cretans = KREE-tuhnz
Arabs = AIR-uhbz (not AY-rabz)

Pontus and *Asia*, *Phrygia* and *Pamphylia*,
Egypt and the districts of *Libya* near *Cyrene*,
as well as travelers from *Rome*,
both *Jews* and *converts* to Judaism, *Cretans* and *Arabs*,
yet we hear them speaking in our own *tongues*
of the mighty acts of *God*."

READING II Romans 8:8–17

A reading from the Letter of Saint Paul to the Romans

The opening is a strong negative; notice that it sets us up for a stronger positive!

Brothers and sisters:
Those who are in the *flesh* cannot *please* God.
But you are *not* in the flesh;
on the *contrary*, you are in the *spirit*,
if only the *Spirit* of *God* dwells in you.
Whoever does *not* have the Spirit of *Christ* does not *belong* to him.

But if Christ *is* in you,
although the *body* is dead because of *sin*,
the *spirit* is *alive* because of *righteousness*.
If the *Spirit* of the one who *raised* Jesus from the *dead* dwells in you,
the one who *raised* Christ from the *dead*
will give life to *your* mortal bodies *also*,
through his *Spirit* that *dwells* in you.

Consequently, brothers and sisters,
we are *not debtors* to the flesh,
to live *according to* the flesh.

READING II **ROMANS. The point Paul makes in this reading is that the transforming power of the Spirit is awesome and complete. The point is not that we are lumps of nasty flesh without the Spirit, but that we are helpless to know God without the Spirit's prompting. And that Spirit is always available to us, eager to dwell in us.**

The Spirit dwelling in us ennobles us and enables us. It ennobles us by giving us a direct share in the life of God. In enables us to see beyond the "slings and arrows of outrageous fortune" and into the spiritual existence that transcends the negatives of our bodily existence.

And another important thing: The transforming power of the Spirit is not something we must do without until after death. No, the life of the Spirit within us makes this present existence totally different. The Spirit enables us to "put to death the deeds of the body" *now* (sin, greed, selfishness, despair, and so on) and live this bodily existence in a spiritual way. We celebrate our transformation *now*—and experience a foretaste of the complete transformation that will take place when we see God face to face. Our sufferings now are a prelude to glory—just as they were for Christ.

1 CORINTHIANS. To understand this reading, realize that Paul is addressing a community that struggled mightily with factions and divided loyalties. Paul's here is to encourage them to unify themselves under the one true Lord, Jesus the Christ.

Squabbling over who has the greatest gift or charism from the Spirit makes no sense at all for Christians. All true gifts come from the one God, and the test of their authenticity is the degree to which they

Here is the main point: We are not powerless in the face of limitations.

For if you *live* according to the *flesh*, you will *die*,
but if by the *Spirit* you put to *death* the deeds of the *body*,
you will *live*.

For those who are *led* by the *Spirit* of *God* are *sons* of God.
For you did *not* receive a spirit of *slavery* to fall back into *fear*,
but you received a spirit of *adoption*,
through whom we cry, "*Abba*, Father!"

Abba = AH-bah ; a warm and intimate form of "Father." It relates to what follows: "When we cry, 'Abba! Father!' it is that very Spirit bearing witness"

The Spirit *himself* bears witness with *our* spirit
that we are *children* of *God*,
and if *children*, then *heirs*,
heirs of God and *joint heirs* with *Christ*,
if only we *suffer* with him
so that we may *also* be *glorified* with him.

Identification with Christ's suffering is always the prelude to sharing his glory.

Or:

READING II 1 Corinthians 12:3b–7, 12–13

A reading from the first Letter of Saint Paul to the Corinthians

The reading begins abruptly. Be sure the assembly is settled and ready before you begin. The first sentence is crucial.

The very effective structure should be stressed: "There are . . . but . . . ; there are . . . but . . . ; there are . . . but . . . ."

Brothers and sisters:
No one can say, "Jesus is *Lord*," except by the Holy *Spirit*.
There are different *kinds* of spiritual *gifts* but the *same Spirit*;
there are different forms of *service* but the same *Lord*;
there are different *workings* but the same *God*
who produces *all* of them in *everyone*.
To each *individual* the *manifestation* of the Spirit
is given for some *benefit*.

build up the common good and bring people together in unity of belief.

The matter of speaking in tongues had led the Corinthians to rank themselves inappropriately. Speaking in tongues is a gift; those who do not receive it have no doubt received a different gift, certainly no less important for the community. The one Spirit has filled *all* of us, Jew or Greek, slave or free, rich or poor, woman or man, people of every race, language, and way of life.

Note that there is a choice of gospel readings today.

GOSPEL JOHN 14. Once again we return to the words Jesus spoke at the Last Supper. They are particularly appropriate today, for now we read them in the light of all we have celebrated since Holy Thursday—and they are imbued with greater meaning.

"If you love me" and "Whoever loves me" are words that show us how firmly the Christian life is founded on love. Everything depends on it. Keeping the commandments is both the cause and the effect of loving Jesus. There are many stories of people who learned to love by doing good things, and just as many of people who learned to do good things by loving. Either way, love is the challenge, the method, and the reward. And to keep the commandments of Jesus is identical with loving him. Loving Jesus is identical with keeping his commandments.

This reading is part of the farewell discourse of Jesus, and so prepares us for the celebration of the coming of the Holy Spirit.

Take special care—and plenty of time—in reading this paragraph. It is complex and rich with meaning.

As a *body* is *one* though it has many *parts*,
and all the *parts* of the body, though *many*, are one *body*,
so also *Christ*.
For in one *Spirit* we were all *baptized* into one *body*,
whether *Jews* or *Greeks*, *slaves* or *free* persons,
and we were all given to *drink* of *one Spirit*.

GOSPEL John 14:15–16, 23b–26

A reading from the holy Gospel according to John

The entire text is made up of the words of Jesus, speaking in the first person. The solemnity is tempered with intimacy.

Jesus said to his *disciples*:
"If you *love* me, you will keep my *commandments*.
And I will ask the *Father*,
and he will give you another *Advocate* to *be* with you *always*.

This paragraph is complex. It must be read slowly. Notice, though, that it makes the single point: The word you keep, or choose not to keep, has come from the Father in love. Jesus encourages us to accept the word.

"Whoever *loves* me will keep my *word*,
and my *Father* will love *him*,
and we will *come* to him and make our *dwelling* with him.
Those who do *not* love me do not keep my words;
yet the word you *hear* is not *mine*
but that of the *Father* who *sent* me.

The sense here is: "I am telling you these things now even though you will not completely understand them; the Holy Spirit will enable you to understand fully."

"I have *told* you this while I am *with* you.
The *Advocate*, the Holy *Spirit* whom the Father
will *send* in my *name*,
will teach you *everything*
and *remind* you of all that I *told* you."

Or:

The risen Christ returns to the Father from whom he was sent, and in his stead the Holy Spirit now becomes God's way of dwelling among us. Filled with that Spirit, the disciples can continue to carry on Christ's work with confidence and peace, knowing that they are accompanied and guided by the divine presence. The Holy Spirit reminds the disciples of the teachings and deeds of Jesus; it enables them to keep these things in mind.

The important thing about this gospel passage is that it moves us away from the resurrected Jesus to show us his new way of being in the world: as the Spirit of truth. We are prompted more than ever to see life with spiritual rather than material vision. We are taught here how to walk by faith, not by sight.

The charm and attraction we have for the image of Jesus walking the earth in his resurrected body must be transformed by the wisdom and insight that enable us to see, in the coming of the Spirit, an even more intimate union with him. It was not an easy adjustment for the disciples and it is not an easy adjustment for us.

But love makes it possible and that is the point of Jesus' words to us today. The proof of our love is that we obey him, and true obedience is freely given because we love, and are loved by, the one we obey. How far this removes us from any view of Christianity as an ethical code! We submit to the Lord's commandments because we love and trust the one who commands, not because there are reprisals if we don't. It is the Spirit dwelling within us that enables us to obey in love, not fear.

How clear can your proclamation make this to the assembly? Can you communicate

GOSPEL John 20:19–23

This is a brief gospel, but it tells of a major event in the life of the church. Proclaim it with great care and breadth.

Emphasize "Peace" each time, not "with."

A reading from the holy Gospel according to John

On the evening of that *first* day of the *week*,
when the doors were *locked*, where the disciples were,
for fear of the *Jews*,
Jesus came and stood in their *midst*
and said to them, "*Peace* be with you."
When he had said this, he showed them his *hands* and his *side*.
The disciples *rejoiced* when they saw the Lord.

We are sent forth just as Jesus was. Our commission in the world is identical to his commission in the world.

Jesus said to them *again*, "*Peace* be with you.
As the *Father* has sent *me*, so *I* send *you*."

And when he had said this, he breathed on them
and said to them,
"*Receive* the Holy *Spirit*.
Whose sins you *forgive* are *forgiven* them,
and whose sins you *retain* are *retained*."

the revolutionary concept of loving obedience that Jesus asks of us? Remember that he himself recognized that the world cannot accept it because it does not recognize him for who he is. Perhaps the best you can do as proclaimer is to enable your hearers to see Jesus a bit more clearly, to recognize him and, irresistibly, to love him.

JOHN 20. In this brief passage from John's gospel, Jesus breathes the Holy Spirit upon the disciples and the Easter celebration comes full circle. With the gift of the Holy Spirit, Jesus' work on earth is complete. The Spirit empowers the disciples to continue the work of redemption in full awareness of the abiding presence of Christ through the power of the Spirit.

John's painstaking effort to make clear that the Jesus who appears to his disciples is really the same Jesus they knew before his death is fascinating. Jesus shows the disciples his hands and side, which still bear the marks of his wounds. So who or what is this being that stands before the happy disciples? He is clearly not mortal, but he is still the teacher the disciples knew and loved. The most important point John is making is that the risen Christ is *real*.

The author describes the disciples' recognition and subsequent joy with what may be the understatement of the ages: "The disciples rejoiced when they saw the Lord." Your proclamation of this line will have to go beyond the meaning of the literal words.

Finally, we witness the giving of the Holy Spirit. Jesus' mission is accomplished, but his work of redemption continues through those he now sends forth in the power of the Holy Spirit.

HOLY TRINITY

Lectionary #166

READING I Proverbs 8:22–31

A reading from the Book of Proverbs

This reading is poetry, and like much of Hebrew poetry it relies on the poetic structure of parallelism to work its effect. Every line is echoed or elaborated upon in the line that follows. The final three lines add a feeling of closure and resolution.

Thus says the *wisdom* of *God*:
"The LORD *possessed* me, the *beginning* of his *ways*,
the *forerunner* of his *prodigies* of long *ago*;
from of *old* I was poured *forth*,
at the *first*, before the *earth*.
When there were no *depths* I was brought *forth*,
when there were no *fountains* or springs of *water*;
before the *mountains* were settled into *place*,
before the *hills*, I was brought *forth*;
while as yet the *earth* and *fields* were not *made*,
nor the first *clods* of the *world*.

Though technically this text is composed of only two complete sentences, every two lines complete an image or thought. And each is beautifully constructed. Let the poetry work its magic.

"When the LORD established the *heavens* I was *there*,
when he marked out the *vault* over the face of the *deep*;
when he made *firm* the skies *above*,
when he fixed *fast* the foundations of the *earth*;
when he set for the *sea* its *limit*,
so that the *waters* should not *transgress* his *command*;
then was I *beside* him as his *craftsman*,
and I was his *delight* day by *day*,
playing before him all the *while*,
playing on the surface of his *earth*;
and I found *delight* in the human *race*."

READING I Our belief in God as a trinity of persons—Father, Son, Spirit—is represented in our catechisms in language that is philosophical and analytical. This is a language very different from that of the scriptures. The challenge before us is to avoid interpreting this reading as a description of part of God. God has no parts. Rather, Wisdom is personified (given human traits) in an attempt to describe the ways in which God chooses to reveal the divine nature. Wisdom is certainly presented here as something very intimately involved with God, and in later writings is perceived as the quality human beings need to discern God's activity in the world.

So is this reading about Wisdom or about God? Well, both, really—although we miss the point if we force the distinction. Wisdom is certainly a God-like virtue, and our scriptures are full of the notion that true wisdom sees more clearly and is necessary for faith. It is the wise who seek God. And those who find God are blessed with true wisdom.

The lovely poetry of Proverbs is meant to give us a sense of the beauty and the permanence—indeed, the eternal quality—of wisdom. And in all those attributes, wisdom is God-like. It is also God's gift to human beings, the gift that enables them to see beyond the literal and into the deeper significance of life's events.

Wisdom is in no way equated with intellectual prowess or an accumulation of information. It is more closely associated with experience and discernment. It is, above all, a spiritual entity, not independent of thought and logic, but far superior to it. It is, finally, an elusive reality, but very, very real—much like the God who is Three-in-One.

READING II Romans 5:1–5

Paul is writing exalted prose here—loosely crafted, but tightly thought out. Wide vocal variety is the secret of an effective proclamation.

Note the strong contrast. Of course we can boast of our hopes. But we can even boast of our afflictions! It is a striking thought. Let it be striking!

A reading from the Letter of Saint Paul to the Romans

Brothers and sisters:
Therefore, since we have been *justified* by *faith*,
we have *peace* with *God* through our *Lord* Jesus *Christ*,
through whom we have gained *access* by faith
to this *grace* in which we *stand*,
and we *boast* in hope of the *glory* of God.

Not only *that*, but we even boast of our *afflictions*,
knowing that *affliction* produces *endurance*,
and *endurance*, proven *character*,
and proven *character*, *hope*,
and *hope* does not *disappoint*,
because the *love* of God has been poured *out* into our *hearts*
through the Holy *Spirit* that has been *given* to us.

READING II Paul presents us here with a fabric of belief, each thread interwoven with the others, each pattern flowing into the next, so that the design is ultimately simple. If we were to reduce Paul's words to a formula here, we could repeat a description of salvation history often heard in religious education classrooms: "From the Father, through the Son, and in the Holy Spirit, to return to the Father." In other words, the love with which God moves toward us is expressed through Jesus, the Son, and is perpetuated by the indwelling of the Holy Spirit to draw us back to the love of God. Today we celebrate the unity of divine persons in which that circular movement of love continues.

The second sentence of the reading (there are only two sentences) is almost playful. The logic represented here is not rigid. It is more the logic of experience and wisdom (as in the first reading). Paul gives us something more useful than an intellectual syllogism. He gives us a formulation of how suffering, for the Christian, is an experience that leads to the very opposite of what we might think. Are those who suffer understandably edging toward despair? Just the opposite! Suffering enables us to endure, to develop character, and to hope for victory over suffering (with Jesus as model). And our hope is firmly grounded because it is guaranteed by the very love of God manifested in the Holy Spirit who lives in us.

A lively approach to this text—communicating something of its playfulness—will probably be most successful in getting its message across. There is nothing trivial about the message, of course, just a healthy delight in the solidity of our faith, the fervor of our love, and the bright outlook of our

GOSPEL John 16:12–15

A reading from the holy Gospel according to John

A brief gospel reading requires careful proclamation; slow, but also dynamic.

Jesus said to his *disciples*:
"I have much *more* to tell you, but you cannot *bear* it now.
But when *he* comes, the Spirit of *truth*,
he will guide you to *all* truth.
He will not speak on his *own*,
but he will speak what he *hears*,
and will *declare* to you the things that are *coming*.
He will *glorify* me,
because he will *take* from what is *mine* and *declare* it to *you*.
Everything that the *Father* has is *mine*;
for this *reason* I told you that he will *take* from what is *mine*
and *declare* it to *you*."

The "things that are coming" are not prophecies of future events, but ever fuller understanding of Jesus as the long-promised Messiah.

Father, Son, and Spirit are all implied in this final sentence.

hope. And there's another "trinity" we can celebrate today!

GOSPEL Once again we return to the scene of the Last Supper and hear Jesus' words in the clarity that hindsight brings. In the light of the resurrection and ascension, the promise of the Spirit and its activity in our life make complete sense.

The disciples could not bear all that Jesus had to tell them. They needed first the assurance that only his triumph over death could bring. And with the coming of the Spirit, they are assured of ever-increasing clarity of understanding. That is the Spirit's function in our lives: to make the mission and message of Jesus more and more clear in every age. The Spirit's guidance adds nothing to the full revelation of God's love in Jesus; that revelation is complete in Jesus' life, death, resurrection and ascension. But our understanding and acceptance of Jesus as the Messiah promised long ago needs the Spirit's presence. The Spirit is Advocate, Counselor, Comforter—the abiding presence of God, who continues to fill our hearts with love and peace.

There is nothing static about God, our faith, the church or our hope. All are dynamic. God's revelation in the Son and through the Spirit continues. Our faith seeks ever greater understanding, the church strives for ever greater integrity and holiness, and our hope struggles toward ever greater assurance.

BODY AND BLOOD OF CHRIST

Lectionary #169

READING I Genesis 14:18–20

A brief reading demands a slow and deliberate proclamation.
Melchizedek = mel-KIZ-ih-dek
Salem is another name for Jerusalem.

A reading from the Book of Genesis

In those days, *Melchizedek*, king of *Salem*,
brought out *bread* and *wine*,
and being a *priest* of God Most *High*,
he blessed *Abram* with these *words*:
"Blessed be *Abram* by God Most *High*,
the *creator* of heaven and *earth*;
and blessed be *God* Most High,
who delivered your *foes* into your *hand*."
Then *Abram* gave him a *tenth* of *everything*.

The final short sentence records Abram's response. Pause before it and read it deliberately. Otherwise, it could be unintentionally humorous.

READING II 1 Corinthians 11:23–26

A reading from the first Letter of Saint Paul to the Corinthians

Relating these solemn and treasured words must be done with great care and intensity.

Brothers and sisters:
I received from the Lord what I also handed on to you,
that the Lord Jesus, on the night he was handed over,
took bread, and, after he had given thanks,
broke it and said, "This is my body that is for you.
Do this in remembrance of me."

READING I The reading from Genesis is chosen because of its mention of Melchizedek, a king and priest of old Jerusalem (Salem) who offers bread and wine and blesses Abram for a long-sought war victory. In these images we can recognize many parallels with Christ's function as priest, king, and provider. We also see identity with Abram, "blessed by God Most High." And we are reminded of a text from one of the messianic psalms: "You are a priest forever, according to the order of Melchizedek."

The choice of this reading for today's feast illustrates the reading of the Hebrew scriptures from a typological point of view—interpreting past events as prefiguring the person and work of Jesus the Christ.

READING II This is the same reading we heard on Holy Thursday. It gives us an account of the tradition of the eucharist in Paul's words. How rich is this word "tradition," from the Latin *tradere!* It means "to hand on," or "to hand over," and is used in both senses here. Paul has handed on to us what Jesus did at the Last Supper. And Jesus in turn was using the context of the ancient ceremony that was handed on to

In the same way also the cup, after supper, saying,
"This cup is the new covenant in my blood.
Do this, as often as you drink it, in remembrance of me."
For as often as you eat this bread and drink the cup,
you proclaim the death of the Lord until he comes.

The final sentence is Paul speaking, not Jesus. Pause before it.

GOSPEL Luke 9:11b–17

A reading from the holy Gospel according to Luke

Jesus spoke to the *crowds* about the kingdom of *God*,
and he *healed* those who needed to be *cured*.

As the day was drawing to a *close*,
the *Twelve* approached him and said,
"*Dismiss* the crowd
so that they can go to the surrounding *villages* and *farms*
and find *lodging* and *provisions*;
for we are in a *deserted* place here."

Here we have a short story and all its literary elements: situation, characters, conflict, climax, and resolution.

He said to them, "Give them some food *yourselves*."
They replied, "Five *loaves* and two *fish* are all we *have*,
unless we *ourselves* go and buy food for all these *people*."
Now the men there *numbered* about five *thousand*.

This sounds like a set-up so that the resolution of the problem is all the more dramatic.

Then he said to his *disciples*,
"Have them sit down in *groups* of about *fifty*."
They *did* so and made them all sit *down*.

him through his Jewish culture. Even more, Jesus did all this on the night that he was handed over in betrayal by Judas. The point of all this is that a good lector is sensitive to an intricately woven text!

Paul's main emphasis here is not on what Jesus did, but on what the assembled community does when it gathers to do what it does in memory of Christ. We know this because of the difficulties among the Corinthians, difficulties that had led to rival factions and the exclusion of the poor from the agape meal. Paul is reminding the church at Corinth that this holy meal is for the purpose of proclaiming the Lord's death until the end of time—a duty that must certainly not be exclusive, and must certainly not be confused with less significant gatherings.

GOSPEL Luke's account of the miraculous feeding of the multitude is replete with images and words we now associate with the eucharistic banquet: "taking the loaves," "said the blessing," "broke them," and "gave them to the disciples." We also hear that "all ate and were satisfied," filled," and that there was an abundance left over.

Some say the real miracle here is that Jesus, by example, got the people to share what they had with them—and to discover that, despite their selfish fears, there was plenty for everyone.

That all were satisfied and had plenty left over seems to be a foretaste of the heavenly banquet. It certainly says something about the overflowing providence of God.

Then taking the five *loaves* and the two *fish*,
and looking up to *heaven*,
he said the *blessing* over them, *broke* them,
and gave them to the *disciples* to set before the *crowd*.

They all *ate* and were *satisfied*.
And when the leftover *fragments* were picked up,
they filled *twelve* wicker *baskets*.

There can be no doubt that Luke had the Christian eucharistic celebration in mind when he wrote of this event from Jesus' life. But Luke also hints at the final banquet—the eschatological banquet—the fulfillment of every promise in heaven, made accessible by Jesus' death and resurrection. Whenever when we see Jesus at a meal in Luke's writing, there are hints of the wider and fuller significance of the act. There is also frequently a specific mention of inclusion of society's marginal characters. Notice that the feeding of the multitude is preceded by the healing of the sick among them.

For our purposes on today's feast, this reading serves to remind us of the promise of that eternal banquet that our daily bread, our eucharist, signifies for us today. The words of an ancient text used on this feast sums it up: "O sacred banquet, in which Christ is received, the memorial of his passion is celebrated, our hearts are filled with grace, and a pledge of future glory is given us!"

12TH SUNDAY IN ORDINARY TIME

Lectionary #96

READING I Zechariah 12:10–11; 13:1

Zechariah = zek-uh-RĪ-uh

A reading from the Book of the Prophet Zechariah

It is the Lord God who speaks. Let this proclamation ring out bold and clear.

Thus says the *Lord*:
I will *pour out* on the house of *David*
and on the inhabitants of *Jerusalem*
a *spirit* of *grace* and *petition*;
and they shall *look* on him whom they have *pierced*,
and they shall *mourn* for him as one mourns
for an only *son*,
and they shall *grieve* over him as one grieves
over a *firstborn*.

Hadadrimmon = hay-dad-RIM-uhn
Megiddo = meh-GID-oh

On that *day* the mourning in *Jerusalem* shall be as great
as the mourning of *Hadadrimmon* in the plain
of *Megiddo*.
On that *day* there shall be *open* to the house of *David*
and to the *inhabitants* of *Jerusalem*,
a *fountain* to *purify* from *sin* and *uncleanness*.

A periodic sentence. The subject is withheld until the end. Build up to—and pause slightly after—the word "fountain."

READING I The reading from the prophet Zechariah is chosen today in the Christian tradition of seeing in this prophecy a prefiguring of the sufferings of Christ, and the redemptive cleansing from sin that Christ's suffering accomplished. Zechariah's vision did not include the person of Jesus Christ, certainly, but it did look forward—through the sufferings of Israel—to that day when redemption and forgiveness would be offered to those who rejected God's message and those who delivered it.

This text is clearly in the tradition of the Suffering Servant theme we find elsewhere in the Hebrew scriptures. Several of the prophets wrote of the chosen one (it could be one person or the entire people of Israel) who would suffer unjustly at the hands of the wicked but ultimately be vindicated by God. The Suffering Servant speaks for God and yet the people do not listen. Instead, they reject both God and the Servant. When the Servant has been vindicated, however, the people see their wickedness and repent of their blindness. In response, the all-merciful God offers a fountain to purify from sin and uncleanness.

READING II There is no stronger defense of our equality in Jesus than this passage. Baptism is the subject of this reading—and the consequences of belonging to (being clothed with) Christ. Once the image and character of Christ have been imprinted on us in baptism, any differences that would seem to rank us according to worthiness are obliterated. Paul specifically lists such perceived differences: race, social

READING II Galatians 3:26–29

A reading from the Letter of Saint Paul to the Galatians

Brothers and sisters:

A bold assertion of our unity and equality. Read with conviction!

Through *faith* you are all children of *God* in Christ *Jesus*.

"Baptized" and "clothed" should receive equal emphasis.

For *all* of you who were *baptized* into Christ
have *clothed* yourselves with Christ.

Proclaim this series of parallels deliberately.

There is neither *Jew* nor *Greek*,
there is neither *slave* nor *free* person,
there is not *male* and *female*;
for you are all *one* in Christ *Jesus*.

And if you belong to *Christ*,
then you are *Abraham's* descendant,

A sense of closure is necessary—slow down, but retain the intensity.

heirs according to the *promise*.

GOSPEL Luke 9:18–24

A reading from the holy Gospel according to Luke

The quiet setting and the cosmic questions make for effective contrast.

Once when *Jesus* was praying in *solitude*,
and the *disciples* were with him,
he *asked* them, "Who do the *crowds* say that I *am*?"

The replies are simple and straightforward.

They said in reply, "John the *Baptist*;
others, *Elijah*;
still others, 'One of the ancient *prophets* has *arisen*.'"

Jesus' next question is a zinger! Craft it carefully to signal its importance.

Then he said to them, "But who do *you* say that I am?"
Peter said in reply, "The *Christ* of *God*."

position, gender. Incorporation into the body of Christ through baptism eliminates all of these as sources of distinction. And by extension, of course, those who belong to the body of Christ see that discrimination or prejudice against those who have not been baptized is equally unthinkable. We are not members of an exclusive group. Through his sacrifice, Christ has redeemed the entire world for all time, and in some way we do not yet understand. All humankind is included in that redemptive act.

In the first reading we see that God's chosen one is persecuted. In the gospel we hear Jesus call us toward the cross. It is apparent that the cost of discipleship is uppermost in our minds today. One of those costs is to live according to the rule Paul lays down in this reading for all Christians: surrender of prejudice. The church is less than Christian until it is an "equal opportunity" community. Christian churches might consider publishing this reading in every Sunday's bulletin, followed by: "This Christian community is an equal opportunity community. You are invited to follow Christ with us, and you will never be excluded here because of your race, color, national origin, ethnicity, gender, sexual orientation, or any of those other things often used to rate, rank and exclude people!" Nothing less than this degree of inclusiveness is truly Christian. Anyone who belongs to Christ, Paul says, is an heir according to the promise made to Abraham, our father in faith. And Christians believe that all the world belongs to Christ.

GOSPEL Jesus' question to his disciples, "Who do you say that I am?" is the question asked of every disciple in every age and at every moment of a

Peter's response seems immediate and spontaneous. Has he been watching Jesus more closely than the rest?

Jesus is going to be a different kind of Messiah than many are expecting. It will take the disciples a long time to realize this.

These words come as a shock and explain Jesus' stern order.

The balance and parallelism here make the passage memorable.

He *rebuked* them
and *directed* them not to *tell* this to *anyone*.
He said, "The Son of *Man* must *suffer greatly*
and be *rejected* by the *elders*, the chief *priests*,
and the *scribes*,
and be *killed* and on the *third* day be *raised*."

Then he said to *all*,
"If anyone wishes to come after *me*,
he must *deny* himself
and take up his cross *daily* and *follow* me.
For whoever wishes to *save* his life will *lose* it,
but whoever *loses* his life for *my* sake will *save* it."

Christian's life. The quality of our response to this question is the best gauge of the quality of our discipleship. If we can say, "You are the Christ, the Messiah of God," and be fully aware of what that implies, then we have arrived at mature faith—and have adopted an unfailing measure for every thought, word and deed.

This passage in Luke signals the beginning of the long journey to Jerusalem. From this point on, Jesus is on the way to the cross. Everything he says and does is another step toward Golgotha—where he will demonstrate perfect obedience, love and self-giving. If that picture seems too grim, we need only thank God that we know more than the first disciples did when they heard the dire prediction we read in this text. We know that beyond Golgotha lies the empty tomb.

Taking up the cross and following Jesus is difficult. It is also non-negotiable. But it should not come as a shock that so much is required of us. This is the same Jesus about whom it was predicted at his birth: "This child will be the rise and fall of many." Jesus is a "sign of contradiction." And baptism places the same sign on us.

As we make our way through Ordinary Time, guided this year by Luke's gospel, we will be challenged again and again toward a fundamental conversion. We will be asked over and over to give up old ways of thinking, to open ourselves to the vulnerability of discipleship—in short, to lose our lives so that we may save them. We need not lose heart in the face of such a challenge; it has been met before—by the one who says, "Come after me."

13TH SUNDAY IN ORDINARY TIME

Lectionary #99

READING I 1 Kings 19:16b, 19–21

Elijah = ee-LĪ-juh
Elisha = ee-LĪ-shuh (the names are similar; enunciate them distinctly)
Shaphat = SHAY-fat
Abel-meholah = AY-b'l-muh-HOH-lah

The reading is a short story, with introduction, plot, conflict, and resolution. Let vocal variety distinguish each section.

A reading from the first Book of Kings

The *LORD* said to *Elijah*:
"You shall anoint *Elisha*, son of *Shaphat* of *Abelmeholah*,
as *prophet* to *succeed* you."

Elijah set *out* and came upon *Elisha*, son of *Shaphat*,
as he was *plowing* with twelve yoke of *oxen*;
he was *following* the *twelfth*.

Elijah went *over* to him and threw his *cloak* over him.
Elisha *left* the oxen, *ran* after *Elijah*, and said,
"*Please*, let me kiss my *father* and *mother* goodbye,
and I will *follow* you."

This dialogue seems strange to us. The meaning is indirect, but clear: "Make the choice with your entire heart."

Elijah *answered*, "Go *back*!
Have I *done* anything to you?"
Elisha *left* him, and taking the yoke of *oxen*, *slaughtered* them;
he used the *plowing* equipment for *fuel* to boil their *flesh*,
and gave it to his *people* to *eat*.
Then Elisha *left* and *followed* Elijah as his *attendant*.

READING I All the readings today deal with the cost of discipleship, the consequences and implications of dedicating one's life to God. Those who speak for God in the Hebrew scriptures—the prophets—come to realize quickly that their calling means personal sacrifice. And there is plenty of evidence that their response is not always immediate or unquestioning. When the call comes to Moses, for example, a long dialogue with God ensues, revealing a strong reluctance on Moses' part to accept the challenge. Not surprisingly, God wins out, but not by force; it is the promise "I will be with you" that enables the prophet to say yes. The call itself creates the prophet and the promise enables the prophet to respond.

In Elisha's case, the assent seems to come easily, though even he asks permission to tie up some loose ends—to say goodbye to his parents. Divine commission does not obliterate our natural existence. The two are always interwoven at first. Conversion may be immediate, but we still have to work out the practicalities of a changed life.

One of the striking things about this reading is the totality of Elisha's assent once it is given. He uses the implements of his trade as firewood to prepare a farewell meal for his people. But there are two lessons implied here: First, the call to be a disciple comes to ordinary people doing ordinary things (farmers farming, fishermen fishing, shepherds shepherding, tax collectors collecting). We should expect God to reveal the divine will in the ordinary tasks of our lives—not necessarily in smoke and thunder. Second, though our assent is total, we can use the implements (talents, gifts, resources) of our former lives in the exercise of, or as a springboard to, our newly committed lives.

READING II Galatians 5:1, 13–18

A reading from the Letter of Saint Paul to the Galatians

The opening sentence is a bit of wordplay, clarified later.

Brothers and sisters:
For *freedom* Christ set us *free*;
so stand *firm* and do not *submit* again to the yoke of *slavery*.

The wordplay continues. Paul is using "freedom," "slavery," and "serve" in different ways with different meanings. Your vocal inflection can assist the hearers.

For you were called for *freedom*, brothers and sisters.
But do not *use* this freedom
as an *opportunity* for the *flesh*;
rather, serve one another through *love*.
For the whole *law* is fulfilled in one *statement*,
namely, "You shall love your *neighbor* as *yourself*."
But if you go on *biting* and *devouring* one another,
beware that you are not *consumed* by one another.

Here is the answer to the problem described above.

I *say*, then: live by the *Spirit*
and you will certainly not *gratify* the desire of the *flesh*.
For the *flesh* has desires *against* the Spirit,
and the *Spir*it against the *flesh*;
these are *opposed* to each other,
so that you may not *do* what you *want*.

The last sentence is a banner statement.

But if you are guided by the *Spirit*, you are *not* under the *law*.

READING II Freedom versus slavery. It is the perception of many, no doubt, that following Jesus is a kind of enslavement: Christians agree to be bound by a set of beliefs, a catalogue of doctrines, a code of ethics, and a list of rules. Nothing could be further from the truth. Christians agree to be intimately united with the person of Jesus and are therefore brought into a kind of freedom that cannot be understood apart from faith. It is the freedom to do what our best nature (our redeemed nature) is eager to do.

The seemingly endless struggle for genuine freedom is part of the Christian life. As faith matures, it becomes clearer that we do not practice our beliefs out of a sense of obligation to God. The gift of salvation is precisely that—a gift. There are no strings attached. The accepting of gifts given in pure love does not create in the recipient an obligation to reciprocate. It creates an eagerness to respond with a like love. What could be more free than an eager response to love?

Paul is a realist. He sees that our unredeemed nature ("flesh," he calls it) keeps trying to replace spontaneous love with something more codified. Thus, there is the constant tendency to enslave ourselves again—to rules, laws, ethical codes, even non-essential religious practices. He appeals to our redeemed nature, now endowed with clearer vision (wisdom) and able to apply the Golden Rule (the "whole law") to every part of our existence.

Christians who feel they must have an elaborate rulebook to guide them have merely traded their old slavery to sin for a new slavery. Christians who are guided by

GOSPEL Luke 9:51–62

A reading from the holy Gospel according to Luke

The opening sentence is cryptic, so proclaim it with great deliberation, hinting at the deeper significance.

When the days for Jesus' being *taken up* were *fulfilled*,
he resolutely *determined* to journey to *Jerusalem*,
and he sent *messengers* ahead of him.

Samaritans = suh-MAIR-uh-tuhns. They do not welcome Jesus because they feel racially superior to him. Jesus shows us how to respond to such prejudice.

On the *way* they entered a *Samaritan* village
to prepare for his *reception* there,
but they would not *welcome* him
because the *destination* of his *journey* was *Jerusalem*.

When the disciples *James* and *John* saw this they *asked*,
"*Lord*, do you want us to call down *fire* from *heaven*
to *consume* them?"
Jesus *turned* and *rebuked* them, and they journeyed
to *another* village.

Two different responses to "Follow me." Separate them with pauses and renewed inflection, so they are distinctly different for your hearers.

As they were *proceeding* on their journey someone *said* to him,
"*I* will follow you *wherever* you go."
Jesus *answered* him,
"*Foxes* have *dens* and *birds* of the sky have *nests*,
but the Son of *Man* has *nowhere* to rest his *head*."

And to *another* he said, "*Follow* me."
But *he* replied, "*Lord*, let me go *first* and bury my *father*."
But he *answered* him, "Let the *dead* bury their *dead*.
But *you*, go and proclaim the *kingdom* of *God*."

The final sentence contains a revered proverb, giving the story an effective sense of closure.

And *another* said, "*I* will follow you, Lord,
but *first* let me say *farewell* to my family at *home*."
To *him* Jesus said, "No one who sets a *hand* to the *plow*
and *looks* to what was left *behind* is *fit* for the kingdom
of *God*."

the Spirit have a kind of "sixth sense"; they are free to model their relationships with others on the person and behavior of Jesus.

GOSPEL In the opening sentence of this reading we hear Luke make explicit where Jesus is headed. He is on his way to Jerusalem where, as we heard last week, he will be put to death. And he invites all of those along the way to follow him.

There are varied responses to the invitation. Some (the Samaritans) will not even listen because they are prejudiced against the one who issues the invitation. Are we, like James and John, to lash out at these ingrates? Of course not. Invitations are not commands. They may be refused, regardless of the loss such a refusal implies.

Some respond to the invitation without fully realizing what it entails. Jesus wants us to know up front that following him will lead to the crucifixion. Discipleship is a total commitment.

Others respond without understanding that their choice eliminates other choices. It must be made clear to them that *this* invitation is to a total conversion, involving all of one's energy, loyalty and devotion.

And still others follow with the mistaken impression that their new life can be somehow combined with their previous way of life.

To all these varied responses Jesus addresses himself clearly. The kingdom of God, which he has come to establish, must be our permanent and only dwelling place. We cannot vacation elsewhere during the oppressive summer heat or the bitter winter cold.

14TH SUNDAY IN ORDINARY TIME

Lectionary #102

READING I Isaiah 66:10–14c

A reading from the Book of the Prophet Isaiah

The tone of this reading is unrestrained joy, and poetry is the means of expressing it.

Thus says the LORD:
Rejoice with *Jerusalem* and be *glad* because of her,
all you who *love* her;
exult, exult with her,
all you who were *mourning* over her!

Some readers may be uncomfortable with the earthy imagery here, but there's no denying its vivid power.

Oh, that you may suck *fully*
of the *milk* of her *comfort*,
that you may nurse with *delight*
at her abundant *breasts*!

From a command to rejoice, we move to a promise of "shalom."

For *thus* says the LORD:
Lo, I will spread *prosperity* over Jerusalem like a *river*,
and the wealth of the *nations* like an overflowing *torrent*.
As *nurslings*, you shall be carried in her *arms*,
and *fondled* in her *lap*;
as a *mother* comforts her *child*,
so will *I* comfort *you*;
in *Jerusalem* you shall *find* your comfort.

The Lord has prophesied; it *will* come true.

When you *see* this, your *heart* shall *rejoice*
and your *bodies* flourish like the *grass*;
the LORD's *power* shall be *known* to his *servants*.

READING I Those who selected and arranged the scripture readings in the lectionary choose the first reading from the Hebrew scriptures to coincide thematically with the gospel reading. In some cases, it is difficult to see a clear connection. In others, the connection is very clear. In all cases, however, we should avoid evaluating the significance of the first reading merely in the light of the gospel. The history of our salvation is a long sweep through both Testaments—and the God who reaches out to us in love is equally present in both. The idea that the Hebrew scriptures have value only in light of their fulfillment in Christ is woefully misguided. Abraham is our father in faith, and the human history of God's movement toward us in love begins in Genesis.

Though the idea of peace appears in all three readings today, the intended connection between the first reading and the gospel may be the spirit of rejoicing that characterizes the return of exiled Israel to Jerusalem and the return of the disciples after a successful mission. Or is it the final joy of finding maternal comfort in renewed Jerusalem (first reading) and having our names written in the heavenly Jerusalem (gospel)?

Since the connection seems flexible, allow me to suggest another. Isaiah's poetry celebrates the return of the people from exile and imagines their triumphant return to the nurturing arms of Jerusalem, the mother of cities. Luke's guiding theme in this section of his gospel is that Jesus is also journeying toward Jerusalem—where he too will be welcomed by the city, but then rejected. It is in Jerusalem that Jesus will inaugurate the new kingdom of God by his passion and death. This is not to say that Luke had Isaiah's

READING II Galatians 6:14–18

A reading from the Letter of Saint Paul to the Galatians

To appreciate the full effect of Paul's boasting, we must remember that the cross was a hideous instrument of torture.

The new creation has changed everything. Let go of outmoded and limited customs.

Brothers and sisters:
May I never *boast* except in the *cross* of our *Lord* Jesus *Christ*,
through which the *world* has been *crucified* to me,
and *I* to the *world*.
For neither does *circumcision* mean *anything*,
nor does *uncircumcision*,
but only a *new* creation.
Peace and *mercy* be to all who *follow* this *rule*
and to the *Israel* of *God*.
From now *on*, let no one make *troubles* for me;
for I bear the marks of *Jesus* on my *body*.

Pause before the blessing, which concludes the reading.

The *grace* of our *Lord* Jesus *Christ* be with your *spirit*,
brothers and sisters. *Amen*.

song in mind in any specific way. But we can see the parallel and the contradiction, and we can marvel at the bitter irony.

READING II **Paul must deal with a people who are slowly moving from one way of believing to another. Some of them naturally tend to hold on to former practices which, in the light of the new way of Jesus, have diminished significance. Some Jewish converts to Christianity felt that the rite of circumcision had to be preserved. Paul has to say, "No, the 'new creation' transcends all that. The great sign of contradiction (a torture instrument that brings life—the cross) is the subject of our own boast. Whether circumcised or uncircumcised, we are the Lord's!"**

The marks that Paul bears on his body are the scars left from imprisonment and persecution. For him they signify the validity of his faith and are proof of his authority to teach the new creation. Suffering for Christ and the church is a hallmark of Christian leadership and authority. Though we may never suffer for the faith as Paul did, there are those around the world who still do. And, on the other hand, if we experience no suffering whatever as a result of living our faith, we probably need to ask how well we're living it.

This reading is the conclusion of the letter to the Galatians. The note of finality comes before the blessing, and it is strong. In modern idiom Paul would be saying something like this: "Please, no more about this circumcision matter! The issue is dead,

GOSPEL Luke 10:1–12, 17–20

A reading from the holy Gospel according to Luke

At *that* time the Lord *appointed* seventy-two *others*
whom he sent *ahead* of him in *pairs*
to every *town* and *place* he intended to *visit*.
He said to them,
"The *harvest* is *abundant* but the *laborers* are *few*;
so ask the *master* of the harvest
to send out *laborers* for his harvest.
Go on your *way*;
behold, I am sending you like *lambs* among *wolves*.
Carry no *money* bag, no *sack*, no *sandals*;
and greet *no one* along the *way*.

"Into whatever *house* you enter, *first* say,
'*Peace* to this household.'
If a *peaceful* person *lives* there,
your peace will *rest* on him;
but if *not*, it will return to *you*.
Stay in the *same* house and *eat* and *drink* what is *offered* to you,
for the *laborer* deserves his *payment*.
Do not move *about* from *one* house to *another*.

The harvest quote sounds like an old proverb. Single it out.

The "lambs among wolves" refers as much to the missionaries' behavior as to the dangers they will encounter. They imitate Jesus in both respects.

and the suffering I have endured on behalf of Jesus give me the authority to say so."

Then follows the customary blessing, which closes the letter and restores a sense of unity and peace after the heated debate.

GOSPEL The number seventy-two has a symbolic value. In the mind of Luke and his contemporaries it stood for the number of all the nations of the world. So the significance of sending out that many disciples is that the message of Jesus' arrival and the inauguration of his kingdom is to reach to the ends of the earth. This theme of universalism is strong in Luke, both here in his gospel and in his second volume, the Acts of the Apostles.

We are reminded here of another great missionary who was "sent before the Lord to prepare his way." The seventy-two are performing much the same work that John the Baptist did. The difference, of course, is that they have experienced the good news in the person of Jesus, whereas John was only vaguely aware that someone greater than himself was coming.

The harvest is great; indeed, it is the harvest of the entire human race that is in need of harvesters. And those who follow Jesus are called to help by their presence and their prayers. The urgency in Jesus' command to pray for harvesters is unmistakable. Now is the time, the day of salvation.

"Whatever *town* you enter and they *welcome* you,
eat what is set *before* you,
cure the *sick* in it and say to them,
'The kingdom of *God* is at *hand* for you.'

The point of these specifics is that time is of the essence. Communicate the urgency.

"Whatever town you *enter* and they do *not* receive you,
go out into the *streets* and say,
'The *dust* of your town that *clings* to our *feet*,
even *that* we shake off *against* you.'
Yet know *this*: the kingdom of *God* is at *hand*.
I *tell* you, it will be more *tolerable* for *Sodom* on that day
than for that *town*."

This is a comment full of sadness rather than rancor.
Sodom = SOD-uhm

The *seventy-two* returned *rejoicing*, and said,
"*Lord*, even the *demons* are *subject* to us because
of your *name*."
Jesus said, "I have observed Satan *fall* like *lightning*
from the *sky*.
Behold, I have given you the *power* to 'tread upon *serpents*'
and *scorpions*
and upon the full force of the *enemy*
and *nothing* will *harm* you.
Nevertheless, do not *rejoice* because the *spirits* are *subject* to you,
but *rejoice* because your *names* are written in *heaven*."

[Shorter: Luke 10:1–9]

The kingdom of God is at hand. Thus the missionaries must move quickly and unencumbered by anything that will slow them down or distract them.

For their sustenance, they are to depend on the goodness of those who receive them. But they are not to stay long, moving from house to house. They are not to tarry where they are not accepted. There is no instruction try to convince the reluctant. No, the mission is urgent, so the missionaries must keep moving. Those who refuse the good news are simply reminded that, regardless of their rejection, the kingdom of God is near.

Finally, their missionary joy is not to be misplaced. Yes, they will find that great power accompanies them, and even the spirit world will be subject to the word they preach. But the cause of their joy is their heavenly inheritance, not their earthly successes. There are no notches in the belt of the Christian missionary who truly understands what the good news is all about. In other words, it is *God* who reaps the harvest and it is *God* who is the reward of the harvesters.

15TH SUNDAY IN ORDINARY TIME

Lectionary #105

READING I Deuteronomy 30:10–14

A reading from the Book of Deuteronomy

Moses said to the *people*:
"If *only* you would heed the *voice* of the LORD, your *God*,
and keep his *commandments* and *statutes*
that are *written* in this book of the *law*,
when you *return* to the LORD, your God,
with all your *heart* and all your *soul*.

The text is formulaic and ritualized. The poetic structure demands an exalted proclamation.

"For this *command* that I *enjoin* on you today
is not too *mysterious* and *remote* for you.
It is not up in the *sky*, that you should say,
'Who will go up in the *sky* to *get* it for us
and *tell* us of it, that we may carry it *out*?'

Eight or nine lines of what the command is *not* are followed by two or three lines of what the command *is*. The effect is a long build-up followed by a sudden resolution.

"Nor is it across the *sea*, that you should say,
'Who will cross the *sea* to *get* it for us
and *tell* us of it, that we may carry it *out*?'

"*No*, it is something very *near* to you,
already in your *mouths* and in your *hearts*;
you have *only* to carry it *out*."

READING I Religious practices can sometimes make faith seem like a very complex business. Imagine someone of another faith looking at us as we celebrate our liturgies. The initial impression might well be that our beliefs are "mysterious and remote." But, of course, they are not. The scripture readings today remind us that our faith—and the practice of it—is as near to us as our hearts, and as accessible as our nearest neighbor.

The faith of the Old Testament centers on love of God and love of neighbor. The history of Israel's struggle to live out that faith is immensely complex and led to very elaborate rule books and guidelines and ethical codes. The history of Christianity has seen a similar evolution. It is perhaps inevitable that organized religious groups develop such codes and rules. And there is nothing essentially wrong in such development. There is, however, a temptation to rely on the code instead of upon the covenant of love that originally inspired the code. And in the face of that temptation we need to be reminded once again that "love of God and love of neighbor" sums up the law and the prophets.

It has been wisely said that if all our decisions and behavior were based on this twofold commandment, there would be no need for any others. Our hearts seem naturally to embrace the rightness of this commandment—even at the moment we transgress it! This is how we know we have a conscience. The commandment to love is already a part of us. We need only to carry it out.

READING II Colossians 1:15–20

Notice the structure of this reading: "Christ Jesus is . . . For in him . . . He is . . . He is . . . He is . . . For in him . . . ." The rhythmic pattern should aid your proclamation.

A reading from the Letter of Saint Paul to the Colossians

Christ *Jesus* is the *image* of the invisible *God*,
the *firstborn* of all *creation*.
For in *him* were created *all* things in *heaven* and on *earth*,
the *visible* and the *invisible*,
whether *thrones* or *dominions* or *principalities* or *powers*;
all things were *created* through *him* and for *him*.

Pause. A new section begins. Renew the emphasis.

He is *before* all things,
and in *him all* things hold *together*.
He is the *head* of the *body*, the *church*.
He is the *beginning*, the *firstborn* from the *dead*,
that in *all* things he *himself* might be *preeminent*.

A long sentence. Do not let your voice gradually fall throughout. Rather, let your intensity build.

For in *him* all the *fullness* was pleased to *dwell*,
and through *him* to *reconcile* all things for him,
making *peace* by the *blood* of his *cross*
through *him*, whether those on *earth* or those in *heaven*.

READING II Here we have an exultant hymn disguised as a theological treatise. Or is it the other way around? No matter; you should proclaim it as a hymn. It has some very important things to say about Jesus the Christ (Anointed One).

First of all, Jesus existed from all eternity, was present at the creation of the world and is the principle upon which heaven and earth exist. It is the cosmic Christ we see in these words—the Lord of heaven, the eternal Word of God, destined to become flesh in order to redeem the fallen world.

Too often, perhaps, our thinking about Jesus is limited to his early mission and ministry. Here, and elsewhere in scripture, Jesus is revealed as the eternal God—a belief unique to Christianity. Islam, for example, reveres Jesus as one of the greatest of the prophets, a man sent from God to reveal the nature of God's loving providence and to model obedient service. But the divinity of Jesus, so essential to Christianity, is an affront to the strictness of Islamic monotheism: the conception of God as one spiritual being without emanations or manifestations beyond himself. Christianity is also monotheistic, of course. We believe in one God, but manifest in three Persons—Father, Son, and Spirit. Today we catch a glimpse of the Son as the fullness of divinity.

Second, Jesus is the ruler of material creation as well. He is the head of the body we call church. In his risen body we see the first and final victory over death and the reason for our hope in everlasting life. In Jesus Christ we see the fullness, the entirety of the God who reconciled the world by taking on

GOSPEL Luke 10:25–37

A reading from the holy Gospel according to Luke

Be sure to begin with energy. We need to have the scene clearly set. In the lawyer's first question, emphasize "do," rather than "eternal life."

There was a scholar of the *law* who stood up to *test* him and said,
"*Teacher*, what must I *do* to inherit eternal *life*?"
Jesus said to him, "What is *written* in the *law*?
How do you *read* it?"
He said in *reply*,

Let each line in the series be distinct.

"You shall *love* the LORD, your *God*,
with *all* your *heart*,
with *all* your *being*,
with *all* your *strength*,
and with *all* your *mind*,
and your *neighbor* as *yourself*."

He replied to him, "You have answered *correctly*;
do this and you will *live*."

The plot thickens. The scholar is testing Jesus, remember. Consider a pregnant pause before Jesus' reply in order to communicate the weight of what is to come.

But because he wished to *justify* himself, he said to Jesus,
"And who *is* my neighbor?"

Renew the energy and tone of your voice to show the beginning of a narrative.

Jesus replied,
"A man fell *victim* to *robbers*
as he went down from *Jerusalem* to *Jericho*.
They *stripped* and *beat* him and went *off* leaving him half-*dead*.
A *priest* happened to be going down that road,
but when he *saw* him, he passed *by* on the opposite *side*.

The priest and Levite are avoiding the ritual impurity that would come from touching a corpse, which is what they take the man to be. They are, ironically here, obeying the law.

Likewise a *Levite* came to the place,
and when *he* saw him, *he* passed by on the opposite side.

human flesh and shedding the blood of self-sacrifice. The reconciliation thus effected involved the heavenly creatures as well, though in what way and for what reason we are uncertain.

In short (and in far more beautiful words than mine), this poetic text reaches for something of the vastness of Christ, something hinting at the limits of the mind to understand but not exceeding the ability of the heart to imagine. Proclaim it boldly and with joy.

GOSPEL Today's gospel reading presents us with one of our most treasured parables, the story of the Good Samaritan. It is surely one of the most effective lessons Jesus ever taught. Applied to our modern world and its problems of racial and ethnic conflict, it gives us the perfect solution. Yet it is not heeded. It is difficult to comprehend, in an age so advanced in technology and science, how the horror of ethnic cleansing is still considered justifiable by some, how major cities cannot find room for their homeless, how corporate greed feeds on the lives of those who built the corporation. Our best hope seems to be to emphasize the lesson of this parable on the individual level, as indeed it is told. It is apparently too early in Christian history for whole peoples and nations and groups to behave consistently toward each other like the Good Samaritan.

The lawyer who responds to Jesus' counter-question is a good and noble man. Unfortunately, the words "wished to justify himself" are often interpreted negatively, as

"But a *Samaritan* traveler who came upon him
was moved with *compassion* at the sight.
He *approached* the victim,
poured *oil* and *wine* over his *wounds* and *bandaged* them.
Then he lifted him *up* on his own *animal*,
took him to an *inn*, and *cared* for him.

"The next *day* he took out two silver *coins*
and gave them to the *innkeeper* with the *instruction*,
'Take *care* of him.
If you spend *more* than what I have *given* you,
I shall *repay* you on my way *back*.'

"*Which* of these three, in *your* opinion,
was *neighbor* to the robbers' *victim*?"

The scholar must pause. This is a difficult lesson to accept.

He answered, "The one who *treated* him with *mercy*."

The final word of Jesus must be full of warmth, not challenge. Jesus respects the difficulty of changing our ways.

Jesus said to him, "*Go* and do *likewise*."

though the lawyer were trying to find a loophole or to demonstrate his worthiness. No, he wants to be sure he understands what "love your neighbor" really implies. We could all do ourselves a favor by asking the same kinds of questions. And the wider context in which this story is recorded in Luke tells us more: it tells us that the lawyer's question, "Who is my neighbor?" is racially motivated. He is asking, "Who are the chosen of God? For these are my neighbors!" And that is how the lawyer is testing Jesus.

Jesus answers the question with an enormously shocking story. Samaritans were hated vociferously by the lawyer's racial group. Priests were expected to be law-abiding role models. Levites would be expected to have a special dedication to the law. And yet, it is a vile Samaritan who proves himself a genuine neighbor. It would not be difficult for each of us to construct a similar story—in which the person (or kind of person) that most repulses us outdoes us in compassion and love.

It is not a pretty scene. It is not a pretty story. The lawyer is not entirely convinced. In response to Jesus' final question, "Who was neighbor to the victim?" he cannot bring himself to say, "The Samaritan." He must resort to a description, "The one who treated him with mercy." So deeply rooted, so much in control of us, so hideous are our prejudices!

16TH SUNDAY IN ORDINARY TIME

Lectionary #108

READING I Genesis 18:1–10a

A reading from the Book of Genesis

terebinth = TAIR-uh-binth
Mamre = MAM-ree

The *LORD* appeared to *Abraham* by the terebinth of *Mamre*,
as he sat in the entrance of his *tent*,
while the *day* was growing *hot*.
Looking *up*, Abraham saw *three* men standing *nearby*.
When he *saw* them, he ran from the entrance of the *tent*
to *greet* them;
and bowing to the *ground*, he said:
"*Sir*, if I may ask you this *favor*,
please do not go on *past* your servant.

The rituals of hospitality are closely adhered to. Each is important.

Let some *water* be brought, that you may bathe your *feet*,
and then *rest* yourselves under the *tree*.
Now that you have come this *close* to your servant,
let me bring you a little *food*, that you may *refresh* yourselves;
and *afterward* you may go on your *way*."
The men *replied*, "Very *well*, do as you have *said*."

These details give the story vividness; but they also emphasize Abraham's eagerness to be a good host.

Abraham *hastened* into the tent and told *Sarah*,
"*Quick*, three measures of fine *flour*! *Knead* it and
make *rolls*."
He ran to the *herd*, picked out a tender, choice *steer*,
and gave it to a *servant*, who quickly *prepared* it.
Then Abraham got some *curds* and *milk*,
as well as the *steer* that had been prepared,

READING I The Lord appears in the form of three men coming toward Abraham's tent. Abraham is the perfect host, showering attention, food, and drink upon them. His hospitality may seem excessive, but we must remember the far more demanding code of the East. It is the tradition from which springs the Christian conviction regarding hospitality: In the guest, Christ is seen.

The significance of this text is, of course, the presence of God in the history of Israel and at work through Abraham's family to establish a covenant with the chosen people. Thus, the promised child is far more than a reward for solicitous hospitality.

The captivating variation of persons in this story inspired the painting of a lovely fifteenth-century icon. It depicts Abraham and three identical young men in the shade of the terebinth, and a table set with food and drink. To the medieval mind, the three persons whom Abraham addresses with the singular "Sir," formed a mysterious revelation of the Trinity, three persons in one God. In any case, it is the wealth of detail and the vividness of the story that make it so charming.

But it is the sheer goodness of God's wish to intervene in human history and reconcile heaven and earth that makes the story significant. Abraham is our father in faith. The promised son, Isaac, will be a central figure in the test of Abraham's obedient faith (and a prefiguring of Christ's sacrifice). We hear in this reading the beginning of our own salvation history. The God of Abraham, Isaac, and Jacob has plans for us—and they begin in the book of Genesis, not the gospel of Matthew.

and *set* these before the three *men*;
and he *waited* on them under the *tree* while they *ate*.

They *asked* Abraham, "Where is your *wife Sarah*?"
He replied, "*There* in the *tent*."
One of them said, "I will surely *return* to you
about this time *next* year,
and *Sarah* will then have a *son*."

Here is the point. End the reading on a high, bright tone.

READING II Colossians 1:24–28

A reading from the Letter of Saint Paul to the Colossians

Brothers and sisters:
Now I *rejoice* in my *sufferings* for *your* sake,
and in my *flesh* I am filling up
what is *lacking* in the afflictions of *Christ*
on behalf of his *body*, which is the *church*,
of which I am a *minister*
in accordance with God's *stewardship* given to me
to bring to *completion* for you the *word* of God,
the *mystery* hidden from *ages* and from generations *past*.

This is a very difficult reading, a long string of mostly abstract concepts. Prepare it very carefully.

But *now* it has been *manifested* to his *holy* ones,
to whom God *chose* to make *known* the riches of the *glory*
of this *mystery* among the *Gentiles*;
it is *Christ* in you, the hope for *glory*.
It is *he* whom we *proclaim*,
admonishing *everyone* and *teaching* everyone
with all *wisdom*,
that we may *present* everyone *perfect* in *Christ*.

If you proceed slowly, letting each assertion carry its own weight, the effect will be a kind of meditation on the presence of Christ in us.

READING II This is a difficult reading. It lacks the concrete imagery that would make it more accessible. But, of course, the writer is concerned with a mysterious thing: the manifestation of Christ through the church and its mission. Paul is writing from prison, so it is natural that he should refer to his sufferings. He is pointing out that his sufferings are clear evidence of Christ at work in the Christian mission—because suffering is an inevitable part of being a disciple. In other words, he is not saying that Christ's sufferings for us were defective or insufficient in some way.

To understand the fervor of this text, we must approach it with the earliest Christian belief about the identity we achieve with Christ through suffering. Then we can understand how Paul sees his afflictions as physical evidence of what the eyes of faith know about Christ's redemptive suffering.

To proclaim Christ is Paul's mission, but his objective is to gather all who hear the proclamation and to present them to God as mature (or even perfect) disciples. Thus the mystery of "Christ in you," only recently manifested, is the good news in a nutshell. That's it: *Christ in us.*

How very different from what we sometimes think being a Christian means! It's not a form of behavior, adherence to rules, avoidance of evil, or even doing good. Being a Christian means confronting the mystery that Christ is in you—that your faith is the result of a personal encounter with Christ the person, not Christianity the religion. Only when we see the difference will we be ready to be brought to completion (maturity) in Christ.

GOSPEL Luke 10:38–42

A reading from the holy Gospel according to Luke

The brief narrative is complete with characters, plot, conflict, and resolution. Don't rush through it.

Jesus entered a *village*
where a woman whose name was *Martha welcomed* him.
She had a *sister* named *Mary*
who *sat* beside the Lord at his *feet* listening to him *speak*.

Martha should not sound like a shrew here. Her concern is that the Lord be served well. She is not malicious. She has simply missed the point.

Martha, burdened with much *serving*, came to him and *said*,
"*Lord*, do you not *care*
that my *sister* has left me by *myself* to do the *serving*?
Tell her to *help* me."

Mary's silence throughout this dialogue says as much as her position at the Lord's feet!

The Lord said to her in *reply*,
"*Martha, Martha*, you are *anxious* and *worried*
about *many* things.
There is *need* of only *one* thing.

Not a stern rebuke. More like a gentle reminder.

Mary has chosen the *better* part
and it will *not* be *taken* from her."

GOSPEL Now is a good time to remember that Jesus is on his way to Jerusalem. The gospel of Luke relates the teachings of Jesus "on the road." It is Luke's literary and theological device to show us Jesus as he journeys toward Jerusalem, where he will bring his earthly mission to a close.

In today's gospel narrative, Jesus stops to take a rest from his journey. The way in which he is received becomes an occasion for him to teach us an important lesson. As the first reading for today's celebration was concerned with hospitality, so is the gospel. In both we hear quite a lot of bustling about providing for the guest's needs and comfort. Such solicitude for the guest is commendable and appreciated. However, Jesus takes the occasion to point out to Martha that she may have forgotten momentarily *why* hospitality is important. It certainly seems that Martha was more concerned with the serving than with the one served.

Imagine a similar situation: You are privileged to have a famous writer in your home to discuss her latest book over dinner. As host, you are so concerned that everything be done right that you end up spending most of the meal in the kitchen. What a pity! You've missed the author's words of wisdom—which were, after all, the purpose of the gathering. The meal was only the scenery, not the script.

So Jesus is cautioning Martha about anxiety. It is advice we hear often on Jesus' lips as he warns his followers not to encumber themselves on this journey with him toward glory. Mary has apparently realized that a simple sandwich is better than a four-course meal if it lets the cook out of the kitchen to enjoy the company of the special guest.

17TH SUNDAY IN ORDINARY TIME

Lectionary #111

READING I Genesis 18:20–32

The formulaic structure of this lengthy reading is part of its delight. Let the predictable stages of Abraham's progressive pleading work their magic. The story has a fable-like quality. We know what's coming, and when it does we are gratified.

Sodom = SOD-uhm
Gomorrah = guh-MOHR-ah

See last week's first reading for context.

A reading from the Book of Genesis

In *those* days, the *LORD* said:
"The *outcry* against *Sodom* and *Gomorrah* is so *great*,
and their *sin* so *grave*,
that I must go *down* and see whether or not
their *actions* fully *correspond* to the *cry* against them
that *comes* to me.
I mean to find *out*."

While *Abraham's visitors* walked on *farther* toward *Sodom*,
the *LORD* remained *standing* before Abraham.
Then Abraham drew *nearer* and said:
"Will you sweep away the *innocent* with the *guilty*?
Suppose there were fifty *innocent* people in the city;
would you wipe *out* the place, rather than *spare* it
for the sake of the fifty *innocent* people within it?

Though Abraham's words may seem brash, do not shy away from them. We are being taught how to pray.

The disclaimer in deference to the Lord results in greater boldness!

Far be it from you to *do* such a thing,
to make the *innocent* die with the *guilty*
so that the *innocent* and the *guilty* would be treated *alike*!
Should not the *judge* of all the world act with *justice*?"
The LORD *replied*,
"If I find *fifty* innocent people in the city of *Sodom*,
I will spare the whole *place* for *their* sake."

READING I Today's first reading presents us with a fable-like story that teaches us something about God's mercy—even toward those who do not know God. To take the bargaining between Abraham and God literally would be to miss the point. Indeed, to do so is misleading and makes the *wrong* point. God is not reluctant to show justice and mercy. God does not drive a hard bargain when it comes to sparing the lives of the innocent or, for that matter, punishing the wicked.

The Middle Eastern approach to divine attributes is very different from our own. We in the West tend to be rational, syllogistic, and literal. This reading shows us the opposite approach: intuitive, picturesque, parabolic. Since everything we think, write, or say about God must be done through metaphor, by using human characteristics in an attempt to comprehend the incomprehensible, perhaps the poetic and intuitive is nearer the truth than the scientifically rational. Any logical argument we employ in describing God is bound to be far afield of the mystery. The more intuitive approach at least leaves the mystery open to several possibilities.

Some readers and listeners will find the narration tedious. The pattern is repeated over and over, becoming predictable before the third repetition. But we have the same kind of literary technique in Western literature—in our fables, fairy tales, jokes, and morality tales. It is a way of telling a story and making a point so that the moral or lesson or experience will be memorable. Those who prefer dissertation and syllogism instead of poetry may be challenged to relax and let the *way* the story is told be as much a part of the experience as the point it makes.

Abraham spoke up *again*:
"See how I am presuming to speak to my *Lord*,
though I am but *dust* and *ashes*!
What if there are five *less* than fifty innocent people?
Will you destroy the whole *city* because of those *five*?"
He answered, "I will *not* destroy it, if I find *forty-five* there."

But Abraham *persisted*, saying "What if only *forty* are found there?"
He replied, "I will forbear *doing* it for the sake of the *forty*."
Then Abraham said, "Let not my Lord grow *impatient* if I go *on*.
What if only *thirty* are found there?"
He replied, "I will forbear *doing* it if I can find but *thirty* there."

By now you are tired of the game! Renew your energy; let the formula work.

Still Abraham went *on*,
"Since I have thus *dared* to speak to my Lord,
what if there are no more than *twenty*?"
The LORD answered, "I will not *destroy* it, for the sake of the *twenty*."
But he *still* persisted:
"*Please*, let not my Lord grow *angry* if I speak up this *last time*.
What if there are at least *ten* there?"
He replied, "For the sake of those *ten*, I will *not destroy* it."

The secret to benefiting from this story is to let it work its ultimate effect and reveal a God who is patient with human weakness, attentive to human needs, and eager to show justice and mercy in boundless measure to all the nations of the world. From Abraham's behavior in the story we can learn that our approach to God is best typified by candor and persistence. Humility, too, of course, but no shrinking violets, please! The gospel teaches the same lesson.

READING II **In a rush of striking images, this section of the letter to the Colossians gives us a summary of the redemption Christ has won for us through his death. To see our baptism as an imitation of the death, burial, and resurrection of Jesus is an effective way to remind ourselves of the degree to which this sacrament changes us. We have died. We have been raised from the dead. And now a whole new kind of existence is ours.**

Held prisoner by our sinfulness we were, in effect, entombed. There was no hope of union with the all-holy God. Until spiritual circumcision established us in a new covenant relationship with God (just like the literal circumcision did), we were hopeless. But the decree of guilt (the bond) that condemned us to this awful separation from God has been rendered null and void. Jesus nailed it to his cross. Or, to use the imagery of Colossians more accurately, Jesus *became* that guilt and was nailed to the cross in our stead. Because he died, our sins died. Because sin has died, we have been forgiven. And—now for the really good news!—because he rose from the dead, we have become a new kind of being, fully justified and established in a new loving relationship with God.

READING II Colossians 2:12–14

A reading from the Letter of Saint Paul to the Colossians

Brothers and sisters:

Make the most of this strong image: "*buried* with Christ."

You were *buried* with him in *baptism*,
in which you were *also raised* with him
through *faith* in the power of *God*,
who *raised* him from the *dead*.

"Even when you were *dead*"—no limits on God's will to save.

And even when you were *dead*
in *transgressions* and the *uncircumcision* of your *flesh*,
he brought you to *life along* with him,
having *forgiven* us all our *transgressions*;
obliterating the *bond* against us, with its *legal* claims,
which was *opposed* to us,

The text ends on a triumphant note.

he also *removed* it from our *midst*, *nailing* it to the *cross*.

GOSPEL Luke 11:1–13

A reading from the holy Gospel according to Luke

A very sensitive opener; Jesus at prayer is a familiar image in Luke.

Jesus was *praying* in a certain *place*, and when he had *finished*,
one of his *disciples* said to him,
"*Lord*, teach *us* to pray just as *John* taught *his* disciples."
He said to them, "When you *pray*, say:

The words are different from what we are accustomed to. Take the opportunity to give them a fresh rendering.

Father, *hallowed* be your *name*,
your *kingdom come*.
Give us each *day* our daily *bread*
and *forgive* us our *sins*

It is up to the homilist to expound upon the rich imagery in this text. But a careful proclamation will prepare the way for the homilist's explanation. In fact, an effective proclamation will do more than that. It will communicate the joy and conviction that inspired the rich imagery in the first place. It is not difficult to *understand* that God raised us to new life in company with Christ. But to *revel* in this good news we need the poetry of the human spirit and the enthusiasm of a good reader eager to share it.

GOSPEL The model Jesus provides his disciples when they ask him to teach them to pray has become the Christian prayer *par excellence*. The Lord's Prayer is the disciple's prayer, and in providing it, Jesus shows us not only what to say but how to say it. We are to pray with persistence and with boldness, confident that we are addressing an "Abba," a very intimate word for "father," who is eager to provide his children with all good things.

It would have been difficult for Jesus' contemporaries to hear him use the word "Abba" in reference to God. They were much more comfortable with euphemisms for God and, in fact, felt that the actual name of God was far too holy to be pronounced aloud. Thus we find names like "Most High," and "Most Holy," and "Lord of All" in the Hebrew scriptures. "Abba" is a term of great respect, too, but also of much greater intimacy. It is the word a child uses to get the attention of his or her natural parent. So the Lord's Prayer begins with a word that says something new about our relationship with God.

For the most part, however, there is nothing fundamentally new about the prayer

for we *ourselves* forgive *everyone* in *debt* to us,
and do not *subject* us to the final *test*."

Pause. Now that the special prayer has been given, teaching about prayer in general follows.

And he said to them, "Suppose one of you has a *friend*
to whom he goes at *midnight* and says,
'*Friend*, lend me three loaves of *bread*,
for a *friend* of mine has arrived at my *house* from a *journey*
and I have nothing to *offer* him,'
and he says in *reply* from *within*,
'Do not *bother* me; the *door* has already been *locked*
and my *children* and I are already in *bed*.
I cannot get *up* to give you *anything*.'

"I *tell* you,
if he does *not* get up to give the visitor the loaves
because of their *friendship*,
he will get up to give him whatever he *needs*
because of his *persistence*.

The point being made is how God answers requests differently.

"And I tell you, *ask* and you will *receive*;
seek and you will *find*;
knock and the *door* will be *opened* to you.

We're into poetic language here. Make the most of it. The final question is rhetorical; it should not sound like a literal question.

For everyone who *asks*, *receives*;
and the one who *seeks*, *finds*;
and to the one who *knocks*, the door will be *opened*.

"What *father* among you would hand his son a *snake*
when he asks for a *fish*?
Or hand him a *scorpion* when he asks for an *egg*?

"If *you* then, who are *wicked*,
know how to give *good gifts* to your *children*,
how much *more* will the Father in *heaven*
give the Holy *Spirit* to those who *ask* him?"

Jesus teaches his disciples. All the petitions have their counterparts in the Hebrew scriptures. But the orientation of the Lord's Prayer toward the future kingdom (already present but yet to be fulfilled) makes it special. Each petition looks ahead to that final day when the reign of God will be fully realized. The bread we pray for is the bread of the heavenly banquet. The forgiveness we pray for is what we need to belong to the eternal kingdom. The forgiveness we give is an ongoing response to the forgiveness we receive—as well as the condition that brings God's forgiveness. The deliverance we pray for is what we will need when the great trial that precedes the end time is upon us. The Lord's Prayer draws us toward triumph!

The example of persistence that Jesus relates following the prayer can easily be misinterpreted to say that we can wear God down with our pleas and extract from God what is really only given grudgingly. But this is a parable of contrast, not similarity. What follows makes it clear that God is different from the reluctant sleepy neighbor. We ask confidently because we know God is eager to give. We knock confidently because we know God is eager to open to us. And because we all know that a doting father will give his children even better things than they ask for, we can only imagine how eager the all-holy God is to favor our requests.

As we progress toward maturity in prayer, we learn that the Father's eagerness to supply our needs renders prayers of petition almost unnecessary—and prayers of thanksgiving and praise spontaneous.

18TH SUNDAY IN ORDINARY TIME

Lectionary #114

READING I Ecclesiastes 1:2; 2:21–23

A reading from the Book of Ecclesiastes

The bleakest of bleak readings! But it is also a thought provoker and prepares for what we hear in the other readings today. Relish it!

Vanity of *vanities*, says *Qoheleth*,
vanity of *vanities*! *All* things are *vanity*!

Pause here. The reading is in three short sections. Let each one sink in.

Here is one who has *labored* with *wisdom* and *knowledge* and *skill*,
and yet to *another* who has *not* labored over it,
he must leave *property*.
This *also* is vanity and a great *misfortune*.

The rhetorical question adds to the feeling of futility.

For what *profit* comes to man from all the *toil* and anxiety of *heart*
with which he has *labored* under the *sun*?

End slowly and quietly. Don't shy away from the bleakness!

All his days *sorrow* and *grief* are their *occupation*;
even at *night* his mind is not at *rest*.
This *also* is *vanity*.

READING I We often speak of knowledge of the Word of God as Wisdom. The Word instills the kind of wisdom that enables us to see deeper into things, to put the events of life in perspective, to rearrange our value systems, to discern what really counts and what doesn't matter quite so much.

Qoheleth understands—the "vanity of vanities" poet who provides our first reading. There is wisdom in his advice, no matter how bleakly he states it. In another place in his poetry he is less bleak, counseling us to enjoy youth, appreciate it, so that the natural process of old age can be embraced with a calm and peaceful heart. Wisdom enables us to see the body's decline as a gradual, almost seamless, transition back to the Creator who receives back the breath of life that was given at birth. Wisdom shows us that material possessions either crush the soul or liberate it, depending upon how we gain them, use them, and share them.

Someone has said that life's choices are all preparation for the final choice we make—to surrender life—to take the next natural step and give our breath back to God. For we do make that choice, apparently. Perhaps even when life is snatched away suddenly, there is an instant when we choose to let go. It will certainly be easier to let go if we have avoided a clutching, grasping approach to life as we lived it. The same insight has been expressed in these words: The only thing we take with us at the end of life is what we have given away during our earthly sojourn.

Wisdom teaches us to avoid greed in all its forms—even greed for our earthly life itself, which by its nature is impermanent. And if life itself is not worth hoarding, how

READING II Colossians 3:1–5, 9–11

A reading from the Letter of Saint Paul to the Colossians

Brothers and sisters:
If you were *raised* with *Christ*, *seek* what is *above*,
where Christ is *seated* at the right hand of *God*.

This text is something of an antidote to the first reading. Make it upbeat.

Think of what is *above*, not of what is on *earth*.
For you have *died*,
and your life is *hidden* with *Christ* in *God*.
When Christ your life *appears*,
then you *too* will appear with him in *glory*.

"You have died"—in baptism. Your life is hidden until you rise with the risen Christ.

Put to *death*, then, the *parts* of you that are *earthly*:
immorality, *impurity*, *passion*, evil *desire*,
and the *greed* that is *idolatry*.

Bring out the relationship between the "death" we have died and "putting to death" what is still evil in us.

Stop *lying* to one another,
since you have taken *off* the *old* self with *its* practices
and have put on the *new* self,
which is being *renewed*, for *knowledge*,
in the *image* of its *creator*.

Very strong advice. Almost a scolding, but plead rather than nag. Don't hold back.

Here there is not *Greek* and *Jew*,
circumcision and *uncircumcision*,
barbarian, *Scythian*, *slave*, *free*;
but *Christ* is *all* and *in* all.

The ending is very upbeat. It means to obliterate every ounce of prejudice.

much less should we exhaust ourselves with amassing lesser things?

READING II **As complicated as it may seem sometimes, the good news of Jesus Christ can be put in few words: Christ has died, Christ is risen, Christ will come again. Sometimes we need to remind ourselves how beautifully simple our faith can be, and how liberating it can be to live it simply. The first part of this reading we heard on Easter Sunday. It should remind us of what we said in the renewal of our baptismal vows on that day.**

Paul's words make it clear that we are living an entirely new life as a result of our baptism. When he says that our life is hidden now with Christ, he means there is more to come and the work of salvation is not complete until the end of time. Scholars speak of "partially realized eschatology," a formidable phrase meaning that the kingdom of God is fully established on earth but has not reached perfection. Another way of putting it is "already, but not yet!" Christ's reign is already victorious but it is not yet fully visible to us. It will no longer be hidden when Christ returns in glory. When Christ appears, our lives, too, will appear for what they really are—completely transformed through the waters of baptism.

Living in faith is a matter of realizing what we are in spite of what we sometimes seem to be. It is a matter of living out our true identity in Jesus rather than the false identity of sinfulness. By faith we know that we are already raised up to eternal life with Christ. By setting our hearts on this higher realm we can lessen the evidence that it has not yet appeared!

GOSPEL Luke 12:13–21

A reading from the holy Gospel according to Luke

Jesus is not rude to the person who made the request. It was common to ask rabbis to help settle disputes. Jesus simply says that he is not in a position to do so. Notice that his remarks are then to the crowd, not the individual who made the request.

Someone in the *crowd* said to Jesus,
"*Teacher*, tell my *brother* to share the *inheritance* with me."
He replied to him,
"*Friend*, who appointed *me* as your *judge* and *arbitrator*?"

A strong statement. A warning, in fact.

Then he said to the *crowd*,
"Take care to *guard* against all *greed*,
for though one may be *rich*,
one's *life* does not consist of *possessions*."

The parable is brief and almost brutal. Take it slowly.

Then he told them a *parable*.
"There was a *rich* man whose *land* produced a bountiful *harvest*.
He *asked* himself, 'What shall I *do*,
for I do not have *space* to *store* my harvest?'

The man's sin is not in being rich. It is in not figuring out a more generous way to handle his riches.

And he said, '*This* is what I shall do:
I shall tear *down* my *barns* and build *larger* ones.
There I shall store all my *grain* and *other* goods
and I shall *say* to myself, "Now as for *you*,
you have so many *good* things stored *up* for many *years*,
rest, *eat*, *drink*, be *merry*!"'

Jesus' contemporaries would not find God's reprimand harsh. The obligation to give alms was a cardinal virtue for them. It is still one of the five pillars of Islam.

The final question is rhetorical.

"But *God* said to him,
'You *fool*, this *night* your *life* will be *demanded* of you;
and the things you have *prepared*, to whom will they *belong*?'

Being rich toward God is feeding the hungry, taking care of the widow and orphan, and so on.

Thus will it *be* for all who *store up* treasure for *themselves*
but are *not* rich in what *matters* to *God*."

GOSPEL Today's readings. aren't simply about swollen bank accounts, the futility of life, or a literal understanding of that old spiritual value *terrena despicere* (despising the things of earth). They are about perspective, proportion, true riches, gospel values, and the challenge of being Christian all the way down to our toes—instead of being Christian only from the neck up.

The rich man in the gospel doesn't seem evil. He seems more interested in a guarantee of security against hard times. But there is no such security in material riches. There is every such security in spiritual treasure—in the true riches of generosity, sensitivity to others' needs, in the freedom to live beyond one's own small self.

There are many ways to be greedy. We can be greedy with our efforts and lament that to expend our energies is fruitless; nothing will ever be quite the way we want it. But we are told to avoid greed in all its forms, so we love the time we have, the gifts we have, the people in our lives, and we spend all we have in the service of God and neighbor.

We can be greedy with our tolerance and our acceptance. But in Christ there is no Greek or Jew, no native or foreigner, no slave or free. Christ is everything in everyone. How can we withhold our tolerance, our acceptance, our love from Christ? Avoid greed in *all* its forms.

If you would be truly rich, seek true riches. Seek the kingdom of Christ on earth, where every human being is the greatest treasure, the greatest gift, the most precious of riches.

19TH SUNDAY IN ORDINARY TIME

Lectionary #117

READING I Wisdom 18:6–9

A reading from the Book of Wisdom

Much is implied rather than clearly stated. Proclaim the text slowly and carefully, leaving the rest to the homilist.

The night of the *passover* was known *beforehand* to our *fathers*,
that, with sure *knowledge* of the *oaths* in which they
put their *faith*,
they might have *courage*.

Your people *awaited* the *salvation* of the *just*
and the *destruction* of their *foes*.
For when you *punished* our *adversaries*,
in this you glorified *us* whom you had *summoned*.

The text is poetry, not prose. It is elusive, but not incomprehensible.

For in *secret* the holy children of the *good* were offering *sacrifice*
and putting into *effect* with one *accord* the divine *institution*.

READING II Hebrews 11:1–2, 8–19

A reading from the Letter to the Hebrews

The opening definition of faith sets the scene for all that follows.

Brothers and sisters:
Faith is the *realization* of what is *hoped* for
and *evidence* of things not *seen*.
Because of it the *ancients* were well *attested*.

By *faith Abraham obeyed* when he was *called* to go out to a place
that he was to *receive* as an *inheritance*;
he went *out*, not knowing *where* he was to go.

READING I When Israel went forth from Egypt, escaping into the desert in pursuit of freedom, the journey was preceded by that first Passover meal. It took place at night, after sundown. In Jewish tradition, it is believed that the Messiah will appear on a night when the commemoration of that Passover is celebrated. The tradition continues in our own celebration of Passover, the sacred Triduum culminating in the Easter Vigil. And in the gospel today we hear Jesus tell us that the Son of Man will come at the end of time like a thief in the night.

Night is special for Jews and Christians alike. It is the time when we watch and pray. The vigilant are those who keep vigil, that is, those who keep awake and alert watching for the coming of the Messiah. The historical event of the Passover created a people of God, bonding them into a body of believers even until now. So we do far more than remember the event when we keep vigil. We celebrate the effect of that event. We celebrate our communion with God and with one another.

This reading from the Book of Wisdom celebrates the long-promised deliverance that came to Israel on that fateful night. It celebrates the fidelity of God in fulfilling that promise. It celebrates the faith of our ancestors for believing in that promise. And it looks ahead confidently to the time when our final deliverance will come—when the promised Messiah will come in glory to restore and establish Israel in complete fullness.

READING II In this masterfully written passage from Hebrews, the author first defines what faith is and then demonstrates how the faith of Abraham is

Let the refrain "By faith" ring out each time.

By *faith* he sojourned in the *promised* land as
in a foreign *country*,
dwelling in *tents* with *Isaac* and *Jacob*,
heirs of the same *promise*;
for he was looking *forward* to the city with *foundations*,
whose *architect* and *maker* is *God*.

By *faith* he received power to *generate*,
even though he was *past* the *normal* age
—and *Sarah herself* was *sterile*—
for he thought that the one who had made the *promise*
was *trustworthy*.

This sentence shows the glorious result of Abraham's faith.

So it *was* that there came *forth* from *one* man,
himself as good as *dead*,
descendants as *numerous* as the *stars* in the *sky*
and as *countless* as the *sands* on the *seashore*.

All these died in *faith*.
They did not *receive* what had been *promised*
but *saw* it and *greeted* it from *afar*
and *acknowledged* themselves to be *strangers* and *aliens*
on earth,
for those who speak *thus* show that they are seeking
a *homeland*.
If they had been thinking of the land from which they had *come*,
they would have had opportunity to *return*.
But *now* they desire a *better* homeland, a *heavenly* one.
Therefore, *God* is not *ashamed* to be *called* their God,
for he has prepared a *city* for them.

After an interlude describing the reward of the faithful, "By faith" rings out a final time!

By *faith Abraham*, when put to the *test*, offered up *Isaac*,
and he who had *received* the promises was ready
to offer his only *son*,
of whom it was said,

a perfect model for our own. To say that "faith is the realization of what is hoped for" sounds like a contradiction. If we are hoping for something, how can it be real? The terms seem like opposites. Nevertheless, we know that in living out what we believe in faith we already have a foretaste of what faith ultimately promises.

Our experience in the liturgy is probably the best example of how the apparent paradox works. In the celebration of the eucharist, we recall the events of our salvation and we see them continuing in our own time. In the eucharistic banquet we experience in sign and symbol a foretaste of the ultimate banquet, when all that we hope and pray for will be fully realized. To believe—to have faith—is to experience (make real here and now) the things we hope for in the future, things that are not yet clearly seen.

Abraham exercised his faith in obedience. He was called to a place he did not know, believing that the God who called him would be faithful. He believed, despite all natural evidence to the contrary, that God would bring a son from his loins; God has promised, so God will deliver. And the ultimate test of Abraham's faithful obedience was the command to offer his son Isaac in sacrifice. He passed the test and the command was rescinded. In all the instances, Abraham, who is called our father in faith, believed with the faith that makes hopes become realities and unseen things become evident.

The author of this reading alludes to other great believers in our history as well, showing that their belief in what they could not see was the faith that kept them in union with God. Faith makes us able to see that

"Through *Isaac descendants* shall bear your *name*."
He reasoned that *God* was able to raise *even* from the *dead*,
and he received Isaac *back* as a *symbol*.

[Shorter: Hebrews 11:1–2, 8–12]

GOSPEL Luke 12:32–48

A reading from the holy Gospel according to Luke

Jesus said to his *disciples*:

The reading is in three sections. Here we are encouraged.

"Do not be afraid any *longer*, little flock,
for your Father is *pleased* to give you the *kingdom*.
Sell your belongings and give *alms*.
Provide *money* bags for yourselves that do not wear *out*,
an *inexhaustible* treasure in *heaven*
that no *thief* can *reach* nor *moth destroy*.

"For where your treasure is . . ." A much loved text. Let it ring out.

For where your *treasure* is, there *also* will your *heart* be.

"*Gird* your *loins* and *light* your *lamps*
and be like servants who await their master's *return*
from a *wedding*,
ready to open *immediately* when he comes and *knocks*.
Blessed are those servants
whom the master finds *vigilant* on his *arrival*.

This is a striking image: The master is waiting on the slaves!

Amen, I say to you, he will *gird* himself,
have them recline at *table*, and proceed to *wait* on them.
And should he come in the *second* or *third* watch
and find them *prepared* in this way,
blessed are those servants.

In this second section we are instructed.

"Be sure of *this*:
if the master of the house had *known* the hour
when the *thief* was coming,

The "thief in the night" image is a favorite.

he would not have let his *house* be broken *into*.

our hopes are being realized; it presents us with evidence of things that are yet to come. It enables us to see what cannot be seen.

GOSPEL Dynamic and lively vigilance is the idea that ties together all three readings today. Our ancestors in faith were those who watched and waited for the fulfillment of all the Lord had promised them. And their faith was not in vain. We continue to look forward to the fulfillment of our hopes, when the glory we now glimpse in the eucharistic celebration will be complete in the heavenly banquet.

Jesus teaches us what a vigilant attitude looks like. It is, first of all, unencumbered and not distracted by other concerns. Like the Israelites of old who had to have their loins girt (be dressed for action) when the moment for their deliverance came, so we must likewise be always prepared. We, too, are awaiting deliverance. And we are awaiting the arrival of the Lord of Glory at the end of time. If our eyes are trained incessantly on the material things of this world, we can hardly keep them focused on the world to come.

And how will it come? Suddenly, and by stealth—like a thief in the night. The more we become engrossed in lesser concerns, the more likely it is that we will be taken by surprise. Jesus does not counsel us to neglect the realities of our earthly life. On the contrary, in answer to Peter's question, he counsels industriousness and dedication to the task at hand. There is also the implication that we take responsibility for our

"You *also* must be *prepared*, for at an *hour* you do not *expect*,
the Son of *Man* will *come*."

Then *Peter* said,
"*Lord*, is this parable meant for *us* or for *everyone*?"
And the Lord replied,

And in this final section, as Jesus answers Peter's question, we are challenged.

"*Who*, then, is the *faithful* and *prudent* steward
whom the master will put in *charge* of his *servants*
to distribute the *food* allowance at the proper *time*?
Blessed is that servant whom his master on *arrival* finds *doing* so.
Truly, I say to you, the master will put the servant
in charge of *all* his property.
But if that servant says to himself,

A timeless insight into lower human nature ("When the cat's away . . .").

'My master is *delayed* in coming,'
and begins to *beat* the menservants and the maidservants,
to *eat* and *drink* and get *drunk*,
then that servant's *master* will come
on an *unexpected* day and at an unknown *hour*
and will *punish* the servant *severely*
and assign him a *place* with the *unfaithful*.

"That servant who *knew* his master's will
but did not make *preparations* nor act in *accord* with his will
shall be beaten *severely*;
and the servant who was *ignorant* of his master's will
but acted in a way *deserving* of a severe beating
shall be beaten only *lightly*.

We're into proverbs here. Rich ore, but not particularly easy to mine.

"*Much* will be *required* of the person *entrusted* with much,
and still *more* will be demanded of the person *entrusted*
with more."

[Shorter: Luke 12:35–40]

actions without having to be supervised. Nothing is more unchristian than service rendered in fear. And yet fear of retribution or punishment seems to be the motivating force in many who bear the name Christian. Jesus counsels us to do our service in love for and loyalty to the master, not in fear of him. Loving service does not slacken when the master seems to be taking his time about coming.

There are times, of course, when we all get weary of the wait. The more difficult life seems to us, the more difficult it is to wait with patient but energetic hope. And yet, these are the times when we most need to let Christ's promise encourage us. How do we prepare for the Lord's return? How do we prepare for death? How do we prepare for the Lord's coming in mystery every moment of every day? Well, first of all we must think about it. We must see that Advent, that time of hopeful waiting, is a year-round season. Every task, every little job, every good word, every kind deed—all of these are the Lord at work in us, preparing us, enabling us to prepare for his coming—now and finally. Blessed is that servant whom the master finds ready—busily waiting.

If we give in to discouragement, then we will become passive—at a loss as to how to hasten his coming. The heart that is merely waiting will find a thousand excuses; the heart that is truly waiting will find a thousand ways.

ASSUMPTION VIGIL

Lectionary #621

READING I 1 Chronicles 15:3–4, 15–16; 16:1–2

A reading from the first Book of Chronicles

"*All* Israel"—this is quite a throng! And it says something about the importance of the event.

Notice the progression: "David assembled . . . David called together . . . David commanded . . ."

Aaron = AIR-uhn

Levite = LEE-vīt

David assembled all *Israel* in *Jerusalem* to bring the *ark*
of the LORD
to the place that he had *prepared* for it.
David *also* called together the sons of *Aaron* and the *Levites*.

The *Levites* bore the ark of God on their *shoulders* with *poles*,
as *Moses* had *ordained* according to the word of the LORD.

Make this list impressive.

lyres = līrz

David commanded the *chiefs* of the *Levites*
to appoint their *kinsmen* as *chanters*,
to play on musical *instruments*, *harps*, *lyres*, and *cymbals*,
to make a loud *sound* of *rejoicing*.

They *brought* in the ark of God and set it within the *tent*
which David had *pitched* for it.
Then they offered up burnt *offerings* and *peace* offerings to God.
When David had *finished* offering up the burnt offerings
and peace offerings,
he *blessed* the people in the *name* of the LORD.

David's blessing brings the reading to a quiet close.

READING I One of Mary's titles is "ark of the covenant," which explains why this text was chosen for the vigil of the Assumption. The comparison is obvious. Since the ark contained the stone tablets of the ten commandments and symbolized God's presence among the people of Israel, so Mary carried within her body the incarnation of God in Jesus Christ. The difference is also important: No longer is the law inscribed on stone tablets; it is now flesh and blood in the person of Jesus. It is for the homilist to make the typology clear.

Clearly the scene here is one of great joy. David had prepared a special place for the ark, and now it is borne into the city amid the noisy rejoicing of the crowd. Notice the detail in the chronicler's report. The descendants of Aaron and the Levites are the priestly clan, charged by Moses in accord with God's directive to carry the ark. Their descendants provide the liturgy that accompanies this joyous occasion: harps, lyres, cymbals, singers, and so on. The scene is vivid, and your proclamation should take advantage of every detail to make it so.

READING II The significance of today's feast is that Mary is the first human being (besides Jesus himself, of course) in Christian tradition to experience fully that total union with God that is the final destiny of us all. God accords Mary that privilege because of her unique role in salvation history.

Paul quotes scripture to make his point about the fruits of Christ's resurrection—and a powerful and poetic text it is! Two rhetorical questions constitute one of the most popular acclamations in Christian literature:

READING II 1 Corinthians 15:54b–57

A reading from the first Letter of Saint Paul to the Corinthians

Take a deep breath and bring out the two sets of contrasting words with strong vocal inflection.

This is a strong and comforting victory cry.

Brothers and sisters:
When that which is *mortal* clothes itself with *immortality*,
then the *word* that is *written* shall come *about*:
"*Death* is swallowed up in *victory*.
Where, O death, is your *victory*?
Where, O death, is your *sting*?"

"But" is an important word here. It's different for us because of Jesus.

The sting of *death* is *sin*,
and the *power* of sin is the *law*.
But thanks be to *God* who gives *us* the victory
through our *Lord* Jesus *Christ*.

GOSPEL Luke 11:27–28

This reading will be over before the assembly begins to listen unless you prepare them for it with a pause after the announcement.

The woman ecstatically praises Jesus, not Mary. She herself would wish to have such a son.

A reading from the holy Gospel according to Luke

While *Jesus* was *speaking*,
a *woman* from the crowd *called out* and said to him,
"Blessed is the *womb* that *carried* you
and the *breasts* at which you *nursed*."

He replied,
"*Rather*, *blessed* are those
who *hear* the word of *God* and *observe* it."

"O death, where is thy victory? O death, where is thy sting?"

The sting of death is sin. Death comes to us through disobedience of the law. But Christ has freed us from the law and its condemnation and so has taken the sting out of death and swallowed up death itself by his own victory on the cross. Mary is the first to reap the benefits of her son's triumph.

GOSPEL There is power in the brevity of this gospel because its few words formulate a description of the true follower of Jesus. As with all brief proclamations, the reader must pause more than usual after the announcement of the reading and then read it with great deliberateness and care. It should not be stilted or artificial, of course, and certainly not rattled off.

It is possible that some will feel these words of Jesus about his mother are harsh and unfeeling. Does he deny that Mary was blessed because she was privileged to bear the Messiah? Jesus does not deny that she is blessed, but he clarifies what it is that makes her, and all his followers, so blessed. Perhaps the best translation here would be "Happy are those," for that is what the word means in this context. Yes, those who hear the word and keep it have received a blessing but, more to the point, they have found the source of true happiness.

Mary is happy, no doubt, that she was chosen to be the mother of Jesus. But her greatest happiness, as we read elsewhere in scripture, comes from her obedience to the word of God. Mary is the perfect model of openness to God's will. This brief gospel text is the perfect choice for the vigil of the feast that celebrates the reward of her openness.

ASSUMPTION

Lectionary #622

READING I Revelation 11:19a; 12:1–6a, 10ab

A reading from the Book of Revelation

The text is broad in its themes and images. Let your proclamation be expansive throughout.
This is more like poetry than prose. Let the images work their magic.

God's *temple* in *heaven* was *opened*,
and the ark of his *covenant* could be seen in the temple.
A great *sign* appeared in the sky, a *woman* clothed with the *sun*,
with the *moon* beneath her *feet*,
and on her *head* a crown of twelve *stars*.
She was with *child* and wailed *aloud* in *pain* as she *labored*
to give *birth*.

Recognize the transitions: The sign appears; the labor begins; the dragon appears.

Then *another* sign appeared in the sky;
it was a huge red *dragon*, with seven *heads* and ten *horns*,
and on its heads were seven *diadems*.
Its *tail* swept away a third of the *stars* in the sky
and hurled them down to the *earth*.

The scene is horrific: The dragon waits to devour the newborn.

Then the dragon *stood* before the woman about to give *birth*,
to *devour* her *child* when she gave birth.

The resolution is an enormous relief.

She gave birth to a *son*, a *male* child,
destined to *rule* all the *nations* with an iron *rod*.
Her child was *caught up* to *God* and his *throne*.
The woman *herself* fled into the *desert*
where she had a place *prepared* by God.

READING I I've always loved the epitaph that Benjamin Franklin wrote for his own tomb:

> The body of Benjamin Franklin, Printer (like the cover of an old book, its contents torn out and stripped of its lettering and gilding), lies here, food for worms; but the work shall not be lost, for it will (as he believed) appear once more in a new and more elegant edition, revised and corrected by the Author.

On the feast of Mary's assumption we are reminded that we are to follow her into glory, as she has followed Christ. We are reminded that what we call death is nothing more than the last thing we do in life. And it will be the best and finest thing we do, for in dying we are introduced into the presence of the one who conquered death. In Christ, death itself dies.

Mary has been taken up into heaven, body and soul. The promise brought to fulfillment in her is a promise we all share. Celebrating her triumph in Christ should give us pause, and it should give us hope as well. We pause to examine the fervor of this revolutionary belief, and we rejoice in the hope we receive from that belief.

The first reading is a classic example of apocalyptic literature in which metaphor and symbol are used to meditate on eternal truths. Mary has long been called "ark of the

The reading ends with a triumphant cry, demanding a significant pause before proclaiming strongly, "The word of the Lord."

Then I heard a loud *voice* in heaven say:
"*Now* have *salvation* and *power* come,
and the *kingdom* of our *God*
and the *authority* of his *Anointed* One."

READING II 1 Corinthians 15:20–27

A reading from the first Letter of Saint Paul to the Corinthians

Brothers and sisters:
Christ has been *raised* from the *dead*,
the *firstfruits* of those who have fallen *asleep*.
For since *death* came through man,
the *resurrection* of the dead came *also* through man.
For just as in *Adam* all *die*,
so too in *Christ* shall all be brought to *life*,
but each one in proper *order*:
Christ the *firstfruits*;
then, at his *coming*, those who *belong* to Christ;
then comes the *end*,
when he *hands over* the kingdom to his God and *Father*,
when he has *destroyed* every *sovereignty*
and every *authority* and *power*.

For he must *reign* until he has put all his *enemies* under his *feet*.
The *last* enemy to be destroyed is *death*,
for "he subjected *everything* under his *feet*."

covenant" (see the first reading for yesterday's vigil). The woman clothed with the sun symbolizes at least three persons: the corporate person of Israel, triumphant in the fulfillment of God's promises; the church, through which the reign of God is expressed most vividly; and Mary, the mother of the Messiah, through whom the messianic promises were fulfilled and for whom a special place has been prepared.

Clearly the choice of this text for today's liturgy has the last of these three persons in mind, though not to the exclusion of the other two. The struggle between good and evil is personified in the woman and the dragon and the rescued child. Centuries of study have revealed that the various elements of this vision are taken from many sources. The drama presented here is effective on its own terms if it is read with conviction and great care.

READING II Today's feast deals with revolutionary beliefs, and there's nothing more revolutionary than what Paul says here: "Christ has been raised from the dead, the first fruits of those who have fallen asleep." We Christians believe in a great many revolutionary things. The challenge, of course, is to believe in them in a revolutionary way. There's nothing new about that for the Christian, but the *way* in which the Christian believes and lives is supposed to be always new.

We have Christ's promise that the world will be divided as a result of his word and his life; we should expect nothing else. We have his word that to follow him, to believe what he believes and does, will make us signs of contradiction in the world. That is

GOSPEL Luke 1:39–56

A reading from the holy Gospel according to Luke

The sense of urgency here should be communicated. This is the first "missionary journey" of the new age of Jesus the Messiah.

Mary set *out*
and traveled to the *hill* country in *haste*
to a town of *Judah*,
where she entered the house of *Zechariah*
and greeted *Elizabeth*.

When Elizabeth *heard* Mary's greeting,
the *infant leaped* in her *womb*,
and *Elizabeth*, filled with the Holy *Spirit*,
cried out in a loud *voice* and said,
"*Blessed* are you among *women*,
and blessed is the *fruit* of your *womb*.

Elizabeth's cry is the cry of generations of expectant people. The baby who stirs in her womb is John the Baptist, whose cry will be, "Behold, the Lamb of God!"

And how does this happen to *me*,
that the mother of my *Lord* should come to me?
For at the moment the sound of your *greeting* reached my *ears*,
the *infant* in my womb *leaped* for *joy*.
Blessed are you who *believed*
that what was *spoken* to you by the *Lord*
would be *fulfilled*."

The second part of the reading begins here. Pause before it.

The canticle of Mary (the Magnificat) has two parts. The first few lines are about Mary's blessedness; the larger portion is about God's saving power.

And *Mary* said:
"My *soul* proclaims the *greatness* of the Lord;
my *spirit rejoices* in God my *Savior*
for he has *looked* upon his lowly *servant*.
From this *day* all *generations* will call me *blessed*:
the *Almighty* has done great *things* for me,
and *holy* is his *Name*.
He has *mercy* on those who *fear* him
in every *generation*.

probably a good test of the fervor of our belief: How much of a sign of contradiction are we? How radically different are our Christian values? Is it obvious how different they are even to the casual observer? Perhaps you have heard the provocative question: "If you were brought to trial for being a Christian, would there be enough evidence to convict you?" It's a timely question in every age, but perhaps especially in our own.

In Christ's resurrection we see the promise of our own resurrection. In Mary's assumption we see that promise already fulfilled in one like ourselves. In Mary's triumph we see the reign of God already triumphant over every other sovereignty and power. God is putting all enemies (the dragon of the first reading) under the sovereignty of Christ.

GOSPEL It was on the feast of All Saints only 53 years ago that Pope Pius XII proclaimed to all the world that the mother of Jesus, having completed her earthly life, was taken up into heaven body and soul. Christians have believed in Mary's assumption from the earliest times. We find it in the writings of the early church Fathers; we even find it depicted by a ninth-century artist in the subterranean basilica of St. Clement in Rome.

Our faith often turns the world upside down, presents a topsy-turvy view of things, and makes revolutionary statements about life, death, life-after-death, and values in general. There's nothing any more revolutionary about what Pius XII said in 1950 than

The world is turned upside down. The powerful fall; the humble rise; the rich go hungry; the hungry are filled. Relish the revolution God's mercy brings.

"He has shown the *strength* of his *arm*,
and has *scattered* the *proud* in their *conceit*.
He has cast down the *mighty* from their *thrones*,
and has *lifted up* the *lowly*.
He has filled the *hungry* with *good* things,
and the *rich* he has sent away *empty*.
He has come to the *help* of his servant *Israel*
for he has *remembered* his promise of *mercy*,
the promise he made to our *fathers*,
to *Abraham* and his children for *ever*."

The final assertion of the song extols the fidelity of God.

The narrative detail at the end lends a gentle feeling of closure.

Mary *remained* with her about three *months*
and then *returned* to her *home*.

what Mary said a long time before: God has deposed the mighty from their thrones and raised the lowly to high places. God has given every good thing to the hungry, and sent the rich away empty.

This beloved gospel story is about women, and more than just about Mary and Elizabeth. The words and accomplishments of women from the Hebrew scriptures (Jael, Judith, and Hannah) are placed in the mouth of Mary and her cousin so that Luke can demonstrate the completion of a long period of preparation for the Messiah's coming. "Leaping in the womb" is a traditional sign of recognition by the unborn of God's intervention in human history.

Mary's exultant song of praise is Israel's hymn, bursting forth in utter joy at the inauguration of the long-awaited messianic age. Notice that Mary's singular "my" becomes the plural "our" in the final words of her song. This is an obvious indication that Mary is the mouthpiece for the chosen people of all ages.

The thing to remember in proclaiming this reading is that the event described here is Luke's way of bringing a much larger reality into focus. It is the inauguration of God's reign and the fulfillment of God's promise to send us a redeemer.

21ST SUNDAY IN ORDINARY TIME

Lectionary #123

READING I Isaiah 66:18–21

A reading from the Book of the Prophet Isaiah

Thus says the *LORD*:
I know their *works* and their *thoughts*,
and I come to gather *nations* of every *language*;
they shall *come* and see my *glory*.

A strong opener. Begin big—and don't let up!

I will set a *sign* among them;
from them I will send *fugitives* to the nations:
to *Tarshish*, *Put* and *Lud*, *Mosoch*, *Tubal* and *Javan*,
to the distant *coastlands*
that have never *heard* of my fame, or seen my *glory*;
and they shall *proclaim* my glory among the *nations*.

Tarshish = TAHR-shish
Put = puht
Lud = luhd
Mosoch = MOH-sok
Tubal = TOO-bahl
Javan = JAY-vuhn
All the nations! *All* the nations!

They shall bring all your *brothers* and *sisters* from all the nations
as an *offering* to the LORD,
on *horses* and in *chariots*, in *carts*, upon *mules*
and *dromedaries*,
to *Jerusalem*, my holy *mountain*, says the LORD,
just as the *Israelites* bring *their* offering
to the *house* of the LORD in clean *vessels*.

Even the mode of arrival is diverse!

Some of these I will take as *priests* and *Levites*, says the LORD.

Almost an afterthought, the final sentence indicates the necessity of God's presence through human touch in the community.

READING I Today's first reading (and gospel) remind us that God's plan encompasses the redemption and salvation of all humankind throughout the world. It is unfortunate that even in our own times we hear attitudes expressed that can only be described as exclusive. God-centered communities must be relentlessly inclusive. This is perhaps the most difficult lesson to be learned by those who claim the Bible as their book and the worshiping community as their home.

In poetic language Isaiah makes very clear how all-encompassing God's intention is. The breadth of God's vision expressed here reveals how narrow our own vision can be. Our preoccupation with the petty faults of others or ourselves is given a much-needed shock when we realize that we are part of a vast eternal plan.

Only a vision on a cosmic level like the one expressed by Isaiah will enable us to get our priorities straight. Only the kind of universalism expressed here will cure us of prejudices and judgments that not only delay unity under God but actually keep it at bay. Ultimate unity will come only at the end of time, but God clearly wills our involvement in the process today.

READING II The author of the letter to the Hebrews (not Paul) is writing to a Christian community living in a religiously diverse society. The "discipline" they are experiencing is probably the difficulties encountered in a mixed society. Certainly it is the same kind of "discipline" experienced by any serious Christian living in the world today. Christianity is not an easy life, if lived with commitment, and tests

READING II Hebrews 12:5–7, 11–13

A reading from the Letter to the Hebrews

Brothers and sisters,
You have *forgotten* the *exhortation* addressed to you as *children*:
"My son, do not *disdain* the discipline of the Lord
or lose *heart* when *reproved* by him;
for whom the Lord *loves*, he *disciplines*;
he *scourges* every son he *acknowledges*."

The tone here is, "Remember what you learned at your mother's knee."

Endure your *trials* as "*discipline*";
God treats you as *sons*.
For what "*son*" is there whom his *father* does not *discipline*?

At the *time*,
all discipline seems a cause not for *joy* but for *pain*,
yet *later* it brings the *peaceful* fruit of *righteousness*
to those who are *trained* by it.

The word "discipline" is closely related to the word "disciple," one who is taught.

So *strengthen* your drooping *hands* and your weak *knees*.
Make straight *paths* for your *feet*,
that what is *lame* may not be *disjointed* but *healed*.

After the instruction, encouragement is offered.

GOSPEL Luke 13:22–30

A reading from the holy Gospel according to Luke

Jesus passed through *towns* and *villages*,
teaching as he went and making his *way* to *Jerusalem*.
Someone *asked* him,
"*Lord*, will only a *few* people be *saved*?"

Emphasize Luke's controlling theme: "making his way to Jerusalem."

of our fidelity abound. Considering the "discipline" undergone by Jesus, our supreme model, we should not be surprised.

But we should also not be surprised when we feel discouraged. This reading is a call to rally in the face of such feelings. The writer first instructs and then encourages—a technique used throughout this letter. And it is a technique founded on a firm reliance on faith—believing in a way that enables us to see through difficult times and ahead to God's reliable promises.

Living by faith means not having any guarantees except one: that faithful service, despite adversity, will be rewarded. The straight path of faith is simple and unadorned, streamlined and uncluttered. It cuts through adversity and accepts inevitable "discipline" and suffering with equanimity. It is, perhaps above all else, detached. There are no tributaries or feeder lanes to distract and confuse us. Staying on that straight path is difficult, and that is perhaps the ultimate discipline.

GOSPEL This passage from Luke's gospel may well be a loose collection of sayings of Jesus, uttered in different contexts but brought together here under the general heading of "who will be saved." In any case, the overall tenor of Jesus' meaning is clear: The salvation he offers is offered to all, but cannot be accepted in part. The good news is offered whole and entire and must be accepted in the same way. The implication of the narrow gate is that the passage is not built to accommodate throngs indiscriminately, as a wider

He *answered* them,
"*Strive* to enter through the *narrow* gate,
for *many*, I tell you, will *attempt* to enter
but will not be *strong* enough.

A little parable begins here. Pause to prepare for it.

"After the *master* of the *house* has *arisen* and locked the *door*,
then will *you* stand outside *knocking* and saying,
'*Lord*, open the *door* for us.'
He will say to you in *reply*,
'I do not *know* where you are *from*.'

"And *you* will say,
'We *ate* and *drank* in your *company* and you *taught*
in our *streets*.'
Then he will say to you,
'I do not *know* where you are *from*.
Depart from me, all you *evildoers*!'

A new section begins here. Pause after the parable.

"And there will be *wailing* and grinding of *teeth*
when you see *Abraham*, *Isaac* and *Jacob*
and all the *prophets* in the kingdom of *God*
and you *yourselves* cast *out*.
And people will come from the *east* and the *west*
and from the *north* and the *south*
and will recline at *table* in the kingdom of *God*.

Obviously, this is a proverb. Relish the re-telling of it.

"For *behold*, some are *last* who will be *first*,
and some are *first* who will be *last*."

entrance would. The narrow gate is open to all, but only those who seek it (rather than the easier wider gate) are admitted. In other words, if you are entering by the narrow gate, you'll know it! There's no gaining entrance unawares, as might be the case with the wider gate. The kingdom of God is a choice to be made.

Latecomers are denied entrance, too. We have a taste of *carpe diem* literature here. Seize the day! The mini-parable makes the point that we must acknowledge Jesus as master when the opportunity, call, or challenge comes. It's possible that if we pass up enough opportunities we will no longer recognize them when they come. God will never stop offering moments of grace, and the Spirit will prompt us all our lives with impulses to reform and do the right thing. The danger is not that grace will dry up and the opportunity for eternal happiness will be withdrawn. No, God is faithful. The danger is that we will dry up and will develop such a thick crust of insensitivity that grace will have difficulty soaking in. And yet, in the end, it is God's will to save us. This is the good news. It is never too late.

The goodness of God issues invitations to all the world. Luke's recurring theme of universalism sounds again. No one is excluded from this banquet except those who exclude themselves. And, finally, there will be surprises in the heavenly kingdom, just as there were constant surprises during Jesus' earthly ministry. Luke is fond of pointing out sudden reversals. Here he tells us that we need to re-think whatever notions we have about who is fit for the reign of God. Those we think least likely to enter may be the first to do so, and vice versa.

AUGUST 29, 2004

22ND SUNDAY IN ORDINARY TIME

Lectionary #126

READING I Sirach 3:17–18, 20, 28–29

Sirach = SEER-ak

These are the words of a wise and experienced parent, offered in love.

Humility is always realism, not fanciful virtue.

A reading from the Book of Sirach

My *child*, conduct your *affairs* with *humility*,
and you will be *loved* more than a *giver* of *gifts*.
Humble yourself the *more*, the *greater* you are,
and you will find *favor* with *God*.
What is too *sublime* for you, seek *not*,
into things beyond your *strength search* not.

Being a good listener is certainly a sign of humility.

The poetic device here is parallelism. Read, "[Just as] water quenches a flaming fire, [so do] alms atone for sins."

The mind of a *sage* appreciates *proverbs*,
and an *attentive* ear is the *joy* of the *wise*.
Water quenches a flaming *fire*,
and *alms atone* for *sins*.

READING II Hebrews 12:18–19, 22–24a

There are two peaks in this poetic text. It rises to the middle with a list of what we have not approached. Then it begins again and rises to the end with a list of what we have approached. The contrast will be clear if your proclamation follows this design. To make this work, you will have to employ a great deal of vocal energy and variety. Bring it to life.

A reading from the Letter to the Hebrews

Brothers and sisters:
You have *not* approached that which could be *touched*
and a blazing *fire* and gloomy *darkness*
and *storm* and a *trumpet* blast
and a *voice* speaking words such that those who *heard*
begged that *no* message be further *addressed* to them.

READING I Here is a selection from the wisdom literature, that rich collection of experience and sage advice that appears too infrequently in our lectionary. Today's excerpts from the book of Sirach concentrate on the virtue of humility and are clearly chosen to complement today's gospel reading.

Humility may well be one of the most misunderstood of all virtues. We do well to examine the images that come to mind when we think of the humble person. One of the most bitter caricatures of humility in Western literature was vividly portrayed by Charles Dickens in the character of Uriah Heep in the novel *David Copperfield.* Uriah Heep protests his humility often, but beneath his fawning exterior is a devious and ambitious man who takes advantage of the weak and defenseless. False humility is the worst kind of pride.

A more common notion is that humility means weakness. Sirach implies that such is not the case: "Humble yourself the more, the greater you are." The apparent paradox here is that truly great leaders with power at their command exercise their influence with humility—and therefore do not need to call upon the power they have.

There is nothing fawning or shrinking about true humility that finds favor with God. It is simply honesty, after all. The etymology of the word is instructive: It comes from the Latin *humus,* meaning earth. The common origin and the common destiny of all men and women should be enough to keep us humble, in the best sense of the word.

READING II In this exalted passage from the second to last chapter of

No, *you* have approached Mount *Zion*
and the city of the living *God*, the heavenly *Jerusalem*,
and countless *angels* in festal *gathering*,
and the assembly of the *firstborn* enrolled in *heaven*,
and *God* the judge of *all*,
and the spirits of the *just* made *perfect*,
and *Jesus*, the *mediator* of a new *covenant*,
and the sprinkled *blood* that speaks more *eloquently* than that of *Abel*.

GOSPEL Luke 14:1, 7–14

A reading from the holy Gospel according to Luke

The first paragraph sets the scene. Don't rush through it.

On a *sabbath* Jesus went to *dine*
at the home of one of the leading *Pharisees*,
and the *people* there were *observing* him *carefully*.

He told a *parable* to those who had been *invited*,
noticing how they were choosing the places of *honor* at the *table*.

Try to hint by your tone that Jesus has a deeper meaning in mind. It is a parable, not a lesson in etiquette.

"When you are *invited* by someone to a wedding banquet,
do not recline at table in the place of honor.
A more distinguished guest than you may have been invited by him,
and the host who invited both of you may approach you and say,

You can't avoid the harshness here. That's the point.

'Give your place to this man,'
and then you would proceed with embarrassment
to take the lowest place.

Hebrews, the writer contrasts the new covenant with the old covenant, encouraging his readers to rejoice in the differences. The signs of the old covenant are material (touchable); those of the new covenant are spiritual. The signs of the old covenant provoked feelings of awe and trepidation; those of the new prompt us to peace and joy.

The images the writer uses here in describing the covenant made with Moses on Mount Sinai are recorded in the book of Exodus. A literal translation of these images onto film resulted in the more dramatic scenes from Cecil B. DeMille's *The Ten Commandments,* a movie that made a noble attempt to tell the story of Israel's experience vividly. Unfortunately, the film also entrenched many in mistaken notions about "the God of the Old Testament," a vengeful deity to be feared more than loved. The Hebrew scriptures reveal far more than such a stereotype.

Nevertheless, the writer of today's second reading employs thunder and smoke to point out the different relationship we have with God as a result of the life and mission of Jesus, the mediator of the new covenant. True enough, in Jesus we find God more approachable than ever before. And the heavenly Jerusalem is truly a city of peace, the Mount Zion dreamed of by the prophets who foretold the coming restoration of the chosen people.

It is not God who has changed from the old covenant to the new covenant. It is we who have been changed and brought into closer union with God through the atoning sacrifice (the sprinkled blood) of Jesus. In this new covenant, initiated by baptism, we joyfully approach the God who is judge of all through Jesus, who has justified us in faith.

"*Rather*, when you are invited,
go and *take* the *lowest* place
so that when the host *comes* to you he may say,
'My *friend*, move up to a *higher* position.'
Then you will enjoy the *esteem* of your *companions* at the *table*.
For every one who *exalts* himself will be *humbled*,
but the one who *humbles* himself will be *exalted*."

A treasured proverb. It means, "*God* humbles the self-exalted, and exalts the self-humbled."

Then he said to the host who *invited* him,
"When you hold a *lunch* or a *dinner*,
do not invite your *friends* or your *brothers*
or your *relatives* or your wealthy *neighbors*,
in case they may invite you *back* and you have *repayment*.
Rather, when you hold a banquet,
invite the *poor*, the *crippled*, the *lame*, the *blind*;
blessed *indeed* will you be because of their *inability*
to *repay* you.
For you will be *repaid* at the *resurrection* of the *righteous*."

The words to the host are also in parable form; not to be taken literally. Parables are stories laid alongside (parallel to) life for the purpose of revealing insights. If taken literally, they cease to be parables and lose their power to reveal.

GOSPEL **Once again Luke finds Jesus at table, but not with social outcasts this time. Here he dines with religious leaders and takes the opportunity to teach some important qualities of discipleship and holiness. Even more, he teaches us about the nature of God.**

Jesus teaches through parables. It is the nature of parables that they use one situation to examine a second, different situation. The meaning of the word "parable" reveals how it works: to lay one thing alongside another and draw parallels. If we interpret parables literally, we interpret them wrongly.

So Jesus teaches us about a special kind of humility here—and goes far beyond rules of etiquette. Every meal in Luke has a greater significance than eating and drinking with others. It is the eternal banquet that is imaged—an image not new with Jesus, but brought into clearer focus by him. We are all called to this heavenly banquet, invited there by God. And the invitation comes regardless of our station in life or any merit of our own. It is a purely gratuitous (gracious, free) invitation. Such is the goodness of God. In the light of such goodness, scrambling for places of honor is ludicrous. Ironically, the more we are aware of our undeserving nature, the more exalted we are in accepting the invitation.

In the second half of today's reading, Jesus offers instruction—but, again, it is parabolic instruction, not to be taken literally. "The poor, the crippled, the lame"—this is God's invitation list, and it must be our own. The gift of salvation is entirely free, expecting nothing in return. God-like love and charity are the same. In our relationship to God, "the poor, the crippled, the lame, the blind" describes all of us.

23RD SUNDAY IN ORDINARY TIME

Lectionary #129

READING I Wisdom 9:13–18b

A reading from the Book of Wisdom

The reading is a series of rhetorical questions that enables the writer, in the answers, to praise God for the gift of Wisdom.

Who can *know* God's *counsel,*
or who can *conceive* what the LORD *intends*?
For the deliberations of *mortals* are *timid,*
and *unsure* are our *plans.*

We're all familiar with this struggle.

For the corruptible *body burdens* the *soul*
and the earthen *shelter* weighs down the *mind*
that has many *concerns.*

Be sure to emphasize the "things on earth" in contrast with the "things in heaven."

And *scarce* do we guess the things on *earth,*
and what is within our *grasp* we find with *difficulty;*
but when things are in *heaven,* who can search *them* out?
Or who ever knew your *counsel,* except you had given *wisdom*
and sent your holy *spirit* from on *high*?

And now for the resolution. God-given Wisdom enables us to live peacefully with uncertainty.

And thus were the *paths* of those on *earth* made *straight.*

READING I The age-old distinction between the body (including the mind/brain) and the soul is not what the Wisdom writer is dealing with in this reading. That old distinction (dualism) presumes a stand-off between the two parts of ourselves, each opposed to the other. The view of human nature in the Hebrew scriptures is not dualistic, even though it is clearly recognized that the limitations of human nature make it impossible for us to comprehend fully the mysteries of God.

The point, then, is that Wisdom brings an intuitive kind of knowledge and insight that enables us, in the words of the poet John Keats, to "rest in the midst of doubt and uncertainty, with no irritable grasping after fact and reason." It is not difficult to see how closely allied Wisdom is to faith—believing without seeing. Analytical reasoning will never by itself enable us to arrive at faith. And Wisdom is a long way off from the hard evidence of logic.

Anti-intellectualism is not the alternative, of course. We were created with an intellect and we must use it in our search for an authentic Christian life. But in matters of faith, faith takes the lead. The one who assents to faith is better equipped in the pursuit of understanding of divine matters than the one who pursues the conviction of faith solely through the mind. When belief and understanding work together, the whole person is involved. Faith and reason are fellow servants, each assisting the other, and both in service to the Master.

READING II The letter to Philemon is unique among Paul's letters. It is a piece of personal correspondence to an individual instead of to a community.

READING II Philemon 9b–10, 12–17

A reading from the Letter of Saint Paul to Philemon

Communicate the deeply personal tone of this passage.

I, *Paul,* an *old* man,
and *now* also a *prisoner* for Christ *Jesus,*
urge you on behalf of my child *Onesimus,*
whose *father* I have become in my *imprisonment;*
I am *sending* him, that is, my own *heart, back* to you.

There is real sacrifice on Paul's part here.

I should have *liked* to *retain* him for *myself,*
so that he might *serve* me on your *behalf*
in my *imprisonment* for the *gospel,*
but I did not want to do *anything* without your *consent,*
so that the *good* you do might not be *forced* but *voluntary.*

The point is that this converted slave now shares the dignity of Christian faith with his master, and must be treated accordingly.

Perhaps *this* is why he was *away* from you for a *while,*
that you might have him *back forever,*
no *longer* as a *slave*
but *more* than a slave, a *brother,*
beloved especially to *me,* but even *more* so to *you,*
as a *man* and in the *Lord.*

So if you regard *me* as a *partner,* welcome *him* as you would *me.*

Onesimus was a runaway slave who converted to Christianity and took care of Paul during his imprisonment. Paul refers to himself as an old man here, not an ambassador—the title he gives himself at the beginning of the letter. An old man probably stands a better chance of having his request granted.

At any rate, Paul is asking Philemon, one of Paul's converts, to take back his converted runaway slave as a beloved brother. It is quite a request when we realize that slavery was accepted as normal and natural in the world of Paul's day. But we must also remember what Paul has to say about slaves elsewhere in his writing: "In Christ there is neither slave nor free . . . all are one in Christ." So it is on the basis of the slave's new-found Christian faith—which he now shares with his master—that Paul recommends a new relationship between them.

And he does so with considerable tact, offering the noblest possible reason why the slave had been away from his master illegally for a time: So that now the master could see him in a new light, not only as a man but "in the Lord."

Paul is asking a great deal of a slave owner who could justly charge him with a serious crime—harboring a runaway. But he is asking it in virtue of their common faith, and that makes any demand a different matter. Paul, seems confident that his request will be honored—no doubt because he knows the person to whom he writing, and he knows that that person holds him in high esteem. In any event, we see here (as we do in the gospel) something of what it costs to be a disciple.

GOSPEL Luke 14:25–33

A reading from the holy Gospel according to Luke

The scene is a confrontation with the serious consequences of following Jesus. There is no harshness here, just the boldness of the truth!

Great *crowds* were *traveling* with *Jesus*,
and he turned and *addressed* them,
"If anyone *comes* to me without *hating* his *father* and *mother*,
wife and *children*, *brothers* and *sisters*,
and even his own *life*,
he *cannot* be my *disciple*.

A series of sayings, somewhat disjointed, but all about the cost of following Jesus.

Whoever does not carry his own *cross* and come after me
cannot be my *disciple*.

"*Which* of you wishing to construct a *tower*
does not *first* sit down and calculate the *cost*
to see if there is *enough* for its *completion*?

Jesus is counseling wisdom here. And discretion. And careful planning.

Otherwise, after laying the *foundation*
and finding himself unable to *finish* the work
the *onlookers* should *laugh* at him and say,
'*This* one *began* to build but did not have the *resources*
to *finish*.'

"Or what *king* marching into *battle* would not *first* sit down
and decide whether with *ten* thousand troops
he can successfully *oppose another* king
advancing upon him with *twenty* thousand troops?
But if *not*, while he is still far *away*,
he will send a *delegation* to ask for *peace* terms.

The final sentence seems disconnected, and indeed it is. But it circles back to the theme of renunciation and priorities: To be my disciple, Jesus is saying, you must be ready to give up everything else.

"In the same *way*,
anyone of you who does not *renounce* all his *possessions*
cannot be my *disciple*."

GOSPEL What does it take to be a follower of Jesus? Must we really turn our backs on the people we love most? Well, sometimes that is necessary, but the more common experience for sincere Christians may be that of having others turn their backs on them! Either way, there is a terrific cost involved. The consequences of following Jesus are real—and perhaps nowhere more dramatically outlined than in this gospel passage.

To understand the meaning of this text, note two things that might easily go unnoticed. First, it is a special kind of leader who gives such fair warnings of the price involved in following him. There is an honest sincerity here that is rare in our experience of leadership. Without being too cynical, we can say that many leaders are less concerned about what it costs their followers to follow than about what it would cost the leaders to be without followers! And second, note that it is the relationships that Jesus holds in the highest regard that he holds up as possible losses for his disciples. It is precisely because Jesus reveres the relationships he mentions (parents, spouse, children) that he uses them to assert the cost of discipleship.

Finally, realize that these words are most often heard by those who are already followers. What do such warnings mean to us? Well, true discipleship is a lifelong goal, not a one-time choice. Insofar as we can still number prejudice, bigotry, haughtiness, cowardice, lukewarmness, dishonesty, or any one of a thousand other subtle sins among our possessions, we still have unpaid bills in this business of being a Christian.

24TH SUNDAY IN ORDINARY TIME

Lectionary #132

READING I Exodus 32:7–11, 13–14

A reading from the Book of Exodus

God speaks in the first half of the reading. There is no need to imitate what you think an angry God would sound like. Just proclaim the text with strength, dignity, and conviction.

The *LORD* said to *Moses*,
"Go down at *once* to your *people*,
whom you brought *out* of the land of *Egypt*,
for they have become *depraved*.
They have soon turned *aside* from the way I pointed *out* to them,
making for themselves a molten *calf* and *worshiping* it,
sacrificing to it and crying out,
'*This* is your God, O *Israel*,
who brought you *out* of the land of *Egypt*!'

"I see how *stiff-necked* this people is," continued the LORD to Moses.
"Let me *alone*, then,
that my *wrath* may blaze *up* against them to *consume* them.
Then I will *make* of you a great *nation*."

After a pause, Moses responds. Here too, strength and dignity are most appropriate. Certainly nothing like fawning or begging would do!

But Moses *implored* the LORD, his God, saying,
"*Why*, O LORD, should your *wrath* blaze up against your own *people*,
whom you brought *out* of the land of *Egypt*
with such great *power* and with so strong a *hand*?
Remember your *servants Abraham*, *Isaac*, and *Israel*,
and how you *swore* to them by your own *self*, saying,
'I will make your *descendants* as *numerous* as the *stars* in the *sky*;

READING I The point of this reading is not that God is angry or that the people have sinned or that God relents. The point is that Moses is a successful intercessor on behalf of the people. Does this make God seem capricious? No. From the beginning of salvation history, we see God moving toward the chosen people with offers of covenant relationship. This means that both parties in the relationship have a say. God is revealed neither as an arbitrary deity nor an uncompromising one. There are many instances in scripture where human beings apparently change God's mind. And who set things up so this could be the case? God, of course. That's the difference between the Judeo-Christian God and deities who seem unapproachable and aloof from the affairs of their people.

God loses nothing by dealing with us on our own terms. On the contrary, such a divine nature calls forth a loving response rather than obeisance out of fear. Those who wish God to be more remote and objective may be the same kind of people who criticize Jesus in today's gospel for consorting with sinners!

Though *God* does not need to be reminded of the covenant made with Abraham, Isaac, and Jacob, Moses *does* and so do we. For in being mindful of the everlasting covenant, we are not discouraged by our own shortcomings and tempted toward hopelessness. Perhaps even more significant, we are less likely to judge the authenticity of religion by the infidelities of those

and all this *land* that I promised,
I will give your *descendants* as their perpetual *heritage*.'"

Finally, with a strong sense of closure—slowing, but keeping up the intensity—the resolution of the situation is announced.

So the LORD *relented* in the punishment
he had threatened to *inflict* on his *people*.

READING II 1 Timothy 1:12–17

A reading from the first Letter of Saint Paul to Timothy

These are personal words and they emphasize a great irony in Christian faith. Wide vocal variety is called for.

Beloved:
I am *grateful* to him who has *strengthened* me, Christ *Jesus* our *Lord*,
because he considered me *trustworthy*
in appointing me to the *ministry*.
I was once a *blasphemer* and a *persecutor* and *arrogant*,
but I have been *mercifully* treated
because I acted out of *ignorance* in my *unbelief*.

Indeed, the *grace* of our Lord has been *abundant*,
along with the *faith* and *love* that are in Christ *Jesus*.

The important division of the text comes here. Here begins the application of what has gone before. What follows must ring out!

This saying is *trustworthy* and deserves full *acceptance*:
Christ *Jesus* came into the *world* to *save sinners*.
Of *these* I am the *foremost*.

Is Paul saying he would not have received mercy had he not been a sinner? No, he is delighting in the way Jesus lavishes mercy and patience in direct proportion to need!

But for that *reason* I was *mercifully* treated,
so that in *me*, as the *foremost*,
Christ *Jesus* might display all his *patience* as an *example*
for those who would come to *believe* in him for everlasting *life*.

The final doxology is a spontaneous response of joy to the great insight we have just seen revealed.

To the king of *ages*, *incorruptible*, *invisible*, the only *God*,
honor and *glory forever* and *ever*. *Amen*.

who do not practice it very well. Such is a common mistake. It is even more common as an excuse!

READING II For the next several Sundays the second reading will be taken from the first and second letters written to Timothy. It may be helpful in preparing readings from these letters to read them in their entirety.

Paul persecuted the Christian community before becoming a member of it. This is no doubt why his ultimate conversion and defense of Christian belief were so intense. Here he points out one of the ironies he is so fond of: The depths of his depravity demonstrate just how merciful and forgiving Jesus is. Again, we have here (as in the first reading) a corrective for those who see a discrepancy between Christian and being a sinner. There is a discrepancy, of course, but it proves the power of Christ's saving love, not the ineffectiveness of it! The marvel underlying our faith is that Jesus died for us while we were still sinners. And now he is our great high priest, making intercession for us (as Moses did for the Israelites) so that our sins may be forgiven.

It is a simplistic view of Christian faith that would reject it because Christians are so imperfect. It is a view that would see religion more akin to magic than the struggle to live a relationship. Those who say

GOSPEL Luke 15:1–32

A reading from the holy Gospel according to Luke

The setting in which Jesus tells these parables is important. The scribes and Pharisees exclude sinners. Jesus includes them—even exalts them!

Tax collectors and *sinners* were all drawing *near* to *listen* to *Jesus*,
but the *Pharisees* and *scribes* began to *complain*, saying,
"*This* man welcomes *sinners* and *eats* with them."

Notice that the story is in the form of a question: "Wouldn't you behave like this in similar circumstances?" It's an effective teaching device.

So to them he addressed this *parable*.
"What *man* among you having a *hundred sheep*
and losing *one* of them
would not *leave* the ninety-*nine* in the *desert*
and go after the *lost* one until he *finds* it?
And when he *does* find it,
he sets it on his *shoulders* with great *joy*
and, upon his arrival *home*,
he calls together his *friends* and *neighbors* and says to them,
'*Rejoice* with me because I have *found* my lost *sheep*.'

A favorite quote for many, this is the essence of Christian hope!

I *tell* you, in just the same *way*
there will be more *joy* in *heaven* over one *sinner* who *repents*
than over ninety-nine *righteous* people
who have no *need* of repentance.

"Or what *woman* having *ten coins* and *losing* one
would not light a *lamp* and sweep the *house*,
searching *carefully* until she *finds* it?
And when she *does* find it,
she calls together her *friends* and *neighbors*
and says to them,
'*Rejoice* with me because I have *found* the coin that I *lost*.'

The point is, as before, that what is lost is most important until it is found.

they no longer go to church because the members are so hypocritical ("they say one thing, but do another") need to take a second look at how Jesus deals with weak human nature. He himself had some harsh things to say about hypocrites, but he was not criticizing their weakness; he was chastising their insincerity and arrogance.

Those who feel they are not good enough to belong to the Christian community should take great comfort from Paul's insights here. He seemed to be beyond all hope of conversion—beyond the reach of Jesus' mercy. And for that very reason he is now an extreme example of how all-encompassing the mercy of Jesus really is!

GOSPEL There are three stories in today's gospel reading, and they are all meant to celebrate how eager God is to find, to forgive, and to save. The word "prodigal" has two uses, adjective and noun. As an adjective, it describes someone who is excessive, extravagant, immoderate, and wasteful. The opposite of "prodigal" is "frugal." As a noun it is a synonym for profligate, spendthrift, squanderer, wastrel. We can see, then, why the third and most familiar story in today's gospel reading has been called the parable of the Prodigal Son. The boy was certainly wasteful of his inheritance and squandered his father's money. He was the opposite of frugal and moderate.

"In just the same *way*, I *tell* you,
there will be *rejoicing* among the angels of *God*
over one *sinner* who *repents*."

Then he said,
"A man had *two sons*, and the *younger* son said to his father,
'*Father* give me the *share* of your *estate* that should *come* to me.'
So the father *divided* the property *between* them.

Tell the familiar story with full animation, so that it will be fresh.

"After a few days, the *younger* son *collected* all his *belongings*
and set *off* to a distant *country*
where he *squandered* his inheritance on a life of *dissipation*.
When he had freely spent *everything*,
a severe *famine* struck that country,
and he *found* himself in dire *need*.
So he *hired* himself *out* to one of the local *citizens*
who sent him to his *farm* to tend the *swine*.
And he *longed* to eat his fill of the *pods* on which the *swine* fed,
but nobody *gave* him any.

A new section begins here. Pause.

"Coming to his *senses* he thought,
'How many of my father's *hired workers*
have *more* than enough *food* to eat,
but here am *I*, *dying* from *hunger*.
I shall get *up* and *go* to my father and I shall *say* to him,
"*Father*, I have *sinned* against *heaven* and against *you*.
I no *longer* deserve to be *called* your *son*;
treat *me* as you would treat one of your *hired workers*."'

But I agree with those who feel that the story could be more appropriately called the parable of the Prodigal Father. Clearly, the point that Jesus makes in this story is not how bad the boy was but how good the father was. It is the father who is excessive and extravagant and immoderate, anything but frugal with his forgiveness and mercy. It is the father who squanders love and reconciliation on the son. The father is the true spendthrift here, sparing no cost or labor to celebrate the homecoming of his wayward son.

And so God deals with us. While we are "still a long way off," still covered with the mire of the pig pen, God rushes toward us with loving compassion, giving orders to prepare the feast before we can even get the words of remorse out of our mouths. The prodigality of God's love and forgiveness is almost too much to be believed. In this area especially the Father needs to remind us over and over that "my ways are not your ways, nor are your thoughts my thoughts." We find it almost impossible to offer forgiveness and reconciliation with such prodigious abandon and love. Yet this is the challenge before each one of us.

Above all, notice that Jesus tells this parable in response to personal criticism. He has scandalized the Pharisees and scribes

Communicate the father's eagerness. It is amazing that the father's compassion is so great even while the son is still "a long way off." Jesus' hearers would see the father's running as very undignified—and sense more of his abandonment to mercy.

"So he got up and went *back* to his *father*.
While he was still a *long way off*,
his *father* caught *sight* of him,
and was filled with *compassion*.
He *ran* to his son, *embraced* him and *kissed* him.
His son said to him,
'*Father*, I have *sinned* against *heaven* and against *you*;
I no longer *deserve* to be called your *son*.'

The son's remorse is not directly acknowledged. It is almost irrelevant in the light of the father's joy.

"But his *father* ordered his *servants*,
'Quickly bring the finest *robe* and put it *on* him;
put a *ring* on his *finger* and *sandals* on his *feet*.
Take the fattened *calf* and *slaughter* it.
Then let us *celebrate* with a *feast*,
because this *son* of mine was *dead*, and has come to *life* again;
he was *lost*, and has been *found*.'
Then the celebration *began*.

The lost and found image is one of Luke's favorites.

"Now the *older* son had been out in the *field*
and, on his way *back*, as he neared the *house*,
he heard the sound of *music* and *dancing*.
He called one of the *servants* and asked what this might *mean*.
The servant said to him,
'Your *brother* has returned
and your *father* has slaughtered the fattened *calf*
because he has him *back* safe and *sound*.'

The older son is jealous; but he is hurt as well. Don't be too hard on him.

He became *angry*,
and when he *refused* to enter the *house*,
his *father* came *out* and *pleaded* with him.

by consorting with sinners. It is necessary for him to show his identity with just this kind of person, even eating with them—which for the people in this historical context meant identification with them. This parable is a forecast of Jesus' ultimate identification with sinners: his death on the cross. So the bottom line here is that Jesus is the prodigal, the spendthrift, the profligate, the one who squanders his love on those who need it most.

If we have difficulty interpreting the parable in this way, perhaps it is because we find our natural inclinations siding with the older brother. "It's not fair," we hear ourselves saying. "The undeserving poor are being treated as though they deserved special favors." It is then that we need to remind ourselves that Jesus' notion of poverty is different from ours. We betray our spiritual poverty, as the older brother did, by our inability to be prodigals ourselves—our inability to squander our love and concern, our tendency to be frugal with mercy. Our horror at seeing ourselves in this new light need not make us despair. For the Prodigal Father squanders love even on our pettiness. "You are here with me always; everything I have is yours."

He said to his father in reply,
'*Look*, all these *years* I *served* you
and not *once* did I disobey your *orders*;
yet you never gave *me* even a young *goat* to feast on
with my *friends*.
But when your son returns,
who *swallowed* up your *property* with *prostitutes*,
for *him* you slaughter the fattened *calf*.'

"He said to him,
'My *son*, *you* are here with me *always*;
everything I *have* is *yours*.
But *now* we *must* celebrate and rejoice,
because your *brother* was *dead* and has come to *life* again;
he was *lost* and has been *found*.'"

[Shorter: Luke 15:1–10]

The father is the soul of kindness, even toward the mean-spirited elder son.

25TH SUNDAY IN ORDINARY TIME

Lectionary #135

READING I Amos 8:4–7

The structure of the text is poetic. Be sensitive to such poetic devices as parallelism, the rhetorical question, and exaggeration for the sake of effect.

The money-grubber finds the festivals tiresome and the day of rest unproductive.

These tricks of the trade all cheat the consumer and pursue wealth at the expense of the poor. We have our contemporary equivalents of these horrors.

ephah = EE-fah

The final sentence is a strong promise of retribution!

A reading from the Book of the Prophet Amos

Hear this, you who *trample* upon the *needy*
and destroy the *poor* of the land!
"When will the *new* moon be *over*," you ask,
"that we may *sell* our *grain*,
and the *sabbath*, that we may *display* the *wheat*?
We will *diminish* the *ephah*,
add to the *shekel*,
and fix our *scales* for *cheating*!
We will buy the *lowly* for *silver*,
and the *poor* for a pair of *sandals*;
even the *refuse* of the wheat we will *sell*!"

The LORD has sworn by the *pride* of *Jacob*:
Never will I forget a *thing* they have *done*!

READING I One of the greatest injustices is when the powerful take advantage of the weak. Throughout the Hebrew scriptures we hear "defense of the lowly and the poor" as a pivotal condition of right relationship with God. Widows and orphans and the destitute are the responsibility of all who consider themselves aligned with the covenant between God and the chosen people. Amos is a vociferous champion of the poor—probably because he was poor himself, a shepherd before God chose him for prophecy.

In this reading Amos deals with the most heinous of sins against humanity. The culprits here not only do not defend the poor; they actually exploit them. Such ghoulish greed brings down the white-hot wrath of God. The fiends are eager for a holiday that was being celebrated to be over so they can get back to their dishonest labors. We are dealing with a poetic description of the crime here so the exaggeration is understandable—and perhaps not even all that exaggerated.

We should have no trouble seeing the relevance of this text today, though exploitation of fellow human beings can take more subtle and complex forms. Corporate greed seems to be on the rise. Businesses restructure themselves and lay off minimum-wage workers at the same time they provide bigger and bigger bonuses to those in the executive offices. Municipal, state, and federal legislators vote themselves substantial salary increases while public school funding remains mired in inequity. Many view the plight of the homeless as old news, and

READING II 1 Timothy 2:1–8

A reading from the first Letter of Saint Paul to Timothy

Beloved:
First of all, I ask that *supplications*, *prayers*,
petitions and *thanksgivings* be offered for *everyone*,
for *kings* and for all in *authority*,
that we may lead a *quiet* and *tranquil* life
in all *devotion* and *dignity*.

Listing the various forms of prayer adds emphasis to the urging.

This is *good* and *pleasing* to God our *savior*,
who wills *everyone* to be *saved*
and to come to *knowledge* of the *truth*.

God wills *all* to be saved! No one is excluded.

For there is *one* God.
There is also one *mediator* between *God* and *men*,
the *man* Christ *Jesus*,
who *gave* himself as *ransom* for *all*.
This was the *testimony* at the proper *time*.

"There is one God" echoes the *shema*, the daily prayer of every pious Jew. "Hear, O Israel, the Lord our God is one."

For *this* I was *appointed preacher* and *apostle*
—I am speaking the *truth*, I am not *lying*—
teacher of the *Gentiles* in *faith* and *truth*.

It is my *wish*, then, that in *every* place the men should *pray*,
lifting up holy *hands*, without *anger* or *argument*.

a little boring. We need to hear Amos' words today perhaps more than ever.

READING II In this section of the letter we hear recommendations that those in civil authority are to be supported by our prayers. The writer clearly realizes that the church and the state must occupy the same space and the good or ill of one affects the other. The Christian community will thrive in any political climate, but domestic tranquility is best. Thus, to pray for "the king and those in authority" is to ask God's blessing on those whose work has a direct bearing on our lives.

Clearly, the intent of the writer throughout this letter is to prescribe general norms of liturgical prayer and practice. But such norms do not emerge from a vacuum; they arise from the actual situation in which the praying community finds itself. The worshiping community is not isolated from the wider political community. When we assemble for prayer we come from that wider community and we bring it with us. And to some extent, the freedom we enjoy in gathering for worship is dependent on those in authority. Thus, it is more than courtesy that prompts us to pray for those who play a role in making it possible for us to "lead quiet and tranquil lives."

This reading reminds us that we live our faith in a real world. Though our beliefs and religious convictions certainly provide us with a hope that transcends the world, that hope must exercise itself in the nitty-gritty of everyday life. The tendency to view ourselves as being above it all is seriously

GOSPEL Luke 16:1–13

A reading from the holy Gospel according to Luke

This story is packed with human emotion and complexity. Tell it energetically.

Jesus said to his *disciples*,
"A *rich* man had a *steward*
who was *reported* to him for *squandering* his *property*.

"He *summoned* him and said,
'What is this I *hear* about you?
Prepare a full *account* of your *stewardship*,
because you can no *longer* be my *steward*.'

"The steward *said* to himself, 'What shall I *do*,
now that my *master* is taking the position of steward
away from me?

An older poetic rendering of the manager's words is: "To dig I am unable; to beg I am ashamed." There's no doubting his self-knowledge!

I am not *strong* enough to *dig* and I am *ashamed* to *beg*.
I *know* what I shall *do* so that,
when I am *removed* from the *stewardship*,
they may *welcome* me into their *homes*.'

His aims are thoroughly selfish, but undeniably clever.

"He called in his master's *debtors one* by *one*.
To the *first* he said,
'How much do you *owe* my *master*?'
He replied, 'One hundred *measures* of *olive* oil.'
He said to him, 'Here is your promissory *note*.
Sit down and quickly write one for *fifty*.'

Do not rush through this dialogue. The formulaic repetition makes it memorable.

Then to *another* the steward said, 'And *you*,
how much do *you* owe?'
He replied, 'One hundred *kors* of *wheat*.'
The steward said to *him*, 'Here is *your* promissory note;
write one for *eighty*.'

far afield of authentic Christianity. Indeed, this reading goes on to make the point that our faith propels us into the workaday world in ever more profound ways. By our witnessing presence we promote God's will that "all be saved and come to knowledge of the truth."

GOSPEL This parable is uniquely qualified to teach us how to read and interpret all parables. They are not to be taken literally. As the word itself implies, a parable is a story laid alongside a life situation so that parallels can be drawn. The parable does not mimic or match the situation to which it applies. It casts new light upon it by being similar in some ways, divergent in others.

The old name for this story is the parable of the unjust steward. And the shocker is that the unjust steward (or manager) receives praise for his cleverness. The parallel is this: If Jesus' disciples were only half as clever at promoting his kingdom as this manager was at promoting his own welfare, that kingdom would flourish. It's a strange comparison, and that is why it makes the point so well.

How can we be more clever in living and promoting our faith? It is a question that deserves some prayerful thought. Certainly we are not being counseled to imitate the dishonesty of the unjust steward. The words of Jesus that follow the parable are a collection of sayings about the appropriate use

"And the master *commended* that dishonest steward
for acting *prudently*.
For the children of *this* world
are more *prudent* in dealing with their own *generation*
than are the children of *light*.

Here's the point of the parable. Proclaim it carefully.

"I *tell* you, make *friends* for yourselves with *dishonest* wealth,
so that when it *fails*, you will be welcomed
into *eternal* dwellings.

Jesus expands on the point.

The person who is trustworthy in very *small* matters
is *also* trustworthy in *great* ones;
and the person who is *dishonest* in very small matters
is also *dishonest* in great ones.

Elusive wealth is material treasure; lasting wealth is the gift of salvation and a life lived in generous gratitude.

If, therefore, you are *not* trustworthy with *dishonest* wealth,
who will trust you with *true* wealth?
If you are not trustworthy with what belongs to *another*,
who will give you what is *yours*?

The final proverb is familiar and much-loved. Proclaim it carefully.

"*No* servant can serve two *masters*.
He will either *hate* one and *love* the other,
or be *devoted* to one and *despise* the other.
You cannot serve both *God* and *mammon*."

[Shorter: Luke 16:10–13]

of wealth. Though they were certainly not part of the original parable, Luke's placement of them here makes it clear that the clever manager's tactics are not to become our own. It is his resourcefulness we praise. It is our lack of resourcefulness in living our faith fully that we need to ponder.

How often have you heard the expression, "Money is the root of all evil"? Actually, that expression is a corruption of the original: *Cupiditas est radix malorum,* which is translated more accurately as, "The *love* of money is the root of all evil." In itself, money is neither good nor bad—it can be used for good or bad purposes. The proverb and the words of Jesus show us that we cannot love money to the exclusion of everything else and avoid evil. One follows the other as the day the night. And now we have come full circle with today's readings: The prophet Amos provided us with a vivid sketch of the ugly deeds done by those who love money more than their fellow human beings.

26TH SUNDAY IN ORDINARY TIME

Lectionary #138

READING I Amos 6:1a, 4–7

A reading from the Book of the prophet Amos

Thus says the LORD the God of *hosts*:
Woe to the *complacent* in *Zion*!

A lament, a prediction of sorrow and regret, not an angry condemnation.

Lying upon beds of *ivory*,
stretched *comfortably* on their *couches*,
they eat *lambs* taken from the *flock*,
and *calves* from the *stall*!

These images are vivid! Sacrilege is involved.

Improvising to the *music* of the *harp*,
like *David*, they devise their own *accompaniment*.
They drink *wine* from *bowls*
and *anoint* themselves with the best *oils*;
yet they are not made *ill* by the collapse of *Joseph*!

Conspicuous consumption and self-indulgence.

Therefore, now they shall be the *first* to go into *exile*,
and their wanton *revelry* shall be done *away* with.

The conclusion is strong, and explains the woeful end awaiting the complacent.

READING II 1 Timothy 6:11–16

A reading from the first Letter of Saint Paul to Timothy

But *you*, man of God, pursue *righteousness*,
devotion, *faith*, *love*, *patience* and *gentleness*.
Compete *well* for the *faith*.

Be sure to give each virtue its due. Lists are difficult to read.

READING I Here is Amos' lament for the complacent and insensitive! And it is in poetic form, replete with vivid imagery that demands an exquisitely careful and well-modulated proclamation. If anything less than your best efforts are used with a text like this, there is the risk that it will sound either trivial or unintentionally humorous. An exalted tone is appropriate, but avoid sounding harsh. The prophet *laments* the sad fate of the wicked, even as he accuses them.

Amos is serious about these complacent folk who pamper themselves at the expense of others and have apparently lost interest in the sufferings of their fellow human beings. And yet there is nothing here that could be called ranting and raving. An author who uses poetry to make a point is several steps above uncontrolled rage. The overall tone is dignified, solemn, and even sad. "Woe" is always a lament!

Amos is a great champion of the poor. The idle rich are the target of his wrath primarily because their conspicuous consumption of delicacies is always at the expense of those who lack even the bare necessities. The lambs from the flock and calves from the stall upon which they feast are supposed to be set aside for sacrifice to the Lord; thus, they add sacrilege to gluttony. They do not lament the imminent moral collapse of Joseph (meaning the whole people); indeed, they are contributing to it.

The entire scene is exaggerated and capitalizes on the stereotypes we recognize even in our own day. But there is nothing exaggerated about the promise of divine

Lay hold of *eternal* life, to which you were *called*
when you made the noble *confession* in the presence
of many *witnesses*.

Here is the main point: "our noble confession of faith."

I *charge* you before *God*, who gives life to *all* things,
and before Christ *Jesus*,
who gave testimony under Pontius *Pilate*
for the noble *confession*,
to *keep* the commandment without *stain* or *reproach*
until the *appearance* of our *Lord* Jesus *Christ*
that the *blessed* and *only* ruler
will make *manifest* at the proper *time*,
the *King* of kings and *Lord* of lords,
who *alone* has *immortality*, who dwells
in unapproachable *light*,
and whom no human *being* has *seen* or *can* see.
To *him* be *honor* and eternal *power*. *Amen*.

A long sentence. Vocal variety will meet the challenge of subordinate clauses.

The brief hymn of praise emphasizes the nobility of discipleship.

GOSPEL Luke 16:19–31

A reading from the holy Gospel according to Luke

Jesus said to the *Pharisees*:
"There was a *rich* man who dressed in purple *garments*
and fine *linen*
and dined *sumptuously* each *day*.
And lying at his *door* was a *poor* man named *Lazarus*,
covered with *sores*,
who would *gladly* have eaten his fill of the *scraps*
that fell from the *rich* man's *table*.
Dogs even used to come and lick his *sores*.

The story is a literary masterpiece complete with all the elements that make a good story, including a surprise ending.

The details of the story make it memorable. Don't rush through them.

retribution—not for mere excess and self-indulgence, but for the neglect of the hungry and the poor which it not only represents but fosters. The social revolution inherent in Christianity is scheduled for the next world, but it begins here: "God puts down the mighty and exalts the humble."

READING II Timothy is the leader of a Christian community. Here he is being counseled in the essentials of Christian living—the consequences of having been initiated into the faith through baptism. There is a theme that emerges clearly from this text. It is the "noble confession of faith" that recalls Jesus' profession before Pilate: "The reason I have come into the world is to bear witness to the truth." The truth is God's plan to bring the world into unity and peace through the gift of eternal redemption.

We have all made our "noble confession of faith" at baptism. The challenge now is to live it out and to avoid the cynicism that would compromise it. The list of virtues that begins the reading can be seen as an antidote to cynicism: integrity (righteousness), piety (devotion), faith, love, steadfastness (patience), and a gentle spirit. Taken together, these qualities guarantee the nobility of spirit that mark the authentic disciple of Jesus.

GOSPEL Here is a parable told only by Luke. It does not appear in the other gospel narratives, and Luke himself is drawing on similar stories when he

"When the poor man *died*,
he was carried away by *angels* to the bosom of *Abraham*.
The *rich* man *also* died and was *buried*,
and from the *netherworld*, where he was in *torment*,
he raised his *eyes* and saw *Abraham* far *off*
and *Lazarus* at his *side*.

The tormented man's plea is heartrending. He has seen his error.

And he cried out, 'Father *Abraham*, have *pity* on me.
Send *Lazarus* to dip the tip of his *finger* in *water* and cool my *tongue*,
for I am suffering *torment* in these *flames*.'

"Abraham *replied*,
'My *child*, *remember* that you received
what was *good* during *your* lifetime
while *Lazarus* likewise received what was *bad*;
but now *he* is *comforted* here, whereas *you* are *tormented*.

The saddest words of all: It might have been. Now the opportunity is gone forever.

Moreover, between *us* and *you* a great *chasm* is established
to prevent *anyone* from *crossing* who might wish to go
from *our* side to *yours* or from *your* side to *ours*.'

"He said, 'Then I *beg* you, father,

Even more poignant is the sufferer's wish to spare others the same misery.

send him to my *father's* house, for I have five *brothers*,
so that he may *warn* them,
lest they *too* come to this place of *torment*.'

"But Abraham replied, 'They have *Moses* and the *prophets*.
Let them listen to *them*.'
He said, 'Oh *no*, father Abraham,
but if someone from the *dead* goes to them, they will *repent*.'
Then *Abraham* said, 'If they will not listen to *Moses* and the *prophets*,

Not even miracles will soften the heart of those blinded by selfishness.

neither will they be persuaded if someone should *rise* from the *dead*.'"

records the telling of it by Jesus. Like all parables, this one reveals more than the obvious. Yes, it is clear that we are meant to learn how to treat the poor. The intention is that we look at our lives and compare them with the lives of the less fortunate.

But the kicker of this story comes at the very end. In effect, we are told that there are no clearly stated formulas to live by that will secure us a place in the afterlife—in Abraham's bosom. We have "Moses and the prophets" to guide us as we figure out for ourselves how to reconcile the gulf that separates the self-absorbed and indulgent from the disadvantaged and the destitute. To "compete well for the faith" (second reading) is to engage in this struggle with the inequities that surround us. There is no overwhelming sign (not even a resurrected Messiah) that will automatically convert the world to social justice. If this were so, the world would be a different place.

The rich man is a poignant figure when we hear him, even in torment, plead for a better outcome for his brothers. It is not easy to hear the response to his plea: "No, it is too late, for the vast gulf that separates you from them makes it impossible to spare them the struggle." There does come a time when lost opportunities cannot be regained, when the realization that being a disciple involves choices that come and go. Not to choose is to choose.

We must be content with knowing that ultimately the social revolution proclaimed in Moses and the prophets will take place. The lowly will be lifted up, the mighty put down from their thrones. The way we conduct our lives now will determine which group we find ourselves in when the revolution comes.

27TH SUNDAY IN ORDINARY TIME

Lectionary #141

READING I Habakkuk 1:2–3; 2:2–4

A reading from the Book of the prophet Habakkuk

A cry of the heart, couched in the solemn dignity of poetry.

How *long*, O LORD? I *cry* for *help*
but you do not *listen*!
I cry *out* to you, "*Violence*!"
but you do not *intervene*.

The exalted language does not permit a literal acting out of the emotions here.

Why do you let me see *ruin*;
why must I look at *misery*?
Destruction and *violence* are before me;
there is *strife*, and clamorous *discord*.

Pause before the Lord's response. Utter calm and assurance is in sharp contrast to the exhaustion expressed in the opening lines.

Then the LORD *answered* me and said:
Write down the vision *clearly* upon the *tablets*,
so that one can read it *readily*.
For the *vision* still has its *time*,
presses *on* to *fulfillment*, and will not *disappoint*;
if it *delays*, *wait* for it,
it will surely *come*, it will not be *late*.

Rashness is the opposite of patience.

The *rash* one has no *integrity*;
but the *just* one, because of his *faith*, shall *live*.

READING I The poetry of Habakkuk will find a place in the heart of every believer who faces the challenge of discipleship head-on. Though many of us are reluctant to express our prayer in such dramatic terms, there is no reason why we should not. It is undeniable that our feelings often match those of the prophet. The ills of the world seem sometimes to be completely beyond a cure. For every dragon slain there seems to be yet another waiting in the next cave. And the same is true for many on the level of individual experience. Whether the struggle is a personal one with weakness or the challenges of hardship from without, enduring faith is never without its test.

Enduring faith—that is what is counseled here. Habakkuk is lamenting specific troubles that confront him and his people, not the generally flawed state of human existence. It is easy for us to indulge in platitudes about our faith and repeat the comforting thought that it enables us to see the larger picture. It is not easy to apply faith when real, personal, and senseless tragedy becomes an all-consuming force in our lives. The strongest among us can be reduced to helplessness; that's when we hear Habakkuk's cry escape our own lips: "Why? Why?"

And that's when we hear in response: "The vision will not disappoint; if it delays, wait for it." It's as much as we get, and often it seems woefully insufficient. That's why our faith must be a living, growing, developing part of us. It cannot be shelved until we need it, for then we will discover that it has grown weak and flabby from disuse and will not sustain us. Our response to tragedy then is rash. The virtue of integrity involves a well-exercised faith that will enable us to survive even the most awful challenges.

READING II 2 Timothy 1:6–8, 13–14

A reading from the second Letter of Saint Paul to Timothy

Beloved:
I *remind* you, to stir into *flame*
the gift of *God* that you have through the *imposition*
of my *hands*.

Such a vivid image: Stoke the fires of faith so that they burn brightly.

For God did not give us a spirit of *cowardice*
but rather of *power* and *love* and *self-control*.

Speak the three virtues slowly: power . . . love . . . and self-control.

So do *not* be *ashamed* of your *testimony* to our *Lord*,
nor of *me*, a *prisoner* for his *sake*;
but *bear* your share of *hardship* for the *gospel*
with the *strength* that comes from *God*.

Note the presumption here: Believing the gospel automatically involves hardship.

Take as your *norm* the sound *words* that you *heard* from me,
in the *faith* and *love* that are in Christ *Jesus*.
Guard this rich *trust* with the help of the Holy *Spirit*
that dwells *within* us.

The Holy Spirit can be relied upon to keep our faith whole and sound.

READING II **Enduring and bold faith is at the heart of this reading. This kind of faith is revealed in (and is nourished by) the boldness of lives lived in power (strength), love, and self-control.**

It would be difficult to imagine a set of words more appropriate to describe the life of an authentic Christian. And there is no better collection of qualities than strength, love, and self-control to ensure effective leadership in the church. This reading is directly concerned with such leadership, as Paul counsels Timothy to be a model of good leadership in the infant church.

Consider strong religious leaders: They uphold the gospel truths with which they are entrusted—and not defensively, for that is a sign of weakness. And certainly not stubbornly because a stubborn spirit is blinded by entrenchment in one position or view of complex issues. Real strength is revealed in openness and dialogue, sustained by conviction and never threatened by challenge. Real strength is empathetic and calm, peaceful and conciliatory, broad-minded and inclusive. It is different from authoritarianism—a weakness that masquerades as strength, blustering a defense that convinces no one.

All good leadership is loving. Unloving leadership is a sham, bad shepherding that does not have the good of the flock at heart.

All effective leadership is disciplined, showing mastery of self that comes from genuine wisdom. Ultimately, wisdom is a gift of God, the gift most like God, and the quality that reveals God most clearly to the world. Perhaps above all else, wisdom shows itself in the peaceful heart, the heart that has mastered its lesser inclinations and fostered its noblest impulses.

GOSPEL Luke 17:5–10

A reading from the holy Gospel according to Luke

The apostles feel the need for greater faith to understand and accept what they are being taught. Jesus lets them know that their faith is sufficient.

The point is elusive. We are all the servants of faith. And faith is greater than those who serve it.

The *apostles* said to the *Lord*, "Increase our *faith*."
The Lord *replied*,
"If you have faith the size of a *mustard* seed,
you would say to this *mulberry* tree,
'Be *uprooted* and planted in the *sea*,' and it would *obey* you.

"*Who* among you would say to your *servant*
who has just come in from *plowing* or tending *sheep*
in the *field*,
'Come here *immediately* and take your place at *table*'?

Our sensitivity to the slave/master relationship must be set aside so we can understand this image from a culture in which slavery was accepted.

Would he not *rather* say to him,
'*Prepare* something for me to *eat*.
Put on your *apron* and *wait* on me while I *eat* and *drink*.
You may eat and drink when I am *finished*'?
Is he *grateful* to that servant because he did what
was *commanded*?
So should it be with *you*.
When you have done *all* you have been *commanded*,
say, 'We are *unprofitable* servants;
we have *done* what we were *obliged* to do.'"

The point is that doing one's duty is to be taken for granted. This is realism, not false humility.

GOSPEL **The parable of the mustard seed shows us what a powerful item faith is. Though the smallest of all the seeds, mustard can be cultivated into the largest of shrubs where the birds of the air build their nests. In using the image of the mustard seed here, Jesus may be making the same point. The disciples ask for an increase of faith and Jesus responds by saying, in effect, "Don't worry about how much faith you have. It is such a powerful thing that even a tiny bit of it makes you potential miracle workers. You have plenty of faith. Now nourish it and make it grow."**

All of us have at times wished for an increase of faith, or have blamed our weakness and doubt on insufficient faith. So it is good to hear that what little faith we have is sufficient for moving mountains and uprooting trees. We need to trust the faith we have. The miracles that result from exercised faith are far greater than the exaggerated signs and wonders Jesus uses as examples here. The fact that he uses such images to describe the power of faith leads us to ponder what faith can achieve in the realm of the spirit and the evangelization of the world. We need to have more faith in our faith!

The second half of the gospel text is also about the gift of faith, though the connection may not be immediately obvious. Faithful service is precisely the kind of service that can work miracles. And the faithful servant knows that whatever is accomplished for the master is because of the relationship of trust between them. When we have done all that faith in us can achieve, we are delighted to say: "This was the understanding from the beginning; we have merely done what was expected of us."

28TH SUNDAY IN ORDINARY TIME

Lectionary #144

READING I 2 Kings 5:14–17

A reading from the second Book of Kings

Naaman = NAY-uh-muhn (note: three syllables)
Elisha = ee-LĪ-shuh

Naaman went down and plunged into the *Jordan seven times*
at the word of *Elisha,* the man of *God*.
His *flesh* became again like the flesh of a little *child*,
and he was *clean* of his *leprosy*.

Naaman *returned* with his whole *retinue* to the man of *God*.
On his *arrival* he *stood* before Elisha and said,
"Now I *know* that there is no *God* in all the *earth*,
except in *Israel*.
Please accept a *gift* from your servant."

Here the skeptic has become a believer.

Elisha *replied*, "As the LORD *lives* whom I *serve*, I will not
take it,"
and despite Naaman's *urging*, he still *refused*.

Elisha's reward is that Naaman has come to the truth about God. It is enough.

Naaman said: "If you will not *accept*,
please *let* me, your *servant*, have two *mule-loads* of *earth*,
for I will no *longer* offer holocaust or sacrifice
to any *other* god except to the *LORD*."

The earth will enable him to pray on Israel's soil. It is a touching image, though perhaps difficult for the modern ear to appreciate.

READING I To proclaim this reading with full understanding, you need to read all of chapter five of Second Kings. The story of Naaman the Syrian as abbreviated here is missing some elements that make it all the more striking. After being told by the prophet Elisha (through a messenger!) that he should bathe in the Jordan River to be healed of his leprosy, Naaman is angry. He wanted the man of God to perform a much more dramatic sign. In fact, he doubted that the prescription he had received would heal him. He protests that the rivers of his own land are far nobler than the Jordan. Why couldn't he wash in them? It was with great reluctance that he finally gave in to the pleading of his servants to do what the prophet said. And, of course, the despised muddy trickle of the Jordan River did cleanse him of leprosy—and of his arrogance as well.

He returns humbly to Elisha and, in effect, wishes to pay for the great healing he has received. True prophet and servant that he is, Elisha refuses to take credit or payment for God's merciful work. Thus Naaman learns another lesson. Genuine grace (and the healing that comes with it) is free.

The two mule-loads of earth Naaman requests will enable him to take a bit of Israel's land back to his native Syria—where he uses it to stand upon when he prays to Israel's God. Naaman has seen the power of the God of Israel and will worship none other. This is the final lesson he learns.

Yet another message in this story will elude us if we fail to appreciate what it means for Naaman to be a foreigner, not a member of the chosen people. God's plan to save the world excludes no one.

READING II 2 Timothy 2:8–13

A reading from the second Letter of Saint Paul to Timothy

Beloved:
Remember Jesus *Christ*, *raised* from the *dead*,
a descendant of *David*:
such is my *gospel*, for which I am *suffering*,
even to the point of *chains*, like a *criminal*.
But the word of *God* is *not* chained.

Therefore, I bear with *everything* for the sake of those
who are *chosen*,
so that they *too* may obtain the *salvation* that is
in Christ *Jesus*,
together with eternal *glory*.

This saying is *trustworthy*:
If we have *died* with him
we shall also *live* with him;
if we *persevere*
we shall also *reign* with him.
But if we *deny* him
he will deny *us*.
If we are *unfaithful*
he remains faithful,
for he *cannot* deny *himself*.

To remember is to be mindful, that is, to keep in mind.

This insightful contrast must be carefully proclaimed. "You can chain me, but you cannot chain the Word of God!"

His sufferings have the power to save others. The same is true for us.

The acclamation has four parallel structures; emphasize the pattern.

The reversal is effective and striking. We expect a fourth match (he will be unfaithful to us), but it does not come. Jesus has pledged fidelity no matter what, and cannot deny himself.

READING II **Paul reminds us in this reading how simple the essence of the good news really is: Christ has died, Christ is risen, Christ will come again! The consequences of preaching this simple gospel are not at all simple, however. They have landed Paul in jail. The insights his imprisonment provides are important and provocative.**

First, he makes the memorable comparison between the limitations placed on his person and the impossibility of placing limitations on the gospel he preaches. Such an observation can come only from a person who is filled with faith and hope. And he goes further: He asserts that even his imprisonment furthers the growth of the Christian community, since he believes in the solidarity of all believers. This is something of the doctrine we express in the creed: "We believe in the communion of saints." We are never alone in our journey toward God. We are surrounded by a cloud of witnesses whose sufferings build up the community life we share, whose shortcomings affect us as well, and whose lives are affected by the way we live our own.

Christians who believe they can exercise their faith in isolation from the believing and worshiping community do not yet understand the nature of their calling. Personal faith and private devotion are essential, of course, but the truly Christian life can only be lived in community with one's fellow believers. Yes, there are saints who are hermits. Saint Benedict in his *Rule for Monasteries* acknowledges such a calling—but it is to be pursued only after a long and successful experience in the proving ground of communal life.

GOSPEL Luke 17:11–19

A reading from the holy Gospel according to Luke

Samaria = suh-MAIR-ee-uh
Galilee = GAL-ih-lee
The point is that Jesus is near foreign territory.

As *Jesus* continued his *journey* to *Jerusalem*,
he traveled through *Samaria* and *Galilee*.

They keep their distance because by law they were forbidden contact with others. And those who came into contact with them became ritually unclean.

As he was entering a *village*, ten *lepers* met him.
They stood at a *distance* from him and raised their *voices*, saying,
"*Jesus, Master*! Have *pity* on us!"

And when he *saw* them, he said,
"Go *show* yourselves to the *priests*."
As they were *going* they were *cleansed*.

Note the details: "loud voice" and "fell at the feet of Jesus."

And *one* of them, *realizing* he had been *healed*,
returned, glorifying *God* in a loud *voice*;
and he fell at the *feet* of Jesus and *thanked* him.
He was a *Samaritan*.

Jesus said in *reply*,
"*Ten* were cleansed, were they *not*?
Where are the other *nine*?

There is no insult to the foreigner here, as the saving words of Jesus that follow make clear.

Has none but this *foreigner* returned to give thanks to *God*?"

Then he said to him, "*Sta*nd up and *go*;
your *faith* has *saved* you."

GOSPEL Luke is the gospel writer who emphasizes more than the others the principle of universality. That is, the good news of Jesus is to cover the earth. It is intended for all the nations of the world. It is not a notion that arrived new on the scene with Jesus. The same point is made throughout the Hebrew scriptures, and we have an example of it in today's first reading. Naaman the Syrian was a foreigner, like the Samaritan leper in this gospel narrative.

The healing of ten lepers expands on the theme of universalism, however, by implying that the foreigner was the only one to return and give thanks to God for the healing received. The implication is clear, and is made at other times by Jesus as well: If those to whom the word of salvation came first do not accept it, it will nevertheless be broadcast to all the world. It is a bitter irony of history, but an important lesson for all of us, that it was the leaders of Jesus' own people who rejected him. It is all the more bitter when we remember that it was the prime duty of those same leaders to watch for, be sensitive to, and announce the arrival of the Messiah when he appeared.

Yet another insight into God's plan is revealed in the ungrudging generosity with which mercy is showered upon all, both the grateful and the ingrate. Nine of the ten lepers healed did not return to praise God for their healing. Nevertheless, they are healed and the liberality of God's mercy is exalted even in their ingratitude. Or perhaps they were simply forgetful. In which case, many of us can identify with them more closely!

29TH SUNDAY IN ORDINARY TIME

Lectionary #147

READING I Exodus 17:8–13

A reading from the Book of Exodus

Amalek = AM-uh-lek

In those days, *Amalek* came and waged *war* against *Israel*.
Moses, therefore, said to *Joshua*,
"Pick out certain *men*,
and *tomorrow* go out and *engage* Amalek in *battle*.
I will be standing on top of the *hill*
with the staff of *God* in my hand."

Emphasize the staff of God.

So Joshua *did* as Moses *told* him:
he *engaged* Amalek in *battle*
after Moses had climbed to the top of the *hill*
with *Aaron* and *Hur*.

Read the "as long as" parallel structure with deliberateness.

As long as Moses kept his *hands* raised *up*,
Israel had the *better* of the *fight*,
but when he let his hands *rest*,
Amalek had the better of the fight.
Moses' *hands*, however, grew *tired*;
so they put a *rock* in place for him to *sit* on.
Meanwhile *Aaron* and *Hur supported* his hands,
one on *one* side and one on the *other*,
so that his hands remained *steady* till *sunset*.

And Joshua mowed down *Amalek* and his *people*
with the edge of the *sword*.

READING I Though this story of Moses and his uplifted arms has been interpreted as a lesson in constancy at prayer, and though it was apparently chosen for the lectionary to match Jesus' words in the gospel about praying constantly, it is not the best choice. It is never referred to by writers of the New Testament. Out of context, it presents a view of a God who is too easily manipulated against one's enemies. It concludes with a brutal image that draws a shudder from even the less squeamish.

The intent by the Exodus writer is no doubt to show that the role of the prophet is to make God present among the people. Moses has demonstrated time and again to the Israelites that he speaks with God's authority. His staff has been shown to be especially powerful (stretched over the waters of the Red Sea, bringing forth water from the rock in the desert, and so on) in alleviating Israel's fear that God may have abandoned them. It is certainly true that the fidelity of God is seen in the spokespersons who are chosen throughout the ages to speak the divine will.

The threat of Amalek is a recurring theme. The writer clearly shows that Israel's only hope of victory lies in reliance on the help of God. And that help is signified in the upraised hands of Moses, holding the revered staff. The necessity for constancy in prayer and dependence on God is also real, for the threat of more subtle enemies is ever present. Any notion, however, that we can mow our enemies down with prayer (or by any other means) is far from an acceptable interpretation. It stems from a defensive view of faith and religion (us against the

READING II 2 Timothy 3:14—4:2

A reading from the second Letter of Saint Paul to Timothy

This strong admonition is appropriate for all of us.

Paul mentions Timothy's mother (Eunice) and grandmother (Lois) by name elsewhere in the letter (1:5) as those who first taught Timothy the faith.

Note: It is what we call the Old Testament that is being referred to here.

Beloved:
Remain *faithful* to what you have *learned* and *believed*,
because you *know* from whom you *learned* it,
and that from *infancy* you have known the sacred *Scriptures*,
which are capable of giving you *wisdom* for *salvation*
through *faith* in Christ *Jesus*.

All Scripture is *inspired* by *God*
and is *useful* for *teaching*, for *refutation*, for *correction*,
and for training in *righteousness*,
so that one who belongs to *God* may be *competent*,
equipped for every good *work*.

"I charge you" is strong. The strength of the final sentence demands even more sense of closure than usual.

I *charge* you in the presence of *God* and of Christ *Jesus*,
who will judge the *living* and the *dead*,
and by his *appearing* and his kingly *power*:
proclaim the *word*;
be *persistent* whether it is *convenient* or *inconvenient*;
convince, *reprimand*, *encourage* through all *patience*
and *teaching*.

world). Hardly a stance from which one can plausibly proclaim good news!

READING II In this second reading we are counseled to think of ourselves as a people of the book, capable of drawing from the revealed word what we need to equip ourselves for good works done in strong, informed faith. Though the letter is addressed to the teaching authority in the Christian community, every devout disciple can hear these words with profit.

The last paragraph emphasizes the awesome responsibility laid upon all who would embrace ministry in the church: Their task, above all else, is to proclaim the word. Organized religion can easily become caught up in many activities that are necessary but actually peripheral to the church's central mission. Preaching the good news is the duty, privilege, and goal that outweighs all other ecclesiastical business.

Finally, the word of God is never preached for personal gain—whether that be financial, personal, or emotional profit. The honest preacher knows that the pulpit is never to be a platform for private convictions or personal agenda. Nor is the preaching of the word to be subjected to the whim of the preacher. As Paul says clearly: "I charge you to stay with this task."

GOSPEL The short parable that makes up today's gospel reading is a gem. Who are the central characters? The judge appears as a world-weary sort who sometimes makes decisions on the basis of his own convenience and comfort—or safety. The persistent widow (the plaintiff)

GOSPEL Luke 18:1–8

A reading from the holy Gospel according to Luke

The introductory sentence explains what the parable is going to be about. This is unusual. Be sure the people hear it.

Jesus told his *disciples* a *parable*
about the *necessity* for them to pray *always*
without becoming *weary*.

He said, "There was a *judge* in a certain *town*
who neither *feared God* nor *respected* any human *being*.
And a *widow* in that town used to come to him and say,
'Render a just *decision* for me against my *adversary*.'

"For a long *time* the judge was *unwilling*, but *eventually*
he thought,
'While it is *true* that I neither fear *God* nor respect
any human *being*,

There is almost a sense of wry humor here.

because this *widow* keeps *bothering* me
I shall deliver a just *decision* for her
lest she finally come and *strike* me.'"

Pause before continuing with "The Lord said."

The *Lord* said, "Pay *attention* to what the dishonest judge *says*.
Will not *God* then secure the *rights* of his *chosen* ones
who call *out* to him *day* and *night*?

Exploit the power of these rhetorical sentences. They should ring in the ears of the members of the assembly long after you've finished the proclamation.

Will he be *slow* to answer them?
I *tell* you, he will *see* to it that justice is done for them *speedily*.
But when the Son of *Man* comes, will he find *faith* on earth?"

is presented as a demanding person who may not make her request with much courtesy. The opponent, whoever it is that the widow is suing, is in the background, and we must presume that the defendant is in the wrong. The point of the story depends on such a presumption.

So, here we have three unlikable characters cast in a drama that will reveal to us the necessity of praying always and not losing heart. It's an odd parable, though not unique. Remember the story of the unjust steward we read just three weeks ago. He was praised for his cleverness, despite his dishonesty.

The persistent widow shows us that persistence in prayer is necessary. We are the widow. The world-weary judge shows us that our prayers will be answered, even if that answer is delayed. God is the judge, but now it is the difference, not the similarity, that makes the parable work. God will give swift justice! The widow's opponent can even teach us something: that it is futile to engage in conflict with someone who knows how to get results through persistent prayer.

We should cast one other character in this story, however. And it is not a person, but the virtue of faith. Only faith enables the persistent widow to persevere until justice is done her. Only faith is able to persevere when the answer to our prayers seems long in coming. Faith knows that God will answer prayer, and gives us the strength and patience to persevere. The final sentence of the reading (a rhetorical question) could, in referring to the parable that has preceded it, be read this way: "When the Son of Man comes, will he find any [of this kind of] faith on the earth?"

30TH SUNDAY IN ORDINARY TIME

Lectionary #150

READING I Sirach 35:12–14, 16–18

The poetry here makes the content memorable. Notice how the poetic device of parallelism is consistent throughout the text. Every line is echoed and restated in the line that follows.

The second paragraph teaches us about the kind of prayer that finds favor with God.

A reading from the Book of Sirach

The *LORD* is a God of *justice*,
who knows no *favorites*.
Though not *unduly* partial toward the *weak*,
yet he hears the *cry* of the *oppressed*.
The LORD is not *deaf* to the wail of the *orphan*,
nor to the *widow* when she pours out her *complaint*.

The one who serves God *willingly* is *heard*;
his *petition* reaches the *heavens*.
The prayer of the *lowly* pierces the *clouds*;
it does not *rest* till it reaches its *goal*,
nor will it *withdraw* till the Most High *responds*,
judges *justly* and affirms the *right*,
and the LORD will not *delay*.

READING I Here in poetic form we see a summary of the way God responds to those who approach in humble prayer. God does not show partiality to the weak; nevertheless, notice that it is the oppressed, the widow and the orphan, and the lowly who receive specific mention. Perhaps we can understand the meaning better here if we think of the word "automatically." One's state in life does not, in and of itself, automatically guarantee divine approval of one's requests. It is the state of our interior life that does that. And the one who serves God willingly is the one who is guaranteed a hearing.

Above all else, the point being made here is that a humble stance before God is what gives power to our prayers. Humility is not necessarily abject breast-beating, however. Humility is honesty. Coming to God in prayer with an open and honest realization of both our need and God's fidelity puts us in a truly humble stance.

We can never hear too frequently how necessary it is to approach God simply and directly. Nor can it be too often repeated that God always sides with those who have no one else to side with them. The weakest of the weak have the strongest possible ally in the God who has always been revealed as their special patron.

READING II Perhaps the most striking thing about this poignant text is that it shows how closely Paul has identified with Jesus, the suffering servant. He speaks of his approaching martyrdom in terms like those used by Jesus when he foretold his own death. To be "poured out like a libation" is to see one's life as

READING II 2 Timothy 4:6–8, 16–18

A reading from the second Letter of Saint Paul to Timothy

Beloved:
I am *already* being poured *out* like a *libation*,
and the time of my *departure* is at *hand*.
I have competed *well*; I have finished the *race*;
I have kept the *faith*.

The first five statements are brief and vivid. Read them slowly and with deliberation. Each one is a gem.

From now *on* the crown of *righteousness* awaits me,
which the *Lord*, the just *judge*,
will *award* to me on that day, and not only to *me*,
but to *all* who have *longed* for his *appearance*.

After five short statements, a long one—with several levels of subordination. Vocal variety will do it justice.

At my *first defense no* one appeared on my *behalf*,
but everyone *deserted* me.
May it not be held *against* them!
But the *Lord* stood by me and gave me *strength*,
so that through *me* the *proclamation* might be *completed*
and all the *Gentiles* might *hear* it.
And I was *rescued* from the *lion's* mouth.

The reading moves from concern with ultimate realities to specific and painful personal experience.

The Lord will *rescue* me from *every* evil threat
and will bring me *safe* to his heavenly *kingdom*.
To him be *glory forever* and *ever*. *Amen*.

The faith and trust here are clear. Let your voice do justice to Paul's confidence.

a memorial act. And somehow Paul senses that his years of toil and struggle in behalf of the good news are about to end—and has resigned himself to it, knowing that he has done a good job. The imagery is athletic: competed well, finished the race, kept the faith.

The great Day of the Lord, when Jesus returns to establish the fullness of his reign on earth, will be the day when Paul is crowned with the laurel wreath that victorious athletes were awarded. And the apostle hastens to add that all who have joined him in his mission will receive the same. Here, too, there are echoes of Jesus' assurance that his followers would join him one day in paradise.

The second half of the reading is one of the most beautiful and strong professions of faith ever written—thoroughly practical, as though hope and trust in the Lord have become second nature to him. Even when abandoned at his trial (like Jesus) Paul prays for forgiveness for those who deserted him—again, in the manner of Jesus begging forgiveness for those "who know not what they do." And finally, like Jesus, Paul will complete his preaching task, so that all the nations might hear the gospel. In every way, Paul has identified his life and his death with that of the Lord he served so faithfully. Perhaps such identity with Jesus is the mark of every dedicated disciple.

GOSPEL The controlling device in this wonderful parable is irony, or reversal of expectations. The people who heard this parable spoken would be shocked by it, and that of course is the intention. The Pharisees were very devout and holy disciples of the law. It is a shame that

GOSPEL Luke 18:9–14

A reading from the holy Gospel according to Luke

In the first sentence we are already told the meaning of the parable.

Jesus addressed this *parable*
to those who were *convinced* of their own *righteousness*
and *despised* everyone *else*.

"Two *people* went up to the *temple* area to *pray*;
one was a *Pharisee* and the *other* was a *tax* collector.
The *Pharisee* took up his *position* and spoke this *prayer*
to himself,

Do not make the Pharisee sound ill-willed or deceptive. He isn't.

'O *God*, I *thank* you that I am *not* like the *rest* of humanity—
greedy, *dishonest*, *adulterous*—or even like this *tax* collector.
I *fast* twice a *week*, and I pay *tithes* on my whole *income*.'

"But the *tax* collector stood off at a *distance*
and would not even raise his *eyes* to *heaven*
but beat his *breast* and prayed,

The tax collector is sincere, but he should not sound timid and cowed.

'O *God*, be *merciful* to me a *sinner*.'

The familiar proverb suffers from any attempt to modernize it.

"I *tell* you, the *latter* went home *justified*, *not* the *former*;
for whoever *exalts* himself will be *humbled*,
and the one who *humbles* himself will be *exalted*."

their name has almost completely negative connotations for us. To understand this parable we have to realize that the Pharisee who spoke of himself as being better than the rest was telling the truth. He was not grasping, crooked, or adulterous. He was, from all external appearances, a much better man than the tax collector, who belonged to a group deserving of the bad name attached to them. They were seen as traitors to their own kind, collecting taxes from their own people in the name of the pagan conquerors.

And we must realize that the people who heard this parable would be repulsed even by the mention of a tax collector. Their presumption while hearing the parable would be that the Pharisee will be praised and the tax collector condemned.

Suddenly, the tables are turned. Because sincerity of heart and humility before God are what make prayer acceptable, the tax collector becomes the hero. Yes, he had faults, but he knew he had faults and asked for mercy and forgiveness. The Pharisee was so busy talking about himself and his good deeds, and comparing himself favorably with others less worthy, that his prayer was little more than self-congratulation.

The tax collector, on the other hand, was clearly concerned with his unworthiness in the sight of God, but had the courage to beg forgiveness anyway. Thus, he is the one who receives the commendation. His humility exalts him. Unfortunately, the opposite is true for the Pharisee: His self-exaltation crushes him. The only way we can earn God's favor is to realize that it cannot be earned. It is a gift to the humble.

OCTOBER 31, 2004

31st SUNDAY IN ORDINARY TIME

Lectionary #153

READING I Wisdom 11:22—12:2

A reading from the Book of Wisdom

You are privileged to read an exceptionally beautiful poem here. It will require extra preparation and your most attentive efforts.

Before the Lord the whole *universe* is as a *grain* from a *balance*
or a drop of morning *dew* come down upon the *earth*.
But you have *mercy* on *all*, because you can do *all* things;
and you *overlook* people's *sins* that they may *repent*.

Each thought is echoed or restated in the thought that follows it. Make the most of the parallelism with effective vocal variety.

The rhetorical question creates emphasis; the indirect response to the question creates resolution.

For you *love* all things that *are*
and loathe *nothing* that you have *made*;
for what you *hated*, you would not have *fashioned*.
And how could a thing *remain*, unless you *willed* it;
or be *preserved*, had it not been called *forth* by you?

But you spare *all* things, because they are *yours*,
O Lord and lover of *souls*,
for your imperishable *spirit* is in *all* things!
Therefore you *rebuke offenders little* by *little*,
warn them and *remind* them of the *sins* they are committing,
that they may *abandon* their wickedness and *believe* in you,
O *Lord*!

READING I The Wisdom literature in the Hebrew scriptures provides us with some of the loveliest and most profound poetry in our tradition. In this first reading we have a meditation on the nature of God that surpasses any doctrinal treatise in its power to draw us. How can we resist being attracted to a God whose greatness is surpassed only by the wish to forgive?

This text was written no more than fifty years before the appearance of Jesus on the earth. As a precursor of the message of mercy that Jesus taught, it serves to dispel further the notion that the "old" testament reveals a god of vengeance and the "new" testament reveals a god of mercy. Such a mistaken view of our tradition is explained only by a selective and arbitrary choice of texts. The truth is that the God of Genesis who pronounced all creation "good" is the same God of Wisdom who "loves all things that are" and who, according to the beloved disciple, John, "so loved the world that he sent his only-begotten Son."

The poet here is obviously charmed by an apparent oxymoron (a juxtaposition of opposites). How can the Lord, for whom "the whole universe is as a drop of morning dew" be so acutely and affectionately aware of the most insignificant part of creation? How can transcendence be so compatible with the intimacy of mercy? The rhetorical questions that characterize this text are inspired by wonder, uttered in praise, and offered in gratitude. In effect, then, we have a model of prayer. Though our minds cannot wrap themselves around such apparent contradictions, our hearts can embrace them—and rejoice!

READING II In this reading we are reminded that the liturgical

READING II 2 Thessalonians 1:11—2:2

A reading from the second Letter of Saint Paul to the Thessalonians

Paul assumes the royal plural here. "We" pray for you.

Brothers and sisters:
We always *pray* for you,
that our *God* may make you *worthy* of his *calling*
and *powerfully* bring to *fulfillment* every good *purpose*
and every *effort* of *faith*,
that the *name* of our Lord *Jesus* may be *glorified* in you,
and *you* in *him*,
in accord with the *grace* of our *God* and *Lord* Jesus *Christ*.

Note that both Jesus *and* his followers are glorified in good works of faith.

We *ask* you, brothers and sisters,
with regard to the *coming* of our Lord Jesus Christ
and our *assembling* with him,
not to be *shaken* out of your *minds* suddenly, or to be *alarmed*
either by a "*spirit*," or by an oral *statement*,
or by a *letter* allegedly from *us*
to the *effect* that the *day* of the *Lord* is at *hand*.

Relax, Paul says, the day of the Lord is yet to come, and it is cause for joy not terror.

year is not a patchwork quilt but a seamless fabric. As we approach the end of Ordinary Time, we begin to hear Advent themes. It is only a hint today—as Paul seeks to quiet the agitated minds of those who were fearful of the Day of the Lord. He is also addressing a peculiar notion that plagued the early church—the idea that some who believed the good news were already existing in a spiritual realm of enlightenment that elevated them above all others. They believed that, for them, the Day of the Lord had already come. It is essentially an elitist position that Paul finds himself battling here—and even more energetically later. Though such an idea may seem strange to us, the church is never completely free from the temptation toward elitism. Those who expend too much effort asserting their privileged status as members of a specific Christian tradition need to recall the expansiveness of God, as revealed, for example, in today's first reading.

Paul lovingly assures the Christians at Thessalonica that they have the constant support of his prayers—specifically so that their every good impulse will redound to the glory of the Lord and to their own sanctification. It is the most pastoral of prayers.

In the second paragraph Paul is eager to quiet their hearts with regard to rumors or mistaken notions about the return of Jesus in glory. The best position to take with regard to "the end of the world" is one of calm and hopeful vigilance, expressed in loving and humble service to one another.

GOSPEL The vivid details of this gospel story have made it a favorite with many of us. There is something irresistibly charming about "the little man" Zacchaeus, eager to see Jesus and willing

GOSPEL Luke 19:1–10

A reading from the holy Gospel according to Luke

At that time, *Jesus* came to *Jericho* and intended
to *pass through* the town.

Pay particular attention to the details of this story which make it memorable.

Now a *man* there named *Zacchaeus*,
who was a chief *tax* collector and also a *wealthy* man,
was seeking to *see* who Jesus *was*;
but he could not *see* him because of the *crowd*,
for he was short in *stature*.

So he ran *ahead* and climbed a *sycamore* tree in order to see Jesus,
who was about to *pass* that *way*.

How did Jesus notice Zacchaeus? Perhaps because his whole mission is to seek and save what is lost.

When he *reached* the place, Jesus looked *up* and said,
"*Zacchaeus*, come down *quickly*,
for *today* I must *stay* at your *house*."

The grumblers are genuinely shocked, not just petty and small-minded. Jesus is doing a shocking thing.

And he came down *quickly* and received him with *joy*.
When they all saw this, they began to *grumble*, saying,
"He has gone to stay at the house of a *sinner*."

Zacchaeus offers his defense humbly, perhaps even tearfully. It's a terrible thing to be misjudged.

But Zacchaeus *stood* there and said to the Lord,
"*Behold*, *half* of my *possessions*, Lord, I shall give to the *poor*,
and if I have *extorted* anything from *anyone*
I shall *repay* it four times *over*."

Jesus' response rings out with new hope for all sinners, everybody, everywhere!

And Jesus said to him,
"*Today salvation* has come to this house
because this man *too* is a descendant of *Abraham*.
For the Son of *Man* has come to *seek*
and to *save* what was *lost*."

to risk a lot for the privilege. Though a member of a group widely despised, he appears to us here as a fundamentally honest and humble man who seeks the truth and is open to finding it where he can.

Most of the power of this story stems from the murmurs of those who are scandalized that Jesus would associate with Zacchaeus. As a tax collector, he was perceived by all as a traitor to his own people, willing to work for the oppressor. In short, he was an outcast, the least likely—in the eyes of the people—to receive God's favor.

As so often in Luke, we see here the effect of a reversal of expectations. The grumblers are shocked that Jesus would go to the house—and, even more shocking, to the table—of a sinner. Zacchaeus feels constrained to offer an elaborate defense of himself in the face of such criticism. And it is interesting that Jesus responds to this defense in sweeping words, including Zacchaeus but going far beyond the particulars of the situation. What does it mean to be a child of Abraham? Well, it doesn't mean automatic justification in the eyes of God. It means living according to law and the prophets, namely, what Zacchaeus does: "I give half my belongings to the poor; I make restitution to those I have wronged; I seek God's will in all things."

Though we see Jesus preferring the company of repentant sinners over and over, the church still has difficulty convincing people that their sinful ways are precisely what gains them entrance. The church is made up of errant people who have discovered the joy of knowing the faithful God! Hypocrites and grumblers are welcome too. What better place to learn better ways?

ALL SAINTS

Lectionary #667

READING I Revelation 7:2–4, 9–14

Literature such as this must ring out expansively. Any proclamation that sounds literal or analytical is out of the question.

A new section begins here, following the missing verses. The imagery is vivid and beautiful.

A reading from the Book of Revelation

I, *John*, saw another *angel* come up from the *East*,
holding the *seal* of the living *God*.
He cried out in a loud *voice* to the *four* angels
who were given power to *damage* the *land* and the *sea*,
"Do *not* damage the *land* or the *sea* or the *trees*
until we put the *seal* on the *foreheads* of the servants
of our *God*."
I heard the *number* of those who had been marked with the seal,
one *hundred* and forty-four *thousand* marked
from every *tribe* of the *Israelites*.

After *this* I had a vision of a great *multitude*,
which *no* one could *count*,
from every *nation*, *race*, *people*, and *tongue*.
They stood before the *throne* and before the *Lamb*,
wearing white *robes* and holding *palm* branches in their hands.
They cried out in a loud *voice*:
"*Salvation* comes from our *God*,
who is *seated* on the *throne*,
and from the *Lamb*."

All the *angels* stood around the throne
and around the *elders* and the four living *creatures*.
They *prostra*ted themselves before the throne,
worshiped *God*, and exclaimed:

READING I The observance of a day in honor of all the saints is the result of two church efforts to supplant pagan beliefs with Christian practice. In the seventh century, the Pantheon in Rome (a domed structure built in the second century to honor all the gods of Rome) was renamed in honor of Mary and all martyrs. About 200 years later, Pope Gregory IV made a day for all saints official. November 1 was probably chosen because it was one of the four great seasonal pagan festivals in the north. The Orthodox church celebrates All Saints on the Sunday after Pentecost.

Though in popular culture Halloween seems to have lost its association with All Saints, the proper name for the day is All Hallows' Eve, and "Hallows" means "Holy Ones." Here, too, a pagan observance (a final fling for ghouls and goblins before harvest) was Christianized, but in North America we seem to have returned to a non-religious observance of it for the most part.

There's no mistaking the nature of today's feast once we have heard this first reading from the apocalyptic literature of John. Taken just a bit out of context, this passage conveys the glory of heaven enjoyed by the elect, those who have survived the great ordeal and now rejoice in the presence of Jesus, the Lamb of God.

In context, the scene—a description of the terrible Day of the Lord—is actually quite horrific. Angels wreak havoc on the earth before the chosen ones are united with Christ in glory. Those chosen ones are marked with a special sign to protect them from the wrath to come. Despite the terror described here, John writes to comfort a church under persecution. He shows them that those who have survived the ordeal will ultimately triumph.

These acclamations should not be shouted. The speakers are bowed in humility before the throne.

"*Amen. Blessing* and *glory, wisdom* and *thanksgiving,*
honor, power, and *might*
be to our *God* for*ever* and *ever. Amen.*"

Then one of the *elders* spoke up and said to me,

Make the dialogue lively, the question real.

"Who *are* these wearing white *robes*, and where did they
come from?"
I said to him, "My *lord, you* are the one who *knows.*"
He said to me,
"*These* are the ones who have *survived* the time
of great *distress;*
they have *washed* their robes
and made them *white* in the *blood* of the *Lamb.*"

READING II 1 John 3:1–3

A reading from the first Letter of Saint John

The text begins with an exclamation. Make it sound like one.

Beloved:
See what *love* the *Father* has *bestowed* on us
that we may be called the *children* of God.
Yet *so* we *are.*

The world does not recognize us because we look so much like Jesus.

The reason the *world* does not *know* us
is that it did not know *him.*

Beloved, we are God's children *now;*
what we *shall be* has not yet been *revealed.*
We *do know* that when it is *revealed* we shall be *like* him,
for we shall *see* him as he *is.*

To place our hope in Jesus is to become like him.

Everyone who has this *hope* based on *him* makes himself *pure,*
as *he* is pure.

A word about the numerology here is in order. The number 144,000 is a number of absolute perfection. It is 12 times 12 multiplied by 1,000. The meaning of the number is not that there are only 144,000 chosen; rather, in its perfection, it symbolizes an unlimited number. Literalists will have to abandon any exclusionary interpretations.

An effective proclamation of apocalyptic literature will surrender to the splendor and majesty of the text, reveling in the poetic imagery.

READING II **"In the evening of life we shall be judged on love alone." This is John's theme song. Here he reminds us not of something we shall become but of what we already are: children of God. It is an adoption that has happened to us because of God's immense love. Christians sometimes concentrate so much on their duty that they forget their dignity. John is out to convince us that, although we do not know what eternal life with God will be like, we do know what we are now. We are God's beloved and redeemed children, all evidence to the contrary notwithstanding.**

Realizing our dignity inspires us to behave accordingly. The effect of focusing only on our duty is that we feel only obligation, a far cry from what the love of God intends for us. John seems to understand that the best way to help people be good is to point out how good they already are.

Today's feast reminds us that the destiny in store for us is glorious, and many have already achieved it. Believing in our dignity as children of God is what makes us saints, and saints are quite simply people who live now in accord with their final destiny.

GOSPEL Matthew 5:1–12a

A reading from the holy Gospel according to Matthew

Like Moses, Jesus proclaims the new law from the mountaintop. Like a teacher with authority, he sits down to deliver his important doctrine.

Whether you pronounce it "blest" or "BLES-*d," be consistent and authoritative. I prefer the latter because it more effectively connotes the meaning "happy," which is the meaning here, rather than "having received a blessing."

The text is so important. Let each beatitude stand on its own. Employ vocal variation.

When *Jesus* saw the *crowds,* he went up the *mountain,*
and after he had *sat down,* his *disciples* came to him.
He began to *teach* them, saying:
"*Blessed* are the *poor* in *spirit,*
for *theirs* is the kingdom of *heaven.*
Blessed are they who *mourn,*
for *they* will be *comforted.*

"*Blessed* are the *meek,*
for *they* will inherit the *land.*
Blessed are they who *hunger* and *thirst* for *righteousness,*
for *they* will be *satisfied.*

The list shifts from personal attributes to attributes affecting how we treat, and are treated by, others.

"*Blessed* are the *merciful,*
for *they* will be *shown* mercy.
Blessed are the clean of *heart,*
for *they* will see *God.*

"*Blessed* are the *peacemakers,*
for *they* will be called *children* of God.
Blessed are they who are *persecuted* for the sake
of *righteousness,*
for *theirs* is the kingdom of *heaven.*

The final encouraging admonition is important. Suffering is seen in its true light, and the saints are proof of its value and its reward.

"*Blessed* are *you* when they *insult* you and *persecute* you
and utter every kind of *evil* against you *falsely* because of *me.*
Rejoice and be *glad,*
for your *reward* will be *great* in *heaven.*"

GOSPEL Matthew presents Jesus as the new Moses, the teachings of Jesus as the new law, and the community Jesus gathers as the new Israel. Thus Jesus proclaims the new commandments on a mountaintop, just as Moses proclaimed the old commandments on Mount Sinai. Only the formulation and the lawgiver, however, are truly new. Every one of the so-called "beatitudes" can be found in the Hebrew scriptures that Jesus knew so well. He came, as he himself said, not to destroy the law but to bring it to perfection.

The list of beatitudes is perhaps most revealing when we apply it to Jesus himself and see that his life is an incarnation of each one. God comes to us in human form to restore the divine image within us. Jesus was poor in spirit, meek and lowly, hungry for holiness, merciful, pure in heart, a peacemaker, persecuted, insulted, slandered, and sorrowful. Yet he was the most joyful person who ever lived. It is Jesus' life that gives such power to his teaching. He himself is the Good News.

And it is the life of Jesus that gives us the ability to follow him and his teaching. The saints prove this to us, and we celebrate that proof in today's feast. Our own lives prove the power of Jesus. This need not surprise us, since we ourselves are among those who are called "saints," made so by the love and election of God.

Proclaiming the beatitudes well is not easy. You are challenged to enable the assembly to hear each one in its uniqueness. After all, it is not a list but a series of acclamations, a song of praise, a declaration of independence, and a portrait of Jesus the Christ.

32ND SUNDAY IN ORDINARY TIME

Lectionary #156

READING I 2 Maccabees 7:1–2, 9–14

A reading from the second Book of Maccabees

Notice the formulaic structure of this story. Each brother is given the test, given the opportunity to scorn it and reveal a different aspect of their beliefs.

The first brother proclaims their readiness to die for their beliefs.

It *happened* that seven *brothers* with their *mother* were *arrested*
and *tortured* with *whips* and *scourges* by the *king*,
to force them to eat *pork* in violation of God's *law*.
One of the brothers, speaking for the *others*, said:
"What do you expect to *achieve* by *questioning* us?
We are ready to *die* rather than transgress the *laws*
of our *ancestors*."

The second brother asserts their belief in resurrection.

At the point of *death* he said:
"You accursed *fiend*, you are depriving us of this *present* life,
but the King of the *world* will raise us *up* to *live* again *forever*.
It is for *his* laws that we are *dying*."

The third brother demonstrates the courage that only strong faith can bring—and inspires admiration even in his torturers.

After *him* the *third* suffered their cruel sport.
He put out his *tongue* at *once* when told to *do* so,
and *bravely* held out his *hands*, as he spoke these noble *words*:
"It was from *Heaven* that I *received* these;
for the sake of his *laws* I *disdain* them;
from him I hope to *receive* them again."
Even the *king* and his *attendants marveled*
at the young man's *courage*,
because he regarded his *sufferings* as *nothing*.

After *he* had died,
they *tortured* and *maltreated* the *fourth* brother
in the same *way*.

READING I As the end of the church year draws near, the readings become more and more concerned with eschatological themes—that is, beliefs centering on the end of time and the afterlife. We coast toward Advent, the season that most concretely meditates on the two comings of Jesus—at his birth in a stable, and at the end of time in glory.

The first reading today is from a book of the Bible that was written in the century immediately preceding Christ's birth. It is particularly appropriate today because it shows us the gradual development in the Hebrew scriptures of a hope for an afterlife that was far brighter than Sheol (the underworld, a place of gloom and shadow). The words of the second brother/martyr in the reading make this hope explicit: "The King of the world will raise us up to live again forever."

The text also makes it clear that the afterlife hoped for by the Maccabees is the reward of a life lived in obedience to God's will. Though it may seem strange to us that a dietary law was worth dying for, we must remember that the specific law is essentially symbolic. It is the principle of obedience to the Law that inspires the brothers to die rather than abandon their spiritual heritage. Any distinctions about which part of the Law was worth dying for would have been inconceivable to them. Besides, it was for their faith in God that they were persecuted, not their adherence to certain dietary customs. To compromise at all would be to compromise everything. We might do well to examine ourselves in the light of such fidelity.

The fourth brother points out that resurrection to life is only for the faithful.

When *he* was near death, he said,
"It is my *choice* to *die* at the hands of *men*
with the hope *God* gives of being raised *up* by him;
but for *you*, there will *be* no resurrection to life."

READING II 2 Thessalonians 2:16—3:5

A reading from the second Letter of Saint Paul to the Thessalonians

The reading begins with one of Paul's long subjunctive requests. Take a deep breath.

Brothers and sisters:
May our Lord Jesus Christ *himself* and God our *Father*,
who has *loved* us and given us everlasting *encouragement*
and good *hope* through his *grace*,
encourage your *hearts* and *strengthen* them
in every good *deed* and *word*.

Another long sentence; make the sense lines work for you.

The rescue and deliverance from wicked people here is a plea not to be killed for preaching the good news!

Finally, brothers and sisters, *pray* for us,
so that the word of the *Lord* may speed *forward* and be *glorified*,
as it did among *you*,
and that we may be *delivered* from *perverse* and *wicked* people,
for not *all* have *faith*.

But the *Lord* is faithful;
he will *strengthen* you and *guard* you from the *evil* one.
We are *confident* of you in the *Lord* that what we *instruct* you,
you are *doing* and will *continue* to do.

The final petition is clearly for the wellbeing of a community under persecution.

May the Lord *direct* your hearts to the love of *God*
and to the *endurance* of *Christ*.

READING II This reading, like the first and the gospel, is concerned with the fulfillment and fruition of God's salvific plan. The underlying conviction in all that Paul writes here is that it is God who inexorably furthers the work of the apostle and the community of believers.

The opening injunction (in the subjunctive mood: "May our Lord Jesus Christ") asks that believers be consoled and strengthened for the work they must perform as they seek to establish the kingdom of Christ in their midst. Then Paul asks prayers for himself and his co-workers in their missionary effort. But notice that the prayer is not that *they* will make progress, but that *the word of the Lord* may make progress. This is more than a subtle distinction. It is an assertion that the Lord is the one who moves salvation history toward its inevitable end: the evangelization and salvation of the world.

It is not a bad idea to remind ourselves occasionally that our efforts on behalf of the Christian message are auxiliary, not primary. God has willed that all people believe the good news and return to their creator. If God has willed it, it will come to pass. Our role is to cooperate with God in this cosmic plan. Like John the Baptist, we are not the light; we bear witness to the light. We do not save the world; we lower the hills and raise the valleys to prepare the way for the salvation that comes from God in Jesus.

GOSPEL Luke 20:27–38

A reading from the holy Gospel according to Luke

The beginning is abrupt. Be sure you have the assembly's attention before starting.

Some *Sadducees*, those who *deny* that there is a *resurrection*,
came *forward* and put this *question* to Jesus, saying,
"*Teacher*, *Moses* wrote for us,
'If someone's *brother* dies leaving a *wife* but no *child*,
his *brother* must *take* the wife
and raise up *descendants* for his brother.'

Lay the argument out very carefully, but also like someone trying to confuse the one to whom it is posed.

Now there were *seven* brothers;
the *first* married a woman but died *childless*.

"Then the *second* and the *third* married her,
and likewise all the *seven* died childless.
Finally the woman *also* died.
Now at the *resurrection* whose *wife* will that woman *be*?
For all *seven* had been *married* to her."

Pause before beginning Jesus' response. Then emphasize the difference between "this age" and the age to come.

Jesus said to them,
"The children of *this* age *marry* and *remarry*;
but those who are deemed *worthy* to attain to the *coming* age
and to the *resurrection* of the *dead*
neither *marry* nor are *given* in marriage.

The point is that those who rise participate in God's life—very different from earthly life.

They can no longer *die*,
for they are like *angels*;
and they are the children of *God*
because *they* are the ones who will *rise*.

GOSPEL In the first reading we heard a strong affirmation of resurrection. In the gospel we hear of a strong denial of resurrection. The Sadducees make a mistake that is not unheard of today: They try to apply earthly standards to heavenly ones, apparently unable to deal comfortably with the mysterious and unimaginable. One wonders how such thinkers conceive of God, who is of course about as mysterious and unimaginable as, well, as we can imagine! At any rate, it is apparent that the Sadducees are not so much interested in a search for understanding as they are in a defense of their own position. Defensive arguments often use veiled or outright ridicule to defy the opponent.

The law the Sadducees refer to is a real one, recorded in the sacred writings. And, like any prescription of behavior, it can be taken to the bounds of absurdity by anyone who wishes to interpret it literally and fundamentalistically. Such is the case here. They want the witnesses of this argument with Jesus to chuckle at the humorous image of the oft-married widow trying to figure out which of her resurrected husbands is the real one.

Jesus himself may have chuckled at this conundrum, but he quickly reveals the false assumption (and the less than sincere intent) underlying it. The Sadducees are apparently unable to imagine a life different from this present one. They are not to be

Pause before beginning the second part of Jesus' response and the proof offered by Moses.

"That the dead will *rise*
even *Moses* made known in the *passage* about the *bush*,
when he called out '*Lord,*'
the God of *Abraham*, the God of *Isaac*, and the God of *Jacob*;
and he is not God of the *dead*, but of the *living*,
for to *him all* are alive."

[Shorter: Luke 20:27, 34–38]

seriously faulted for this, since it is certainly a stretch for any of us. But we must engage in the stretch and Jesus helps us by his response. The whole argument becomes irrelevant, he says, if you imagine a life where there is no death. And if no one dies, there is hardly a reason for marriage and the bearing of children.

The further response of Jesus seems perhaps a bit contrived to our modern ears. It introduces another kind of afterlife—the kind perpetuated by memory and legacy. We can say of someone who has died that their memory lives on. This is a different kind of afterlife than resurrection from the dead. But Jesus is saying more than this. He is asserting an even more fundamental truth than resurrection from the dead. He is saying that the relationship God has initiated with us is not subject to death—simply because God is not so subject. In this sense, Abraham, Isaac, and Jacob are as alive today as they ever were. Likewise, resurrection from the dead is simply confirmation that our relationship with God cannot be subject to mere physical death.

33RD SUNDAY IN ORDINARY TIME

Lectionary #159

READING I Malachi 3:19–20a

Malachi = MAL-uh-kī

The poetic opening is an attention getter. The text is brief and demands a slow, exalted, deliberate proclamation.

Read sense lines, not punctuation. We're dealing with poetry here.

A reading from the Book of the prophet Malachi

Lo, the day is *coming*, *blazing* like an *oven*,
when all the *proud* and all *evildoers* will be *stubble*,
and the day that is coming will set them on *fire*,
leaving them neither *root* nor *branch*,
says the LORD of *hosts*.

This sudden twist ("But for you") must be prepared for with a pause.

But for *you* who fear my *name*, there will arise
the sun of *justice* with its healing *rays*.

READING II 2 Thessalonians 3:7–12

A reading from the second Letter of Saint Paul to the Thessalonians

Brothers and sisters:
You *know* how one must *imitate* us.

Paul's humility takes the form of blunt honesty.

For we did *not* act in a *disorderly* way among you,
nor did we eat *food* received *free* from *anyone*.
On the *contrary*, in *toil* and *drudgery*, *night* and *day*
we *worked*, so as not to *burden* any of you.

READING I From the prophet Malachi we hear images of both sides of judgment. The image for the dire side is an effective one. Only those who have watched a farmer burn the stubble from a field in preparation for the next planting can appreciate its vigor. On a dry, hot, early autumn day, a field of stubble is like a tinder box. The short stems left from the harvest are lifeless and stiff and hollow. When the blaze touches them, they don't so much burn up as simply disappear in a flash. The ash that is left is so insubstantial that a touch reduces it to dust.

So it is with the proud evildoer when the Day of the Lord brings judgment and justice to the earth. Dry and stiff and hollow—completely devoid of worth—they will disappear in a flash, leaving no evidence of their passing. It is a horrible image that strikes fear in the heart of any sensitive person.

But for those who reverence the Lord, an entirely different fate is in store. The revealing heat of the sun of justice is to them the opposite of destruction. It brings healing with its rays. Healing implies an illness. It is not perfection or heroic holiness that merits the healing rays; it is that gift of the Spirit we call "fear of the Lord," the kind of humble reverence that enables us to see ourselves honestly—flawed creatures who nonetheless accept and rejoice in the love God has shown us. Such reverence welcomes the final judgment.

READING II There is something ominous in Paul's words in this second reading. There's no denying the strong work ethic revealed in Paul's writing. Here he not only asserts that he more than earned whatever he was given in return for his labors, he also makes it clear that

The choice *not* to make a rightful claim—in order to be an example—is a noble one.

Not that we do not have the *right*.
Rather, we wanted to *present* ourselves as a *model* for you,
so that you might *imitate* us.
In *fact*, when we were *with* you,
we *instructed* you that if anyone was unwilling to *work*,
neither should that one *eat*.

We hear that *some* are conducting themselves among you
in a *disorderly* way,
by not keeping *busy* but minding the business of *others*.
Such people we *instruct* and *urge* in the Lord Jesus *Christ*
to work *quietly*
and to *eat* their own *food*.

The play on the contrast between keeping busy and minding other people's business is effective.

GOSPEL Luke 21:5–19

A reading from the holy Gospel according to Luke

While *some* people were *speaking* about
how the *temple* was *adorned* with costly *stones*
and *votive* offerings,
Jesus said, "All that you *see* here—
the days will *come* when there will not be left
a *stone* upon *another* stone that will not be thrown *down*."

The careful reader will notice from the start that we have a kind of set-up here. The gospel writer is creating a setting in which some important things can be said.

Then they *asked* him,
"*Teacher, when* will this *happen*?
And what *sign* will there be when all these things
are about to *happen*?"

The question is so matter-of-fact because it merely serves as a springboard to the next subject of Jesus' discourse.

he expects labor to the point of exhaustion from everyone.

Even more ominous is Paul's admonition for those who not only do not work, but spend their idle time in playing the busybody. They are enjoined to get busy, earn their food, and not expect a handout. He may also be correcting the mistaken notion that the Lord's second coming was imminent, making any labor senseless. Paul himself had to wrestle with the delay of the Lord's coming in glory. We see the progression of his thought in this regard throughout his letters. We should profit from his experience and realize with him that any speculation about when the end time will come is futile. We don't know. We can't know. And it shouldn't make any difference to us in any case. There is an urgency in Paul's tone. For those who work, the sunset of life will be radiant with peace and hope; for those who do not, the approaching night will seem dark indeed.

GOSPEL There is a subtle form of presumption that afflicts many Christians. They seem to be motivated by the conviction that if they work hard, do the right thing, and avoid the bad thing, then their lives (and the world situation) should "every day, in every way, get better and better." Where this presumption originates is hard to determine, for there are no guarantees or time frames in God's promise to renew the face of the earth. It will happen, but the question of "when" remains unanswered. Times of apparent growth and peace can suddenly be followed by cataclysmic upheaval and disorder. Tragedy is all the more tragic when it strikes at a time of prosperity and apparent predictability.

The point is that these calamities are no threat to the faithful.

He answered,
"See that you not be *deceived*,
for *many* will come in my *name*, saying,
'*I* am he,' and 'The *time* has *come*.'
Do not *follow* them!

"When you hear of *wars* and *insurrections*,
do not be *terrified*; for such things *must* happen *first*,
but it will not *immediately* be the *end*."

Treat the list kindly. Let each item have its due.

Then he said to them,
"*Nation* will rise against *nation*, and *kingdom* against *kingdom*.
There will be powerful *earthquakes*, *famines* and *plagues*
from place to *place*;
and awesome *sights* and mighty *signs* will come from the *sky*.

History has shown Jesus' promise to be true, witnessed in the death of martyrs.

"Before all this *happens*, however,
they will *seize* and *persecute* you,
they will hand you *over* to the *synagogues* and to *prisons*,
and they will have you led before *kings* and *governors*
because of my *name*.

"It will *lead* to your giving *testimony*.
Remember, you are not to *prepare* your defense *beforehand*,
for I *myself* shall give you a *wisdom* in *speaking*
that all your *adversaries* will be *powerless* to *resist* or *refute*.

"You will even be handed over by *parents*, *brothers*,
relatives and *friends*,
and they will put *some* of you to *death*.

Bring the awesome text to an effective close: firmly and slowly and joyfully!

You will be hated by *all* because of my *name*,
but not a hair on your *head* will be *destroyed*.
By your *perseverance* you will *secure* your *lives*."

Those who interpret in a literal way the so-called "predictions" of Jesus regarding the end times are usually creating a scenario to match a notion they already embrace. Despite centuries of failed attempts to predict the end of the world or to read current catastrophes as unmistakable signs of the approaching end, the attempts continue.

Literature that deals with the end times is called "apocalyptic." To understand this kind of literature correctly we must realize that it is literature of interpretation, not prediction. It is difficult to understand why a writer would look at past events and then re-tell them in the future tense—like a prediction—but that is precisely the case with much of prophecy. The purpose of this method is clear: With hindsight the prophet can see and relate how the hand of God is at work in history, and continues to be at work in the future. It is much easier to understand such an approach if we remember that the writers of this literature were not historians but theologians. Understanding and instruction is their aim, not historical accuracy or fact finding. And certainly not predicting the future in any literal sense.

The controlling theme of the words of Jesus here is that his name (which is equivalent to his mission and his person) will be the cause of disruption. And how could it be otherwise, since the forces of good and evil must always be squared off in battle? Those associated with the name will endure persecution. How could it be otherwise in a world that often rejects the good and embraces the bad? And finally, all who persevere to the end will be saved. How could it be otherwise, when the God of heaven and earth has promised eternal life to those who call upon the name of Jesus?

CHRIST THE KING

Lectionary #162

READING I 2 Samuel 5:1–3

A reading from the second Book of Samuel

This is a reunification gathering of a divided kingdom.
Hebron = HEB-ruhn

In those days, *all* the tribes of *Israel* came to *David*
in *Hebron* and said:
"Here we *are*, your *bone* and your *flesh*.
In days *past*, when *Saul* was our king,
it was *you* who led the Israelites *out* and brought them *back*.
And the *LORD* said to you,
'You shall *shepherd* my people *Israel*
and shall be *commander* of Israel.'"

Here is the divine commission that confirms David's royalty.

When all the *elders* of Israel came to David in *Hebron*,
King *David* made an *agreement* with them *there*
before the *LORD*,
and they *anointed* him *king* of *Israel*.

The agreement to rule and to be ruled is sealed in the presence of God ("before the Lord").

READING I Jesus was born of Mary, the husband of Joseph, of the house and lineage of David. Because David is considered to be the greatest of the kings of Israel, it was inevitable that the Messiah to come would be a descendant of his household. And just as David was chosen by God to be king over the whole people Israel (formerly divided, but now unified under him), so Jesus was chosen by God to bring all nations together under the divine sovereignty. Such is one of the similarities that explains the choice of this first reading for today's celebration. But there are differences that show us the special kingship proper to Christ.

The kingship of Christ is primarily an eschatological reality. That is, it is in his triumph over the forces of evil and death and his enthronement at the right hand of the Father where we see the kingship of Jesus most vividly. His return in glory at the end of time has been the focus of our readings during these last Sundays of the liturgical year.

READING II Here we have an exultant hymn disguised as a theological treatise. Or is it the other way around? No matter; you should proclaim it as a hymn. It has some very important things to say about Jesus the Christ (the Anointed One), whom today we hail as King.

First of all, Jesus existed from all eternity, was present at the creation of the world and is the principle upon which heaven and earth exist. It is the cosmic Christ we see in Paul's words—the Lord of heaven, the eternal Word of God, destined to become flesh in order to redeem the fallen world.

READING II Colossians 1:12–20

A reading from the Letter of Saint Paul to the Colossians

The admonition to give thanks precedes the great hymn that defines to one to whose kingdom we belong.

Brothers and sisters:
Let us give *thanks* to the *Father*,
who has made you *fit* to share
in the *inheritance* of the *holy* ones in *light*.

He *delivered* us from the power of *darkness*
and *transferred* us to the *kingdom* of his beloved *Son*,
in whom we have *redemption*, the forgiveness of *sins*.

Be aware of the structure of this reading: "He is . . . For in him . . . He is . . . and in him . . . He is . . . He is . . . For in him."

He is the *image* of the invisible *God*,
the *firstborn* of all *creation*.
For in *him* were created *all* things in *heaven* and on *earth*,
the *visible* and the *invisible*,
whether *thrones* or *dominions* or *principalities* or *powers*;
all things were *created* through *him* and for *him*.
He is *before* all things,
and in *him* all things hold *together*.

Pause. A new section begins. Renew the emphasis.

He is the *head* of the *body*, the *church*.
He is the *beginning*, the *firstborn* from the *dead*,
that in *all* things he *himself* might be *preeminent*.

A long sentence. Do not let your voice gradually fall throughout. Rather, let your intensity build.

For in *him* all the *fullness* was pleased to *dwell*,
and through *him* to *reconcile* all things for him,
making *peace* by the blood of his *cross*
through him, whether those on *earth* or those in *heaven*.

Second, Jesus is the ruler of material creation as well. He is the head of the body we call the church. In his risen body we see the first and final victory over death and the reason for our hope in everlasting life. In Jesus Christ we see the fullness, the entirety, of the God who reconciled the world to himself by taking on human flesh and shedding the blood of self-sacrifice. The reconciliation thus effected involved the heavenly creatures as well, though in what way and for what reason we are uncertain.

In short (and in far more beautiful words than mine), this poetic text reaches for something of the vastness of Christ, something hinting at the limits of the mind to understand but not exceeding the ability of the heart to imagine. Proclaim it boldly and with joy.

GOSPEL The feast of Christ the King is very new by liturgical standards. It was added to the calendar of feasts by Pope Pius XI in a papal document promulgated on December 11, 1925.

The significance of hailing Christ as King of the universe is not difficult to discern. The imagery of Messiah King is everywhere in the Hebrew scriptures. And the titles of Son of Man, Son of David, and Son of God in the Christian scriptures make the image explicit with regard to Christ.

Though kings who exercise sovereign power in our time are few, our associations with the title reveal much about Christ. We must also remember what a special kind of king our Lord is—as well as the kind of king

GOSPEL Luke 23:35–43

A reading from the holy Gospel according to Luke

The *rulers sneered* at *Jesus* and said,
"He saved *others*, let him save *himself*
if he is the *chosen* one, the Christ of *God*."
Even the *soldiers* jeered at him.
As they approached to offer him *wine* they called out,
"If you are *King* of the *Jews*, *save* yourself."
Above him there was an *inscription* that read,
"*This* is the *King* of the *Jews*."

The jeering and mocking take on a new kind of horror considering the feast we are celebrating today.

Now one of the *criminals* hanging there *reviled* Jesus, saying,
"Are you not the *Christ*?
Save yourself and *us*."

The dialogue between the two criminals should not be bombastic.

The *other*, however, *rebuking* him, said in *reply*,
"Have you no fear of *God*,
for you are *subject* to the same *condemnation*?
And *indeed*, we have been condemned *justly*,
for the *sentence* we received *corresponds* to our *crimes*,
but *this* man has done *nothing* criminal."
Then he said,
"*Jesus*, *remember* me when you come into your *kingdom*."

He *replied* to him,
"*Amen*, I *say* to you,
today you will *be* with me in *Paradise*."

At last Jesus speaks, and they are words only a special kind of king could utter.

he is not. Christ is the shepherd-king par excellence, a role found often in the Hebrew scriptures.

No scene could make it more clear that Jesus Christ is a special kind of king. He reigns here from an instrument of torture, the strangest kind of throne. The crown he wears is thrust upon his head in ridicule. The robe that lies at the foot of the cross was flung over his beaten body in mockery of his claims. And soldiers cast dice to see who would inherit the last remnant of his dignity. The sign above his head proclaims him to be king, but the leaders of those he is presumed to rule object to the proclamation. The subjects around this "throne" are scoffing soldiers and a jeering crowd, challenging him to exercise power on his own behalf. Only one, a criminal, does obeisance—and receives in return the promise of paradise.

Clearly, our liturgical celebration of Christ the King reveals the tension between a "king of shreds and patches" and a king of eschatological glory. It is precisely the kind of tension most appropriate as we stand on the threshold of a new liturgical year and look back upon the old one. In the contradictory images of this strange king we see clearly the personification of a kingdom that has come but is not yet fully revealed. This king rules us in the realm of "already . . . but not yet."